To my understanding and loving wife, Nancy Jo, and our daughters,
Audra Marie and Sarah Tupper, who make my life better
and more enjoyable every year.

Contents

Foreword

"**G**ood dog!" That's the first vivid memory I have of Jack Daniels. I heard that over the telephone after a 3K time trial Jared Scott and I ran in Flagstaff, AZ, in the fall of 2007.

I moved to Flagstaff in the fall of 2007, knowing that I had specific running goals in mind and I wanted to maximize my chances of reaching them. For me, the most important ingredient for success was Jack Daniels, so I began one of the greatest relationships of my life. Over the next few years, I came to know Jack quite well as he coached me to the Olympic Trials 5K in 2008.

It is clear that Jack is the greatest mind in running. His experience in exercise physiology and its application to running is unparalleled. His running philosophy was known to me in college. I actually first saw Jack in 2002 at the SUNYAC Indoor Championships. (He was seated in the Cortland section, with a Donald Duck hat on.) At SUNY Geneseo we competed against SUNY Cortland with frequency. Dr. Daniels was well known to us as his athletes were omnipresent on the awards podium, regardless of the meet.

Several years later, I sought him out, and as we worked closely together, we became good friends. My fondest memories from my time training in Flagstaff are of the stories he would tell as he was riding his bicycle beside me while I was on a recovery jog between quality workouts. The story about a beaver squeezing in under the door of his cabin one Montana winter to warm itself is my favorite.

As I trained under his tutelage, I realized the elegance of his philosophy. Proper training requires specific intensities for specific distances. Overtraining is not to be sought as the pinnacle of a running career; rather it should be scoffed at. The essence of his philosophy is that anyone can benefit from its application, since it allows flexibility based on mileage, pace, and other variables. It is because of Jack Daniels that I had the success I did, and I will be forever grateful.

Without further delay, please enjoy reading this third edition of the definitive training tome for so many athletes. Even now, years after the first edition, Jack provides new, scientifically-based information with your success in mind.

Anthony Gallo, MD
Olympic Trials Qualifier, 2008

Preface

I have learned a great deal about running and runners since the second edition of *Daniels' Running Formula*. It might seem strange to some of you that after so many years of study and coaching, I still find new, more practical, and often simpler ways of prescribing training and racing programs, but it's true. Some of these new ideas and strategies that can be found in this third edition of my book include the following:

- Finding success through different approaches and amounts of running
- Logging the stress of different types of training, which provides a way of keeping track of total stress, rather than just mileage for each season and each type of training
- Thinking of rest as part of training, as opposed to resting in order to avoid training
- Being able to compare runners of different ages based on adjusted VDOT values
- Using a wide variety of marathon training programs for beginners through the elite

The many runners and coaches who so often contact me to say they used my training ideas with considerable success have encouraged me to continue looking for new ideas or simpler ways of improving fitness and performance. In this edition, I have included a list of what I refer to as the basic laws of running; these can be used by individual runners to better prepare for races and by coaches to help their runners perform better.

It has been an interesting journey working with and researching elite (and some not-so-elite) runners over the years. Although we tend to go through phases of what is considered the best approach to improved performance, it all really boils down to following some principles, trying to adjust training to meet individual needs, and prescribing training that is productive yet minimizes the chances of injury. I have always tried to emphasize the importance of consistency in training and to produce the greatest benefit from the *least* amount of training stress, rather than the greatest benefit from the *greatest* amount of stress.

No one has all the answers for how best to train, and there is no single system that works best for everyone. My aim is to present scientific information in a manner that coaches and athletes can understand, appreciate, and use. Then you can decide whether the knowledge and the training and racing programs provided in the pages that follow have a positive impact on you, the runner or running coach.

The chapters are sequenced to build on the previous content. Each new chapter can offer ways to apply what you learned in the earlier chapters to develop an overall plan of running success.

In chapter 1, I review what I have often suggested are the ingredients of success (ability, motivation, opportunity, and direction) and also include my new laws of running.

In chapter 2, I cover key principles of training and running technique. Too often coaches and runners build a training program based on the workouts of a current national champion, world-record holder, or Olympian, without understanding why those people achieved their success—adherence to important principles of training, including how the body reacts to stress and the benefits of various types of training.

Chapter 3 delves into what I refer to as physiological profiles, specifically aerobic and lactate profiles. This information is useful for understanding the relationships between the intensity (speed) at which a person runs and the demands that changes in stress impose on some systems of the body.

Chapter 4 covers the various types of training available to runners and what each type of training is designed to accomplish. You should always be able to answer this very simple question: "What is the purpose of this workout?" Although many runners use various types of training—repetitions, intervals, threshold running, and easy prolonged runs—few are really certain of how the body responds to each.

Chapter 5 gets into the details of the VDOT system, which has proven to be so useful in setting training paces for all types of running. A new aspect of the VDOT system shows runners of all ages (from 6 years to 50 years and beyond) how they compare with runners in what is regarded as the optimal age range for top performance.

In chapter 6, I refer to the information presented in chapter 4 by suggesting some ways of setting up a season of training and how the season may be broken down into smaller segments (phases) that emphasize different types of training and how these different types of training fit together.

Chapter 7 gets into the specifics of training for fitness, from a very basic white program for novice runners, to red and blue plans for experienced runners, to a gold training schedule for those who fit into what I consider the elite group.

Chapter 8 deals with altitude training, an area of special interest to me and something I have spent much of my research and coaching career investigating. Because of the success of some runners who live at altitude, training in this environment has made some runners and coaches feel success is not possible without it.

Chapter 9 provides details of various workouts designed specifically for runners who are concentrating on racing the 800-meter event during track season. The anaerobic aspect of racing the 800 dictates that training should put considerable emphasis on anaerobic workouts.

Chapter 10 deals with training for and racing distances from 1,500 meters to 2 miles. Runners who prefer these race distances need some of the types of training used by 800 specialists as well as what longer-distance specialists consider provides them with their strength.

Chapter 11 presents training needs for runners who select the 5K and 10K distances as their favorites. These race distances are very demanding in terms of intensity and endurance and typically require a high degree of concentration during both training and racing.

Chapter 12 covers cross country running, a type of training that applies to many runners who specialize in shorter events during track season. In fact, it is often during a cross country season that many runners decide what distance they will concentrate on in the coming track season.

Chapter 13 is designed to prepare runners for a half marathon. These events are typically longer than most track events and usually require more concentration on mileage and on training that builds endurance.

Chapter 14 gets into considerable detail about marathon training. There are programs designed for raw beginners and those who are interested in just finishing a marathon. There are also many advanced marathon programs, with some emphasizing more mileage than others and some dealing with a variety of quality sessions. The marathon programs presented in chapter 14 are considerably more detailed than those found in most suggested training plans.

Chapter 15 provides a description of supplemental training and how to return to training after some time off, whether as a result of injury, illness, or a simple decision to take a planned break.

I truly enjoy helping relative beginners improve as much as I enjoy seeing one of my elite runners make it to the Olympic Games. I am a firm believer that the experience of the journey is much greater than any sense of accomplishment that may be realized at the end of the journey. The people I have met in my years as an athlete and as a coach are far more important to me than are the Olympic and world championship medals I have won.

—

Acknowledgments

It certainly is true that a teacher learns more than do the students, and one of the reasons this is so is because the teacher comes in contact with so many students over a lifetime of teaching. In my 50 years of coaching and teaching (and I see coaching as teaching), I have been very fortunate in terms of outstanding mentors, students, and athletes with whom I have spent time. I also want to mention my wife, Nancy Jo, and our two daughters, Audra Marie and Sarah Tupper, because they have been so supportive throughout our lives together.

It's not possible to list all the people who have helped me during my years of teaching and coaching, but a few made such an impact on my learning that I want to say thanks to them by name. Thanks to Dr. Bruno Balke, who was my major professor during doctoral studies. We also worked together in the Federal Aviation Administration and during many altitude research studies in the years leading up to the 1968 Mexico City Olympics. I was especially lucky to get to study one year at the Royal Gymnastic Central Institute in Stockholm, Sweden, where I was taught by, and became friends with, Dr. Per Olaf Åstrand, one of the world's greatest in exercise physiology and in promoting fitness for humans everywhere.

In my years of research involving elite runners, many gave freely of their time and allowed me to run numerous tests on them, and I would like to mention those who seemed to always be there when needed. These elite include Jim Ryun, Tom Von Ruden, Chris McCubbins, Alberto Salazar, Joan Benoit Samuelson, John Mason, Tom Heinonen, Oscar Moore, Dave Chisholm, Conrad Nightingale, and numerous Athletics West and Nike Farm Team runners.

I have also been honored to get to coach some outstanding runners over the years. A coach can't help but learn from the athletes who become particularly successful, and some of note include Penny Werthner (Canadian 1500 Olympian); Ken Martin and Jerry Lawson (both 2:09 marathon runners); Lisa Martin and Magdalena Lewy Boulet (both Olympic marathoners, with times of 2:24 and 2:26); Peter Gilmore and Jeffrey Eggleston (both 2:12 marathon runners); and Janet Cherobon-Bawcom, who ran the 10K in the 2012 London Olympics.

Special thanks to the many collegiate runners I got to coach during my 17 years at SUNY Cortland, because it is seeing young collegiate runners improve that reinforces the notion that what you are doing as a coach really does work. Special thanks to Vicki Mitchell, who went from being a 2:39 high school 800 runner to winning seven NCAA Division III national track and cross country titles and the 10K at Penn Relays in 33:01, with a final 800 of 2:31 (new 800 PR).

I also would like to thank Carl Foster for his longtime support related to research, and Jimmy Gilbert for the tremendous time and effort he put into converting my running research data into the rather popular VDOT tables that have become very useful in setting training paces for runners of all ability levels. Thanks to Bob Sevene and Frank Gagliano for letting me watch them work with athletes at the elite level, and thanks to Graham Covington and Harry Turvey, who played a significant role in helping me put thoughts about training into words and computer programs so that others may find some benefit in what I have to offer.

A final word of thanks to Anthony Gallo, Abdi Abdirahman, and Anthony Famiglietti, who became good friends and also became close friends of my wife and daughters. All those mentioned here have played a role in my coaching success, and many still do; thanks.

1

The Ingredients of Success

Don't waste your time wishing for things you don't have.
Do your best with what you do have.

The four basic ingredients of success I have always referred to will determine how successful any person will be as a runner. These ingredients are, in their order of importance, inherent ability, intrinsic motivation, opportunity, and direction. I think of inherent ability as most important because it is something a person is born with; you don't really have any control over how tall you will be or the design of your cardiovascular system, and some people are just built for running. Intrinsic motivation reflects a person's desire to follow any particular athletic pursuit, and without this ingredient, even a very talented person may not reach true potential. Opportunity varies a great deal and may depend on something as simple as where you live or how what you want to do is influenced by others around you, and direction may involve personal contact with a coach, teacher, or even just something that you read about in a magazine or book. The more time I spend coaching (in person, or by contact with runners via mail, fax, or email), the more I have realized how important each of these ingredients is in determining success in any running event.

INHERENT ABILITY

Think of an ideal distance runner. The image you have may vary a bit depending on who is the current champion or record holder, and certainly there are very successful runners who are tall or short or lean or even fairly muscular. The variation is considerable in terms of anatomical design, but physiologically and biomechanically the better runners have things in common; these may include how far from a joint a muscle tendon is attached and the efficiency of the cardiovascular system, based on heart size and cardiac output.

Because a good deal of what makes a great runner is not outwardly obvious, it is not as easy to see who is designed to be a great distance runner as it is to see who might have potential to play center on an elite basketball team. In fact, there might be two runners on a team who are the same height and same weight, who eat and sleep well, and who follow the same training program, but one beats the other by 30 seconds in a mile race because of unseen physiological or biomechanical (or even psychological) factors. A factor that can greatly affect performance is how much oxygen the blood is carrying with each liter of blood delivered. Hemoglobin (the substance that carries oxygen to the exercising muscles) levels can vary considerably among runners, and I have seen more than a minute difference in 5K race times associated with relatively small differences in hemoglobin levels.

Not all people are designed with equal chances of success in running. In some instances a test in the exercise physiology lab can identify some desirable characteristics, such as high $\dot{V}O_2$max or great running economy, but it is not always easy to see who has ideal characteristics; the person being tested may not be training or may be overweight and not currently capable of demonstrating the ability that lies beneath the surface.

INTRINSIC MOTIVATION

The second ingredient of success is intrinsic motivation, the desire a person has within to achieve success in running. It is important to differentiate between the motivation someone else has for you and the motivation you have within yourself to be a successful runner. It is easy for a high school running coach to be highly motivated for an ideally designed runner who transfers into his school, but if this runner is more interested in being a successful artist or piano player, success as a runner may not be as great as the coach anticipates.

In terms of the people who select running as a sport to pursue and the first two ingredients of success (ability and motivation), runners fall into three different categories:

1. Those with great ability and high motivation to use their outstanding ability

2. Those with outstanding inherent ability and little or no motivation to pursue the sport of running, for which they are nicely designed to be successful

3. Those with little ability for running and high intrinsic motivation to achieve success as a runner

The first group of runners are champions because they are not only nicely designed for running in terms of biomechanical and physiological features, they also have the necessary motivation either because of their interest in following a current champion or need to satisfy the desire to outperform others in the same age group.

Those in group two may be best referred to as coach frustrators because the coach sees their ability, but desire is lacking on the part of the athletes. It is not uncommon for a coach who has such a runner to make a comment such as, "Son, you could be a really great runner if you just had some desire." Sometimes a coach will even yell at some type twos to "give it your all," or "let's get going," or some other outlandish comment that probably will go further in driving these people away from the sport than it will to get them excited about running.

The runners in group two should not be yelled at by a coach who wants them to do better or for not having the motivation the coach believes they should have. My attitude about dealing with any runner under my wing is to provide an environment in which each runner's ability and potential will be realized. Coaches need to provide an encouraging environment for their runners, not a discouraging one. The way I try to develop an encouraging environment is to follow the basic laws of running, which are detailed later in this chapter. I have found that runners who are treated with respect and individually rather than as just part of a group of runners will realize constant improvement and find they are often meeting their personal running goals. Each runner needs to be positively recognized for every improvement that is realized. I much prefer concentrating on individual improvement rather than always comparing one runner with how others are doing.

Over the past 8 or 10 years I have asked high school runners, whom I run into at camps, to answer one question for me, and that question is "Why did you take up the sport of running?" They can choose from one of four answers:

1. I want to get in shape for another sport.
2. I got cut from another sport.
3. Someone pushed me or encouraged me to do it.
4. I wanted to be a runner.

So far the fourth answer applies to about 12 percent of those who are pursuing running in our high school system. This is a sad situation because it indicates that running is not something many youngsters want to try, and our school system is so lacking in physical education that the kids with natural ability don't get the chance to be seen running or realize they have a talent for the sport. Even worse, running is often used as a punishment. It is not unusual to hear a team sport coach tell a player who doesn't perform properly to "give me a lap."

A thoughtful coach can go a long way in instilling some motivation in a group two athlete, and it may also be the coach's job to encourage the person to put more time and effort into whatever future life he is motivated to pursue. A thoughtful coach may even help a talented but not-so-motivated runner become more interested in pursuing the sport. This can happen in several ways, but one thing I focus on is asking my runners to feel the workouts and to feel the same workout getting easier before increasing training stress. When so much focus is placed on increasing training stress to increase fitness, running can become too stressful.

As for those in group three, there are cases of people who were not very good at the high school level who went on to make an Olympic team. One of the subjects in an earlier research project I conducted had a best high school mile of 4:34, and this runner went on to set a world record in an indoor, middle-distance event and also to place ninth in the Olympic 1,500. One of my runners couldn't make the top seven on our team until her junior year of college, but she went on to win seven national collegiate titles and the Penn Relays in the 10K the year after she graduated.

Runners experience success at a variety of times in their careers, and a thoughtful coach can point out some positive facts about progressing as a runner. The fact that some runners progress rather quickly should not discourage those who are taking longer to progress. Every runner should have short-term and long-term goals to shoot for.

As for those runners who fit in group three (lacking ability but high in motivation), I'll take a team of these any day. They may be frustrated with their performances, but they are fun to have on a team and will usually be very supportive of teammates. They will also do anything the coach says. The negative side is they will do whatever is asked of them and will want to do even more, and it is often the coach's job to hold them back so they don't get hurt instead of letting them do extra training. A good approach to avoid overtraining is to always stick with the same amount and intensity of training for about four weeks before demanding or taking on more. Let the body adjust to one level of stress before introducing a harder stress.

Regardless of the types of runners a coach has, the coach needs to treat everyone as an individual, a person with various strengths and weaknesses. The goal is to teach each runner to be an optimist, someone who internalizes good things and externalizes unfortunate things.

OPPORTUNITY

Opportunity shows itself in many different ways, from weather and facilities to training and competing with or against others, and personal financial situations. Fortunately for runners, running is available to just about anyone, in just about any climate and any type of terrain. In fact, one person I coached for a number of years by mail was serving seven years in a state prison and was able to average about 40 miles (65 km) a week in the prison yard while preparing for a marathon that he ran upon release.

Opportunity can be related to how much money a person has, money that can be used to travel to various races, but you certainly don't need a lot of money to pursue running as a sport. Some runners do very well training on their own and often surprise competitors when they seemingly come from nowhere to win a race or two.

No doubt some people have better opportunities to train for running events than do others. Some who live in areas of cold winter weather have access to

Runners can be comfortable and successful training in almost any environment.

Zuma Press/Icon SMI

an indoor facility or a treadmill when running outside is rather difficult. The same could be said for residents of very hot summer climates; a relatively cool indoor facility could be a lifesaver.

When I lived in Sweden and trained outside through some rough winter conditions, I used to enjoy running by myself and often wondered if others, many of whom had nicer weather conditions, would be willing or able to put up with the less than ideal conditions. It is very possible that lacking an opportunity strengthens some runners' dedication to their sport.

One might ask why we in the United States, with every imaginable climate and terrain available for training, do not dominate running around the world. My answer to that is simple: We lack the type of physical education in our school systems that would help identify talented runners, and running is not promoted in the United States like other sports. With regular physical education in our school systems, more potential runners are likely to be spotted while running around playing a variety of games. Also, many of our youngsters see sports only on television, which is usually dominated by football, hockey, basketball, and baseball, and those are the sports these young ones imagine themselves participating in. If children never witness great runners, why should they be interested in becoming one?

In the United States, most young runners are attended to in the school systems rather than in clubs, as is more popular in other countries. Being part of a school team has advantages and disadvantages. One potential disadvantage is that runners may be exposed to several coaches while going through many years of school. There may be a middle school coach, then a high school coach (sometimes even a different coach for cross country and track during the same running season), followed by a college coach (or two).

Having multiple coaches can sometimes work out, but often the runner gets different approaches to how best to train and even how best to run a race. For example, some coaches may be very scientific in their approach, and others use minimal science in their training but may have such a good relationship with, and understanding of, the runners that science is not needed. The best a runner can do is hope that each new coach will provide some little idea that fills a gap in the overall training program. For a coach who has to work with runners influenced by a variety of training philosophies, it's best to determine what each runner has been subjected to in order to understand which techniques to apply. Having a variety of coaches can minimize the opportunity for a sound, continuous training program, something I discuss in the fourth ingredient, direction.

DIRECTION

The ingredient of direction refers to a coach or teacher or training plan to follow, and I tend to list direction as the last and possibly least important of the four ingredients of success. Why is direction least important? Because you can have no direction, some degree of direction, or direction that is worse than none. For example, let's say a runner asks me to coach him for the marathon. My first question would be "How much running have you been doing recently?" If the response is "I haven't been running," then I would ask, "What running have you done in your life up to this time?" If the response to this question is "I have never run," then I would ask, "What sports have you done in your life?" Now if the answer to this is "I have never done any sports," then I might say something like, "Starting right now, I want you to run 150 miles each week." Clearly, that response would be a harmful one—worse than no response, or no direction. Just because I have coached several marathon runners who do or have run 150 miles a week certainly doesn't mean I should impose that amount of stress on a raw beginner.

Training with a dedicated coach is the ideal situation.

A positive coaching approach is definitely more desirable from the athlete's point of view (and often even from the coach's point of view). Saying that progress is being made even when it doesn't seem to be the case will go a long way toward improving a runner's attitude about training. I often have success by emphasizing progress over a longer period of time; for example, I might tell a runner it would be nice to see a certain amount of improvement over the next couple of years rather than insisting on improvement in every season of every year. Some runners progress rapidly and others not so rapidly; understanding and positive thinking can provide a desirable environment for runners.

When I think of all the great runners I have known who suffered through a tough coach–athlete relationship, it amazes me that some of them ever reached high levels of success, and certainly some probably didn't do as well as they might have with more reasonable direction. It is definitely not uncommon for high school runners to be subjected to the same training program regardless of their level of experience or ability.

It is sometimes difficult to make a true evaluation of a coach because assessment is typically based on the performances turned in by the athletes. Further, in the U.S. collegiate system, success is often based more on a coach's ability to recruit athletes than on how much those athletes improved while in the program. If the term *coach* refers to the person who directs the improvement or refinement of running performance, then a good coach can always answer the questions "What is the purpose of this workout" and "Why are we doing this workout today?" A good coach produces beneficial reactions to training, creates positive race results, and transforms the athletes she brings into the program into better runners and better human beings.

Talented athletes who have motivation and opportunity can often perform well enough to mask the job being done by a not-so-great coach. On the other side of the coin, truly great coaches may be overlooked as a result of not having much to work with in terms of ability and motivation, but their day will come.

In addition, it's important that coaches always be available to their runners. Coaches need to care for their athletes as people first and then as runners. When I talk to my college runners at the beginning of each new season, I say something like, "First you are a person, second you are a student, and third you are a runner—and don't ever rearrange that order of importance while you are in school."

What coaches often tend to overlook is the importance of giving positive individual attention to each athlete on the team. Nothing can replace encouraging comments or understanding words from a coach. To become an elite runner, a person needs a support system, and this support system must have the athletes' best interests in mind.

DANIELS' BASIC LAWS OF RUNNING

In addition to the important ingredients of success in running, I have come up with what I call basic laws of running. I have designed these laws in hopes of allowing runners of all levels of achievement to be able to optimize the benefits of training. Since runners respond differently to a particular coaching treatment, training program, or environment, these basic laws help evaluate and enhance individual training situations.

1. Every runner has specific individual abilities.

Each runner has unique strengths and weaknesses. Some runners have a desirable muscle fiber design, with a high fraction of slow-twitch endurance fibers, which leads to a high aerobic power output (high $\dot{V}O_2max$). On the other hand, another runner who does not have a particularly high $\dot{V}O_2$max may have outstanding running economy because of ideal mechanics. I think that runners should spend a good deal of their training time trying to improve any known weaknesses, but when approaching important races, the main emphasis should be taking advantage of known strengths. For example, a runner who feels weak in the area of speed but great in endurance should spend early and even midseason time working on improving speed, but in the latter weeks of training, put more emphasis on endurance to take advantage of what works best for this individual.

2. A runner's focus must stay positive.

Do not dwell on the negative; try to find positives in all training sessions. For example, if a runner says after a workout that her run didn't feel very good, it would not be very wise for a coach, teammate, or training partner to say, "You sure looked bad running today." A better approach is to find something good to refer to, such as "Sorry you weren't feeling great today, but your arm carriage looked like what you've been working toward."

While you should be flexible when weather threatens your training, running under adverse, yet safe, conditions often strengthens confidence.

3. Expect ups and downs; some days are better than others.

Even world-record holders and Olympic champions have some off racing days now and then. Usually the longer the race distance, the less desirable it is to run a race when not feeling well. For example, you will need more time to recover from a marathon that you felt poor running than a 5K. I certainly would recommend even dropping out of a race when not feeling well, as opposed to struggling through a race knowing it will have to be some time before you are able to run well again.

4. Be flexible in training to allow for the unexpected.

Switch days to accommodate weather, for example. If you have a workout scheduled for Monday, and Monday's weather is cold rain and high winds and Tuesday's weather is predicted to be much nicer, put Monday's workout off until Tuesday.

5. Set intermediate goals.

These goals pave the way to long-term goals. Long-term goals are important to have but may take years to achieve, so it is crucial to have some smaller, more readily achievable goals along the way.

6. Training should be rewarding.

It's not always fun, but it should always be rewarding. Sometimes a particular workout may not feel so great, but if you understand the purpose of each workout, it is more likely that you will understand that progress is being made—and that is certainly rewarding.

7. Eat and sleep well.

Rest and good nutrition are parts of training, not things that are done outside of training.

8. Don't train when sick or injured.

Not following this law often leads to a more prolonged setback than if you'd taken a few days to recover from an illness or injury.

9. Chronic health issues should be checked by a professional.

Feeling below par now and then is not a big deal, but feeling consistently out of sorts is usually related to something that needs medical attention.

10. A good run or race is never a fluke.

Sometimes a bad run is a fluke, but if you do run a great race, it is because you are capable of doing it.

Keep these basic laws in mind throughout the training and racing process. Being able to keep training balanced, maintain a positive outlook, and set reasonable and achievable goals will lead to running success.

From a runner's standpoint, consistency in training is the single most important thing that leads to success. That consistency comes from concentrating on the task at hand—neither dwelling on the past nor looking too far forward. The only thing you can control is the present, and when you focus on that and remain consistent in your training, you'll find your greatest success.

The way to take advantage of these basic laws of running is to make them part of your everyday life as a runner. Over time, runners shouldn't have to think about how they are treating themselves; following these laws becomes a part of daily life, and race results will reflect this benefit. On the other hand, not following these laws can lead to disappointment in running performance and even poor relationships with other runners.

Athletes can't be sorted into clear-cut categories. Different amounts and combinations of my four ingredients of success are what give runners their individuality. Whether you are a runner or a coach, be happy with what you have, and use the ability you do have to its fullest. I discuss some training basics in chapter 2, but don't be afraid to make some changes now and then, when you are experiencing success with some alterations I offer. There are as many individual pathways to success as there are individuals, and discovering what works best for each person is what makes running so exciting and fun. Periodically reviewing the basic laws of running can remind runners of some important aspects of training and racing and also can be helpful in avoiding the negative effects of overtraining and not taking care of the body.

2

Training Principles and Running Technique

Eat well, rest often, and maintain a good state of hydration.

What type of training plan do most runners follow? Or maybe the question should be how do most runners train? Often a coach coaches as she was coached, which is not so unusual since many coaches go from being an athlete to being a coach. Some runners and coaches study psychology or biomechanics or physiology, and this provides some scientific background to the practical experiences they had as athletes. Still, it is not unusual to train the way some champion athlete was coached or trained. So, copying what others have done is certainly not uncommon. The question is do runners always understand why they are doing what they are doing?

A friend told me of a not uncommon approach to coaching, a method he referred to as "the eggs against the wall" approach. With this approach, the coach just pounds the athletes and hopes some survive, as if throwing a basket of raw eggs against a brick wall and hoping now and then that one doesn't break. No doubt with enough runners on a team, this method can often reap positive results, even if only a single athlete out of 10 survives. My concern in this case is that some who didn't survive may have been even better than those who did if they hadn't been driven out of the sport by injury or lack of commitment.

In this chapter I will present several topics on training and technique development, including eight significant training principles, how to develop a training plan, proper stride mechanics, and the importance of breathing rhythms. It is always important to understand each training component adds to the entire training program and overall fitness.

EXTREME APPROACHES TO TRAINING

I grew up as a swimmer and had to run to complete the modern pentathlon events I participated in for a number of years. The first running coach I ever had was our fencing master; he was a great fencing master, but he was not very skilled at coaching runners. As a newcomer to running, I did what he said and assumed it was how runners trained.

The first 6 weeks I ran for this coach, I ran a mile warm-up followed by 10 repeat 400s on a cinder track in spikes. Each 400 was about as hard as I could go (trying to keep up with others who knew how to run). I got a 400 jog for recovery between the harder 400s. I did this 5 days a week for 6 weeks. Now, if the purpose of this workout was to produce pain and injury, it was just right. I got such painful shins I didn't know which foot to stand on.

Another negative result of this daily set of hard 400s was that no one bothered to tell me how to run a race that was 4,000 meters in distance, so knowing nothing but all-out running, that's how I ran my 4K races—all out right at the start. Naturally, after about 800 meters I was already in a death trot for the remainder of the event. Not a really great approach.

How about doing what the great runners do—is that a good approach? Here is what one 17-year-old runner did one week in the spring of his junior year in high school.

Sunday was a 10-mile run in 64 minutes, and his only run on Sunday. Each of the other 6 days of every week involved a morning 4-mile run and then afternoon sessions on the track. This week in April I am referring to had the following afternoon workouts:

Monday: 9:55 2 mile + 2 × 5:15 miles + 3 × 2:28 800s + 6 × 65 sec 400s + weights and a 4-mile cool-down

Tuesday: 6 × 400 at 64 sec each + 10 × 140 at 18 sec each + 5 × 200 at 31 sec each

Wednesday: 50 × 400 at 69 sec each on a 3-minute send-off

Thursday: 18 × 800 at 2:45 each

Friday: 1 mile + 1,200 + 800 + 600 + 400 + 3 miles easy cool-down

Saturday: race

I guess this is how we should train our middle-distance runners because this runner broke several world records and made it to three Olympics.

Another national record holder had several 66-mile runs, ran 380 miles one week, averaged 320 a week for 6 weeks, and averaged 240 miles a week for one year. To perform as well as he did, is this the way we need to train? I seriously doubt many runners could do these workouts and live through them. So what is needed? I'd say we need to follow some principles of training.

PRINCIPLES OF TRAINING

It is a good idea to understand how training affects your body and that different kinds of training will stress different systems. Every time you impose a specific stress, there will be some immediate reactions in different parts of your body. Every time you impose that same stress, you get the same reactions, but over time there is a different reaction to a particular repeated stress, and that is the body strengthening itself.

The human body is very good at adapting to a variety of stresses, but it takes a fair amount of time for the body to fully react to some types of stress (e.g., it takes months for muscle fibers to fully adjust to the stress of regular running). It is important to understand different principles of training so you can take advantage of them and avoid overstressing the body with amount, intensity, or frequency of training.

Principle 1: Stress Reaction

Regardless of what running event you decide to engage in, it is worthwhile learning a little about how the human body reacts to various types of physical stress, and believe me it does react. All you have to do to realize there is always some reaction is to go for a simple run once around the block or around the track. At the completion of your one-lap run you can easily recognize some reactions to that stress. Your heart will be beating faster, you will be breathing a little harder, and you may notice a little discomfort in some muscles in your legs. If you take your blood pressure, you will find that it has gone up a little, not to mention that blood flow has been diverted from some parts of your body to other parts to accommodate the task you undertook. Your body does a very good job of adjusting to the stresses placed on it, and you won't even be aware of many of the adjustments made.

Steve Bardens/Action Plus/Icon SMI

By learning to deal with stress, runners like Haile Gebrselassie can strengthen both mind and body to achieve successful results.

Principle 2: Specificity

The second principle of training is directly associated with the first. The principle of specificity simply states that the tissues being stressed are the ones that react to that stress. If you stress your heart muscle, the heart reacts; if you stress some breathing muscles, they react; and if you stress some running muscles in your legs, those muscles will react. Every time you run, or even walk, some parts of your feet will also react to the stress imposed on them.

In addition to the relatively immediate reactions to physical stress, there is a second type of reaction. The parts of the body being stressed become stronger and better prepared to deal with any future stress, as long as the body is in a state of good health. Stress the heart muscle and the heart muscle gets stronger; stress your running muscles and they get stronger; stress the breathing muscles and they get stronger. This response occurs in all muscles, tendons, bones, and other tissues under stress.

Principle 3: Overstress

More stress leads to more adaptation, but another training basic may also come into play here: the principle of overstress. If you overstress some body parts, they may not get tougher; in fact, they may get weaker or break down completely. This brings up a very important part of the equation. When does the body accomplish the strengthening part of the stress reaction? It is during the recovery, or rest time, between bouts of stress that the strengthening takes place.

Rest and recovery are a vital part of a training program, not an attempt to avoid training. There may actually be times when you will benefit more from rest than from going out for another run, and sometimes doing a less stressful workout will produce more benefits than will a harder session. An approach I suggest for runners is that whenever you are not sure which of two training sessions to take on at any particular time, select the less stressful of the two. You are admitting you aren't sure which would be better, so why not eliminate the more demanding one? An example is deciding whether to do a solid set of interval 1,000-meter runs or a not-so-demanding fartlek session; the weather is not desirable, including some heavy winds. Doing the 1,000s will probably be slower than desired because of the wind, and that can be a bit discouraging. On the other hand, the fartlek session will not involve trying to hit any particular times for specific distances, and the overall benefit of the session may be as good as having done the repeat thousands for time.

Success in running relies on being able to make adaptations when necessary, particularly when it comes to coaching a team of young runners. For example, let's say a coach says, based on the fact that his star runner, Bob, has done a similar workout before, "Today I want you all to run eight repeat 400s in 75 seconds each with a 400-meter jog for recovery. If you want to run as well as Bob, you need to train like Bob." So the group goes out in 75 for the first 400, and as time goes by, Bob keeps running 75s, but some of the group can't hold that pace and struggle to run 78, 80, or slower for some of their 400s. Soon enough, those who can't keep up are struggling to run as hard as they can and are not getting as much recovery time between the faster 400s, and technique goes out the window.

What is the purpose of this workout? Probably to develop speed and economy, but if most of the group are struggling with poor technique, good economy is not being practiced, and speed is not developed if the pace keeps getting slower. So who benefits from the workout? Bob is the only one who benefits; all the others are just getting negative feedback as to how well they are progressing.

Coaches and runners must be able to make adjustments to accommodate each athlete who is out there to work out. You never know when the slowest person on the team may eventually become the best, but it will never happen if he is discouraged and quits before he realizes his potential or, worse, is run into the ground and injured so he is not able to run at all.

I feel confident saying that the United States never sends its top runners to any Olympic Games because some of the best are hurt when it comes time to pick the team. As far as coaching a cross country team, I would personally rather have my top seven runners all healthy and a little below their capability than to have three of them in peak shape and the other four injured and not even able to start the championship race. It does not make sense to always strive to produce the top athlete if that ruins the lives of others who may have eventually become great. What produces the best result is to have each member of a team performing at her best, regardless of where on the team each member is ranked.

Reducing stress, be it physical or psychological in nature, is desirable going into championship events. I have mentioned many times in writings and talks how Tom Von Ruden, a good friend of mine, asked for my advice when he was training for the final Olympic trials in South Lake Tahoe in 1968. He told me he was not feeling as ready as he would like to be in the final few weeks leading up to the trials, and he wondered what I thought he should do. Who knows if I gave the best answer, but I told him to leave the training camp and go up to Leadville, Colorado, where he could be by himself for the final couple of weeks before the trials. He took that advice and, somewhat unexpectedly, made the U.S. team. He followed that with a ninth-place finish in the Olympic 1,500. Maybe it was just a matter of reducing psychological stress, but it certainly paid off.

Principle 4: Training Response

Figure 2.1 shows how the body tends to respond to a new stress. Let's say you are starting a training program. You are not in great shape but are capable of running 30 minutes or so during any training session, and you can run

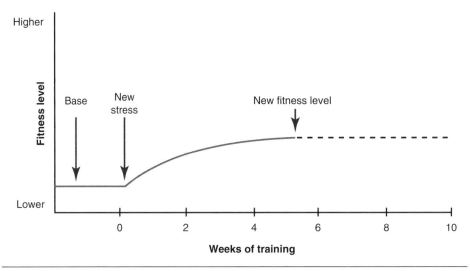

Figure 2.1 Increased fitness as a response to a new level of training stress.

some repeated 1-kilometer runs at 3:45 minutes each without undue stress. Also, let's say your current level of fitness is the one depicted in figure 2.1 as "base fitness," so you start doing the following program (which is more stressful than what you have been doing): 3 × 1 kilometer at 3:40 each, with 3 minutes of rest between the 3:40 kilometers. Also, let's say you do this training session on 3 days of each week. Since this new training program is more demanding than what you have been doing, you rise to a new level of fitness, shown as "new fitness level" in figure 2.1.

The benefit of this new training stress gets less as time goes by, however, and eventually, if you just continue doing the same training week after week, your new fitness level will no longer improve, as shown by the dashed line in figure 2.1. To gain further benefits, the training stress needs to be increased again. There are times when some runners will want to hit a steady state of fitness and not increase the stress until later in the year or when a new competitive season is fast approaching, but when a new level of fitness is desired, the training stress has to increase.

In the sport of running, there are several ways to achieve an increase in stress. Look back at the program you started following in our example—3 × 1 kilometer at 3:40 with 3-minute rests, performed 3 days each week. There are four variables in this program:

- **Workload**, or total amount of work being accomplished, which is 3 kilometers in this case
- **Intensity factor**, which is a speed of 3:40 for each kilometer
- **Recovery**, which is 3 minutes after each 3:40 kilometer being run
- **Frequency**, which in this program is 3 times each week

All training sessions have at least three of these four components: workload, intensity, and frequency. Steady runs (e.g., long easy runs) don't have the recovery factor because the workout involves a single bout of running. When you feel the need to increase the stress level of the training program in figure 2.1, you have all four components to work with:

- You could increase the workload by increasing the number of 1-kilometer runs to 4, or some number more than 3, and leaving the other ingredients as they are.
- You could leave the workload at 3,000 meters and increase intensity to 3:30 per kilometer.
- You could keep load and intensity as is and reduce the recovery time between runs to 2 minutes.
- You could leave load, intensity, and recovery as they are and just increase frequency to 4 or 5 days each week.

It is not a good idea to change more than one of the training variables. A lot depends on the total mileage currently achieved; the number of repeats of a particular training distance in a training session should be a function of weekly mileage. If a runner has a stable weekly mileage, the number of repeats will not usually be changed; more likely the speed of the repeated runs will be increased and recovery time held similar to what it was earlier. Making any of the ingredients of the training session more stressful will usually result in the body moving up to a new level of fitness, and the manner in which this improved fitness is achieved is similar to how the first improvement was achieved—relatively rapidly at first and then tapering off over a period of weeks. Figure 2.2 shows how new levels of fitness are attained.

Principle 5: Personal Limits

Sometimes an increase in training stress may not result in improved fitness, and in figure 2.2 I have put a question mark after the new fitness level (2), suggesting that imposing a new stress (3) may not bring about an increase in fitness. This doesn't mean a person has reached optimal fitness, but it does indicate that another principle of training is coming into play here, namely that everyone has limits. By no means does this imply that anyone ever reaches her absolute limits, but it certainly does suggest that everyone has seasonal limits. By seasonal limits I mean limits that are imposed on a person because of a lifestyle at any given time.

The principle that everyone has limits is most noticeable during college years because of the variations that occur in class schedules. For example, during one term of study a student may have a class at 8:00 a.m. every day of the week, have classes until 2:00 p.m. every afternoon, and attend two labs from 2:15 to 5:15 p.m. on Tuesdays and Thursdays. The labs may even

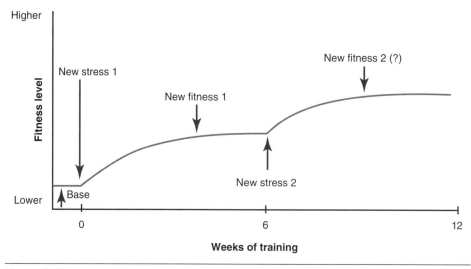

Figure 2.2   Increased fitness as a response to new levels of training stress added to prior training stresses.

prevent the runner from attending practice on Tuesdays and Thursdays, and training may have to be alone. Now, the very next college term this same runner may not have a class until 10:00 a.m. any day of the week and may not have any labs, with the final class of the day ending at 2:00 p.m. This certainly is a better schedule for training, with sufficient time for morning runs and also plenty of time in the afternoons.

Even for runners who are not in college, the demands of daily life can definitely vary from one season of the year to the next. The demands at work, at home, and of other things going on at different periods in a person's life make training more or less difficult.

Something that should definitely be avoided is overtraining, and the best way to prevent this negative scenario is to have constant runner–coach interaction. Training intensities should be determined by current fitness, which is best measured by race performances. With this in mind, my standard answer to a runner who thinks his training needs to be speeded up is "Prove to me in a race that you are ready to train faster." Of course when a runner has been training at a specific intensity for 4 to 6 weeks without feeling any increase in stress, then, without a race to go by, training can be increased slightly in intensity.

I have designed a brief stress table that some runners find useful for tracking life issues (table 2.1). Keeping track of different aspects of daily life can often help athletes and coaches decide what daily activities and stresses are associated with good and bad performances, or even what is associated with variations in how training, or life in general, is going.

Table 2.1 Stress Table

For each of the eight items, for each day, assign one of the following scores: 1 (outstanding), 2 (good), 3 (OK), 4 (not so good), 5 (terrible). Score 1 and 2 within 2 hours of waking; 3 to 6 by early afternoon; 7 and 8 at the end of each day.

Week 1							
	Sun	**Mon**	**Tues**	**Wed**	**Thurs**	**Fri**	**Sat**
1. Last night's sleep							
2. Pains and illness							
3. Today's workout and recovery							
4. Flexibility							
5. Energy and nutrition							
6. Today's physical stress							
7. Today's mental stress							
8. Other							
Day totals							

Week 2							
	Sun	**Mon**	**Tues**	**Wed**	**Thurs**	**Fri**	**Sat**
1. Last night's sleep							
2. Pains and illness							
3. Today's workout and recovery							
4. Flexibility							
5. Energy and nutrition							
6. Today's physical stress							
7. Today's mental stress							
8. Other							
Day totals							

Date of week 1: _____ Week 1 total: _____
Date of week 2: _____ Week 2 total: _____
Enter 2-week total here _____ Make any overall comments below regarding your training:

_____

_____

_____

From J. Daniels, 2014, *Daniels' running formula,* 3rd ed. (Champaign, IL: Human Kinetics).

In arriving at scores for each item in table 2.1, consider the following:

- How desirable was last night's sleep?
- Do you have an injury, an illness, or unusual pains?
- How well do you think you recovered from yesterday's training?
- How is your flexibility?
- Rate the previous 24 hours of rest, energy, and nutrition.
- Rate the physical stress of today's training session.
- How stressful was today, relative to your general mental and emotional state?
- Add any category you would like to include in your daily evaluations.

Principle 6: Diminishing Return

Two other principles of training often associated with each other are the principle of diminishing return and the principle of accelerating setbacks, both of which are depicted in figure 2.3.

Let's first examine the principle of diminishing return. Here we are looking at how fitness improves over time, with increases in intensity of training. In this case, time may be years of training, not just several weeks. When you start training, the benefits are rather substantial relative to the effort put forth. The fitter you get, the less benefit you get from training harder, which is quite logical if you think about it.

For example, as a beginner you may improve your time for a 1-mile race from 6:10 to 5:40 without training very hard, but a 30-second improvement

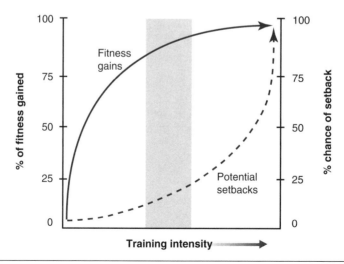

Figure 2.3   Comparison of an increase in fitness level caused by training with the chance of a setback caused by the increased stress from training.

from 5:40 to 5:10 will probably be a bit tougher, and improving from 4:30 to 4:00 will take a lot more work than it took to get from 6:10 to 5:40.

Just imagine how much harder you would need to train to improve your marathon time by 1 minute if you are currently running 2:08 than it would take to improve 4 minutes, from 3 hours to 2:56. Again, the fitter you become, the less benefit you get from training harder. Here's another (and more appealing) way to put it: The worse your state of fitness, the more benefit you will reap from not training very hard, which is reassuring when you have lost fitness because of illness or injury.

Principle 7: Accelerating Setbacks

Now that we have looked at the diminishing return curve, let's look at the accelerating setback curve, represented by the dashed line in figure 2.3. This curve shows that when you are not training very hard, there is less chance of encountering a setback, through injury or lack of interest; but at some point in the training process, as the stress of training increases in intensity, the chance of a setback starts to increase rather rapidly.

When you consider these two responses to training, most of your training must be in the gray shading shown in figure 2.3. Within this ideal intensity zone, there are substantial benefits and relatively minimal chances of being sidetracked by setbacks.

Bear in mind that it is not possible to assign a particular amount of stress to this window because that will vary based on training experience. For example, for one runner this desirable window of training stress may be 30 miles (50 km) per week, and for another runner it may be 120 miles (190 km) per week. What constitutes a good amount of training depends a great deal on years of experience and body design, not to mention time available and commitment to the sport of running. I don't mean to suggest that you never move outside that ideal training zone; but when you do, it is best to stay out there only a short time before going back to the safer, ideal zone.

Principle 8: Maintenance

The last principle of training is the maintenance principle, which states that it is easier to maintain a level of fitness than it was to achieve that fitness. Part of this is a psychological matter because it is typically easier for a runner to repeat a particular performance than it was to achieve that same performance in the first place.

For example, if you have been working for some time to race a 5-minute mile, and you finally make it happen, it won't be as hard to do it again as it was to do it the first time. Physiologically, you have increased your fitness level a notch as well. Your heart has gotten stronger, more blood vessels have opened up to the running muscles, and the muscle cells themselves have become more efficient in converting fuel into energy.

Zuma Press/Icon SMI

Running at a comfortable pace as part of your training program can reap benefits.

Another example of how maintaining fitness is not as hard as it was to achieve it is seen when you taper for races. During a taper, you back off some on the training stress and achieve faster race times. Being able to maintain, or even improve, fitness while reducing stress certainly supports the maintenance principle.

The maintenance principle is particularly important when planning a long-term training program because it allows you to shift from emphasizing one type of training to another while still maintaining the benefits of the previous workouts. For example, you may have been concentrating on interval training for some weeks and then switched over to more threshold work and a little less of the interval-type training. The maintenance principle allows you to keep the benefits you gained from the interval work as you begin to reap the benefits of threshold training.

It is also possible to see the maintenance principle at work when a student has some time off between cross country and track season. During this time off from running, an athlete may do some supplemental training or may even play a little basketball or some other sport, and the stresses imposed on different parts of the body can help maintain some conditioning that the earlier running produced. This is of particular importance for runners who take some time off for injury, for illness, or just to take a break from daily running.

TRAINING PLAN DEVELOPMENT

In discussing these important principles of training, I have shown that there is no one specific route to success as a runner. Some runners respond better to one type of training than do others; some are slow to respond to the same training that others respond to quickly; and it is certainly a good idea to expose all runners to various approaches during a season of training. You must always be open to trying different types of training and to arranging training in different orders of importance throughout a season, but at all times you should be able to answer the question "What is the purpose of this workout?"

Several years ago I was asked by some high school coaches how to best deal with their teams' racing schedule (every Tuesday and every Saturday throughout cross country season). The question was, "If we have to race Tuesday and Saturday every week, when can we train?" My response was twofold.

First, realize that races are a serious part of training and that there are definite physiological and psychological benefits achieved from racing. In addition, when running a 4,000- to 5,000-meter race twice a week, there is little, if any, need for interval training during this time. In other words, a race that lasts 15 to 20 minutes is just about the optimal physiological stress on those systems of the body that are taxed during an interval session.

Second, it might be best to do a workout on Wednesday each week, the day after that midweek race. This has worked out so well over the years that I often used that approach with my collegiate runners. Not that I had a Tuesday race each week, but we would often train hard Tuesday and come back Wednesday for another quality workout. It is true that the muscular discomfort associated with a hard session is realized more about 48 hours after the stress than it is 24 hours afterward. Therefore, a Wednesday quality session can often be performed quite well and even better than it might have been if put off until Thursday.

Here are some additional benefits to scheduling back-to-back training days on Tuesday and Wednesday. First, this means you have 2 easy days before any Saturday races and 2 easy days after a Saturday race before the next Tuesday race or training session. Second, some runners like to run some quality sessions faster than I have asked them to run, and this back-to-back schedule often solves this problem. For example, if I say, "Tuesday you are to run six 1,000-meter runs at 3:20 each, with 3-minute recoveries," they are less likely to try running them in 3:15 (too fast) if I also add, "and tomorrow you will be running six 1-mile runs at 5:44 with 1-minute rests between." Knowing another quality session is coming tomorrow tends to put a damper on overtraining on the first of the two back-to-back days. Third, when you get into track season, you may attend some 2-day meets in which you have to race on two consecutive days, and your back-to-back training sessions will have prepared you for this.

Understanding the principles of training helps you minimize the possibility of overtraining while letting you take full advantage of the work you are doing. Remember to always try to achieve the greatest possible benefit from the least amount of training rather than getting the greatest possible benefit from the hardest training possible.

When increasing the training stress, always stay at a chosen degree of stress for 4 to 6 weeks before making changes. It is a mistake to try to make each week of training, or each specific workout, better than the previous week or the last time you did that specific workout. I would much rather have my runners come to me saying a particular workout is starting to feel too easy than for them to be struggling to go a little faster each time they train.

Training is not always fun, but it should be rewarding, so don't overdo it. Coaches and athletes should be conservative when increasing the training stress. I let race performances tell me when it is time to increase the stress of training rather than increasing the stress level too often in hopes of a performance improvement.

The following are not necessarily principles of training but topics of particular importance that might fit into a talk of training principles: how you stride over the ground and how you breathe when running.

STRIDE RATE

During the 1984 Olympics in Los Angeles, my wife and I spent every day of the running events counting different runners' stride frequency, often several times for the same runner, during prelims and finals and also early and late in the same race. In all we examined about 50 runners, both male and female and in events from the 800 to the marathon.

Of all the runners evaluated, only one took fewer than 180 steps per minute. Turnover was well over 200 per minute in the 800 and sometimes in the 1,500, but from the 3,000 (a women's event in the 1984 Olympics) through the marathon, the rate was quite similar and only stride length was reduced as the race distance became longer.

In our lab one time, I tested an Olympic gold medalist in the marathon. At a 7-minute-per-mile pace, the rate was 184; at a 6-minute pace, it moved up to 186; and at a 5-minute pace, it moved up to 190. This represented a 16.5 percent increase in running speed and a 3 percent increase in rate. It is quite clear that runners seem most comfortable with a particular rhythm, and that rhythm varies little as they change stride length to increase speed during different races.

Adam Davy/Press Association Images

Most elite runners have similar mechanics, including a quick stride rate.

180 Steps per Minute

One reason I strongly emphasize trying to run with a stride rate around 180 steps per minute is to minimize the landing shock associated with running. Keep in mind that the slower the leg turnover, the more time you are spending in the air; the more time you spend in the air, the higher you are elevating your body mass; and the higher you elevate body mass, the harder you hit the ground on the next landing. Believe me, it is during the impact associated with hitting the ground that many little injuries occur.

So, how do you minimize landing shock when running? A simple way of explaining it is to pretend you are rolling over the ground rather than bounding from foot to foot. Try to avoid placing each foot out in front of yourself, which often acts as a braking action, increasing the impact force as you go from one foot to the other. Try to have your feet land closer back, toward your center of gravity, so your body is floating (or rolling) over your feet.

Foot Strike

Another issue is what part of your feet hit the ground first (i.e., where is your foot strike?). Where you strike the ground (relative to your center of gravity) is one concern, and another is how your feet strike the ground.

Foot strike tends to vary, not only among runners but also depending on the event for which you are training. It is most common for those racing in short events (e.g., sprinters and even some middle-distance runners) to hit the ground on the balls of their feet, almost as if they are running on their toes. On the other hand, many longer-distance runners, which certainly includes those who are running a marathon, tend to strike the ground with a heel-first landing or, in some cases, a midfoot landing.

A big advantage of a mid- or rear-foot landing is that it reduces the stress placed on the calf muscles and shifts the landing stress more to the larger thigh muscles. It is not uncommon for beginner runners to develop calf pain, and forefoot landings add to that possibility. If using a heel-first landing, try to imagine you are rolling over your feet as your body moves forward after each landing, as previously stated.

From my years of testing many runners of all ability levels, it has become apparent that some people are more comfortable using a certain type of foot strike. Runners who are relatively new to the sport should experiment with different foot-strike techniques and use the one that is most comfortable, that is the least fatiguing, and that allows for a light and quick turnover rate of about 180 steps per minute.

In particular, if you are experiencing calf or shin discomfort, try to concentrate on a mid- or rear-foot landing technique for a few weeks and see if that solves your problem. Very often, just focusing on taking 180 steps each minute will result in a mid- or rear-foot landing, and you won't have to think about how you are striking the ground.

One final thought about foot strike is to try to avoid turning your toes outward as you land. Have someone watch you from the front as you run toward them, checking to see if your feet are striking the ground with the toes pointing straight forward rather than to the side. A turned-out foot on landing often leads to shin pain along the inside of the lower leg.

Go for 180 steps a minute and learn to roll over the ground with as little effort as possible, and running should be much more enjoyable and leave you more injury free. I sometimes tell runners they should imagine they are running over a field of raw eggs and their goal is to not break any of them; be light on your feet and comfortable in your landing. And one final note—don't count each foot when counting stride rate; just count the right (or left) foot and look for 90 (assuming, of course, that you take as many steps with the left as you do with your right).

BREATHING WHILE RUNNING

It is important to understand your breathing and how it should feel when running. People who have asthma or other breathing-related issues need to discuss their ventilation problems with their doctor so they are doing the best they can to eliminate stressful situations relative to their breathing.

In normal atmospheric conditions, the breathing discomfort that is sometimes associated with exercising (specifically, running) hard is not due to a lack of oxygen (O_2) in your lungs. The feeling of wanting to breathe harder is caused by an increase in the amount of carbon dioxide (CO_2) in your lungs. In normal air (i.e., in a building or outside in open air), there is very little CO_2. In fact only about .04 percent of normal air is CO_2.

Impact of CO_2

In your lungs, because your blood is always delivering CO_2 from functioning tissues throughout your body, there is a much greater fraction of this gas, compared with how much is in the air you breathe in. In fact, at any given time, even during rest, the air in your lungs is about 4.0 percent or even 5.0 percent CO_2. You feel quite comfortable when your lungs contain this much CO_2, but when you start exercising, the muscles you use while running produce much more CO_2 than when at rest, so the fraction of this waste product of exercise is increased.

When your body senses an increase above the normal 4 or 5 percent, you breathe harder to get rid of the excess CO_2. So it is the increase in this gas, not a drop in the amount of O_2, that stimulates you to breathe harder. In fact, you always have plenty of O_2 as long as you are breathing normal air.

An extreme example of how the buildup of CO_2 increases the desire to breathe is when you hold your breath to see how far you can swim underwater. That intense desire to inhale a good breath of fresh air is the increase in CO_2 that results from not breathing; it is not due to a lack of O_2. In fact, if you were to reach a state of insufficient O_2, you would pass out because not enough O_2 is being delivered to the brain. We are quite fortunate that the increase in CO_2 drives us to breathe before the lack of O_2 results in our passing out.

So how does this all relate to breathing while running? Well, the harder you run, the faster you deliver CO_2 to the lungs, and that increase in CO_2 drives you to breathe harder to reduce the concentration of that gas in your lungs, which, of course, also helps you stay well above the concentration of O_2 needed for the work being done.

Breathing Rhythms

The total amount of air that you breathe each minute is the product of the size and number of breaths you take each minute. As you start to run you usually increase both the size and number of breaths, but the rate at which you breathe is typically in rhythm with your stride rate.

When not running very hard, you may breathe in for three steps and breathe out for three steps, and you may stay with this rate even when you feel the need to breathe harder, by just increasing the size of each breath. By running a little harder, you feel the need to ventilate even more, so you switch to a faster breathing rhythm; for runners this is usually by taking two steps while breathing in and two steps while breathing out (referred to as a 2-2 breathing rhythm).

Most accomplished runners breathe with a 2-2 rhythm, especially when running fairly hard, because it is comfortable and allows a sizable amount of air to be breathed in and out of the lungs. I strongly recommend using a 2-2 rhythm during practice and in competition, at least during the first two-thirds of middle-distance races, as I explain later in the chapter. You may be able to breathe at a slower rate when running slowly, but it is usually better to use that good 2-2 rhythm even in easy runs, and in threshold, interval, and repetition workouts, so it becomes natural.

When considering the rate at which you breathe, you must understand that the important aspect of breathing is to ventilate the lungs with fresh air. Let's take, for example, a few different situations. If you breathe with a 4-4 rhythm, you will certainly move a large amount of air into your lungs with each breath you take, but this 4-4 rhythm means you are taking only about 22 breaths per minute (180 steps per minute divided by 8 steps per breathing cycle means you are taking 22.5 breaths per minute). Let's say you are moving 4 liters of air in and out with each breath; this means you are moving 90 liters of air in and out of your lungs per minute, and believe me, if working hard, that is not very much.

Now, let's go to a 3-3 rhythm, which may reduce the amount of each breath to 3.5 liters per breath, which means you are now moving 3.5 liters in and out, 30 times per minute, and $30 \times 3.5 = 105$ liters per minute, 16 percent more air per minute. Now, let's try a 2-2 breathing rhythm, which will give you 45 breaths per minute and about 3 liters per breath. In this case you move 135 liters of air per minute ($3 \times 45 = 135$), which is doing a better job of ventilating the lungs, reducing CO_2 buildup, and increasing the O_2 content of the air in your lungs.

We can go one step further and try a 1-1 breathing rhythm (something you often hear novice runners doing at the end of a hard race). With this rate of breathing, the size of each breath will be greatly reduced, and the total amount of air moved in and out may not even be as much as can be accomplished with a slower yet deeper rate. In addition, realize that a portion of each breath you move through your mouth and nose is dead-space air, the air that does not reach the lungs for gas exchange. The faster the breathing rate, the greater portion of each breath, and of each minute, is *not* involved in O_2 and CO_2 exchange.

Obviously, faster breathing rates are a little more costly in terms of energy expenditure of the breathing muscles, but at some point, the ventilation factor, along with the cost factor, usually ends up favoring a breathing rhythm of somewhere around a 2-2 (or 2-1) rhythm. Taking three steps per breathing cycle (using a 2-1 or 1-2 rhythm) gives you 60 breaths per minute (1 each second). This probably allows for the greatest amount of air to be moved per minute while running, but it is usually not necessary until you are working very hard, such as in the last part of a 5K or 10K race.

Running with a smooth breathing rhythm, as Shalane Flanagan did during her bronze medal 10,000-meter run in the 2008 Beijing Olympics, can be crucial to a runner's success.

John Walton/Press Association Images

Of all the elite runners I have tested in the lab, about 86 percent of them automatically choose a 2-2 rhythm until working at maximum, at which time they go to 2-1 or 1-2. Whether the elite runners have learned over the years that this is the most efficient approach, or whether someone has suggested this to them, it makes sense to adjust to this rhythm early in a career without having to wait for it to become the natural thing to do.

One way I demonstrate the effects of the different breathing rhythms to my runners is to ask them to run five laps on the track (just at moderate intensity, not racing). For the first lap they are to breathe with a 4-4 rhythm, then 3-3 for lap two, 2-2 for lap three, 1-1 for lap four, and back to 4-4 for lap five. Then I ask them which was most stressful and which was most comfortable.

Something that works quite well with younger runners is to have them breathe with a 2-2 rhythm for the first two-thirds of a race (e.g., first 2 miles of a 5K cross country race), then go to 2-1 or 1-2 for the final third of the race. If they can't manage 2-2 for the first two-thirds of the race, it tells them they have gone out too fast, and next time they are to set an easier early pace.

How much air any particular runner moves in and out of the lungs per minute varies a great deal. Two Olympians I tested were similar in size and in performance, but during a maximum-effort test, one breathed 160 liters per minute and the other 224 liters per minute. One was breathing just over 2.6 liters per breath and the other just over 3.6 liters per breath. People definitely vary in minute ventilation and in the size of each breath, but it is not necessarily an advantage or disadvantage to be a heavy or light breather, so do not worry about how you operate.

One situation where a faster breathing rate is a little easier is when running at altitude. The air at altitude is less dense and offers less resistance to flowing in and out of the breathing airways. I have known at least two great runners who used a 1-1 breathing rhythm at altitude when working really hard.

A runner can also use the knowledge of breathing rhythm to determine how hard she is working. If you can breathe comfortably with a 3-3 rhythm during a long steady run, this means you are not working too hard, but if you feel you must breathe 2-2 to get enough air, then you are not working that easily. I am not suggesting that you use a 3-3 breathing rhythm during all easy long runs (2-2 is still probably the way to go), but that giving 3-3 a try for a few minutes would tell you how hard you are working. This is similar to knowing you are going too hard during threshold running (i.e., if you can't use a 2-2 rhythm and have to go to 2-1 or 1-2). I'm not suggesting you need to constantly monitor your breathing, but it is good to know how you can use this information during training and racing to judge the effort you are putting forth.

3

Aerobic and Training Profiles

Don't compare yourself to other runners;
focus on your own fitness and performance.

In this chapter I describe profiles of how various systems of the body react to increasing levels of stress. In other words, as you work harder, or run faster, relationships are seen between the intensity of the work being done and how fast the heart beats, or how much oxygen is being consumed, or the accumulation of blood lactate, or how you envision the workloads you are being exposed to. In some cases equal increases in running speed cause a relatively predictable increase in physiological response, but in other cases the response is not linear. Oxygen consumption, for example, reacts quite predictably to steady increases in running speed (under calm conditions on a flat surface), whereas the accumulation of blood lactate does not show such a predictable, nor linear, response curve.

AEROBIC PROFILE

For many years maximum oxygen consumption ($\dot{V}O_2max$) was considered the most important indicator of endurance. Some 40 years ago a teammate of mine found that his $\dot{V}O_2max$ was 73 ml $\cdot$ min^{-1} $\cdot$ kg^{-1} (milliliters of oxygen consumed per minute per kilogram of body weight). During that same time, I also had my $\dot{V}O_2max$ tested, and it was a disappointing 63 ml $\cdot$ min^{-1} $\cdot$ kg^{-1}. Interestingly, I often beat him in our 4,000-meter modern pentathlon races, so I decided to see how much oxygen he consumed during some submaximal runs.

The measure of energy expended while running aerobically at some submax speeds is a measure of running economy. Just as some cars use less fuel to cover any particular distance of movement, so do some runners consume less oxygen (they are more economical) while running at the same speed.

Figure 3.1 shows the two economy curves that were developed by connecting the V̇O₂ data points collected during repeated 5-minute runs at several submaximal running speeds. By extrapolating the generated economy curves out to each runner's V̇O₂max value (73 for my teammate [runner 1] and 63 for me [runner 2]) and then drawing a vertical line from each max value down to the horizontal axis of the figure, I was able to arrive at a running speed that I termed vV̇O₂max (velocity at V̇O₂max).

If you think about it, vV̇O₂max is a far more important determinant of running ability than are V̇O₂max or economy, individually, because this important variable indicates what running speed is associated with each athlete's aerobic power (V̇O₂max). So, if two runners have the same vV̇O₂max, they should be equal in racing over various distances. Other factors come into play in determining who is better, but vV̇O₂max is certainly a better indicator than V̇O₂max, and I am happy I was able to introduce this term to researchers around the world. I like to think of any runner's economy curve and associated V̇O₂max and vV̇O₂max as that runner's *aerobic profile*, which varies with changes in running fitness.

To carry the results of the tests run on my teammate and me a step further, figure 3.1 shows that a vertical line drawn through both economy curves and down to a speed of 268 meters per minute, which is a 6:00-per-mile pace, indicates both runners are working at the same percentage (81 percent) of their respective V̇O₂max values. Interestingly, runners race at rather predict-

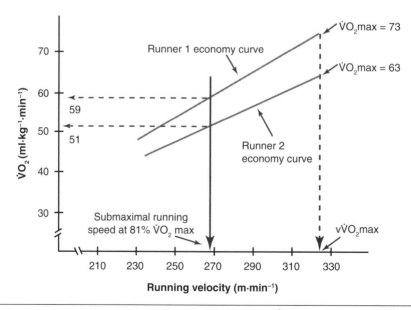

Figure 3.1   Two runners with considerable differences in V̇O₂max and economy with very similar vV̇O₂max and race times.

able fractions (percentages) of their $v\dot{V}O_2max$ speeds, which are determined by the duration (not the distance) of a race. For example, a race that lasts about 30 minutes is run at about 93 percent of a person's $\dot{V}O_2max$, even if one runner is completing 10,000 meters and another only 8,000 meters in that 30-minute period.

Again, $v\dot{V}O_2max$ is the important value, because as that value is increased, either by an increase in $\dot{V}O_2max$ or an improvement in running economy, the same fraction of the improved $v\dot{V}O_2max$ becomes associated with a faster running speed. I will go into more detail about the relationship between aerobic profiles and performance when I discuss the term *VDOT* in chapter 5.

Figure 3.2 and figure 3.3 are examples of how economy can vary among individual runners and under various running conditions. Figure 3.2 shows three elite female runners I tested some years ago. It is easily seen that the three women varied a great deal in $\dot{V}O_2max$ and in running economy, but all three had similar $v\dot{V}O_2max$ values and ran almost identical times for 3,000 meters. Interestingly, the runner with the lowest $\dot{V}O_2max$ was a U.S. collegiate national champion in 10,000 meters, and the one with the highest max was also very successful in international competitions.

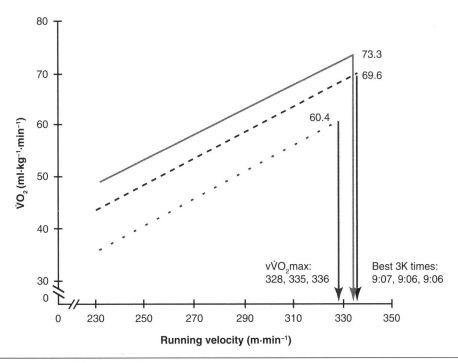

Figure 3.2 Three female runners with different aerobic profiles that produce similar predicted and actual 3,000-meter times.

Adapted from Daniels, J. et al. 1986. "Elite and sub-elite female middle-and long-distance runners." In *Sport and Elite Performers, 1984 Olympic Scientific Congress Proceedings,* Vol. 3, ed. D. Landers. Champaign, IL: Human Kinetics. First published in Daniels, J. 1985. "A case for running economy, an important determinant of distance running," *Track Technique* (92) Spring, 2937-2938, Track & Field News. Los Altos, CA.

Figure 3.3 shows the changes in aerobic, heart rate, and blood lactate profiles of an elite runner I was able to test in the early part of his track season and later in the season when he was in better shape. As shown in figure 3.3, this runner's maximum heart rate (HR) was the same (196) during both test sessions, but his V̇O₂max had increased from about 73 to nearly 78, which is just about a 7 percent increase in a matter of a few months. With the increase he experienced in running economy, his vV̇O₂max rose from 358 to 387 meters per minute, which is an 8 percent increase.

His blood lactate profile also improved a good deal: A 4 mmol value was initially associated with a running speed of 330 meters per minute, and this rose to about 355 meters per minute, another 7.5 percent improvement. During both test sessions, this runner showed a 4.0 blood lactate accumulation when running at about 85 to 87 percent of his V̇O₂max, which is very typical for well-trained runners.

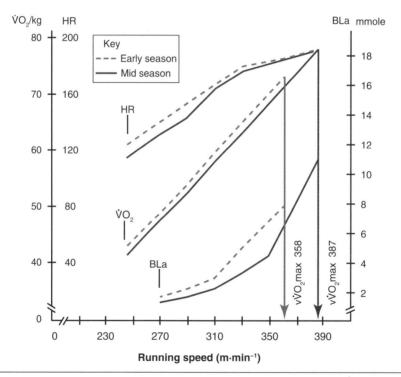

Figure 3.3   The comparison of heart rate (HR), oxygen consumption (V̇O₂), and blood-lactate level (BLa) of an elite runner during the early season and midseason.

Variations in Running Economy

Running economy can vary depending on where you are running. Figure 3.4 shows the results of a group of well-trained runners who were tested under four conditions—at sea level (both on a treadmill and on a track) and at an altitude of 2,000 meters (also both on a treadmill and on a track). $\dot{V}O_2$max values were the same on a track and treadmill, both at sea level and at altitude. It is clear that $\dot{V}O_2$max was lower at altitude under both conditions (track and treadmill), but it is also clear that at altitude the aerobic demand of running is less than it is at sea level. This means that some of the running ability lost at altitude, because of a lower $\dot{V}O_2$max, is regained because of a decreased energy demand (better economy) at altitude.

A closer look at figure 3.4 indicates that upon arrival at altitude, $\dot{V}O_2$max was lower by about 13 percent, but because of less dense air to run against at altitude, economy is improved to the point that $v\dot{V}O_2$max (and performance) differs by only about 6 percent.

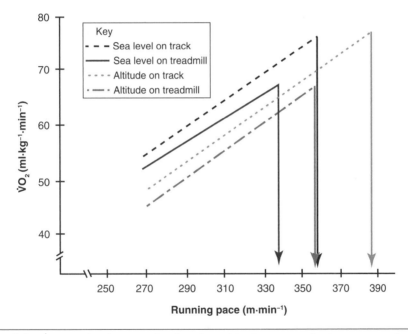

Figure 3.4 $\dot{V}O_2$max levels at sea level and at altitude are equal when measured on the track and on a treadmill. However, economy is much better on a treadmill both at sea level and at altitude than it is on the track.

Gender Differences in $\dot{V}O_2$max and Running Economy

One reason that men race longer distances faster than women is because the best men have higher $\dot{V}O_2$max values than the best women. There is a fair amount of variation among both the top men and the top women, and I have tested Olympic-caliber male runners with max values between 68 and 86 ml·min^{-1}·kg^{-1}. Usually those with lower max values are better at the 800 and 1,500 distances because of the greater anaerobic demand of those events. These 800 and 1,500 types are also more economical at faster speeds than are the longer-distance specialists, most likely because they spend more time perfecting their running mechanics at faster speeds.

How about a comparison of running economy between men and women? I have had the honor of testing large numbers of both male and female elite runners. The men are slightly more economical than the women, but the difference is not much at all. Part of the reason some researchers say women are not as economical as men is that they compare the two while running at the *same* submax speeds. The result shows that when running at any given submax speed, women consume a fair amount more oxygen (per kilogram of body weight per minute) than do men, but this is not being fair to the women, because when running at the same speed, the women are running at a higher fraction of their (lower) $\dot{V}O_2$max values.

The more realistic approach is to compare the genders when both are running at the same fraction of their respective $\dot{V}O_2$max values. So, the better way to compare running economy is to calculate it in terms of $\dot{V}O_2$ per kilogram of body weight per kilometer of running. For example, if a man and a woman both have their $\dot{V}O_2$ tested when running at a speed of 300 meters per minute, the man might be consuming 57 ml of O_2 per kilogram per minute and the woman 60 ml/kg, which is a 5 percent difference in economy. However if the woman's max is 67 and the man's is 73, he is working at only 78 percent of his max and she is at 89.5 percent of her max; the faster you run, the less economical you are, so the woman should be tested at a speed that elicits 78 percent of her max.

Let's say she is at 268 meters per minute when running at 78 percent of her max, and that speed demands a relative $\dot{V}O_2$ of 50 ml/kg. You need to calculate the aerobic demand per kilometer of running, which for her would be 1,000 meters divided by 268 meters per minute, meaning it would take 3.73 minutes to run 1,000 meters, and $3.73 \times 50 = 187$ ml of O_2 per kilogram of body weight per kilometer of running.

If the man, when at 78 percent of his max, is running 300 meters per minute, it would take him 3.33 minutes to complete a kilometer. If his relative $\dot{V}O_2$ at that speed is 56 ml/kg/min, his $\dot{V}O_2$ per kilogram of body weight per kilometer is 56×3.33, which equals 187 ml/kg/km, and the two runners are equal in economy when both run at the same relative intensity.

RUNNING VARIABLES AND IMPROVEMENTS

The important thing for any runner is to improve as many variables as possible in order to perform better. Just looking at figures 3.1 and 3.2, it is obvious that in order to improve running performance, it is necessary to include training that will improve aerobic power ($\dot{V}O_2$max) and running economy, and as either, or both, of these variables improves, there will be an improvement in the important v$\dot{V}O_2$max variable.

Keep in mind that any person can run at various fractions of v$\dot{V}O_2$max for different durations. For example, you can race at about 93 percent of v$\dot{V}O_2$max for any event that lasts about 30 minutes, so as v$\dot{V}O_2$max is improved, so is the speed at which you can race for any specific time. I will show how I have been able to use this information to develop the very popular VDOT tables that I discuss in chapter 5.

It is not uncommon for some runners to plot blood lactate values against running speed, as I did when I compared $\dot{V}O_2$ with running speed. When designing a blood lactate profile, this is also accomplished by testing a runner at a number of submaximal speeds, as shown in figure 3.3.

It is desirable for the curve to shift toward the right with improved endurance, which indicates the runner is running at a faster speed before the lactate value is as high as it was in earlier testing. This right shift in the lactate profile occurs as the body improves its ability to clear the lactate being produced; as well, improvements in $\dot{V}O_2$max and running economy increase the speed at which a given lactate value is reached. As your body becomes better at clearing lactate, a higher fraction of $\dot{V}O_2$max becomes associated with the same blood lactate accumulation value that was previously associated with a lesser intensity of effort; you can endure a faster pace with the same feeling of discomfort.

One way to realize how various changes can affect the lactate profile is to consider that a particular blood lactate value is associated with running at 86 percent of $\dot{V}O_2$max. This being the case, then the same fraction (or percentage) of an increased $\dot{V}O_2$max will be associated with a faster v$\dot{V}O_2$max. Same thing for an increase in running economy—better economy also increases v$\dot{V}O_2$max, so the blood lactate value at the same fraction of an increased v$\dot{V}O_2$max will be associated with a faster speed than it had been earlier in the training cycle.

The same thing can be done with heart rate, for those who are in tune with their heart rates during training. If you have a heart-rate check associated with $\dot{V}O_2$ or speeds of running, then a particular heart rate will also be associated with a specific blood lactate value.

Let's say, for example, that your heart rate is at 164 when you are at a blood lactate value of 4.0 mmol, and that this heart rate is also about 88 to 90 percent of your maximum heart rate. Keep in mind that heart rate is pretty closely associated with how much work you are doing, as well as what your aerobic involvement is at any particular running speed. As you improve your running economy, $\dot{V}O_2$max or v$\dot{V}O_2$max will be associated with a faster speed of running, and the same fraction of that improved v$\dot{V}O_2$max will be associated with the same heart rate that was earlier representative of a slower speed of running.

You could even go a step further and associate your subjective feeling of stress with different fractions of your maximum heart rate, aerobic power, or blood lactate values. One way of doing this is to relate numbers with your feeling of comfort or discomfort. For example, you might assign easy running a number between 1 and 3; comfortable hard work might equal a 4 or 5 ranking, with 6, 7, and 8 related to different degrees of hard work; and 9 and 10 might mean you are working very hard. Or you might just use a 5-point scale, with 1 being easy work and 5 the hardest work you do. Refer to figure 3.3, which shows how a runner's heart rate, $\dot{V}O_2$, and blood lactate values were all related to the speed at which this runner was running.

HEART RATE DURING TRAINING RUNS

Let's now discuss using heart rate during training runs to determine training intensities. You must understand that running intensity is not always the same at the same speed of running. For example, under hot weather

Zuma Press/Icon SMI

Maintaining heart rate can be useful, but it's important to understand that certain factors, such as training in a cool indoor environment versus outdoors in the heat, can influence heart rate.

conditions, the heart has to work harder at any given speed of running than when under cool conditions because more blood is diverted to the skin for cooling purposes.

With more blood going to the skin and the same required amount going to the running muscles, there is an increase in total blood flow and in heart rate. This means that if a runner is trying to use heart rate to monitor a particular speed of running, speed will be slower than anticipated.

The same situation will occur if running into a wind, on hilly terrain, or over rough or muddy footing; shooting for a specific heart rate will result in a slower-than-hoped-for speed of running. It is fair to say that a slower speed of running under less-than-desirable conditions will often still be associated with the desired intensity of exercise, even though not at the same speed.

So, it is always important to be able to answer the question "What is the purpose of this workout?" If the purpose of a specific workout is to spend time at a specific *speed* of running, then it might be necessary to not let heart rate be the guide, but if *intensity* of effort is the most important thing being sought, then heart rate can be very useful. I like to say that monitoring heart rate can be a good thing for runners as long as they understand how heart rates can vary based on conditions.

Maximum Heart Rate

A very important matter relative to using heart rate for monitoring training stress is knowing your personal maximum heart rate because it is very typical to consider training at a variety of fractions of maximum heart rate. A few methods are used to estimate maximum heart rate, primarily based on age, but these formulas can be inaccurate. An example is an often-used formula that involves subtracting your age from 220; so if you are 50 years old, a calculated maximum heart rate would be 170 (220 – 50).

Now, this formula, and others, for that matter, may do a decent job of estimating maximum heart rate for a large group of people, but it could be very misleading for any particular person. I can cite two people, whom I tested on numerous occasions, whose maximum heart rates fell far from their predicted values. One male runner, at age 30, had a carefully measured maximum heart rate of 148, and this same runner, at age 55, had a maximum heart rate of 146. You can imagine how far off you would be if you told this runner, when he was 30 years old, that to run at 86 percent of his maximum heart rate he would need to maintain a heart rate of 163; this would be impossible for a person with a max heart rate of 148.

Another of my subjects had a maximum heart rate of 186 when he was 25 years old (lower than predicted when using 220 – age), and this same runner had a maximum heart rate of 192 when he was 50 years old (far higher than predicted using 220 – age as a formula). My point is that if you do use heart rate as a measure of relative running intensities, you need to have a pretty good idea of what your personal maximum heart rate is.

As a runner, probably the easiest way to determine your maximum heart rate is to run several hard 2-minute uphill runs. Get a heart-rate reading at the top of the first hill run, and if your heart rate is higher the second time up, go for a third time and see if that is associated with an even higher heart rate. If it is not higher, you can be pretty sure that reading is maximum. If the third run is higher than the second, then try a fourth, or as many as needed before you do not see an increase in heart rate compared with the previous run. If no hill is available, you could just do a few 800-meter runs at a solid pace and do the same comparisons between repeated efforts

Resting Heart Rate

Another way that monitoring heart rates can be useful includes noting resting heart rate upon waking in the morning. Your waking heart rate can show how your fitness is progressing; with time, resting heart rate will typically get slower as a result of your heart getting stronger and capable of pumping more blood with each beat (increased stroke volume). As your heart muscle gets stronger, it doesn't have to beat as often to deliver the same amount of blood to various parts of your body because each beat is delivering more. Waking heart rate can also indicate a state of overtraining, and if your morning heart rate is considerably higher than what you normally measure, you might need a rest or to get a health checkup.

Hemoglobin Content

Another factor that will affect heart rate is the status of your blood's oxygen-carrying capacity. Oxygen is carried by hemoglobin in the blood, so having a desirable hemoglobin content is an important consideration, especially for endurance athletes.

When your hemoglobin levels are below normal, you will not feel very good and will certainly not be prepared for an ideal performance as a runner. On the other hand, it is not wise to try to elevate your hemoglobin to very high values because this will increase the thickness of the blood, which puts too much strain on the heart and can actually slow down circulation.

Having a normal hemoglobin value is primarily a matter of good nutrition and consuming foods that have iron in them. Typical normal hemoglobin values are between 13.5 and 16 grams percent, which means you have that many grams of hemoglobin for each 100 grams of blood. People are often considered anemic when they have hemoglobin values below 13, and from a running performance point of view, the difference between a 12 and 13 in hemoglobin could be about 30 to 40 seconds in a 5K run. Again, it is not desirable to try driving that number up high, however.

ABSOLUTE $\dot{V}O_2$

$\dot{V}O_2$max can be expressed in two ways. Up to this point I have been referring to $\dot{V}O_2$max in relative terms, which means relative to your current body mass (body weight as most often referred to). The other way of referring to $\dot{V}O_2$, whether submax or max in nature, is in absolute terms.

When oxygen consumption is measured, the initial calculation is an absolute $\dot{V}O_2$, which is typically expressed in milliliters or liters per minute (1,000 ml = 1 liter). For example, if your absolute $\dot{V}O_2$max is 4,000 ml (4.0 liters), and your body weight is 135 pounds (61.3 kg), this means your relative $\dot{V}O_2$max is 65.25 ml/kg, arrived at by dividing 4,000 ml (absolute value) by 61.3 kg.

Now, as a runner, the more important value is the relative $\dot{V}O_2$ because you must carry your body weight while running. If you are a competitive rower, then the absolute value is more important because it is associated with how much work you can perform. By the way, each liter of $\dot{V}O_2$ is related to about 5 kilocalories of energy expenditure.

Where some people get into trouble is trying to find whatever way possible to increase the relative $\dot{V}O_2$max value. When they understand that relative $\dot{V}O_2$max is the result of dividing absolute $\dot{V}O_2$ by body mass in kilograms, they realize they can either increase the absolute value or decrease body weight.

The early days of $\dot{V}O_2$ testing during a run on a track.

Training increases the absolute value, and even with no change in body weight, the relative value also increases. So, why not just lose as much weight as possible to increase the all-important relative value? If you have unnecessary body tissue that can safely be lost, then this is one way to go. However, if you do not have any tissue that can, or should, be lost and you try to reduce your body weight, you will also be reducing your absolute $\dot{V}O_2$ value and just get weaker, and running will not improve.

Here is an example: Absolute $\dot{V}O_2$max = 3,000 ml and body mass = 60 kg, which produces a relative $\dot{V}O_2$max of 50 ml/kg, which according to my calculation is equal to a 19:56 5K race time. Now, getting body weight down to 50 kg means your relative $\dot{V}O_2$max theoretically should now become 60 ml/kg (3,000 / 50 kg = 60 ml/kg), and a 60 max is associated with a 5K time of 17:02.

However, if while losing weight you lose some valuable muscle, then absolute $\dot{V}O_2$max drops because that $\dot{V}O_2$ value is a function of how much muscle mass you have to do your running for you. So, maybe your weight (and muscle) loss results in a reduced absolute $\dot{V}O_2$max of 2,500 ml (down from the previous 3,000 ml value). This leaves your relative max value at 50 ml/kg, and now you are weaker because of a smaller working muscle mass, and that results in a slower time.

Be very careful when you think the way to go is to lose weight. If it is a reasonable approach, then some loss may be possible, but anytime you are not performing well or feeling good during races or training, pay particular attention to rest and proper diet. For those interested in performing tests in the lab or on a track, the protocols I have used over the years are presented in appendix A, Aerobic Profile Test Protocol.

PERSONAL TRAINING AND RACING PROFILES

Before setting up any training programs, runners or coaches should gather some basic information about the past and current state of fitness and time availability. I gather detailed information from all my runners (figure 3.5), making it much easier to plot a training plan that best fits each individual. This information is critical when dealing with runners by e-mail, and it is also very important for any high school, college, or club coach.

Knowing current or recent mileage and workouts makes it much easier to determine the appropriate training loads and training intensities that will best prepare each athlete for the important race(s) ahead. Clearly, you must also know the types of races that are of most importance in the weeks and months ahead.

FIGURE 3.5
Runner Profile

Name, address, and e-mail: _____

_____

Age: _____ Ht: _____ Wt: _____ Gender: _____

1. What has been your average weekly total run (miles or minutes) over the past 6 weeks? _____ miles per week *or* _____ minutes per week

2. What has been your longest single run in the past 6 weeks? _____ miles _____ min

3. Have you run any races in the past several months? _____ If yes, list distances and times. _____

_____

4. How much free time do you have, on a daily average, for running? _____ hours/day

5. How many days per week are you able to train? _____ days/week

6. What is available for training? (e.g., track, grass, dirt roads, trails, treadmill, indoor track) _____

_____

7. Give details of any specific workouts you have performed over the past 6 weeks. _____

_____

_____

8. List any races you are planning to run (or at least hoping to run) in the coming 4 months. _____

_____

_____

9. What is your most important race in the next 6 to 12 months?
Date: _____ Distance: _____ Site: _____

Comments: _____

_____

From J. Daniels, 2014, *Daniels' running formula,* 3rd ed. (Champaign, IL: Human Kinetics).

Even if you are a school coach and know the facilities available, writing them down helps you plot out training for any kinds of weather conditions. Plotting out a season of training is not as easy as it may seem, and having individual (or team) profiles can go a long way in coming up with the best possible training program. I find myself referring to runner profiles whenever writing out a season's training schedule, such as the ones presented in the later chapters of the book.

4

Training Runs
and Intensities

Focus on the task at hand.

As I often mention, you must always be able to answer the question "What is the purpose of this workout?" If you can't answer this all-important question, then you may be better off not doing any training at this particular time. In this chapter I describe the various types of training a runner engages in and how these different types of training benefit a runner.

E, **M**, **T**, **I**, and **R** refer to intensities of training and stand for the types of training (shown in figure 4.1) that make up most training programs. **E** stands for **E**asy running, **M** for **M**arathon-pace running, **T** for **T**hreshold running, **I** for **I**nterval training, and **R** for **R**epetition training.

Figure 4.1 also indicates typical durations of training (in minutes), both for steady runs and for repeated bouts of work (W/R), during intermittent workouts. Also shown are purposes and benefits of each type of training, the amount of each type that is typically associated with a single session, the percentage of $\dot{V}O_2$max and of maximum heart rate related to each type of training, and work–recovery ratios for intermittent training sessions.

EASY RUNNING

E stands for easy and is typically an intensity about 59 to 74 percent of $\dot{V}O_2$max or about 65 to 78 percent of maximum heart rate. What is the purpose of easy running? There are several benefits, and the first is that you build up a certain degree of resistance to injury by taking it easy in many of your runs. **E** running is especially good for building a base when just starting out in a running program or when returning to running after a break of some weeks or months. Think of **E** runs offering some of the same benefits that taking it easy in any sport offers—performing the specific activity of interest with limited stress on the body or mind.

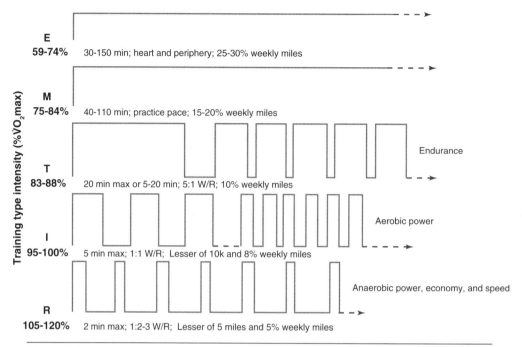

Figure 4.1 The different types of training showing the percent of $\dot{V}O_2$max, the range of time per workout, the benefits, the work to rest ratio, and the percentage of weekly miles.

Adapted, by permission, from J. Daniels and N. Scardina, 1984, "Internal training and performance," *Sports Medicine* 1(4): 327-334.

E running does a good job of developing the heart muscle, since the maximum force of each stroke of the heart is reached when the heart rate is at about 60 percent of maximum. As you run faster, the heart rate and the amount of blood pumped with each heartbeat (referred to as stroke volume) both increase, but stroke volume increases minimally. So, fairly easy running is a good developer of the heart muscle, and although it doesn't feel as if you are working very hard, your heart is.

Another benefit of **E** running is an increase in vascularization (opening of more tiny blood vessels that feed the exercising muscles) and the development of characteristics of the muscles themselves that are involved in running. Even during **E** running, your heart is delivering a good amount of blood and oxygen to the exercising muscles, and these muscles respond by making changes in the muscle fibers that allow the muscles to accept more oxygen and convert more fuel into energy in a given period. In fact, many of the benefits gained as a result of this process are a function of time spent stressing the muscle fibers. You will no doubt spend more time accomplishing this goal by running easily because it is easier to last longer at a comfortable pace than it is at a hard pace.

Training Suggestions

Because 30 minutes of steady running provides considerable benefits for the time spent running, I suggest that 30 minutes be the minimum duration of any **E** run you go out for. I also suggest that your longest steady run (unless preparing for some ultra events) be 150 minutes (2.5 hours), even if preparing for a marathon. Obviously, anyone who is combining walking with running in preparation for a marathon should feel free to stay out longer than 150 minutes, but all long (**L**) runs should be built up to very gradually.

Undoubtedly, most runners spend a majority of their running time working at an easy pace, a conversational pace that is always comfortable to manage. In all the training plans I describe, or that I prepare for runners at any level of performance, I refer to easy running as **E** running. Sometimes I refer to **E** days of training, which means the runner should take it easy on this particular day, and an **E** day may even be a day off from running. In addition to using **E** pace during **L** runs, **E** intensity is also used for a good part of warming up and cooling down and during recovery jogs between bouts of faster and harder running.

It is often good to think of **E** days as opportunities to accumulate the mileage needed to reach your desired weekly mileage goals. For example, if you are trying to total 40 miles in a particular week and you have a 10-mile **L** run one day and a total of 8 miles (including warm-up, some faster quality running, and cool-down) on two other days, this means you have to accumulate another 14 miles on the remaining 4 days.

This could be done by running 3 to 5 **E** miles on each of these 4 days, or you might run 5 or 6 miles on 2 of the 4 days, plus 3 on another day and take one day off completely from running. Sometimes a day off works out best in your weekly schedule (maybe because of difficult weather or an unexpected commitment), and you should think of time off from running as part of training rather than as a missed training day. Remember, the **E** days are included so that you get proper recovery from the quality (Q) sessions, so it is not a good idea to add an additional Q session in place of an **E** session.

Easy Running Pace

Although **E** running is typically performed at about 59 to 74 percent of $\dot{V}O_2$max or about 65 to 78 percent of maximum heart rate, at times you may feel more comfortable going a little faster (or slower). The important thing, especially if going extra slow on an **E** run, is to make every effort to maintain good running mechanics, because losing desirable mechanics may lead to injury. Remember this when you are feeling particularly tired or not quite right with your stride—this may be one of those days when not running will do you more good than forcing yourself to struggle through a run and end up with a minor injury.

You will notice in the VDOT tables in chapter 5 that I list a range of **E**-pace running speeds, and that range is about 2 to 3 minutes per mile slower than you might be able to race for 1 mile, so it should be clear that **E** running is not very stressful.

Long Runs and Increasing Mileage

Relative to **L** runs, which are typically at **E** pace, I like to limit any single **L** run to 30 percent of weekly mileage for runners who are totaling fewer than 40 miles (64 km) per week. For those who are accumulating 40 or more miles per week, I suggest **L** runs be the lesser of 25 percent of weekly mileage or 150 minutes, whichever comes first.

Try to stay with the same weekly mileage for 4 weeks before making an increase, which also means your **L** run will stay similar for several weeks at a time. Also, feel free to reduce the duration of an **L** run if some weeks you are not feeling as good as in others, if conditions make the same **L** run much more stressful, or if you need to back off a little for a coming race.

Kirsty Wigglesworth/PA Archive/Press Association Images

Easy runs are comfortable and conversational in nature.

I often get into some fairly lively discussions about **L** runs for slower marathon runners, and certainly marathon running has become a very popular fund-raising event, with many runners taking 5 hours, or longer, to complete a marathon. It is not uncommon for some runners and coaches to say that in order to complete a marathon you must have some 20-mile (32 km) training runs.

For someone who is going to spend 6 or 7 hours completing a marathon, this means a training run that lasts about 5 hours, and that sure seems like a little too much stress for a beginner. I doubt many elite marathon runners go for 40- or 50-mile training runs, which would take them about 5 hours, so it doesn't make sense for not-so-accomplished runners to spend more time training than do the best.

When you consider that the top runners do go for some 20-mile runs and longer, you must realize that they accomplish these runs in about 2 to 2.5 hours, and that is the main reason I think 2.5 hours is long enough, even if it gets a runner a total of only 15 miles (24 km).

In summary, **E** runs help build resistance to injury, strengthen the heart muscle, improve the delivery of blood, and promote some useful character-istics of the muscle fibers that will help you run at your best. In addition, increasing the duration of **E** runs (and it's much easier to increase mileage or duration of your runs if they are easy) is a good boost for your confidence that you can last a long time if you so desire. Never overlook the mental side of the training you are doing.

MARATHON-PACE RUNNING

Marathon-pace running, as the name implies, is training at your projected marathon race pace. I refer to this as **M**-pace running. For runners who have not previously run a marathon, it can certainly pose a question as to the proper pace to use, which is definitely another benefit of the VDOT tables provided in chapter 5. These tables show the relative performances for a variety of race distances and the corresponding marathon times. It is always best to use a recent longer race for the purpose of predicting your proper **M** pace (e.g., a half marathon is better than a mile for predicting your **M**-pace capability). Another way to estimate **M** pace for runners who have recently finished some serious 10K races is to estimate **M** pace as being about 3 min-utes per 10K slower than 10K race pace.

Figure 4.1 (and table 5.4 in chapter 5) shows some percentages of VDOT and of maximum heart rate that should be reasonable approximates of what to expect based on the time you plan to run in completing a marathon.

Just as I have suggested an upper limit on the distance or amount of time spent on any **L** run, I also suggest limiting an **M** run to the lesser of 110 min-utes or 18 miles (29 km), whichever comes first. I also like to mix **M**-pace running with both **E**- and **T**- (threshold) pace running; the maximum accu-mulated at **M** pace may then be less than the time spent in a steady **M**-pace run. I also suggest that **M**-pace running, in a single session of training, not add up to more than the lesser of 20 percent of your weekly mileage or 18 miles, whichever comes first.

Relative to that important question—"What is the purpose of this work-out?"—the purpose of **M** running, for someone who is training for a marathon, is to adjust to the specific pace to be used in the coming marathon and to practice drinking while at this pace. So, you might say the main benefit of **M** running is mental, helping you gain confidence at the pace you plan to race in a coming marathon. Physiological benefits are really not different from those gained during **E** running. However, some runners who are not training for a marathon may find that **M**-pace runs build confidence that they can handle a fairly prolonged run at something a little faster than a typical **E**-pace run. Table 4.1 shows a number of possible **M**-pace workouts.

Using a lot of fuel in the form of carbohydrate helps teach the body to conserve stored muscle glycogen and rely a little more on fat metabolism. During some long, steady **E** runs, it is suggested that you do *not* take in any energy drinks so your body learns to conserve carbohydrate. However, still take in water occasionally in practice (in the marathon itself, it helps to take in fuel, and these training sessions are a good time to practice this).

Table 4.1   Marathon-Pace (M) Workouts

Workout	Total minutes
*Training session A: for runners totaling up to 70 min **E** and 50 min **M***	
15 min **E**, 50 min **M**, and 10 min **E**	75 min
35 min **E**, 50 min **M**, and 10 min **E**	95 min
60 min **E**, 50 min **M**, and 10 min **E**	120 min
*Training session B: for runners totaling up to 70 min **E** and 60 min **M***	
15 min **E**, 60 min **M**, and 15 min **E**	90 min
35 min **E**, 60 min **M**, and 15 min **E**	110 min
55 min **E**, 60 min **M**, and 15 min **E**	130 min
*Training session C: for runners totaling up to 60 min **E** and 75 min **M***	
15 min **E**, 75 min **M**, and 15 min **E**	105 min
35 min **E**, 75 min **M**, and 15 min **E**	125 min
45 min **E**, 75 min **M**, and 15 min **E**	135 min
*Training session D: for runners totaling up to 45 min **E**, 70 min **M**, and 15 min **T***	
15 min **E**, 30 min **M**, 5 min **T**, 30 min **M**, 5 min **T**, 5 min **M**, and 10 min **E**	100 min
15 min **E**, 5 min **T**, 40 min **M**, 5 min **T**, 15 min **M**, 5 min **T**, 10 min **M**, and 10 min **E**	105 min
15 min **E**, 50 min **M**, 5 min **T**, 20 min **M**, 5 min **T**, and 30 min **E**	125 min
*Training session E: for runners totaling up to 70 min **E** and 80 min **M***	
60 min **E**, 30 min **M**, and 10 min **E**	100 min
60 min **E**, 40 min **M**, and 10 min **E**	110 min
60 min **E**, 50 min **M**, and 10 min **E**	120 min
60 min **E**, 60 min **M**, and 10 min **E**	130 min
30-40 min **E**, 80 min **M**, and 10 min **E**	120-130 min
40-60 min **E**, 70 min **M**, and 10 min **E**	120-140 min

Table created by Jack Daniels' Running Calculator designed by the Run SMART Project.

"Total for session" indicates the actual amount of time run. Some workouts also include time at **T** pace.

THRESHOLD RUNNING

The intensity of **T** (threshold) runs should be comfortably hard, which means you are definitely working relatively hard, but the pace is manageable for a fairly long time (certainly 20 or 30 minutes in practice). Peaked and rested, you can race at **T** pace for about 60 minutes, which means elite runners run right at **T** pace for 20K or even for a half marathon.

As opposed to **M** and **E** runs, which for well-trained runners are usually not intensities that you keep hoping will end soon, **T**-pace runs are of that type—you do look forward to their coming to an end, but they are manageable for a fair number of miles.

The all-important purpose of **T** runs is to allow your body to improve its ability to clear blood lactate and keep it below a fairly manageable level. It is often best to think of the purpose of **T** runs as being to improve your endurance—teaching your body how to deal with a slightly more demanding pace for a prolonged period of time, or increasing the duration of time you can hold at a specific pace. Just as **E** and **M** runs improve your ability to press on mentally at a comfortable pace, **T** runs improve the speed you can keep up for a relatively long time.

Threshold pace would physiologically be at about 86 to 88 percent of $\dot{V}O_2$max (88 to 90 percent of maximum heart rate) for well-trained athletes and still above 80 percent values for lesser-trained runners. When I have a runner who is relatively new to my style of coaching and she is doing a **T**-pace workout for the first time, I will suggest that she ask herself during the run if that pace could be maintained for 30 or 40 minutes if necessary. If the answer to that question is "No," then the pace must be slowed down a little. Remember, the proper pace is comfortably hard, not hard, which is an intensity set aside for **I** (interval) running.

As shown in figure 4.1, I recommend two types of **T**-pace workouts; one is a tempo run and the other is what I refer to as cruise intervals. The difference between these two types of **T**-pace workouts is that the tempo run is a steady run lasting about 20 minutes in duration, and cruise intervals are a series of runs at **T** pace, with a short rest break between the individual runs. Both types of **T**-pace runs have a particular advantage. The steady tempo runs are better at building confidence that you can keep up a fairly demanding pace for a prolonged period of time, whereas a session of cruise intervals subjects your body to a longer session at the desired threshold intensity.

Even though cruise intervals provide little periodic rest breaks, that does not mean you should run them faster. In fact, if you think you are not stressed enough doing cruise intervals, just reduce the recovery time a bit. Do your tempo runs and cruise intervals at the same designated pace as you can find in the VDOT tables in chapter 5.

As with **L** runs and **M** runs, I suggest a limit on how much running to accumulate at **T** pace in a single workout session; for **T**, I suggest not totaling

Zuma Press/Icon SMI

Threshold runs can seem easier when done with a partner.

more than 10 percent of your weekly mileage in a single workout. However, for any runner who can handle a steady 20-minute **T** run, I also suggest a minimum of 30 minutes at **T** pace if the session is broken into cruise intervals. After all, if a steady 20-minute run is doable, then 30 minutes shouldn't be too difficult if broken into shorter 5- or 10-minute work bouts.

One issue that often comes up regarding tempo runs is duration, and differences in the definition of *tempo* cause some concern. Some coaches and runners will talk about a 60-minute or 10-mile (16 km) tempo run, and when you realize elite runners can just about race at **T** pace for 60 minutes (tapered and rested), it is hard to imagine a person going for a 1-hour tempo run just in training.

What I have found regarding what some coaches and runners refer to as tempo runs is that the overall distance may, for example, be 10 miles, but the first 5 or 6 miles of this run are slower than true **T** pace, and there is a gradual increase in speed to the point that the final 3 or 4 miles of the run are actually at **T** pace. So, the overall run may be referred to as a tempo run, but only part of the run is at true **T** pace.

Again, my definition of a tempo run is any run during which the pace of the entire run is performed at **T** pace, and when a runner progresses from an easier pace to true **T** intensity, only the **T**-pace portion of that overall run is tempo. I consider **T**-pace runs that last about a steady 20-minutes in duration as true tempo runs. Sessions that involve running a series of shorter-duration runs at **T** pace, with short recoveries between the **T**-pace runs, I refer to as cruise intervals. A couple examples of typical cruise interval workouts might involve running five 1-mile runs at **T** pace with 1-minute rests after each mile, or three 2-mile runs at **T** pace with 2-minute rests.

Some of the more advanced runners I have coached have accumulated as much as 15 miles (24 km) at **T** pace in a single workout. Typically this is accomplished by runners who are running around 150 miles (240 km) a week. The usual approach is to run 5 miles (8 km) at **T** pace, then a 5-minute break, followed by 4 miles **T** + 4 min rest + 3 miles **T** + 3 min rest + 2 miles **T** + 2 min rest + 1 mile **T**.

Another good approach when training for a marathon is to mix a couple of 1-mile runs at **T** pace in the middle of an **M**-pace workout. For example, try 8 miles **M** + 1 mile **T** + 4 miles **M** + 1 mile **T** + 1 mile **M**. This is to be a nonstop workout, and the runners who have done this type of training typically say it is not particularly hard to speed up to **T** pace after some time at **M** pace, but it is not so easy to drop back to **M** pace after that harder time at **T** pace. This prepares you for any surges or changes in wind or hills that may be encountered in a marathon race.

I typically limit a steady tempo run to about 20 minutes, but you could do more than one 20-minute **T**-pace run in the same training session if you are up to it. In other words, a well-trained runner might run two or three 20-minute runs at **T** pace in the same training session, but one 20-minute run in a single training session is usually enough for most runners.

I usually prescribe 1-mile or 2-mile runs as cruise intervals, and when doing 1-mile runs you get 1-minute rest breaks between the individual **T**-pace runs. For example, I may prescribe a workout in which you are to repeat five 1-mile runs at **T** pace, with 1-minute rest breaks between the individual work bouts (written as 5 × 1 **T** w/1 min rests). If I suggest 2-mile runs, then I would recommend 2-minute rests between the **T**-pace runs, and for three of these 2-mile runs it would be written as 3 × 2 **T** w/2 min rests. As is shown in figure 4.1, the recommended work–recovery time with cruise intervals is about 5 to 1.

See table 4.2 for a number of **T**-pace workouts that could be used or modified to fit your needs.

Table 4.2   Threshold-Pace (T) Workouts

Consider any 5 to 6 min **T** to be the same as 1 mile **T**; 10 to 15 min **T** is the same as 2 miles **T**; and 16 to 20 min **T** is the same as a 3-mile run at **T** pace. Feel free to run appropriate miles, and the time will approximate the times listed in the various sessions below.

Warm up with a 10- to 20-minute **E** run + end with a few 30-second ST + some cool-down.

Workout	Total minutes
Training session A: for runners totaling up to 40 miles (64 km) each week	
Steady 20 min run at **T** pace	20 min
4 × 5-6 min **T** with 1 min rests	20-24 min
Training session B: for runners totaling 41-70 miles (66-113 km) per week	
6 × 5-6 min **T** with 1 min rests	30-36 min
2 × 10-15 min **T** with 2 min rest and 2 × 5-6 min **T** with 1 min rest	30-42 min
3 × 10-15 min **T** with 2 min rests	30-45 min
2 × 16-20 min **T** with 3 min rest	32-40 min
16-20 min **T**, 3 min rest, 10-15 min **T**, 2 min rest, and 5-6 min **T**	31-41 min
20 min **T**, 4 min rest, and 10-15 min **T** (or 2 × 5-6 min **T** with 1 min rest)	30-35 min
Training session C: for runners totaling 71-85 miles (114-137 km) per week	
8 × 5-6 min **T** with 1 min rests	40-48 min
5 × 8 min **T** with 1 min rests	40 min
4 × 10-15 min **T** with 2 min rests	40-60 min
20 min **T**, 3 min rest, 2 × 10-15 min **T** with 2 min rests, and 5-6 min **T**	45-56 min
Training session D: for runners totaling 86-100 miles (138-160 km) per week	
10 × 5-6 min **T** with 1 min rests	50-60 min
5 × 10-15 min **T** with 2 min rests	50-75 min
2 × 15 min **T** with 3 min rest and 2 × 10-15 min **T** with 2 min rest	50-60 min
20 min **T**, 3 min rest, 15 min **T**, 2 min rest, 10 min **T**, 1 min rest, and 5 min **T**	50 min
Training session E: for runners totaling 101-120 miles (163-194 km) per week	
6 × 10-15 min **T** with 2 min rests	60-90 min
4 × 15 min **T** with 3 min rests	60 min
2 × 15 min **T** with 3 min rests, 2 × 10-15 min **T** with 2 min rests, and 2 × 5 min **T** with 1 min rest	60-70 min
Training session F: for runners totaling more than 120 miles (194 km) per week	
25 min **T**, 5 min rest, 20 min **T**, 4 min rest, 15 min **T**, 3 min rest, 10 min **T**, 2 min rest, and 5 min **T**	75 min

Table created by Jack Daniels' Running Calculator designed by the Run SMART Project.

INTERVAL TRAINING

Moving up to the next level of intensity in run training, we arrive at **I** (interval) training, probably the most varying in definition of all types of training. I was once asked to write an article on interval training for a scientific journal, so I started out by asking three runners what their definition of **I** training was.

One said it was "fast" running with intermittent rest breaks, and the fast runs were to be no longer than 2 minutes. The second runner said interval training involved repeated hard runs that had to be at least 2 minutes long, and recovery was until the runner was ready to go again. The third had a different answer, so I asked the coach, who coached all three of these runners, and the coach's answer did not agree with the definitions of any of the three runners. It seems the only point of agreement among these four people was that interval training involves intermittent training, during which there is some hard running and some recovery time.

I decided to develop my own definition based on the purpose of the type of training being carried out. According to my studies in Sweden and in graduate school, the most logical purpose of **I** training is to maximize aerobic power ($\dot{V}O_2max$), and believing that the best way to improve any bodily function is to stress that function, I decided that the intensity had to be at or very close to $\dot{V}O_2max$ (and maximum heart rate), and the work-to-rest ratio had to optimize that purpose.

Studies that Jimmy Gilbert and I did when developing the VDOT tables allowed us to determine the duration a person can exercise at $\dot{V}O_2max$, and that time is about 11 minutes. Obviously it is not desirable to make individual work bouts that long, but since it takes about 90 to 120 seconds to build up to $\dot{V}O_2max$, from complete recovery, a good amount of time to spend running at **I** pace is between 3 and 5 minutes. It can also be less than 3 minutes, as explained in the next section.

Going for longer than 5 minutes would be too demanding because it is hard to run at 3K to 5K race pace a number of times when each of those runs lasts more than 5 minutes. Also, by not allowing too long a recovery between hard runs, $\dot{V}O_2$ will not have recovered completely, and the next work bout will allow reaching max in a shorter period of time, which is an important determinant when using work bouts shorter than 2 or 3 minutes.

Reaching $\dot{V}O_2max$

Figure 4.2 shows how a runner achieves $\dot{V}O_2max$ when running at a speed that elicits max. It takes about 2 minutes to reach $\dot{V}O_2max$ when starting out at a resting $\dot{V}O_2$. In addition to always being able to indicate the purpose of every workout performed, it is wise to always try to gain the maximum benefit out of the least amount of stress rather than trying to achieve the maximum benefit from the most amount of stress.

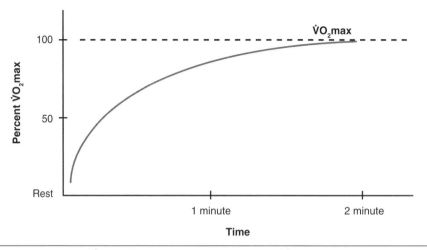

Figure 4.2   The rate $\dot{V}O_2$max is achieved when running at $\dot{V}O_2$max intensity.

Figure 4.3 depicts a good example of getting the most out of the least effort. If a runner's appropriate speed of running for an interval workout is a pace of 5:30 per mile (292 meters per minute or 82.5 seconds per 400 meters), then running faster than an 82.5-second pace (for the first of five 5-minute runs, for example) will not result in any more time at max than will running at an 82.5-second pace. Working beyond your $\dot{V}O_2$max pace (beyond $v\dot{V}O_2$max) will not give you any more benefit relative to the purpose of the workout.

In addition, running too fast on the first of five repeated 5-minute runs may result in the second run just making an 82.5-second pace, but the last three may all be slower than the proper pace because you wiped yourself out working too hard on the first one or two. Further, no matter how much you may be hurting during those later ones, which are too slow (because of so much anaerobic work being done while overworking in the first one or two), you are not spending any time at your max aerobic power.

The result is that you get about 3 minutes at $\dot{V}O_2$max in runs one and two, but you get no time at max in runs three, four, and five. What was the purpose of the workout? If it was to hurt, you accomplished the purpose, but if you had planned to spend 15 minutes or so stressing your aerobic maximum, you missed that completely.

As I have mentioned, it is good to normally use 3- to 5-minute work bouts during an **I** workout because you are guaranteed some time at max, even when it takes a minute or two to reach max. However, it is possible to accumulate a fair amount of time at max even when running much shorter work bouts, but you must keep the recovery time very short between the harder runs.

Figure 4.4 shows how you could accumulate a good amount of time at $\dot{V}O_2$max when using 400-meter work bouts. $\dot{V}O_2$ doesn't quite reach $\dot{V}O_2$max during the first **I**-pace run, but with a short recovery after the first run (about 45 seconds), the second run will be starting at an already elevated $\dot{V}O_2$, and it will take less time to reach max with all additional runs that are followed

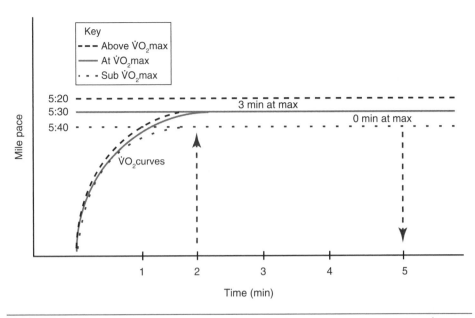

Figure 4.3 The time it takes to achieve $\dot{V}O_2$max when running above and at $\dot{V}O_2$max. $\dot{V}O_2$max is not achieved when running below $\dot{V}O_2$max intensity.

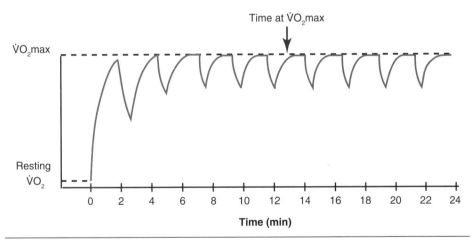

Figure 4.4 To reap the benefits of short interval training, the recovery periods must be kept even shorter.

Adapted, by permission, from J. Karlsson, et al., 1970, *Energikraven vid lopning (Energy requirements vid lopning)* (Stockholm: Trygg), 39.

by short recoveries. The result is that each additional run will reach max rather quickly, and the overall time spent at $\dot{V}O_2$max will accumulate to a fairly good number.

It should now be clear that a person can stress the aerobic system using a variety of workout durations that are ideally between 3 and 5 minutes each, but the bouts can also be shorter if the recovery time is kept short (less than the time at **I** pace that each recovery follows).

Running Hard

I training can also be performed by making the **H** runs just that—hard runs and not necessarily any specific distance for time. For example, you might run six 3-minute **H** runs, with each being followed by 2 minutes of recovery jogging (jg). I would designate this workout as 6 × 3 min **H** w/2 min jg. When doing **H** runs for time, rather than a particular distance for time, it is expected that the **H** pace be one you subjectively feel you could maintain for about 10 to 12 minutes if racing for time.

My suggestion for how much **I**- or **H**-pace running to do in a single session is to make the maximum the lesser of 10K or 8 percent of your weekly mileage. So if you do 40 miles a week, the recommended maximum at **I** pace would be 3.2 miles (8 percent of 40). When doing **H**-pace sessions, consider that 5 minutes of **H** running is equal to a mile for keeping track of how many miles to accumulate in an **I** session. For someone totaling more than 75 miles (120 km) per week, then the maximum at **I** pace would be the previously mentioned 10K (about 30 minutes).

I like to have runners more often do **H**-pace runs when at altitude, rather than the more strictly designed **I**-pace efforts, because the speed of running associated with maximum aerobic power at altitude is considerably slower than it is at sea level, and this can be rather discouraging for a runner. Just running hard and not really worrying about the actual speed effectively stresses the central component of the aerobic system and eliminates the worry about whether this is the optimal pace for the workout.

Another **I**-type workout many runners like is my step-count workout. The standard variation of this workout is to start out running hard for 10 right footfalls, followed by 10 jogging right footfalls. Then you run 20 hard and jog 20, followed by 30/30, 40/40, and so on, increasing by 10 each time until you have run hard for 100 right footfalls and jogged for 100. Then you repeat the 100/100 and come back down—90/90, 80/80, all the way back to 10 run and 10 jog.

This will take about 24 or 25 minutes to complete, and the distance covered will be 3 or 4 miles. Of course a slower runner will cover less distance, and a very good runner may total a little more, but all are spending the same amount of time running hard and jogging, and time spent doing a specific type of training is the best way to make things equal for runners of different ability levels.

When doing an **I** session using the **H**-pace method, it is possible to vary the time spent running hard during the session. For example, to total 20 minutes of **H** running, you might do either of the following:

- 2 × 4 min **H** with 3 min jg plus 4 × 3 min **H** with 2 min jg
- 1 × 4 min **H** with a 3-min jg plus 2 × 3 min **H** with 2 min jg + 3 × 2 min **H** with 1 min jg + 4 × 1 min **H** with 30 sec jg

I typically make the recovery jogs a little shorter than the time of the **H** runs they follow, and the recovery jogs should never be longer than the **H** running portion of the workout.

Another interval session that works well on windy days when it is not easy to hit desired times for interval 1,000s, for example, is to run 20 × 200, starting one each minute, which means if **I** pace is 40 seconds per 200, you get only 20 seconds of rest before starting the next 200. Slower runners could just limit recovery to a set amount of time (about half as long as the faster runs).

Table 4.3 shows a variety of **I**-pace and **H**-pace workouts to consider.

Table 4.3   Interval-Pace (I) and Hard-Pace (H) Workouts

Workout	Total minutes
Training session A: for runners totaling up to 30 miles (48 km) per week	
5-6 × 2 min **H** with 1 min jg	15-18 min
4 × 3 min **H** with 2 min jg	20 min
3 × 4 min **H** with 3 min jg	21 min
4-5 × 800 at **I** pace with 2 min jg	20-25 min
Training session B: for runners totaling 30-40 miles (48-64 km) per week	
7-8 × 2 min **H** with 1 min jg	21-24 min
5 × 3 min **H** with 2 min jg	25 min
4 × 4 min **H** with 3 min jg	28 min
5-6 × 800 at **I** pace with 2 min jg	25-30 min
4-5 × 1,000 at **I** pace with 3 min jg	26-33 min
Training session C: for runners totaling 40-45 miles (64-72 km) per week	
6 × 800 at **I** pace with 2 min jg	27 min
6 × 3 min **H** with 2 min jg	30 min
5 × 1,000 at **I** pace with 3 min jg	33 min
4-5 × 1,200 at **I** pace with 3 min jg	28-35 min
3-4 × 5 min **H** (can be 1 mile runs if **I** pace is under 5:00/mile) with 4 min jg	27-36 min
Training session D: for runners totaling 46-55 miles (74-88 km) per week	
5-6 × 1,000 at **I** pace with 3 min jg	33-39 min
5 × 1,200 at **I** pace (or 5 × 4 min **H**) with 3 min jg	35 min
4 × 1 mile at **I** pace (or 4 × 5 min **H**) with 4 min jg	36 min
5 × 4 min **H** with 3 min jg	35 min
7 × 3 min **H** with 2 min jg	35 min
10 × 2 min **H** with 1 min jg	30 min

(continued)

Table 4.3   Interval-Pace (I) and Hard-Pace (H) Workouts   *(continued)*

Workout	Total minutes
Training session E: for runners totaling 56-70 miles (90-113 km) per week	
6-8 × 1,000 (total 25 min or less) at **I** pace with 3 min jg	39 min
5-6 × 1,200 (total 25 min or less) at **I** pace with 3 min jg	35-42 min
5 × 1 mile (or 5 × 5 min **H** if **I** pace is slower than 5:00/mile) at **I** pace with 4 min jg	45 min
4 × 3 min **H** with 2 min jg and 4 × 2 min **H** with 1 min jg	32 min
3 × 3 min **H** with 2 min jg, 4 × 2 min **H** with 1 min jg, and 5 × 1 min **H** with 30 sec jg	35 min
Training session F: for runners totaling more than 70 miles (113 km) per week	
7-10 × 1,000 at **I** pace with 3 min jg	45-65 min
3 × 5 min **H** (can be miles if fast enough) with 4 min jg and 4 × 1,000 at **I** pace with 3 min jg	54 min
6-8 × 4 min **H** (can be 1,200s at **I** pace if fast enough) with 3 min jg	42-56 min
5-6 × 5 min **H** (can be miles at **I** pace if fast enough) with 4 min jg	45-54 min
2 × 5 min **H** with 4 min jg, 3 × 3 min **H** with 3 min jg, and 4 × 2 min **H** with 1 min jg	48 min
Training session G: hill sessions run on a treadmill for runners of all mileage amounts	
20 × 30 sec at 6 mph/20% grade with 30 sec rests	20 min
5 × 1 min at 6 mph/20% grade with 1 min rests and 10 × 30 sec at 6 mph/20% grade with 30 sec rests	20 min
10 × 1 min at 6 mph/20% grade with 1 min rests	20 min
20 × 30 sec at 7 mph/20% grade with 30 sec rests	20 min
5 × 1 min at 7 mph/20% grade with 1 min rests and 10 × 30 sec at 7 mph/20% grade with 30 sec rests	20 min
10 × 1 min at 7 mph/20% grade with 1-min rests	20 min
Could attempt **H4**, **H5**, and **H6** at 7.5 or 8 mph	

Table created by Jack Daniels' Running Calculator designed by the Run SMART Project.

REPETITION TRAINING

The primary purpose of **R** (repetition) training is to improve anaerobic power, speed, and economy of running. Always remember what you are trying to accomplish when doing an **R** (or any) workout. It makes sense that if you want to improve your speed, you have to practice running fairly fast, and it is particularly important to remember that in order to run fast, you have to be recovered enough to run fast and with good technique. You don't want to be struggling while running fast, or good mechanics will be sacrificed.

Some runners, and even some coaches, believe that if a good workout is 10 × 400 at 70 seconds each, with 3 minutes of recovery between the faster runs, then 10 × 400 at 70 with only 2-minute recoveries would be a better workout. I could argue that the latter could be a worse workout. Consider the purpose of the workout—to improve speed and maintain good mechanics while running fast. However, if you cut the recovery time, you may not be adequately recovered to run a 70-second pace with good mechanics, and struggling is not accomplishing the purpose of the workout.

R sessions are not that conducive to a large group of runners training together. Some in the group are faster than others and will finish and be ready to go on the next run sooner, and if the slower runners are expected to start each run with the faster runners, they (the slower ones) will be struggling to keep up and in fact won't be able to keep up. Guess what the outcome of the workout is? The faster runners benefit and the slower runners suffer and don't accomplish the goal of the workout.

I encourage the distance runners on the team not to make fun of the sprinters who totaled only 2 miles for the day when the distance runners made it to 6 miles. Those sprinters need to spend lots of time recovering so they can run fast and develop speed, and on cold days they need some extra clothes to put on during the recovery time so they won't freeze while waiting for their next fast run. On cold days, even the distance runners may need to put on a jacket between the faster runs to avoid getting cold.

For distance runners, I suggest a recovery time that is about two or three times as long (in time, not in distance covered) as the faster **R**-pace runs they are performing. Another way to determine recovery time in an **R** session is to do an easy jog as far as the fast run just performed. For example, when running **R** 400s, jog an easy 400 between the faster runs, perhaps walking the final 10 or 20 meters before the next fast run.

I suggest that the amount of running to accumulate at **R** pace (in a single training session) be the lesser of 5 miles (8 km) and 5 percent of weekly mileage. For example, a runner totaling 30 miles (48 km) per week would have a maximum of 1.5 miles (.05 × 30) at **R** pace for an **R** session. However, for a runner doing more than 100 miles (160 km) per week, I recommend keeping the maximum at **R** pace to 5 miles, and not 6 miles for someone accumulating 120 miles (190 km), for example. Another rule of thumb I like to follow is that single work bouts (for faster runs at **R** pace) should not last longer than about 2 minutes each, which means most true **R** sessions will be made up of repeated 200s, 300s, 400s, 500s, and 600s for most runners. Rep 800s may be OK if **R** pace is around 60 seconds per 400, but that means we are talking about runners who are near or under 4 minutes for racing a mile.

It is always best to think in terms of time spent running at various intensities, rather than distances covered, or else the slower runners on a team end up spending considerably more time doing the workouts than do the faster runners. In fact, a slower runner whose **R** pace is 90 seconds per 400 would spend 2 minutes more time (not to mention more footsteps and more impact with the ground) running 8 × 400 at **R** pace than would a better runner doing 8 × 400 whose **R** pace is 65. If you think about it, this slower runner may be better off doing just 6 × 400 at 90 each; this would match the total stress time of the faster runner who can complete 8 × 400 in the same amount of total time.

As with **M**, **T**, and **I** running, a number of **R** sessions are listed in table 4.4.

Table 4.4   Repetition-Pace (R) Workouts

Workout	Total minutes
Training session A: for runners totaling up to 30 miles (48 km) per week	
8 × 200 **R** with 200 jg	16 min
2 sets of 200 **R**, 200 jg, 200 **R**, 400 jg, 400 **R**, and 200 jg	16 min
2 × 200 **R** with 200 jg, 2 × 400 **R** with 400 jg, and 2 × 200 **R** with 200 jg	16 min
4 × 300 **R** with 300 jg and 1 × 400 **R**	13 min
4 × 400 **R** with 400 jg	16 min
Training session B: for runners totaling 31-40 miles (50-64 km) per week	
2 sets of 6 × 200 **R** with 200 jg (with 400 jg between sets)	27 min
3 sets of 200 **R**, 200 jg, 200 **R**, 400 jg, 400 **R**, and 200 jg	24 min
4 × 200 **R** with 200 jg, 2 × 400 **R** with 400 jg, and 4 × 200 **R** with 200 jg	24 min
6 × 400 **R** with 400 jg	24 min
2 × 200 **R** with 200 jg, 2 × 600 **R** with 600 jg, and 2 × 400 **R** with 400 jg	24 min
Training session C: for runners totaling 41-50 miles (66-80 km) per week	
2 sets of 8 × 200 **R** with 200 jg (with 800 jg between sets)	37 min
4 sets of 200 **R**, 200 jg, 200 **R**, 400 jg, 400 **R**, and 200 jg	32 min
4 × 200 **R** with 200 jg, 4 × 400 **R** with 400 jg, and 4 × 200 **R** with 200 jg	32 min
4 × 400 **R** with 400 jg and 8 × 200 **R** with 200 jg	32 min
8 × 400 **R** with 400 jg	32 min
2 × 200 **R** with 200 jg, 2 × 600 **R** with 600 jg, and 4 × 400 **R** with 400 jg	32 min
Training session D: for runners totaling 51-60 miles (82-96 km) per week	
2 sets of 10 × 200 **R** with 200 jg (with 800 jg between sets)	45 min
5 sets of 200 **R**, 200 jg, 200 **R**, 400 jg, 400 **R**, and 200 jg	40 min
6 × 200 **R** with 200 jg, 6 × 400 **R** with 400 jg, and 2 × 200 **R** with 200 jg	40 min
6 × 400 **R** with 400 jg and 8 × 200 **R** with 200 jg	40 min
2 × 200 **R** with 200 jg, 8 × 400 **R** with 400 jg, and 2 × 200 **R** with 200 jg	40 min
10 × 400 **R** with 400 jg	40 min
2 × 200 **R** with 200 jg, 4 × 600 **R** with 600 jg, and 3 × 400 **R** with 400 jg	40 min
3 × 200 **R** with 200 jg, 5 × 600 **R** with 600 jg, and 2 × 200 **R** with 200 jg	40 min
2 × 200 **R** with 400 jg and 3 sets of 1 × 800 **R**, 400 jg, 2 × 200 **R** with 400 jg	40 min
2 × 200 **R** with 200 jg, 2 × 800 **R** with 800 jg, 2 × 600 **R** with 600 jg, and 2 × 400 **R** with 400 jg	42 min
2 × 200 **R** with 400 jg, 3 × 800 **R** with 800 jg, and 3 × 400 **R** with 400 jg	43 min
5 × 800 **R** with 800 jg	40 min

Workout	Total minutes
Training session E: for runners totaling 61-75 miles (98-120 km) per week	
2 sets of 8 × 200 **R** with 200 jg (with 400-800 jg between sets)	37 min
6 sets of 200 **R**, 200 jg, 200 **R**, 400 jg, 400 **R**, and 200 jg	48 min
4 × 200 **R** with 200 jg, 8 × 400 **R** with 400 jg, and 4 × 200 **R** with 200 jg	48 min
8 × 400 **R** with 400 jg and 8 × 200 **R** with 200 jg	48 min
4 × 600 **R** with 600 jg, 4 × 400 **R** with 400 jg, and 4 × 200 **R** with 200 jg	52 min
3 × 600 **R** with 600 jg, 3 × 800 **R** with 800 jg, and 3 × 200 **R** with 200 jg	51 min
2 × 800 **R** with 800 jg, 3 × 600 **R** with 600 jg, 2 × 400 **R** with 400 jg, and 3 × 200 **R** with 200 jg	51 min
4 × 200 **R** with 200 jg and 5 × 800 **R** with 800 jg	48 min
2 × 800 **R** with 800 jg, 4 × 400 **R** with 400 jg, and 8 × 200 **R** with 200 jg	48 min
Training session F: for runners totaling 76-80 miles (122-129 km) per week	
4 × 200 **R** with 200 jg, 4 × 400 **R** with 400 jg, 4 × 800 **R** with 800 jg, and 4 × 200 **R** with 200 jg	62 min
2 × 200 **R** with 200 jg, 2 × 800 **R** with 800 jg, 2 × 200 **R** with 200 jg, 4 × 400 **R** with 400 jg, 2 × 200 **R** with 200 jg, 2 × 800 **R** with 800 jg, and 2 × 200 **R** with 200 jg	64 min
2 × 200 **R** with 200 jg, 3 × 800 **R** with 800 jg, 4 × 600 **R** with 600 jg, and 2 × 400 **R** with 400 jg	64 min
2 × 800 **R** with 800 jg, 3 × 600 **R** with 600 jg, 4 × 400 **R** with 400 jg, and 5 × 200 **R** with 200 jg	63 min
4 sets of 4 × 400 **R** with 400 jg (with 800 jg between sets)	79 min
4 sets of 8 × 200 **R** with 200 jg (with 400 jg between sets)	74 min
Training session G: for runners totaling more than 80 miles (129 km) per week	
5 sets of 8 × 200 **R** with 200 jg (with 400 jog between sets)	90 min
20 × 400 **R** with 400 jg	80 min
16 × 400 **R** with 400 jg and 8 × 200 **R** with 200 jg	80 min
4 × 200 **R** with 200 jg, 4 × 800 **R** with 800 jg, 6 × 400 **R** with 400 jg, 1 × 800 **R** with 800 jg, and 4 × 200 **R** with 200 jg	80 min
3 sets of 5 × 200 **R** with 200 jg, 2 × 400 **R** with 400 jg, and 1 × 800 **R** with 800 jg (with 5 min between sets)	88 min

Table created by Jack Daniels' Running Calculator designed by the Run SMART Project.

TREADMILL TRAINING

Train on a treadmill—how boring. Most of us like to think that one of the advantages runners have over other athletes, or, more simply stated, that running has over many other types of aerobic exercise, is the simplicity and freedom of the sport. You really can run just about anywhere and for free. So why train on a treadmill?

I remember coaching a sailor during the Gulf War who was 6 foot 4 and weighed 185 pounds, and he maintained an 80-mile-per-week program for most of a year. This sounds reasonable enough for someone training for a marathon, but when you consider he was limited to doing all his running on the deck of an aircraft carrier, treadmill running doesn't seem quite so limiting after all.

Some inmates I worked with at a state prison held an annual marathon in the yard, and they ran on a 1-mile loop that changed surfaces five times each loop. One of the guys averaged 40 miles a week in that yard. A guy I coached by e-mail a few years back ran to and from work each day (in New York City, by the way). He would sometimes get a ride home on very bad days, so to make up for missing his workout, he would run for an hour and a half, in place, in his apartment. Another guy, in his 70s, ran more than 100 miles a week for 14 consecutive weeks, and it was all done between 2:00 and 5:00 a.m.

Then there was the law student I used to watch run around the outdoor track just outside the lab I worked in during graduate studies. He seemed to go on forever, every day. I finally went down to meet him and ask just what he did each day. It turned out he ran 80 laps on that 400-meter track, but only 6 days each week. He wore high-top basketball shoes, no shirt, and only cotton shorts. Rumor had it that on really cold days he would put on a T-shirt, but I never saw him wear one.

Both he and the gentleman in his 70s were living in Michigan, where it tended to get pretty cold in the winter. When I asked the 80-laps-per-day guy why not fewer laps and a faster pace some of the time, he said, "No, the idea isn't to get in shape; it's to have some time to myself and relax." Does treadmill running still sound like the most humdrum experience a runner could be subjected to?

Let me offer a few more instances when treadmill running might not be such a bad idea. How about Phoenix in July? Minnesota (or Syracuse, New York) in November, December, January, February, and March? Miami in August?

If anyone should give treadmill running—and treadmill competition, for that matter—some consideration, it should be the International Olympic Committee. What a media event that would be—the top marathon racers in the world all in a big gymnasium on their own treadmill, facing each other. The room is held at a constant temperature of 55 °F (or about 15 °C) and 30% humidity. The gun goes off and the winner is the one who covers 42,195 meters in the shortest amount of time. Participants are free to eat and drink at will and even check their body weight now and then to keep an eye on water loss. They are even free to change the speed of the treadmill as often as they wish.

The bottom line is that treadmill running can be useful for all runners, not only on days of adverse weather, but even on nice days when there is a need for control or during injury rehabilitation. There is a lot you can do on a treadmill with minimal boredom.

One of the biggest advantages of treadmill running is that you can very accurately control intensity of exercise. Over flat ground, intensity can be controlled only by varying speed. On the treadmill, practically unlimited combinations of speed and grade can be employed to subject the runner to the desired intensity of exercise. You can run at a pretty slow pace, but with the right grade set on the treadmill, the task can be made equal to the energy demand of just about any faster speed you want.

Possibly one disadvantage of treadmill running is not being able to run along with a partner or group of runners (unless you are in a room with numerous treadmills, of course). Workouts in which two runners share the same treadmill are very good, however. For example, if a treadmill workout involves running for 1 minute up a tough grade followed by a 1-minute rest (off the treadmill), two runners can alternate running and resting by just hopping on and off the treadmill when it is their turn. I have done this with my college teams for many years, with considerable success.

Some people, me included, like to be by themselves on some runs, and treadmills can certainly provide this atmosphere. For some years I used to work full time in a lab, and I would come in an hour before anyone else, turn off the lights (so it seemed particularly calm and so no one would see the lights on and come in to bug me while I was running), turn on the treadmill, and get an hour in before I had to even see anyone else (something I learned from those guys in Michigan, I guess). My biggest worry was that someone else would show up and strike up a conversation or turn on the lights.

No matter how I ran, how I breathed, or how I carried my arms or legs, I always knew the one thing I didn't have to worry about was how fast I was going. When my time was up I knew exactly how far I had run; what could be simpler, or more relaxing, than that?

I coached a guy some years ago who had a marathon personal record (PR) of 2:12 +. He moved to a new city (with some moderate altitude) where he did not particularly like going on long runs, so he did a weekly 20-mile run on his treadmill. He followed that routine with a 2:09 + marathon at New York City. My guess is that the main advantage he had in that New York City marathon was getting to run just a little over two hours outside, instead of just staring at a wall or out a window. The mental benefits of those long treadmill runs may have actually been greater than any particular physiological benefits. You never know what type of training pays off.

Treadmill training by no means has to be limited to steady running at a pace where the stress level is conducive to falling asleep. By the way, I have always preferred a large wall clock, with a sweep second hand, to wearing a wristwatch during treadmill runs. If you are going to give up the freedom of an outside run, at least rid yourself of carrying excess baggage. Not even a shirt (or shorts, for that matter) is necessary if you are on your own treadmill at home. A wall clock that includes a large sweep second hand is best placed off to the side so it is not staring you in the face throughout your run but can still be easily seen when necessary just by turning your head to the side. The clock can help you keep track of work and rest bouts, and the sweep hand allows you to check heart rate now and then if interested.

Steady Running and Intermittent Running

There are really only two types of training a person can do: steady running and intermittent running. By steady running I mean a nonstop run at a consistent intensity. The intensity may be very easy, as at the beginning of a warm-up, during cool-downs, or during recovery runs; or it may be moderate, as when running at **M** pace or **T** pace.

Any intensity faster than **T** pace will usually be associated with intermittent running, such as during **I** or **R** workouts, types of training that stress the aerobic system or that work on mechanics, speed, and economy. Intermittent training simply means the workout alternates between bouts of work and recovery, and the recoveries may or may not be active in nature. Usually with longer work bouts you also take longer periods of recovery, but on a treadmill this is very simple to control for. A single session can also involve a mixture of different intensities and durations of running, along with varying bouts of recovery, something that is typically referred to as fartlek training.

Hill Training

A big advantage treadmill running has over ground running is in the area of hill training. Overground hill work invariably involves both uphill and downhill running, which can be good if that is what you want. However, often a runner wants the uphill aspect of the workout without the negative aspects of running back down, and that is easy to do on a treadmill. You run up for a period of time and then just hop off the treadmill for recovery before starting the next uphill run. This is particularly desirable for a runner who may be nursing a minor injury that is aggravated by running downhill but not by running uphill because of the reduced impact. It is possible to get in some very demanding workouts at a very slow pace provided the grade is steep enough.

For those who want to prepare for a race that involves a good deal of downhill running, as is experienced in the Boston marathon, for example, then some downhill training is a good idea. It is possible to buy a treadmill that can be adjusted to a downhill configuration, but that costs a fair amount more. Another option is to jack up the rear end of a normal treadmill with a railroad tie or some similar chunk of strong wood.

For example, if you have a treadmill that goes up to a 20 percent grade, and a carpenter's level tells you the running belt is level when the dial reads 5 percent, then you know you can go down to –5 percent if you set the dial at 0. You will then have a treadmill that can go from a –5 percent to + 15 percent grade. Of course it is important to make sure your treadmill is firmly attached to the supporting block so that vibration or an unsuspecting person doesn't knock it off its block.

A word of caution about running downhill, be it over ground or on a treadmill. Just as running uphill reduces the impact of landing, so does running downhill increase the impact. It is wise to add bouts of downhill running rather gradually to a training program so you don't bring on an injury associated with the extra landing shock. It is probably best to stay away from downhill training during the final couple of weeks before an important race, and certainly don't start any downhill training unless you have at least 6 weeks of time before an important race.

Always experiment with a new type of training during the off-season or early in your training cycle. The majority of treadmill training is either on a level or positive grade for most people, and negative-grade running need not be of concern for average, or even some elite, runners.

Treadmill Training Intensity

In an effort to minimize boredom and to provide more variety to treadmill training, I have generated some tables that combine speed and grade to equal a variety of flat-ground speed demands. One advantage of using these intensity tables is that it allows runners to achieve the desired intensity of training without necessarily running fast all the time. Some treadmills will not go as fast as may be desired to achieve true interval pace, so by adding some grade to a slower speed, the targeted system of the body is still stressed to its limit.

Tables 4.5 and 4.6 show the relationships among m/min, mph, km/h, and equivalent speeds of running on the flat per mile and per kilometer at different combinations of speed and percent grade on a treadmill. For example, if running at 7 mph on a grade of 10 percent, that would be a similar effort to running on the flat at 5:21 per mile or 3:19 per kilometer.

For people who like to investigate how times over shorter distances are related to times over other distances, up to a full marathon, see appendix B, Times for Varying Distances at the Same Pace, which sheds some light on this issue.

Table 4.5   Treadmill Grade and Speed Combination for 6.0 to 8.5 Miles Per Hour

Speed	6.0 mph (9.7 km/h)		6.5 mph (10.5 km/h)		7.0 mph (11.3 km/h)	
% grade	$\dot{V}O_2$cost	Time per mi (km)	$\dot{V}O_2$cost	Time per mi (km)	$\dot{V}O_2$cost	Time per mi (km)
0	27.4	10:00 (6:13)	30.3	9:14 (5:44)	33.3	8:35 (5:20)
1	29.7	9:23 (5:50)	32.8	8:40 (5:23)	35.9	8:04 (5:01)
2	32.0	8:50 (5:29)	35.3	8:11 (5:05)	38.5	7:37 (4:44)
3	34.3	8:22 (5:12)	37.8	7:45 (4:49)	41.2	7:14 (4:30)
4	36.6	7:56 (4:56)	40.3	7:21 (4:34)	43.8	6:52 (4:16)
5	38.9	7:34 (4:42)	42.8	7:00 (4:21)	46.4	6:33 (4:04)
6	41.2	7:13 (4:29)	45.3	6:42 (4:10)	49.1	6:16 (3:54)
7	43.6	6:54 (4:17)	47.8	6:25 (3:59)	51.7	6:00 (3:44)
8	45.9	6:37 (4:07)	50.2	6:09 (3:49)	54.3	5:46 (3:35)
9	48.2	6:22 (3:57)	52.7	5:55 (3:41)	57.0	5:33 (3:27)
10	50.5	6:08 (3:49)	55.2	5:42 (3:32)	59.6	5:21 (3:19)
11	52.8	5:54 (3:40)	57.7	5:30 (3:25)	62.2	5:10 (3:13)
12	55.1	5:42 (3:32)	60.2	5:18 (3:18)	64.8	5:00 (3:06)
13	57.4	5:31 (3:26)	62.7	5:08 (3:11)	67.5	4:50 (3:00)
14	59.7	5:21 (3:19)	65.2	4:59 (3:06)	70.1	4:41 (2:55)
15	62.0	5:11 (3:13)	67.7	4:50 (3:00)	72.7	4:33 (2:50)
16	64.3	5:02 (3:08)	70.1	4:42 (2:55)	75.4	4:25 (2:45
17	66.6	4:53 (3:02	72.6	4:34 (2:50)	78.0	4:18 (2:40)
18	68.9	4:45 (2:57)	75.1	4:26 (2:45)	80.6	4:12 (2:36)
19	71.2	4:38 (2:53)	77.6	4:19 (2:41)	83.2	4:05 (2:32)
20	73.5	4:31 (2:48)	80.1	4:13 (2:37)	85.9	3:59 (2:28)

Be aware that any running speed (e.g., 10 mph) on a treadmill is slightly less demanding than is that same speed during overground running on a track or flat road. This is because when you run over ground you are creating a headwind, even on a calm day. If you run at 10 mph, for example, and no wind is blowing, you are creating a 10 mph headwind, and that makes the energy demand a little greater than running with no wind resistance on a treadmill.

The lack of air resistance on a treadmill brings up another problem, and that is cooling. As time goes by on a treadmill, you will build up a layer

7.5 mph (12.1 km/h)		8.0 mph (12.9 km/h)		8.5 mph (13.7 km/h)		Speed
$\dot{V}O_2$cost	Time per mi (km)	$\dot{V}O_2$cost	Time per mi (km)	$\dot{V}O_2$cost	Time per mi (km)	% grade
36.3	8:00 (4:58)	39.3	7:30 (4:40)	42.4	7:04 (4:23)	0
39.1	7:33 (4:41)	42.2	7:05 (4:24)	45.4	6:41 (4:09)	1
41.9	7:08 (4:26)	45.2	6:42 (4:10)	48.5	6:20 (3:56)	2
44.7	6:46 (4:12)	48.1	6:22 (3:57)	51.5	6:02 (3:45)	3
47.4	6:27 (4:00)	51.0	6:04 (3:46)	54.6	5:45 (3:34)	4
50.2	6:09 (3:49)	53.9	5:48 (3:36)	57.6	5:30 (3:25)	5
53.0	5:53 (3:39)	56.9	5:33 (3:27)	60.7	5:16 (3:16)	6
55.8	5:39 (3:31)	59.8	5:20 (3:19)	63.7	5:04 (3:09)	7
58.6	5:25 (3:22)	62.7	5:08 (3:11)	66.8	4:53 (3:02)	8
61.4	5:13 (3:14)	65.6	4:57 (3:04)	69.8	4:42 (2:55)	9
64.2	5:02 (3:08)	68.6	4:46 (2:57)	72.9	4:33 (2:50)	10
67.0	4:52 (3:01)	71.5	4:36 (2:51)	75.9	4:24 (2:44)	11
69.8	4:43 (2:56)	74.4	4:28 (2:46)	79.0	4:16 (2:39)	12
72.6	4:34 (2:50)	77.4	4:20 (2:42)	82.0	4:08 (2:34)	13
75.4	4:26 (2:45)	80.3	4:12 (2:37)	85.1	4:01 (2:30)	14
78.2	4:18 (2:40)	83.2	4:05 (2:32)	88.1	3:54/58* (2:25)	15
81.0	4:11 (2:36)	86.1	3:58 (2:28)	91.2	3:48/57* (2:22)	16
83.8	4:04 (2:32)	89.1	3:52/58* (2:24)	94.2	3:43/56* (2:19)	17
86.5	3:58 (2:28)	92.0	3:46/56* (2:20)	97.3	3:37/54* (2:15)	18
89.3	3:52/58* (2:24)	94.9	3:41/55* (2:17)	100.3	3:32/53* (2:12)	19
92.1	3:47/57* (2:21)	97.9	3:36/54* (2:14)	103.4	3:27/51* (2:09)	20

Table created by Jack Daniels' Running Calculator designed by the Run SMART Project.

*400 m times (seconds) are shown for the aerobic demands of higher grades at 7.5, 8.0, and 8.5 mph.

Table 4.6 Treadmill Grade and Speed Combinations for 9.0 to 12.0 Miles per Hour

Speed	9.0 mph (14.5 km/h)		9.5 mph (15.3 km/h)		10.0 mph (16.1 km/h)		10.5 mph (16.9 km/h)
% grade	$\dot{V}O_2$cost	Time per mi (km)	$\dot{V}O_2$cost	Time per mi (km)	$\dot{V}O_2$cost	Time per mi (km)	$\dot{V}O_2$cost
0	45.5	6:40 (4:08)	48.6	6:19 (3:55)	51.8	6:00 (3:44)	55.0
1	48.7	6:19 (3:55)	52.0	5:59 (3:43)	55.4	5:41 (3:32)	58.8
2	51.9	6:00 (3:44)	55.4	5:41 (3:32)	59.0	5:24 (3:21)	62.6
3	55.1	5:43 (3:33)	58.8	5:25 (3:22)	62.6	5:08 (3:11)	66.4
4	58.3	5:27 (3:23)	62.2	5:10 (3:13)	66.3	4:55 (3:03)	70.2
5	61.5	5:13 (3:14)	65.6	4:57 (3:04)	69.9	4:42 (2:55)	73.9
6	64.7	5:01 (3:07)	69.0	4:45 (2:57)	73.5	4:31 (2:48)	77.7
7	67.9	4:49 (3:00)	72.4	4:34 (2:50)	77.1	4:21 (2:42)	81.5
8	71.1	4:39 (2:53)	75.8	4:24 (2:44)	80.8	4:11 (2:36)	85.3
9	74.3	4:29 (2:47)	79.2	4:15 (2:38)	84.4	4:03 (2:31)	89.1
10	77.5	4:20 (2:42)	82.6	4:07 (2:33)	88.0	3:55/59* (2:26)	92.9
11	80.7	4:12 (2:37)	86.0	3:59 (2:28)	91.6	3:48/57* (2:22)	96.7
12	83.9	4:04 (2:32)	89.4	3:52/58* (2:24)	95.3	3:41/55* (2:17)	100.5
13	87.1	3:57/59* (2:27)	92.8	3:45/56* (2:20)	98.9	3:34/53* (2:13)	104.3
14	90.3	3:51/58* (2:23)	96.2	3:39/55* (2:16)	102.5	3:29/52* (2:10)	108.1
15	93.5	3:44/56* (2:19)	99.6	3:33/53* (2:12)	106.1	3:23/51* (2:06)	111.9
16	96.7	3:39/55* (2:16)	103.0	3:28/52* (2:09)	109.7	3:18/50* (2:03)	115.7
17	99.9	3:33/53* (2:12)	106.4	3:23/51* (2:06)	113.4	3:13/48* (2:00)	119.5
18	103.1	3:28/52* (2:09)	109.8	3:18/50* (2:03)	117.0	3:09/47* (1:57)	123.3
19	106.3	3:23/51* (2:06)	113.2	3:14/46* (2:00)	120.6	3:05/46* (1:55)	127.1
20	109.6	3:19/50* (2:04)	116.6	3:09/47* (1:57)	124.2	3:01/45* (1:52)	130.9

of warm and humid air around your body, and a fan can be most pleasing in helping to keep you from overheating by blowing that warm humid air away from your body. Of course, if you are training for a race in warm, humid conditions, then eliminate the fan and face reality and some heat acclimatizing.

Although it is not necessarily a constant, adding a 2 percent grade will increase the demand of running on the treadmill to just about what it would be outside on a calm day at the same running speed. This slight grade makes up for not having any air resistance to deal with. Interestingly, if you are checking heart rate now and then, you may find a slightly higher value on

10.5 mph (16.9 km/h)	11.0 mph (17.7 km/h)		11.5 mph (18.5 km/h)		12.0 mph (19.3 km/h)		Speed
Time per mi (km)	$\dot{V}O_2$cost	Time per mi (km)	$\dot{V}O_2$cost	Time per mi (km)	$\dot{V}O_2$cost	Time per mi (km)	% grade
5:43 (3:33)	58.2	5:27 (3:23)	61.5	5:13 (3:14)	64.8	5:00 (3:06)	0
5:25 (3:22)	62.2	5:10 (3:13)	65.7	4:57 (3:04)	69.2	4:45 (2:57)	1
5:09 (3:12)	66.1	4:55 (3:03)	69.9	4:42 (2:55)	73.5	4:31 (2:48)	2
4:54 (3:03)	70.1	4:41 (2:55)	74.1	4:29 (2:47)	77.9	4:19 (2:41)	3
4:41 (2:55)	74.1	4:29 (2:47)	78.2	4:18 (2:40)	82.2	4:08 (2:34)	4
4:30 (2:48)	78.0	4:18 (2:40)	82.4	4:07 (2:33)	86.6	3:58 (2:28)	5
4:19 (2:41)	82.0	4:08 (2:34)	86.6	3:58 (2:28)	90.9	3:49/57* (2:22)	6
4:09 (2:35)	85.9	3:59 (2:28)	90.8	3:49/57* (2:22)	95.2	3:41/55* (2:17)	7
4:01 (2:30)	89.9	3:51/58* (2:23)	95.0	3:41/55* (2:17)	99.6	3:33/53* (2:12)	8
3:53/58* (2:49)	93.9	3:43/56* (2:19)	99.2	3:34/53* (2:13)	103.9	3:26/51* (2:08)	9
3:45/56* (2:20)	97.8	3:36/54* (2:14)	103.3	3:27/51* (2:09)	108.3	3:20/50* (2:04)	10
3:38/54* (2:15)	101.8	3:30/52* (2:10)	107.5	3:21/50* (2:05)	112.6	3:14/49* (2:00)	11
3:32/53* (2:12)	105.7	3:24/51* (2:07)	111.7	3:15/49* (2:01)	117.0	3:09/47* (1:57)	12
3:26/51* (2:08)	109.7	3:18/50* (2:03)	115.9	3:10/47* (1:58)	121.3	3:04/46* (1:54)	13
3:20/50* (2:04)	113.7	3:13/48* (2:00)	120.1	3:05/46* (1:55)	125.7	2:59/44* (1:51)	14
3:15/49* (2:01)	117.6	3:08/47* (1:57)	124.3	3:01/45* (1:52)	130.0	2:55/21* (1:49)	15
3:10/47* (1:58)	121.6	3:04/46* (1:54)	128.4	2:56/44* (1:49)	134.3	2:51/21* (1:46)	16
3:06/46* (1:56)	125.5	2:59/45* (1:51)	132.6	2:52/21* (1:47)	—	—	17
3:02/45* (1:53)	129.5	2:55/44* (1:49)	136.8	2:49/21* (1:45)	—	—	18
2:58/44* (1:51)	—	—	—	—	—	—	19
2:54/21* (1:48)	—	—	—	—	—	—	20

Table created by Jack Daniels' Running Calculator designed by the Run SMART Project.

*400 m and some 200 m times (seconds) are shown when 400 speeds are faster than 44 seconds.

the treadmill because the warmer conditions your body faces tend to result in an increase in heart rate.

Treadmill Calibration

If you are like me, you want to be accurate in how fast you are running, especially when doing intervals, threshold runs, or other quality workouts. This requires calibrating your treadmill, which is done as follows.

1. On the edge of your treadmill running belt, make a starting mark with a pencil (have the power off at this time), and lay a measuring tape or

ruler on the running belt, starting at this mark. Push the running belt slowly around, making small pencil marks when needed, and record the accumulating distance from your starting point. Continue measuring until you reach the mark where you started, and record the total distance to the nearest quarter inch or .5 centimeter. If you are measuring in feet and inches, calculate the total distance in inches and multiply that value by 2.54 to get centimeters. Let's say, for example that you end up with a running belt that is 542.9 centimeters.

2. Convert the centimeter distance to meters by dividing the centimeter distance by 100—5.429 in the example just given.

3. Multiply belt length by 10 to get the distance traveled in 10 belt revolutions. Example: $5.429 \times 10 = 54.29$ meters.

4. Place an identifying mark on the edge of your treadmill running belt—one that can be seen when the belt is moving fast. If it is your own treadmill, you may want to put a spot of white paint or correction fluid that is easily seen and will stay put for some time. White tape can work, but sometimes it will not stay put when the belt gets going.

5. Exact speed of the treadmill belt is determined by timing 10 revolutions of the belt, as follows.

   a. With the treadmill running at approximately the speed you want, pick a spot at which you will start timing the white mark as it passes that spot. I often just start and stop timing as my white mark disappears over the back of the treadmill, but this is hard to do if timing yourself running. It is best to do the belt timing with the person who is going to train or be tested running on the treadmill, since body weight will slow some treadmill belts down because of the friction of a person on the belt. Have someone else do the timing when you are running.

   b. Start a stopwatch as the white mark reaches the designated spot, and say "zero" to yourself.

   c. Count 1-2-3-4-5-6-7-8-9-10 for the next 10 times the white mark arrives at your designated spot, and stop the watch when you say the number 10. You may want to time 10 revolutions a couple times to see if you are consistent. Remember to start with zero when you start the watch.

   d. Let's say your watch says 13.03 seconds for those timed 10 revolutions. Assign the 10-revolution time the letter T and the distance of the 10 revolutions (54.29 meters in our example) the letter D. Speed in meters per minute is arrived at as follows: $(D \times 60) / T$ = m/min. Example: $(54.29 \times 60) / 13.03 = 250$ m/min

   e. If you want a particular speed, then you can calculate the T needed for that speed as follows: $(D \times 60) / $ m/min = T. Example: for 268 m/min, $54.29 \times 60 / 268 = 12.15$ seconds

In this example, a speed of 268 meters per minute (6:00 mile pace) is achieved by adjusting the treadmill speed until you get the time of 12.15 seconds for 10 revolutions. I usually try to get close to specific speeds, but I don't spend too much time trying to hit a specific speed. Just record the speed that is close to what you want, and when you plot your data on a graph, just use the speed you were actually running at. It is also nice to know what mph to set the treadmill belt. Table 4.7 shows conversions among mph, mile pace, and m/min, and table 4.8 shows the relationship among mph, mile time, and m/min. In addition, for those who want to make more detailed comparisons of different speeds of movement, see appendix C, Time and Pace Conversions.

Table 4.7   Conversions for Miles per Hour, Mile Pace, and Meters per Minute

Miles per hour to mile pace	
Formula	**Example: 9.0 mph**
60 ÷ mph = mile pace	60 ÷ 9.0 = 6.6667 min/mile
Decimal minutes × 60 = seconds	.6667 × 60 = 40 sec, so 6:40 min/mile

Mile pace to miles per hour	
Formula	**Example: 6:40 min/mile**
Seconds ÷ 60 = decimal minutes	40 ÷ 60 = 0.6667 (plus 6 min = 6.6667)
60 ÷ minutes per mile = mph	60 ÷ 6.6667 = 9.0 mph

Meters per minute to miles per hour	
Formula	**Example: 241.4 m/min**
m/min × 60 = m/hr	241.4 × 60 = 14,484 m/hr
m/hr ÷ 1,609.344 m* = mph	14,484 ÷ 1,609.344 = 9.0 mph

Miles per hour to meters per minute	
Formula	**Example: 9.0 mph**
mph × 1,609.344* = m/hr	9.0 × 1,609.344 = 14,484 m/hr
m/hr ÷ 60 = m/min	14,484 ÷ 60 = 241.4 m/min

Meters per min to mile pace	
Formula	**Example: 241.4 m/min**
1,609.344* ÷ (m/min) = min/mile	1,609.344 ÷ 241.4 = 6.6667 min/mile
Decimal minutes × 60 = seconds	.6667 × 60 = 40 sec, so 6:40 min/mile

Mile pace to meters per minute	
Formula	**Example: 6:40 mile pace**
Seconds ÷ 60 = decimal minutes	40/60 = .6667 min
Minutes + decimal minutes = min/mile	6 + .6667 = 6.6667 min/mile
1,609.344* ÷ (min/mile) = m/min	1,609.344 ÷ 6.6667 = 241.4 m/min

Table created by Jack Daniels' Running Calculator designed by the Run SMART Project.

*1,609.344 m is equal to 1 mile.

Table 4.8   Relationship Among Miles per Hour, Mile Time, and Meters per Minute

Speed (mph)	Mile time	Speed (m/min)	Speed (mph)	Mile time	Speed (m/min)	Speed (mph)	Mile time	Speed (m/min)
6.0	10:00	161	8.1	7:24	217	10.1	5:56	271
6.1	9:50	164	8.2	7:19	220	10.2	5:53	274
6.2	9:41	166	8.3	7:14	223	10.3	5:49	276
6.3	9:31	169	8.4	7:09	225	10.4	5:46	279
6.4	9:22	172	8.5	7:04	228	10.5	5:43	282
6.5	9:14	174	8.6	6:59	231	10.6	5:40	284
6.6	9:05	177	8.7	6:54	233	10.7	5:36	287
6.7	8:57	180	8.8	6:49	236	10.8	5:33	290
6.8	8:49	182	8.9	6:44	239	10.9	5:30	292
6.9	8:42	185	9.0	6:40	241	11.0	5:27	295
7.0	8:34	188	9.1	6:36	244	11.1	5:24	298
7.1	8:27	190	9.2	6:31	247	11.2	5:21	300
7.2	8:20	193	9.3	6:27	249	11.3	5:19	303
7.3	8:13	196	9.4	6:23	252	11.4	5:16	306
7.4	8:06	198	9.5	6:19	255	11.5	5:13	308
7.5	8:00	201	9.6	6:15	257	11.6	5:10	311
7.6	7:54	204	9.7	6:11	260	11.7	5:08	314
7.7	7:48	207	9.8	6:07	263	11.8	5:05	317
7.8	7:42	209	9.9	6:04	266	11.9	5:02	319
7.9	7:36	212	10.0	6:00	268	12.0	5:00	322
8.0	7:30	215	—	—	—	—	—	—

Table created by Jack Daniels' Running Calculator designed by the Run SMART Project.

5

VDOT Values

Set realistic goals for every race you run and you will almost always achieve them.

Because of the great popularity, usefulness, and simplicity of the VDOT training tables I have provided for runners and coaches over the past 30 years, I decided to set aside a chapter of this edition of the book to describe the VDOT system in a little more detail.

The term *VDOT* was originally used as a short form for the $\dot{V}O_2$max value, to which it is related. When a person refers to $\dot{V}O_2$ (whether in reference to a submaximal or maximal value of oxygen being consumed), it is correctly pronounced "V dot O2" because there is a dot over the *V* indicating that the volume, which the *V* represents, is a 1-minute volume.

Without a dot over the *V*, the volume represented may be measured over more or less than 1 minute, so to make different volumes comparable, the volume is converted to a 1-minute value. For example, if I collect a 30-second bag of expired air from subject A, who is being tested on a treadmill or track, the collected volume may be 65 liters and the volume of oxygen that this subject consumed during that 30-second collection may be 2,000 ml (2 liters). You could say the V_E (volume of expired air collected during that 30-second period of time) is 65 liters and VO_2 consumption is 2,000 ml.

However, if another subject (subject B) had an expired air collection for a period of 40 seconds, with a V_E of 75 liters and a VO_2 of 2,500 ml, it would not be legitimate to say that B was breathing more air or consuming more oxygen, because the periods of collection were for different amounts of time.

By converting the volumes for both A and B to 1-minute values, then the two subjects can be better compared. In this example, A's $VDOT_E$ would be 130 liters and B's would be 112.5 liters. As for the comparable VDOT O_2 values, A would have a 4,000 ml volume and B a 3,750 ml volume.

The point is that to properly compare different values, whether for different subjects or the same subject under different conditions, the data must first be converted to 1-minute values, and in the case of oxygen consumption, the proper terminology is VDOT O_2.

When Jimmy Gilbert and I used my collection data to generate the original VDOT tables, we just referred to our calculated (pseudo) $\dot{V}O_2$max values as *VDOT* in the computer programs we wrote at that time. I also want to add that Jimmy Gilbert is the person who wrote the programs. He is a guy I coached in college and who later became a computer programmer for NASA in Houston, Texas, where he still lives and has just finished running his 95,000th mile (he has, of course, quite carefully kept track of them all). Our VDOT tables are the result of his careful attention to detail.

USING VDOT TO ESTABLISH TRAINING INTENSITIES

The data we used in constructing the VDOT tables were gathered from years of testing many runners of a variety of ability levels. The three most important variables generated were $\dot{V}O_2$max (that's VDOT O_2max), running economy over a minimum of four submaximal speeds of running, and the fraction of each runner's respective $\dot{V}O_2$max at which each runner performed when racing over a variety of distances, more specifically, over a variety of durations of time.

Figure 5.1 shows the representative economy curve that was the result of all submax economy tests we ran, and figure 5.2 shows the curve that represents the fraction of max that was associated with durations of races run.

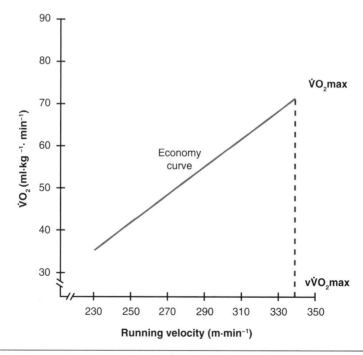

Figure 5.1   Average economy curve and v$\dot{V}O_2$max associated with this curve and a $\dot{V}O_2$max.

Adapted from J. Daniels, R. Fitts, and G. Sheehan. 1978, *Conditioning for distance running: The scientific aspects* (New York, NY: John Wiley and Sons), 31. By permission of J. Daniels.

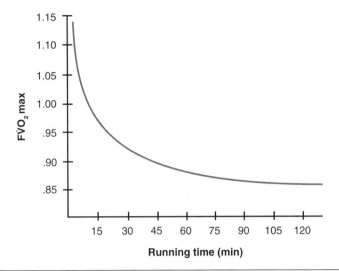

Figure 5.2   Curve relating race time and fraction of $\dot{V}O_2$max.

Adapted from J. Daniels, R. Fitts, and G. Sheehan. 1978, *Conditioning for distance running: The scientific aspects* (New York, NY: John Wiley and Sons), 31. By permission of J. Daniels.

For example, using the regression equation that describes the curve in figure 5.1, the typical aerobic (oxygen) demand for running at a 6-minute-mile pace is about 51.7 ml per minute per kilogram of body weight. Now if a runner ran a 5-mile race in 30 minutes (a pace of 6 minutes per mile), then the formula that describes the curve in figure 5.2 says that the fraction of VDOT O_2max for a 30-minute race is .937 (93.7 percent of max). So, if the cost of the race is 51.7 ml and the runner is working at 93.7 percent of max, then this runner's VDOT (pseudo $\dot{V}O_2$max) will be 51.7 / .937, which equals 55.2.

Now and then a runner will contact me to say my VDOT tables gave him a value of, say, 56.5, but in a recent lab test he was told his $\dot{V}O_2$max was 61.6. I have no problem with this at all. Remember, our values are dependent on a particular (representative) running economy, so this person, with the measured max above the awarded VDOT value, is just not as economical as our formula gave him credit for. If your lab-measured max is less than we determine, then this means you are more economical than we gave you credit for. No problem, because we use the same VDOT data and some considerably more complicated equations along with your actual performance times to calculate proper training intensities and to predict race times for other distances.

Using a person's race times gives a far better prediction of training intensities and other race performances than do tests in the lab. Race times reflect your max, your economy, your threshold, and your mental approach to racing, all in one measure—the time it takes you to run a race.

Naturally, it is not as legitimate to use a time under perfect race conditions to predict another race under poor conditions, and performance in a mile is not as good a predictor of a marathon time as would be a half-marathon

Bennett Cohen/Icon SMI

Better race times determine higher VDOT values.

time. Think of the VDOT values as good predictors of physiological capability and they will do a great job when used to estimate times for race distances for which you are currently training.

When we devised the VDOT tables, some world records were not as great as the VDOT values predicted they should be. For example, for women, the 1,500 meter and 3,000 meter world records at that time both represented VDOT values of 71+, and the marathon record was associated with a considerably lower VDOT value, which prompted us to say, "It can be predicted that, based on relative VDOT values, women's times in the marathon will come down to the low 2:20s before a noticeable improvement takes place in men's marathon times."

Not a bad prediction at all, and all world records for men and for women are quite close in VDOT values, with men's times associated with VDOT values that are a little more than 11 percent greater than are the women's. It is also true that a female runner with a 70 VDOT will outperform a male runner whose VDOT is in the mid-60s. The higher VDOT value is associated with the better runner, regardless of age or sex, simply because VDOT represents performance in the first place.

Let's face it, we already use performance to place marathon runners in different starting boxes, with slower people farther back in the starting area. We may as well use VDOT values to separate the runners; performance over other distances could be used to determine starting points in a race that the runners have not even run before.

Oxygen Power, the book that Jimmy Gilbert and I wrote in 1979, contains 81 pages of VDOT tables for more than 40 different distances, including values for distances run in meters, yards, kilometers, and miles, and even for a 1-hour run time. Table 5.1 shows VDOT values for some more popular race distances.

Table 5.1   VDOT Values Associated With Running Times of Popular Distances

VDOT	1,500	Mile	3,000	2 mile	5,000	10K	15K	Half marathon	Marathon	VDOT
30	8:30	9:11	17:56	19:19	30:40	63:46	98:14	2:21:04	4:49:17	30
31	8:15	8:55	17:27	18:48	29:51	62:03	95:36	2:17:21	4:41:57	31
32	8:02	8:41	16:59	18:18	29:05	60:26	93:07	2:13:49	4:34:59	32
33	7:49	8:27	16:33	17:50	28:21	58:54	90:45	2:10:27	4:28:22	33
34	7:37	8:14	16:09	17:24	27:39	57:26	88:30	2:07:16	4:22:03	34
35	7:25	8:01	15:45	16:58	27:00	56:03	86:22	2:04:13	4:16:03	35
36	7:14	7:49	15:23	16:34	26:22	54:44	84:20	2:01:19	4:10:19	36
37	7:04	7:38	15:01	16:11	25:46	53:29	82:24	1:58:34	4:04:50	37
38	6:54	7:27	14:41	15:49	25:12	52:17	80:33	1:55:55	3:59:35	38
39	6:44	7:17	14:21	15:29	24:39	51:09	78:47	1:53:24	3:54:34	39
40	6:35	7:07	14:03	15:08	24:08	50:03	77:06	1:50:59	3:49:45	40
41	6:27	6:58	13:45	14:49	23:38	49:01	75:29	1:48:40	3:45:09	41
42	6:19	6:49	13:28	14:31	23:09	48:01	73:56	1:46:27	3:40:43	42
43	6:11	6:41	13:11	14:13	22:41	47:04	72:27	1:44:20	3:36:28	43
44	6:03	6:32	12:55	13:56	22:15	46:09	71:02	1:42:17	3:32:23	44
45	5:56	6:25	12:40	13:40	21:50	45:16	69:40	1:40:20	3:28:26	45
46	5:49	6:17	12:26	13:25	21:25	44:25	68:22	1:38:27	3:24:39	46
47	5:42	6:10	12:12	13:10	21:02	43:36	67:06	1:36:38	3:21:00	47
48	5:36	6:03	11:58	12:55	20:39	42:50	65:53	1:34:53	3:17:29	48
49	5:30	5:56	11:45	12:41	20:18	42:04	64:44	1:33:12	3:14:06	49
50	5:24	5:50	11:33	12:28	19:57	41:21	63:36	1:31:35	3:10:49	50
51	5:18	5:44	11:21	12:15	19:36	40:39	62:31	1:30:02	3:07:39	51
52	5:13	5:38	11:09	12:02	19:17	39:59	61:29	1:28:31	3:04:36	52
53	5:07	5:32	10:58	11:50	18:58	39:20	60:28	1:27:04	3:01:39	53
54	5:02	5:27	10:47	11:39	18:40	38:42	59:30	1:25:40	2:58:47	54
55	4:57	5:21	10:37	11:28	18:22	38:06	58:33	1:24:18	2:56:01	55
56	4:53	5:16	10:27	11:17	18:05	37:31	57:39	1:23:00	2:53:20	56
57	4:48	5:11	10:17	11:06	17:49	36:57	56:46	1:21:43	2:50:45	57
58	4:44	5:06	10:08	10:56	17:33	36:24	55:55	1:20:30	2:48:14	58
59	4:39	5:02	9:58	10:46	17:17	35:52	55:06	1:19:18	2:45:47	59
60	4:35	4:57	9:50	10:37	17:03	35:22	54:18	1:18:09	2:43:25	60
61	4:31	4:53	9:41	10:27	16:48	34:52	53:32	1:17:02	2:41:08	61
62	4:27	4:49	9:33	10:18	16:34	34:23	52:47	1:15:57	2:38:54	62
63	4:24	4:45	9:25	10:10	16:20	33:55	52:03	1:14:54	2:36:44	63
64	4:20	4:41	9:17	10:01	16:07	33:28	51:21	1:13:53	2:34:38	64
65	4:16	4:37	9:09	9:53	15:54	33:01	50:40	1:12:53	2:32:35	65

(continued)

Table 5.1   VDOT Values Associated With Running Times of Popular Distances   *(continued)*

VDOT	1,500	Mile	3,000	2 mile	5,000	10K	15K	Half marathon	Marathon	VDOT
66	4:13	4:33	9:02	9:45	15:42	32:35	50:00	1:11:56	2:30:36	66
67	4:10	4:30	8:55	9:37	15:29	32:11	49:22	1:11:00	2:28:40	67
68	4:06	4:26	8:48	9:30	15:18	31:46	48:44	1:10:05	2:26:47	68
69	4:03	4:23	8:41	9:23	15:06	31:23	48:08	1:09:12	2:24:57	69
70	4:00	4:19	8:34	9:16	14:55	31:00	47:32	1:08:21	2:23:10	70
71	3:57	4:16	8:28	9:09	14:44	30:38	46:58	1:07:31	2:21:26	71
72	3:54	4:13	8:22	9:02	14:33	30:16	46:24	1:06:42	2:19:44	72
73	3:52	4:10	8:16	8:55	14:23	29:55	45:51	1:05:54	2:18:05	73
74	3:49	4:07	8:10	8:49	14:13	29:34	45:19	1:05:08	2:16:29	74
75	3:46	4:04	8:04	8:43	14:03	29:14	44:48	1:04:23	2:14:55	75
76	3:44	4:02	7:58	8:37	13:54	28:55	44:18	1:03:39	2:13:23	76
77	3:41+	3:58+	7:53	8:31	13:44	28:36	43:49	1:02:56	2:11:54	77
78	3:38.8	3:56.2	7:48	8:25	13:35	28:17	43:20	1:02:15	2:10:27	78
79	3:36.5	3:53.7	7:43	8:20	13:26	27:59	42:52	1:01:34	2:09:02	79
80	3:34.2	3:51.2	7:37.5	8:14.2	13:17.8	27:41	42:25	1:00:54	2:07:38	80
81	3:31.9	3:48.7	7:32.5	8:08.9	13:09.3	27:24	41:58	1:00:15	2:06:17	81
82	3:29.7	3:46.4	7:27.7	8:03.7	13:01.1	27:07	41:32	:59:38	2:04:57	82
83	3:27.6	3:44.0	7:23.0	7:58.6	12:53.0	26:51	41:06	:59:01	2:03:40	83
84	3:25.5	3:41.8	7:18.5	7:53.6	12:45.2	26:34	40:42	:58:25	2:02:24	84
85	3:23.5	3:39.6	7:14.0	7:48.8	12:37.4	26:19	40:17	:57:50	2:01:10	85

Table created by Jack Daniels' Running Calculator designed by the Run SMART Project.

If you look up the relative VDOT values for several race times, it is usually just fine to use your highest value when using the VDOT training tables to determine the appropriate speeds at which to do different types of training. Table 5.2 then lets you use the VDOT value that represents your best recent performance in order to determine the appropriate paces for the types of training that make up your current program.

For example, let's suppose your best current performance is a 5:44 mile, which from table 5.1 is associated with a 51 VDOT value. Then you go to table 5.2 to get appropriate training paces for a 51 VDOT. Easy runs and long runs (**E** pace) can best be performed at 4:52 to 5:29 per kilometer or between 7:49 and 8:49 per mile, which should be very comfortable, conversational running speeds.

The next couple of columns indicate the appropriate training speed for a runner training for a marathon (**M** pace), with a current VDOT of 51 (4:27 per kilometer and 7:09 per mile pace). For threshold training (**T** pace), there are three columns describing the proper training paces, expressed in times per 400 meters, per kilometer, and per mile. For the runner with a 51 VDOT, these training paces would be 1:40/400, 4:11/km and 6:44/mile.

When it comes to interval (**I**) training, remember that my recommendation is not to include individual work bouts that are longer than 5 minutes. For this reason, the training speeds for various distances at **I** pace will not be associated with any distances for which each individual run will last longer than 5 minutes.

In the current example, which is for a 51 VDOT, 92/400 (3:04/800), 3:51/km, and 4:36/1,200 would be the right training speeds. It would not be appropriate to run **I** miles because it would take more than 5 minutes to complete a mile at the appropriate speed. You will see from the VDOT training-intensity table that the lowest VDOT value that should be used in running **I** miles is a 66.

A similar situation is associated with training at repetition (**R**) pace, which is shown in the final five columns of the table. For our current example of a person with a 51 VDOT, the proper **R** training speeds are 43/200, 64/300, and 86/400. With **R** training, it is not desirable to include individual work bouts that last longer than 2 minutes, so it would be pushing it a little to include 600s or 800s for a person whose VDOT is only 51. A 56 VDOT runner could include some **R** 600s in the program; a runner's VDOT would have to be about 77 in order for 800-meter **R** work bouts to be appropriate.

In all honesty, it is perfectly fine to go a little outside the recommended ranges now and then, and a person with a 70 VDOT would probably not have a big problem running **R** 800s in 2:10, which is not far outside the suggested 2-minute maximum duration for **R** work bouts.

Daniels' 6-Second Rule

When it comes to determining **R** training speed, of particular interest is how close **R** pace is to mile or 1,500 race ability and the typical association between **R**, **I**, and **T** training speeds. For example, a person with a 60 VDOT should have a current mile race time of about 5:00 (table 5.1 shows a 4:57 mile), which is a pace of about 75 seconds per 400, and table 5.2 lists a 75/400 pace as appropriate for 60-VDOT **R** training.

Now, if you follow a 60-VDOT runner's training paces back to **I** and **T** speeds in table 5.2, you will find **I** pace to be 81 seconds per 400 (6 seconds slower per 400 than is the proper **R** pace for a 60 VDOT). Going to the **T** column, you find the pace per 400 to be 7 seconds slower than is **I** pace for this runner. Further, if you look down to higher VDOT values, you will find that **T** pace is typically 6 seconds per 400 slower than **I** pace and **I** pace 6 seconds per 400 slower than **R** pace. I refer to this as my 6-second rule for training, but it applies most accurately to better runners. However, you can make it into a 7- or 8-second rule for runners in the 50 or 40 VDOT categories.

Table 5.2 Training Intensities Based on Current VDOT

VDOT	E (easy)/L (long)		M (marathon pace)		T (threshold pace)		
	Km	Mile	Km	Mile	400 m	Km	Mile
30	7:27-8:14	12:00-13:16	7:03	11:21	2:33	6:24	10:18
31	7:16-8:02	11:41-12:57	6:52	11:02	2:30	6:14	10:02
32	7:05-7:52	11:24-12:39	6:40	10:44	2:26	6:05	9:47
33	6:55-7:41	11:07-12:21	6:30	10:27	2:23	5:56	9:33
34	6:45-7:31	10:52-12:05	6:20	10:11	2:19	5:48	9:20
35	6:36-7:21	10:37-11:49	6:10	9:56	2:16	5:40	9:07
36	6:27-7:11	10:23-11:34	6:01	9:41	2:13	5:33	8:55
37	6:19-7:02	10:09-11:20	5:53	9:28	2:10	5:26	8:44
38	6:11-6:54	9:56-11:06	5:45	9:15	2:07	5:19	8:33
39	6:03-6:46	9:44-10:53	5:37	9:02	2:05	5:12	8:22
40	5:56-6:38	9:32-10:41	5:29	8:50	2:02	5:06	8:12
41	5:49-6:31	9:21-10:28	5:22	8:39	2:00	5:00	8:02
42	5:42-6:23	9:10-10:17	5:16	8:28	1:57	4:54	7:52
43	5:35-6:16	9:00-10:05	5:09	8:17	1:55	4:49	7:42
44	5:29-6:10	8:50-9:55	5:03	8:07	1:53	4:43	7:33
45	5:23-6:03	8:40-9:44	4:57	7:58	1:51	4:38	7:25
46	5:17-5:57	8:31-9:34	4:51	7:49	1:49	4:33	7:17
47	5:12-5:51	8:22-9:25	4:46	7:40	1:47	4:29	7:09
48	5:07-5:45	8:13-9:15	4:41	7:32	1:45	4:24	7:02
49	5:01-5:40	8:05-9:06	4:36	7:24	1:43	4:20	6:56
50	4:56-5:34	7:57-8:58	4:31	7:17	1:41	4:15	6:50
51	4:52-5:29	7:49-8:49	4:27	7:09	1:40	4:11	6:44
52	4:47-5:24	7:42-8:41	4:22	7:02	98	4:07	6:38
53	4:43-5:19	7:35-8:33	4:18	6:56	97	4:04	6:32
54	4:38-5:14	7:28-8:26	4:14	6:49	95	4:00	6:26
55	4:34-5:10	7:21-8:18	4:10	6:43	94	3:56	6:20
56	4:30-5:05	7:15-8:11	4:06	6:37	93	3:53	6:15
57	4:26-5:01	7:08-8:04	4:03	6:31	91	3:50	6:09
58	4:22-4:57	7:02-7:58	3:59	6:25	90	3:46	6:04
59	4:19-4:53	6:56-7:51	3:56	6:19	89	3:43	5:59
60	4:15-4:49	6:50-7:45	3:52	6:14	88	3:40	5:54
61	4:11-4:45	6:45-7:39	3:49	6:09	86	3:37	5:50
62	4:08-4:41	6:39-7:33	3:46	6:04	85	3:34	5:45

| I (interval pace) | | | | R (repetition pace) | | | | | |
400 m	Km	1,200 m	Mile	200 m	300 m	400 m	600 m	800 m	VDOT
2:22	—	—	—	67	1:41	—	—	—	30
2:18	—	—	—	65	98	—	—	—	31
2:14	—	—	—	63	95	—	—	—	32
2:11	—	—	—	61	92	—	—	—	33
2:08	—	—	—	60	90	2:00	—	—	34
2:05	—	—	—	58	87	1:57	—	—	35
2:02	—	—	—	57	85	1:54	—	—	36
1:59	5:00	—	—	55	83	1:51	—	—	37
1:56	4:54	—	—	54	81	1:48	—	—	38
1:54	4:48	—	—	53	80	1:46	—	—	39
1:52	4:42	—	—	52	78	1:44	—	—	40
1:50	4:36	—	—	51	77	1:42	—	—	41
1:48	4:31	—	—	50	75	1:40	—	—	42
1:46	4:26	—	—	49	74	98	—	—	43
1:44	4:21	—	—	48	72	96	—	—	44
1:42	4:16	—	—	47	71	94	—	—	45
1:40	4:12	5:00	—	46	69	92	—	—	46
98	4:07	4:54	—	45	68	90	—	—	47
96	4:03	4:49	—	44	67	89	—	—	48
95	3:59	4:45	—	44	66	88	—	—	49
93	3:55	4: 40	—	43	65	87	—	—	50
92	3:51	4:36	—	43	64	86	—	—	51
91	3:48	4:32	—	42	64	85	—	—	52
90	3:44	4:29	—	42	63	84	—	—	53
88	3:41	4:25	—	41	62	82	—	—	54
87	3:37	4:21	—	40	61	81	—	—	55
86	3:34	4:18	—	40	60	80	2:00	—	56
85	3:31	4:14	—	39	59	79	1:57	—	57
83	3:28	4:10	—	38	58	77	1:55	—	58
82	3:25	4:07	—	38	57	76	1:54	—	59
81	3:23	4:03	—	37	56	75	1:52	—	60
80	3:20	4:00	—	37	55	74	1:51	—	61
79	3:17	3:57	—	36	54	73	1:49	—	62

(continued)

Table 5.2   Training Intensities Based on Current VDOT   *(continued)*

VDOT	E (easy)/L (long)		M (marathon pace)		T (threshold pace)		
	Km	Mile	Km	Mile	400 m	Km	Mile
63	4:05-4:38	6:34-7:27	3:43	5:59	84	3:32	5:41
64	4:02-4:34	6:29-7:21	3:40	5:54	83	3:29	5:36
65	3:59-4:31	6:24-7:16	3:37	5:49	82	3:26	5:32
66	3:56-4:28	6:19-7:10	3:34	5:45	81	3:24	5:28
67	3:53-4:24	6:15-7:05	3:31	5:40	80	3:21	5:24
68	3:50-4:21	6:10-7:00	3:29	5:36	79	3:19	5:20
69	3:47-4:18	6:06-6:55	3:26	5:32	78	3:16	5:16
70	3:44-4:15	6:01-6:50	3:24	5:28	77	3:14	5:13
71	3:42-4:12	5:57-6:46	3:21	5:24	76	3:12	5:09
72	3:40-4:00	5:53-6:41	3:19	5:20	76	3:10	5:05
73	3:37-4:07	5:49-6:37	3:16	5:16	75	3:08	5:02
74	3:34-4:04	5:45-6:32	3:14	5:12	74	3:06	4:59
75	3:32-4:01	5:41-6:28	3:12	5:09	74	3:04	4:56
76	3:30-3:58	5:38-6:24	3:10	5:05	73	3:02	4:52
77	3:28-3:56	5:34-6:20	3:08	5:02	72	3:00	4:49
78	3:25-3:53	5:30-6:16	3:06	4:58	71	2:58	4:46
79	3:23-3:51	5:27-6:12	3:03	4:55	70	2:56	4:43
80	3:21-3:49	5:24-6:08	3:01	4:52	70	2:54	4:41
81	3:19-3:46	5:20-6:04	3:00	4:49	69	2:53	4:38
82	3:17-3:44	5:17-6:01	2:58	4:46	68	2:51	4:35
83	3:15-3:42	5:14-5:57	2:56	4:43	68	2:49	4:32
84	3:13-3:40	5:11-5:54	2:54	4:40	67	2:48	4:30
85	3:11-3:38	5:08-5:50	2:52	4:37	66	2:46	4:27

The advantage of realizing the relationship between training paces for the various types of training is that you can do a very good job of determining all proper training paces if all you have to go by is a recent mile or 1,500 race time. The mile or 1,500 pace for 400 is used for **R** pace, and that pace can easily be converted to proper **I** and **T** paces, without having the VDOT tables in hand. There is also a faster **R** pace (which I refer to as "fast rep" pace) that is part of training programs for 800-meter specialists, covered later in chapter 9.

Novice and Low-VDOT Training Intensities

In recent years it has become more and more popular to train for and participate in half marathons and full marathons. I offer some suggested marathon

I (interval pace)				R (repetition pace)					
400 m	Km	1,200 m	Mile	200 m	300 m	400 m	600 m	800 m	**VDOT**
78	3:15	3:54	—	36	53	72	1:48	—	63
77	3:12	3:51	—	35	52	71	1:46	—	64
76	3:10	3:48	—	35	52	70	1:45	—	65
75	3:08	3:45	5:00	34	51	69	1:43	—	66
74	3:05	3:42	4:57	34	51	68	1:42	—	67
73	3:03	3:39	4:53	33	50	67	1:40	—	68
72	3:01	3:36	4:50	33	49	66	99	—	69
71	2:59	3:34	4:46	32	48	65	97	—	70
70	2:57	3:31	4:43	32	48	64	96	—	71
69	2:55	3:29	4:40	31	47	63	94	—	72
69	2:53	3:27	4:37	31	47	63	93	—	73
68	2:51	3:25	4:34	31	46	62	92	—	74
67	2:49	3:22	4:31	30	46	61	91	—	75
66	2:48	3:20	4:28	30	45	60	90	—	76
65	2:46	3:18	4:25	29	45	59	89	2:00	77
65	2:44	3:16	4:23	29	44	59	88	1:59	78
64	2:42	3:14	4:20	29	44	58	87	1:58	79
64	2:41	3:12	4:17	29	43	58	87	1:56	80
63	2:39	3:10	4:15	28	43	57	86	1:55	81
62	2:38	3:08	4:12	28	42	56	85	1:54	82
62	2:36	3:07	4:10	28	42	56	84	1:53	83
61	2:35	3:05	4:08	27	41	55	83	1:52	84
61	2:33	3:03	4:05	27	41	55	82	1:51	85

Table created by Jack Daniels' Running Calculator designed by the Run SMART Project.

training plans later in this book for many levels of ability and fitness, including people who have little or no running experience (see chapters 13 and 14) Many of these participants are not able to find training paces associated with very low VDOT values, so I have added an applicable VDOT table (table 5.3).

This table shows race times for 1 mile and 5,000 meters and their associated VDOT values, followed by recommended training paces for people who fit into this range of current performance categories. You will notice that the final column shows **M** training paces and the total time for a marathon associated with the VDOT values. For example, if your VDOT is 28 and you want to train for a marathon, **M** pace is 7:27 per kilometer and 12:02 per mile, and the total marathon time associated with that average pace is 5 hours and 15 minutes.

Table 5.3 Training Intensities for Novice Runners and Others Starting With Slow Performances

Race times			R		I		T			M		
Mile	5K	VDOT	200 m	300 m	200 m	400 m	400 m	Km	Mile	Time (hr:min)	min/ km	min/ mile
9:10	30:40	30	1:08	1:42	1:11	2:24	2:33	6:24	10:18	4:57	7:03	11:21
9:27	31:32	29	1:10	1:45	1:14	2:28	2:37	6:34	10:34	5:06	7:15	11:41
9:44	32:27	28	1:13	1:49	1:17	2:34	2:42	6:45	10:52	5:15	7:27	12:02
10:02	33:25	27	1:15	1:53	1:19	2:38	2:46	6:56	11:10	5:25	7:41	12:24
10:22	34:27	26	1:18	1:57	1:22	2:44	2:51	7:09	11:30	5:35	7:56	12:47
10:43	35:33	25	1:21	2:02	1:24	2:48	2:56	7:21	11:51	5:45	8:10	13:11
11:06	36:44	24	1:24	----	1:27	2:55	3:02	7:35	12:13	5:56	8:26	13:36
11:30	38:01	23	1:27	----	1:30	3:01	3:08	7:50	12:36	6:08	8:43	14:02
11:56	39:22	22	1:30	----	1:33	3:07	3:14	8:06	13:02	6:19	8:59	14:29
12:24	40:49	21	1:33	----	1:36	3:13	3:21	8:23	13:29	6:31	9:16	14:57
12:55	42:24	20	1:37	----	1:40	3:21	3:28	8:41	13:58	6:44	9:34	15:26

Table created by Jack Daniels' Running Calculator designed by the Run SMART Project.

TRACKING TRAINING INTENSITIES

Most distance runners are careful to record the total amount of mileage they accomplish each week. This is useful information to keep track of because it helps prevent overtraining and allows the runner to look back on previous training and associated performances. I showed earlier that it is good to stay with a particular amount of training stress for several weeks before increasing the stress to a higher level, but it is also a good idea to make note of how much of the different types of stress are being included in an overall program.

The first step I took in trying to monitor types of stress was to get other coaches and experienced runners to consider how to relate different intensities of running with other intensities. For example, in terms of overall training stress, how much running at **I** intensity would be equal to how much running at **T** intensity? I arrived at some comparative multiplication factors that allow a runner to compare different intensities, or speeds, of running in terms of overall stress. Table 5.4 summarizes this information.

• **E zone (easy runs):** Although a variety of running speeds qualify as **E** runs (see **E** zone in table 5.4), I have assigned an average **E** run intensity as being worth .2 points per minute of running at a speed that represents 66 percent of any runner's VDOT. I consider **E**-zone running to range in intensity from 59 percent to 74 percent of your VDOT value, and the relative percentages of maximum heart rate (HR) are also shown throughout each zone.

Keep track not only of weekly mileage but also the intensity level and stress included in your program.

For those who monitor HR during some training sessions, I have left this column blank. Entering HR data will provide even more precise monitoring of training intensities.

• **M zone (marathon-pace runs):** These are usually performed between about 75 percent and 84 percent of VDOT. For simplifying the recording of stress associated with **M**-pace running, assign .4 points (.5 for faster marathon runners) for each minute run at **M** pace.

In the **M** zone of table 5.4, I have entered typical marathon race times associated with the percentages of VDOT and HR found here. You can see that faster runners will be working at higher fractions of their max data because they are racing for shorter periods of time, and duration of a race is what is most closely associated with intensity, as mentioned earlier.

• **T zone (threshold running):** The next more intense zone is related to typical **T**-pace running and represents running at intensities in the mid- to upper 80 percent of VDOT values. **T** running is best for improving the body's ability to clear lactate and in simple terms is great for improving endurance. I consider .6 points for each minute as a simple point-calculation multiple in the **T** zone.

• **10K zone:** Some runners like to train in the 10K zone, which in my way of looking at training, falls between **T** and **I** intensity of effort, and for each minute in this zone .8 points are awarded.

• **I zone (intervals):** The **I** zone is best for improving aerobic power and makes the body function at, or nearly at, V̇O₂max. When training in this zone, in most cases you can roughly consider each minute at **I** intensity to be worth 1 point. I have shown some durations considered the longest time that can be raced at the corresponding VDOT percentages.

The typical races associated with the **I** zone are in the range of 2 miles to 5 miles (3 km to 8 km). One thing of note in the **I** zone is that the percentages of VDOT and maximum heart rate merge at 100 percent. You will notice that in the earlier zones, percentage of maximum heart rate is somewhat higher than is percentage of VDOT.

• **R zone (repetitions):** In the final training zone (**R** zone), no percentages of maximum HR are indicated. When running this fast, you are working at an intensity that will always elicit maximum heart rate if you stay at that speed of running for a couple minutes or longer.

It is in the **R** zone that a runner spends time working on speed, anaerobic power, and running economy. When you are training or racing at the 105 percent to 110 percent VDOT intensities, these running speeds are associated with races that last about 4:40 to 7:00, which are close to what many runners will race for 1,500 meters or 1 mile. When working at about 115 percent to 120 percent of VDOT, then you are running at speeds more closely associated with 800-meter race times.

The other columns of table 5.4 show how many points are awarded for various durations of time spent in each zone. If not worried about being too detailed in recording points associated with various intensities of training, you could use the following rough estimates—.2 points per minute of **E** running, .4 points per minute at **M** pace, .6 points per minute at **T** pace, 1.0 point per minute at **I** pace, and 1.5 points per minute at **R** pace.

Even if the relative values for times spent in the different zones may not be perfectly accurate in relation to each other, the numbers provided could be useful for logging training performed. For example, you might finish a season having accumulated a total of 100 points in the **I** zone, and the next season you will try for 110 points in that zone.

You can also see the total number of points (using the sum of all zones) you accumulate each week, and next season you can try to increase that number by a certain percentage—similar to increasing weekly mileage from one season to the next. A possible starting point may be to suggest that beginning high school runners try to accumulate 50 points a week and a year or two later go for 100 points per week.

During college the point totals may go up to 150 points a week and to 200 or more points per week after graduation. No doubt some runners will be capable of accumulating more points than are others while still avoiding injury, just as is the case with total weekly mileage. See table 5.5 for workouts that accumulate 10, 15, 20, 25, and 30 points.

Table 5.4 Tracking Intensity Training

Points awarded per number of minutes shown. Add your HR in the appropriate row for each intensity.

E zone (easy running)

%VDOT	%HRmax	HR	1 min	5 min	10 min	20 min	30 min	60 min
59	65		.100	.500	1.00	2.00	3.00	6.0
60	66		.110	.550	1.10	2.20	3.30	6.6
61	67		.122	.610	1.22	2.44	3.66	7.3
62	68		.135	.675	1.35	2.70	4.05	8.1
63	69		.150	.750	1.50	3.00	4.50	9.0
64	70		.167	.835	1.67	3.34	5.00	10
65	71		.183	.915	1.83	3.66	5.50	11
66	72		.200	1.000	2.00	4.00	6.00	12
67	73		.217	1.085	2.17	4.34	6.50	13
68	74		.233	1.165	2.33	4.66	7.00	14
69	75		.250	1.250	2.50	5.00	7.50	15
70	75.5		.267	1.335	2.67	5.34	8.00	16
71	76		.283	1.415	2.83	5.66	8.50	17
72	77		.300	1.500	3.00	6.00	9.00	18
73	78		.317	1.585	3.17	6.34	9.50	19
74	79		.333	1.665	3.33	6.66	10.00	20

M zone (marathon-pace)

%VDOT*	%HRmax	HR	1 min	5 min	10 min	20 min	30 min	60 min
75 (5:00)	80		.350	1.750	3.5	7.0	10.5	21
76 (4:40)	81		.367	1.835	3.7	7.4	11.1	22
77 (4:20)	82		.392	1.960	3.9	7.8	11.7	23.5
78 (4:00)	83		.417	2.090	4.2	8.4	12.6	25
79 (3:40)	84		.442	2.210	4.4	8.8	13.2	26.5
80 (3:20)	85		.467	2.340	4.7	9.4	14.1	28
81 (3:00)	86		.492	2.460	4.9	9.8	14.7	29.5
82 (2:50)	87		.517	2.590	5.2	10.4	15.6	31
83 (2:20)	88		.550	2.75	5.5	11.0	16.5	33
84 (2:05)	89		.583	2.92	5.8	11.6	17.4	35

T zone (threshold/tempo)

%VDOT	%HRmax	HR	1 min	5 min	10 min	20 min	30 min	60 min
83	88		.550	2.75	5.5	11.0	16.5	33
84	89		.583	2.92	5.8	11.6	17.4	35
85	89.5		.600	3.00	6.0	12.0	18.0	36
86	90		.617	3.09	6.2	12.4	18.6	37
87	91		.650	3.25	6.5	13.0	19.5	39
88	92		.683	3.42	6.8	13.6	20.4	41

(continued)

Table 5.4   Tracking Intensity Training   *(continued)*

10K zone

%VDOT**	%HRmax	HR	1 min	2 min	5 min	10 min	20 min	30 min
89 (60:00)	92.5		.700	1.40	3.5	7.0	14.0	21.0
90 (50:00)	93		.723	1.45	3.6	7.2	14.4	21.7
91 (40:00)	94		.763	1.53	3.8	7.6	15.2	22.9
92 (35:00)	95		.800	1.60	4.0	8.0	16.0	24.0
93 (30:00)	96		.840	1.68	4.2	8.4	16.8	25.2
94 (27:00)	97		.883	1.77	4.4	8.8	17.6	26.5

I zone (interval)

%VDOT***	%HRmax	HR	1 min	2 min	5 min	10 min	20 min	30 min
95 (21:00)	97.5		.900	1.80	4.5	9.0	18.0	27.0
96 (18:00)	98		.917	1.83	4.6	9.2	18.4	27.5
97 (15:30)	98.5		.940	1.88	4.7	9.4	18.8	28.2
98 (13:30)	99		.960	1.92	4.8	9.6	19.2	28.8
99 (12:15)	99.5		.983	1.97	4.9	9.8	19.6	29.5
100 (11:00)	100		1.000	2.00	5.0	10.0	20.0	30.0

R zone (repetition)

%VDOT****	%HRmax	HR	1 min	2 min	5 min	10 min	20 min	30 min
105 (7:02)			1.25	2.5	3.75	6.25	12.5	25
110 (4:40)			1.50	3.0	4.50	7.50	15.0	30
115 (3:00)			1.75	3.5	5.25	8.75	17.5	35
120 (1:43)			2.10	4.2	6.301	0.50	21.0	42

Table created by Jack Daniels' Running Calculator designed by the Run SMART Project.

*Times (hr:min) are approximate marathon times associated with %VDOT.

**Times (min) shown are approximate 10K times associated with %VDOT.

***Times (min) shown are race times (distance irrelevant associated with %VDOT.

****Times (min) shown are race times (distance irrelevant associated with %VDOT.

Presented in table 5.5 are examples of how much time is required to achieve different point totals when running at different intensities (easy **L** runs, **M** pace, **T** pace, **I** and **R** workouts). In addition to the maximum number of minutes that should be spent at each intensity (relative to the number of points associated with each workout), I list how much distance would be suitable in order to accumulate a desired number of points in any particular workout. In addition, the total distance to be covered in various workouts is also a function of your current VDOT.

For example, a runner with a 52 VDOT would have 6.5 miles as an appropriate 10-point **L** run. This runner would also have to total 2.5 miles of running at **T** pace to achieve a 10-point workout at that intensity of running. For this same 52 VDOT runner to get 25 points for a **T** workout would require totaling 6 miles of running at **T** pace (maybe 6 × 1 mile, 3 × 2 miles, or 2 × 3 miles at **T** pace, with appropriate recoveries between the **T**-pace runs). You must remember that current mileage will affect how much of each type of training should be included.

Table 5.5   Varying Point Workouts

	10-point workouts										
	L	**M**	**T**		**I**			**R**			
	50 min	33 min	16 min		10 min			7 min			
VDOT	Miles	Miles	K	Miles	400 m	K	1,200 m	200 m	400 m	600 m	800 m
<40	5	4	3	2	5+	2	—	8	4	—	—
40-45	5	4	3	2	6	2	—	8	4	—	—
46-50	6	4.5	4	2.5	6	2	2	10	5	—	—
51-55	6.5	5	4	2.5	7	3	2	10	5	3	—
56-60	7	5	5	3	7	3	2	12	6	3	—
61-65	7.5	5.5	5	3	8	3	3	12	6	3	—
66-70	8	6	5	3	8	3	3	12	6	4	3
71-75	8.5	6.5	5	3	9	3	3	14	7	4	3
76-80	9	7	6	3.5	9	4	3	14	7	4	4

	15-point workouts											
	L	**M**	**T**		**I**				**R**			
	75 min	50 min	25 min		15 min				10 min			
VDOT	Miles	Miles	K	Miles	400 m	K	1,200 m	Miles	200 m	400 m	600 m	800 m
<40	7.5	6	5	3	8	3	—	—	12	5	—	—
40-45	8	6	5	3	9	3	—	—	12	6	—	—
46-50	9	7	6	4	9	3	3	—	14	7	—	—
51-55	10	7.5	6	4	10	4	3	—	15	7	5	—
56-60	11	8	7	4	11	4	3	—	16	8	5	—
61-65	11	8.5	8	5	12	4	4	3	17	8	5	—
66-70	12	9	8	5	12	5	4	3	18	9	6	4
71-75	13	10	8	5	13	5	4	3	19	9	6	5
76-80	13	10	9	5	14	5	4	3	20	10	6	5

(continued)

Table 5.5   Varying Point Workouts   *(continued)*

20-point workouts

VDOT	L 100 min Miles	M 45 min Miles	T 33 min K	T 33 min Miles	I 20 min 400 m	I 20 min K	I 20 min 1,200 m	I 20 min Miles	R 14 min 200 m	R 14 min 400 m	R 14 min 600 m	R 14 min 800 m
<40	10	5	6+	4	10	4	—	—	14	7	—	—
40-45	11	5.5	7	4	11	4	—	—	16	8	—	—
46-50	12	6	8	5	12	5	4	—	19	9	—	—
51-55	13	6.5	8	5	13	5	4	—	20	10	7	—
56-60	14	7	9	5	15	6	5	—	22	11	7	—
61-65	15	7.5	9	6	15	6	5	4	24	12	8	—
66-70	16	8	10	6	17	7	6	4	26	13	8	5
71-75	17	8.5	11	6	18	7	6	4	26	13	9	6
76-80	18	9	12	7	18	7	6	4	28	14	9	7

25-point workouts

VDOT	L 125 min Miles	M 60 min Miles	T 40 min K	T 40 min Miles	I 25 min 400 m	I 25 min K	I 25 min 1,200 m	I 25 min Miles	R 16 min 200 m	R 16 min 400 m	R 16 min 600 m	R 16 min 800 m
<40	13	7	8	5	13	5	—	—	19	9	—	—
40-45	13	7	8	5	14	6	—	—	20	10	—	—
46-50	15	8	10	6	16	6	5	—	23	11	—	—
51-55	16	8.5	10	6	17	7	5	—	25	12	8	—
56-60	18	9	12	7	18	7	6	—	26	13	8	—
61-65	19	10	13	7	20	8	6	5	27	13	9	—
66-70	20	11	13	8	21	8	7	5	29	14	9	7
71-75	21	12	14	8	22	9	7	6	30	15	10	7
76-80	22	12	15	9	23	9	8	6	32	16	10	8

30-point workouts

VDOT	L 150 min Miles	M 70 min Miles	T 50 min K	T 50 min Miles	I 30 min 400 m	I 30 min K	I 30 min 1,200 m	I 30 min Miles	R 20 min 200 m	R 20 min 400 m	R 20 min 600 m	R 20 min 800 m
<40	15	8	10	6	16	6	—	—	22	11	—	—
40-45	16	12	11	7	17	7	—	—	25	12	—	—
46-50	18	13	12	8	19	7	6	—	27	13	—	—
51-55	19	15	13	8	20	8	7	—	30	15	10	—
56-60	20	16	14	9	22	8	7	—	32	16	10	—
61-65	21	17	15	9	23	9	8	5	34	17	11	—
66-70	23	18	16	10	25	10	8	6	36	18	12	9
71-75	24	19	17	11	26	10	8	6	40	20	13	9
76-80	25	20	18	11	26	10	9	6	40	20	13	10

Table created by Jack Daniels' Running Calculator designed by the Run SMART Project.

ACHIEVING PERFORMANCE LEVELS BASED ON VDOT

Many coaches and young (even some not so young) runners have told me they enjoy achieving higher and higher levels of performance based on VDOT values. It has become somewhat common for me to hear "Our cross country team has a top five who all have a VDOT over 50," which would mean they have a top five who have all broken 20 minutes in a 5K race. Some can say they have a top five all with a 60 VDOT or higher (17:03 5K or faster).

What I have done to make this a little more interesting for young runners is to calculate comparative VDOT values for male and female runners, with basic increments of about five VDOT values per performance category. Table 5.6 shows how male and female runners can be compared over 10 performance levels. So now a coach could say, "We have 7 level-6 girls on our team," or "We have 7 level-6 guys on our team," and so on. Naturally, having a bunch of level-7 or level-8 runners would be quite an achievement; there are probably not many level-9 runners on the same team, and level-10 types are few and far between.

My most recent calculations are associated with comparing performances over a wide range of ages, based on some research done on young runners and some runners up to those in masters categories. Table 5.7 shows male (M) and female (F) adjusted VDOT values, along with associated 1,600-meter times for ages 18 down to 6. Naturally, the provided VDOT values can be looked up in table 5.1 for distances other than the 1,600. You may have to do

Table 5.6   Performance Levels for Females and Males Based on VDOT and Race Times

Level	1	2	3	4	5	6	7	8	9	10
Female VDOT	31.4	35.8	40.2	44.6	49.0	53.4	57.8	62.2	66.6	71.0
Male VDOT	35.0	40.0	45.0	50.0	55.0	60.0	65.0	70.0	75.0	80.0
800 m										
Female	3:59	3:33	3:12	2:55	2:41	2:29	2:19	2:10	2:02	1:56
Male	3:37	3:13	2:54	2:38	2:26	2:14	2:05	1:57	1:50	1:44.4
1,500 m										
Female	8:10	7:17	6:34	5:59	5:30	5:05	4:44	4:26	4:11	3:57.2
Male	7:25	6:35	5:56	5:24	4:57	4:35	4:16	4:00	3:46	3:34.0
1 mile										
Female	8:49	7:52	7:05	6:28	5:56	5:30	5:07	4:48	4:31	4:16.2
Male	8:01	7:07	6:25	5:50	5:21	4:57	4:37	4:19	4:04	3:51.1
1.5 mile										
Female	13:41	12:14	11:03	10:05	9:17	8:36	8:00	7:30	7:03	6:40.1
Male	12:28	11:06	10:01	9:07	8:22	7:45	7:13	6:45	6:21	6:00.4

(continued)

Table 5.6 Performance Levels for Females and Males Based on VDOT and Race Times *(continued)*

Level	1	2	3	4	5	6	7	8	9	10
Female VDOT	31.4	35.8	40.2	44.6	49.0	53.4	57.8	62.2	66.6	71.0
Male VDOT	35.0	40.0	45.0	50.0	55.0	60.0	65.0	70.0	75.0	80.0
					3K					
Female	17:15	15:27	13:59	12:46	11:45	10:54	10:10	9:31	8:58	8:28.0
Male	15:45	14:02	12:40	11:33	10:37	9:50	9:09	8:34	8:04	7:37.6
				2 mile and 3,000 m Steeple						
Female	18:36	16:39	15:04	13:46	12:41	11:46	10:58	10:17	9:41	9:08.8
Male	16:58	15:08	13:40	12:28	11:28	10:37	9:53	9:16	8:43	8:14.4
					4K					
Female	23:22	20:57	18:59	17:22	16:01	14:54	13:52	13:00	12:15	11:35
Male	21:21	19:04	17:14	15:44	14:29	13:25	12:31	11:44	11:03	10:27
					5K					
Female	29:32	26:29	24:01	21:59	20:17	18:50	17:36	16:31	15:34	14:44
Male	26:59	24:07	21:49	19:56	18:22	17:02	15:54	14:55	14:03	13:18
					6K					
Female	35:46	32:04	29:05	26:38	24:35	22:50	21:20	20:02	18:54	17:53
Male	32:41	29:13	26:26	24:10	22:16	20:40	19:18	18:06	17:04	16:09
					4 mile					
Female	38:31	34:32	31:19	28:41	26:28	24:35	22:59	21:35	20:21	19:16
Male	35:11	31:27	28:28	26:01	23:59	22:15	20:47	19:30	18:23	17:25
					8K					
Female	48:27	43:25	39:22	36:02	33:15	30:54	28:52	27:07	25:35	24:14
Male	44:15	39:32	35:46	32:41	30:07	27:58	26:07	24:31	23:08	21:54
					10K					
Female	1:01:24	55:00	49:51	45:37	42:04	39:05	36:31	34:17	32:20	30:37
Male	56:03	50:03	45:16	41:21	38:06	35:21	33:01	31:00	29:14	27:41
					15K					
Female	1:34:35	1:24:44	1:16:46	1:10:13	1:04:44	1:00:05	56:06	52:38	49:37	46:58
Male	1:26:22	1:17:06	1:09:41	1:03:36	58:34	54:18	50:40	47:32	44:48	42:25
					10 mile					
Female	1:41:57	1:31:21	1:22:46	1:15:42	1:09:47	1:04:46	1:00:28	56:44	53:28	50:36
Male	1:33:07	1:23:07	1:15:07	1:08:34	1:03:07	58:32	54:36	51:13	48:17	45:41
					20K					
Female	2:08:26	1:55:10	1:44:24	1:35:30	1:28:02	1:21:42	1:16:15	1:11:32	1:07:25	1:03:46
Male	1:57:22	1:44:50	1:34:46	1:26:30	1:19:38	1:13:49	1:08:51	1:04:34	1:00:49	57:33

Level	1	2	3	4	5	6	7	8	9	10
Female VDOT	31.4	35.8	40.2	44.6	49.0	53.4	57.8	62.2	66.6	71.0
Male VDOT	35.0	40.0	45.0	50.0	55.0	60.0	65.0	70.0	75.0	80.0
Half marathon										
Female	2:15:55	2:01:54	1:50:31	1:41:06	1:33:13	1:26:30	1:20:45	1:15:45	1:11:22	1:07:31
Male	2:04:13	1:50:59	1:40:19	1:31:36	1:24:19	1:18:09	1:12:54	1:08:21	1:04:23	1:00:55
25K										
Female	2:42:30	2:25:53	2:12:21	2:01:09	1:51:44	1:43:43	1:36:49	1:30:49	1:25:35	1:20:57
Male	2:28:39	2:12:55	2:00:14	1:49:48	1:41:05	1:33:43	1:27:24	1:21:57	1:17:11	1:13:00
30K										
Female	3:16:33	2:56:40	2:40:27	2:26:59	2:15:38	2:05:57	1:57:37	1:50:22	1:44:00	1:38:22
Male	2:59:59	2:41:07	2:25:52	2:13:18	2:02:47	1:53:52	1:46:13	1:39:36	1:33:48	1:28:43
Marathon										
Female	4:39:07	4:11:26	3:48:49	3:30:00	3:14:05	3:00:29	2:48:43	2:38:27	2:29:26	2:21:25
Male	4:16:02	3:49:45	3:28:26	3:10:49	2:56:01	2:43:25	2:32:35	2:23:10	2:14:55	2:07:39

Table created by Jack Daniels' Running Calculator designed by the Run SMART Project.

a little guessing for the proper race times associated with the VDOT values that are not whole numbers. If interested in detail, our book, *Oxygen Power*, lists times for more than 40 different metric and English distances and for every VDOT value to the nearest .1, from 25.0 to 85.0.

Looking at table 5.7, you can see that a 10-year-old girl would qualify for level-6 ability with a 1,600 time of 7:18, which makes her equal in quality to an 18-year-old girl with a 5:28 1,600 or a guy who has run 4:55 at age 18.

Table 5.8 shows the VDOT values associated with different quality levels for ages up to 58 years. I have ranked all participants from age 18 to 38 in the same fitness category, but from 39 on up, there is an adjustment for each additional year of aging. This table suggests that a 58-year-old female runner who runs 1,600 meters in 7:00 is equal to a younger female runner (between 18 and 38 years of age) who runs 1,600 in 5:04. I am currently at level 7, which is exactly where I was 15 years ago. I guess I am not destined to move up to level 8.

Table 5.7 VDOT Levels for Male and Female Runners Aged 6 to 18 for 1,600-Meter Times

	Novice				*Intermediate*					
Level	**1**		**2**		**3**		**4**		**5**	
Age	**M**	**F**	**M**	**F**	**M**	**F**	**M**	**F**	**M**	**F**
18	35.0	31.4	40.0	35.8	45.0	40.2	50.0	44.6	55.0	49.0
	7:58	8:46	7:05	7:49	6:22	7:03	5:48	6:25	5:19	5:54
17	33.5	30.2	38.4	34.6	43.3	38.9	48.2	43.2	53.1	47.5
	8:17	9:04	7:20	8:03	6:36	7:15	5:59	6:36	5:29	6:04
16	32.0	29.0	36.8	33.3	41.5	37.5	46.2	41.7	50.9	45.9
	8:37	9:23	7:37	8:20	6:51	7:30	6:13	6:49	5:42	6:15
15	30.5	27.8	35.1	31.9	39.7	36.0	44.3	40.1	48.9	44.2
	8:59	9:44	7:57	8:39	7:08	7:46	6:28	7:04	5:55	6:28
14	28.9	26.5	33.3	30.5	37.7	34.5	42.1	38.5	46.5	42.5
	9:25	10:08	8:20	8:59	7:28	8:04	6:46	7:19	6:11	6:42
13	27.3	25.2	31.5	29.1	35.7	33.0	39.9	36.9	44.1	40.8
	9:53	10:35	8:44	9:22	7:50	8:24	7:06	7:36	6:29	6:57
12	25.7	23.9	29.8	27.7	33.8	31.5	37.8	35.3	41.8	39.0
	10:24	11:03	9:10	9:46	8:13	8:44	7:27	7:55	6:48	7:14
11	24.1	22.6	28.0	26.2	31.8	29.8	35.6	33.4	39.4	37.0
	10:59	11:35	9:41	10:14	8:40	9:10	7:51	8:18	7:10	7:35
10	22.5	21.3	26.2	24.8	29.8	28.3	33.4	31.8	37.0	35.2
	11:37	12:09	10:14	10:43	9:10	9:35	8:18	8:40	7:35	7:56
9	20.9	20.0	24.3	23.3	27.7	26.6	31.1	29.9	34.5	33.2
	12:20	12:46	10:54	11:17	9:46	10:06	8:50	9:09	8:04	8:21
8	19.3	18.7	22.5	21.8	25.7	24.9	28.9	28.0	32.1	31.1
	13:08	13:28	11:37	11:55	10:24	10:41	9:25	9:41	8:36	8:50
7	17.7	17.4	20.7	20.3	23.6	23.2	26.5	26.1	29.4	29.0
	14:03	14:14	12:26-	12:37	11:10	11:20	10:08	10:16	9:17	9:23
6	16.1	16.1	18.8	18.8	21.5	21.5	24.2	24.2	26.9	26.9
	15:06	15:06	13:25	13:25	12:03	12:03	10:56	10:56	10:01	10:01

Good						Elite				
6		7		8		9		10		Level
M	F	M	F	M	F	M	F	M	F	Age
60.0	53.4	65.0	57.8	70.0	62.2	75.0	66.6	80.0	71.0	18
4:55	5:28	4:35	5:05	4:18	4:46	4:03	4:29	3:50	4:15	
58.0	51.8	62.9	56.1	67.7	60.4	72.5	64.7	77.3	69.0	17
5:04	5:37	4:43	5:14	4:25	4:54	4:10	4:36	3:57	4:21	
55.6	50.1	60.3	54.3	65.0	58.5	69.7	62.7	74.4	66.9	16
5:16	5:47	4:54	5:23	4:35	5:02	4:19	4:44	4:04	4:28	
53.4	48.3	57.9	52.4	62.4	56.5	66.9	60.6	71.4	64.7	15
5:28	5:59	5:05	5:33	4:45	5:12	4: 28	4:53	4:13	4:36	
50.9	46.5	55.3	50.5	59.7	54.5	64.0	58.5	68.3	62.4	14
5:42	6:11	5:18	5:45	4:57	5:22	4:39	5:02	4:23	4:45	
48.3	44.7	52.5	48.6	56.7	52.4	60.9	56.2	65.1	60.0	13
5:59	6:24	5:33	5:57	5:11	5:33	4:51	5: 13	4:35	4:55	
45.8	42.7	49.8	46.4	53.8	50.1	57.8	53.8	61.8	57.5	12
6:16	6:41	5:49	6:12	5:26	5:47	5:05	5:26	4:48	5:07	
43.2	40.6	47.0	44.2	50.8	47.8	54.6	51.4	58.4	54.9	11
6:36	6:59	6:08	6:28	5:43	6:02	5:21	5:39	5:03	5:20	
40.6	38.6	44.2	42.0	47.8	45.4	51.4	48.8	55.0	52.2	10
6:59	7:18	6:28	6:47	6:02	6:19	5:39	5:55	5:19	5:35	
37.9	36.5	41.3	39.8	44.7	43.0	48.1	46.2	51.5	49.4	9
7:26	7:41	6:53	7:07	6:24	6:38	6:00	6:13	5:39	5:51	
35.3	34.2	38.5	37.3	41.7	40.4	44.8	43.5	47.9	46.5	8
7:55	8:08	7:19	7:32	6:49	7:01	6:24	6:34	6:01	6:11	
32.3	31.9	35.2	34.8	38.2	37.7	41.2	40.6	44.2	43.5	7
8:33	8:39	7:56	8:01	7:22	7:28	6:54	6:59	6:28	6:34	
29.6	29.6	32.3	32.3	35.0	35.0	37.7	37.7	40.4	40.4	6
9:13	9:13	8:33	8:33	7:58	7:58	7:28	7:28	7:01	7:01	

Table created by Jack Daniels' Running Calculator designed by the Run SMART Project.

Table 5.8 VDOT Levels for Male and Female Runners Aged 18 to 58 for 1,600-Meter Times

	Novice				Intermediate					
Level	1		2		3		4		5	
Age	M	F	M	F	M	F	M	F	M	F
18-38	35.0	31.4	40.0	35.8	45.0	40.2	50.0	44.6	55.0	49.0
	7:58	8:46	7:05	7:49	6:22	7:03	5:48	6:25	5:19	5:54
39	34.1	30.4	39.1	34.8	44.1	39.3	49.1	43.8	54.1	48.2
	8:09	9:01	7:13	8:01	6:29	7:11	5:53	6:32	5:24	5:59
40	33.2	29.5	38.2	33.9	43.2	38.4	48.2	42.9	53.2	47.3
	8:21	9:15	7:22	8:12	6:36	7:20	5:59	6:39	5:29	6:05
41	32.4	28.7	37.4	33.1	42.4	37.6	47.4	42.1	52.4	46.5
	8:32	9:28	7:31	8:22	6:43	7:29	6:05	6:46	5:33	6:11
42	31.5	27.8	36.5	32.2	41.5	36.7	46.5	41.2	51.5	45.6
	8:44	9:44	7:41	8:34	6:51	7:38	6:11	6:54	5:39	6:18
43	30.6	26.9	35.6	31.3	40.6	35.8	45.6	40.3	50.6	44.7
	8:58	10:01	7:51	8:47	6:59	7:49	6:18	7:02	5:44	6:24
44	29.7	26.0	34.7	30.4	39.7	34.9	44.7	39.4	49.7	43.8
	9:12	10:18	8:02	9:01	7:08	7:59	6:24	7:10	5:50	6:32
45	28.8	25.1	33.8	29.5	38.8	34.0	43.8	38.5	48.8	42.9
	9:27	10:37	8:13	9:15	7:16	8:10	6:32	7:19	5:55	6:39
46	28.0	24.3	33.0	28.7	38.0	33.2	43.0	37.7	48.0	42.1
	9:40	10:54	8:24	9:28	7:25	8:21	6:38	7:28	6:01	6:46
47	27.1	23.4	32.1	27.8	37.1	32.3	42.1	36.8	47.1	41.2
	9:57	11:15	8:36	9:44	7:34	8:33	6:46	7:37	6:07	6:54
48	26.2	22.5	31.2	26.9	36.2	31.4	41.2	35.9	46.2	40.3
	10:14	11:37	8:48	10:01	7:44	8:46	6:54	7:48	6:13	7:02
49	25.3	21.6	30.3	26.0	35.3	30.5	40.3	35.0	45.3	39.4
	10:33	12:01	9:02	10:18	7:55	8:59	7:02	7:58	6:20	7:10
50	24.4	20.7	29.4	25.1	34.4	29.6	39.4	34.1	44.4	38.5
	10:52	12:26	9:17	10:37	8:05	9:13	7:10	8:09	6:27	7:19
51	23.6	19.9	28.6	24.3	33.6	28.8	38.6	33.3	43.6	37.7
	11:10	12:49	9:30	10:54	8:16	9:27	7:18	8:20	6:33	7:28

	Good						Elite				
	6		7		8		9		10		Level
	M	F	M	F	M	F	M	F	M	F	Age
	60.0	53.4	65.0	57.8	70.0	62.2	75.0	66.6	80.0	71.0	18-38
	4:55	5:28	4:35	5:05	4:18	4:46	4:03	4:29	3:50	4:15	
	59.1	52.7	64.1	57.2	69.1	61.6	74.1	66.1	79.1	70.5	39
	4:59	5:32	4:39	5:08	4:21	4:49	4:05	4:31	3:52	4:16	
	58.2	51.8	63.2	56.3	68.2	60.7	73.2	65.2	78.2	69.6	40
	5:03	5:37	4:42	5:13	4:24	4:52	4:08	4:34	3:54	4:19	
	57.4	51.0	62.4	55.5	67.4	59.9	72.4	64.4	77.4	68.8	41
	5:07	5:42	4:45	5:17	4:26	4:56	4:10	4:37	3:56	4:22	
	56.5	50.1	61.5	54.6	66.5	59.0	71.5	63.5	76.5	67.9	42
	5:12	5:47	4:49	5:21	4:30	5:00	4:13	4:41	3:59	4:25	
	55.6	49.2	60.6	53.7	65.6	58.1	70.6	62.6	75.6	67.0	43
	5:16	5:53	4:53	5:26	4:33	5:04	4:16	4:44	4:01	4:28	
	54.7	48.3	59.7	52.8	64.7	57.2	69.7	61.7	74.7	66.1	44
	5:21	5:59	4:57	5:31	4:36	5:08	4:19	4:48	4:04	4:31	
	53.8	47.4	58.8	51.9	63.8	56.3	68.8	60.8	73.8	65.2	45
	5:26	6:05	5:01	5:36	4:40	5:13	4:22	4:52	4:06	4:34	
	53.0	46.6	58.0	51.1	63.0	55.5	68.0	60.0	73.0	64.4	46
	5:30	6:10	5:04	5:41	4:43	5:17	4:24	4:55	4:08	4:37	
	52.1	45.7	57.1	50.2	62.1	54.6	67.1	59.1	72.1	63.5	47
	5:35	6:17	5:09	5:46	4:46	5:21	4:27	4:59	4:11	4:41	
	51.2	44.8	56.2	49.3	61.2	53.7	66.2	58.2	71.2	62.6	48
	5:40	6:24	5:13	5:52	4:50	5:26	4:31	5:03	4:14	4:44	
	50.3	43.9	55.3	48.4	60.3	52.8	65.3	57.3	70.3	61.7	49
	5:46	6:31	5:18	5:58	4:54	5:31	4:34	5:08	4:17	4:48	
	49.4	43.0	54.4	47.5	59.4	51.9	64.4	56.4	69.4	60.8	50
	5:51	6:38	5:22	6:04	4:58	5:36	4:37	5:12	4:20	4:52	
	48.6	42.2	53.6	46.6	58.6	51.0	63.6	55.5	68.6	59.9	51
	5:57	6:45	5:27	6:10	5:02	5:40	4:40	5:17	4:22	4:56	

(continued)

101

Table 5.8   VDOT Levels for Male and Female Runners Aged 18 to 58 for 1,600-Meter Times   *(continued)*

	Novice				Intermediate					
Level	1		2		3		4		5	
Age	M	F	M	F	M	F	M	F	M	F
52	22.7	19.0	27.7	23.4	32.7	27.9	37.7	32.4	42.7	36.8
	11:32	13:18	9:46	11:15	8:28	9:42	7:28	8:32	6:41	7:37
53	21.8	18.1	26.8	22.5	31.8	27.0	36.8	31.5	41.8	35.9
	11:55	13:49	10:03	11:37	8:40	9:59	7:37	8:44	6:48	7:48
54	20.9	17.2	25.9	21.6	30.9	26.1	35.9	30.6	40.9	35.0
	12:20	14:22	10:20	12:01	8:53	10:16	7:48	8:58	6:56	7:58
55	20.0	16.3	25.0	20.7	30.0	25.2	35.0	29.7	40.0	34.1
	12:46	14:57	10:39	12:26	9:07	10:35	7:58	9:12	7:05	8:09
56	19.2	15.5	24.2	19.9	29.2	24.4	34.2	28.8	39.2	33.3
	13:11	15:31	10:56	12:49	9:20	10:52	8:08	9:27	7:12	8:20
57	18.3	14.6	23.3	19.0	28.3	23.5	33.3	27.9	38.3	32.4
	13:42	16:13	11:17	13:18	9:35	11:13	8:20	9:42	7:21	8:32
58	17.4	13.7	22.4	18.1	27.4	22.6	32.4	27.0	37.4	31.5
	14:14	16:58	11:40	13:49	9:51	11:34	8:32	9:59	7:31	8:44

Good						Elite				
6		7		8		9		10		Level
M	F	M	F	M	F	M	F	M	F	Age
47.7	41.3	52.7	45.8	57.7	50.2	62.7	54.7	67.7	59.1	52
6:03-	6:53	5:32	6:16	5:06	5:46	4:44	5:21	4:25	4:59	
46.8	40.4	51.8	44.9	56.8	49.3	61.8	53.8	66.8	58.2	53
6:09	7:01	5:37	6:23	5:10	5:52	4:48	5:26	4:29	5:03	
45.9	39.5	50.9	44.0	55.9	48.4	60.9	52.9	65.9	57.3	54
6:15	7:09	5:42	6:30	5:15	5:58	4:51	5:30	4:32	5:08	
45.0	38.6	50.0	43.1	55.0	47.5	60.0	52.0	65.0	56.4	55
6:22	7:18	5:48	6:37	5:19	6:04	4:55	5:36	4:35	5:12	
44.2	37.8	49.2	42.2	54.2	46.6	59.2	51.1	64.2	55.5	56
6:28	7:27	5:53	6:45	5:23	6:10	4:59	5:41	4:38	5:17	
43.3	36.9	48.3	41.4	53.3	45.8	58.3	50.3	63.3	54.7	57
6:36	7:36	5:59	6:52	5:28	6:16	5:03	5:46	4:42	5:21	
42.4	36.0	47.4	40.5	52.4	44.9	57.4	49.4	62.4	53.8	58
6:43	7:46	6:05	7:00	5:33	6:23	5:07	5:51	4:45	5:26	

Table created by Jack Daniels' Running Calculator designed by the Run SMART Project.

6

Season Training

Smile some during every run you go on.

Of all aspects of training for different running events, the most difficult to find a common approach to is setting up a training season. So many factors come into play that it is almost impossible to say there is a standard approach that will work best for everyone. Take a typical high school cross country season, for example. The coach will be working with new runners (some of whom have never run a step before working with the school coach), while others vary in previous training, from 20 or 30 miles a week and a few races to some who are very experienced and capable of placing in or winning a conference or state championship.

Probably one of the most challenging decisions for the coach is how to fit everyone into the program. For runners who are training alone or without a coach, it is very important to approach a new season carefully and certainly not too intensely. Remember, the less fit you are the less intense the training has to be to benefit. I offer some suggestions that may minimize both the frustration and the number of injuries that are always lurking around the corner.

There is no one way of training that is best for every runner; we are not all the same and need to be treated as individuals. That being said, there are definitely some principles of training that apply to everyone, and I discuss those in chapter 2. When I am setting up a season of training for any athlete or team I am working with, I like to make things as simple as possible so I don't have to be at each runner's side every time he goes out for a training session.

Before setting up a season of training, runners and coaches must gather some essential information. Once all this information is acquired, it is easier to set up a season plan that will work best for all runners involved. First determine level of fitness based on current mileage and speeds of any workouts that make up training sessions, which allows runners to establish the proper VDOT value for all types of training.

Identifying the most important goal race of the current training season is also important, as well as what races are available or desired along the way to reaching that final goal race. Some runners like competing more often in races that are shorter than the season's goal race, and others prefer racing in over-distance events. This season's race information will influence the training that is set up for each week of the season.

It is also useful to understand what facilities are available for training; for example, is there an indoor track you can use in times of poor weather, or is it possible to get on a treadmill to avoid really cold, windy, or hot days outside? Some workouts are fun to do on a smooth grass course; is such a facility available?

One additional consideration when setting up a season program is how much time is available for training and which days of the week provide the most time. It can also be useful to consider what times of different days work best for training, based on other commitments. During high school years, daily schedules are fairly consistent, but in college, class schedules can vary a great deal; for those who run after college, most runners have jobs that dictate available time.

BREAK YOUR SEASON INTO PHASES

I like to break a season of training into four phases, as shown in figure 6.1.

- Phase I is B/FIP, which stands for base training with foundation and injury-prevention emphases.
- Phase II has an IQ emphasis, which stands for initial quality training phase.
- Phase III is for TQ (transition quality) training, and this is generally the most demanding of the four phases.
- Phase IV is designed to provide the runner with peak performances and is identified as FQ (final quality).

Training is designed so that phase I, at the left side of figure 6.1, is the start of the season, which for students in high school and college may take place during the summer before school begins for the year. Runners who are not currently involved in studies and a school season of running have the freedom to start phase I training whenever it best prepares them for the most important races in the coming season. This means that phase IV is the final stage of the current season and the time when races are most important. The middle two phases advance fitness and racing ability from the early part of the season to the most important part.

At the bottom of each training phase I have listed a number from 1 to 4; these indicate the order in which I consider what type of training will go into each phase. As can be seen, phase I training is first to be considered,

Phase I	Phase II	Phase III	Phase IV
B/F IP	IQ	TQ	FQ
1	4	3	2

←————————————————→
Potential
altitude
training

Figure 6.1   Dividing the season into four progressive phases of training, including considerations for altitude training.

as indicated by the number 1 at the bottom of that phase. It's necessary to first determine what each runner needs to do in the earliest part of each season of training.

So, it is during phase I that each runner's profile (the information gathered before the start of the season) must most carefully be considered. For example, how much running has each runner been doing each week? What has been the longest training run performed in the past several weeks, and have any races been run that may provide information as to current state of fitness and what needs to be worked on before progressing into the other phases of training?

I always make a point of asking each runner what type of workouts they have been doing recently; in some cases phase I is not even necessary before going on to phase II. If a runner has been running regularly for 6 or more weeks, it is OK to go into phase II. In fact, if the previous 3 or 4 weeks have included some relatively demanding workouts and the runner has not experienced any setbacks, it is fine to go into phase III.

You will notice in figure 6.1 that the number 2 is at the bottom of phase IV. The reason is that I believe the next phase of training to be considered the final one—that period of time when you expect your best performance. In other words, what specific training types and amounts of training do you think will produce the best possible performances? Clearly, an 800 runner and a 10K runner would be concentrating on different types of training during that final (FQ) peak phase of preparation, so each athlete must be considered separately.

Having determined what to include in phase IV, I step back to phase III, with the goal of deciding what type of training will best prepare each runner for the training that will be taking place in phase IV. For example, an 800 runner will need more emphasis on speed work, and a 10K runner will need more **T** workouts. Both these runners will need some solid **I** training in phase III, but in each phase there needs to be some variation from the primary focus. After that, I move back to phase II, with the same goal in mind—what should I be doing in phase II that will best prepare the runner for what lies ahead in phase III, the most demanding of the four phases of training?

A coach or a self-training runner must always consider what races may be involved along the way in the earlier phases, and I always try to record the dates and distances of all races that fall during the season so that daily training can be arranged accordingly.

Phase I Training

My typical approach to setting up the four phases of training is to include mostly **E** running during phase I. If there are more than 3 weeks available for phase I, I would start adding some light strides (10- to 15-second light, quick runs, with full recoveries) to daily **E** runs, along with some supplemental training, such as light resistance training and dynamic flexibility work, after some of these runs. I also suggest one weekly easy **L** run that is 25 to 30 percent of each week's total mileage.

Phase II Training

After phase I is completed, I prefer to include **R** training in phase II. I try to add just one new stress to a new phase of training, and going from **E** running to **R** workouts is adding only a speed stress, with little being asked of the aerobic or lactate-clearance systems. If I were to go from **E** running to **I** training, I would be adding two new stresses—faster running and more stress on the aerobic system.

I like to add the light, fast running first so that when moving forward to the **I** phase (phase III), the speed of the intervals is not a new stress, since the previous repetitions were actually faster. It is important to not use the previous season's best race times for identifying proper **R** training paces; use a current race time or best estimate of what you think you could currently race for 1 mile. A weekly **L** run should be continued throughout phase II, and plan on two **R** sessions each week, with two **E** days of running between the **R** sessions.

Phase III Training

The third phase (primarily **I**) adds an aerobic stress but not any faster running speeds, which would be an additional new stress for the body to deal with. Phase III training will vary a fair bit based on the events being trained for. The shorter-distance specialists may get in just one good **I** session each week and also continue with an **R** session, with the idea that speed needs to be better maintained throughout. For longer-distance runners, it is often better to get in two **I** sessions each week, but keep in mind that if a 3,000-meter or longer race will be run in any of the phase III weeks, that counts as a tough aerobic workout, and just one **I**-training session is adequate for that week. I also encourage the inclusion of an easy **L** run each week during phase III.

Phase IV Training

I then typically move to some **T** running in phase IV. This is still quality training but not as stressful as the previous **I** sessions were, and the runner will be feeling better for the important races that are typical during phase IV.

During phase IV, training will vary a fair amount based on the most important events being prepared for. Longer-distance specialists usually do best by concentrating on **T** workouts and discontinuing **I** sessions (unless a race is the type that stresses the aerobic system to its maximum). With an **L** run and a race each week, one **T** session per week is enough because races at this time are usually fairly important. Even for the longer-distance specialists, it is a good idea to include a few short **R** runs (four to six **R** 200s would be good) at the end of each **T** session. Shorter-distance specialists may be better off combining a Q session with some **T** and **R** work so they are sharp for shorter races that may take place in this phase of training.

To summarize, I prefer going from **E** running to **R** workouts to **I** sessions and finally to **T** training. However, when I move from **E** running to **R** training, I continue doing **E** runs most days of the week during the **R** phase, and when moving from **R** to **I**, I may still schedule occasional **R** sessions to maintain what was gained in the earlier **R** phase.

It might be simplest to think of each phase as including a primary type of training plus secondary training to maintain what was accomplished in the previous phase. Definitely, when moving to phase IV, when the emphasis is primarily on **T** workouts, I continue to add some **R** training, usually at the end of a **T** session.

Remember as well that races are part of training, and the duration of a race determines what training benefit is reaped. Races that last between about 5 and 20 minutes are stressing the aerobic system to its fullest, so these races are the ultimate benefit in terms of what **I** training does for you, so it is easy to back off on the **I** training when you have regular races of medium distance. This is why I tend to drop **I** training from a typical school program during phase IV training, because the races accomplish what a hard **I** session would normally do for you.

ADAPT THE PHASE LENGTHS AS NECESSARY

I have set up the four phases of a training season to last 24 weeks—6 weeks in each of the four phases. However, especially during high school and college cross country seasons, there are not always 24 weeks available in order for there to be four 6-week phases of training. I have two ways of dealing with this shortage of time.

My first approach is to get the first two phases accomplished during the summer months, before the start of cross country season in the fall. In other words, after the completion of a spring track season, start the summer with phase I base training, which is then followed by phase II training, still during the latter part of summer break. This means that as school starts in the fall, the first 6 weeks of that academic year are set aside for phase III training, the toughest part of the season, but this phase is completed before the more important races held during the final 6 weeks of the season.

For runners who have the time and who want to include some altitude training in their season plan, figure 6.1 shows when I think is the best time for altitude training. With only enough time for a couple weeks at altitude, I suggest concentrating on **R** sessions along with **E** long runs during the altitude stay, which is before the major sessions of **I** work. You'll learn more about altitude training in chapter 8.

The other approach to dealing with lack of time for four solid training phases in a season program is to set aside fewer than 6 weeks for each phase. Figure 6.2 shows how I evaluate the season and where I prefer to reduce time in various phases of training. I have placed 6 numbers in each of the four phases of training to guide you.

If you look at numbers 1 through 12, you will see 1, 2, 3 in phase I; followed by 4, 5, 6 in phase IV; 7, 8, 9 in phase II; and 10, 11, 12 in phase III. What this indicates is that if you have only 3 weeks for an entire season, all three of those weeks will be spent doing phase I–type training.

For example, if you had a runner come out for the team with only 3 weeks left in the cross country season, and this runner had not been training at all, and there was a place for her on your team, it seems logical to simply ask this runner to do easy foundation training. No sense asking a runner in this situation to get involved in more stressful quality training for just 3 weeks.

Phase I			Phase II			Phase III			Phase IV		
1	2	3	7	8	9	10	11	12	4	5	6
	13			18			14			17	
		21			19			15			22
		23			20			16			24
	B/F IP			IQ			TQ			FQ	

Figure 6.2 Numbering system to determine the number of weeks of training per phase according to how many weeks you have available.

This approach should also be used with any runner who had to take a break for some time because of an injury or illness. The worst thing to subject one of these runners to would be a somewhat demanding workout with the idea that you have to make up for lost time. Remember, the less your body has been stressed recently in training, the more benefit it gets from not imposing much stress on it. You are always better off a little below optimum and healthy than unable to race because of overtraining or illness.

Now, if a runner had only 6 weeks for the entire season, figure 6.2 shows that I'd spend weeks 1, 2, and 3 doing foundation phase I training, followed by 3 weeks of phase IV (weeks 4, 5, 6) training. With only 9 weeks available, I opt to not even get involved with any phase III training; after 3 weeks in phase I, I'd go to phase II for 3 weeks, followed by the final 3 weeks in phase IV.

You could also use figure 6.2 to work backwards, relative to how many weeks you had in a season. For example, if you had only 23 weeks available, I'd drop a week in phase IV (number 24). If I had 20 weeks available, I'd go 4 weeks in phase I, followed by 6 weeks in phases II and III, and reduce phase IV to 4 weeks (by dropping 22 and 24). This approach is arrived at by dropping the weeks that would probably have the least effect on ideal performance, based on how many weeks are available.

SAMPLE WEEKLY PLAN

Presented in figure 6.3 is a sample week of training. I like to have **L** runs on the first day of every week (considered to be Sunday). If in phase II of training, then Q1, Q2, and Q3 (Q stands for quality days of training) may all be **R** sessions, or Q1 and Q2 **R**s and Q3 a **T** session. This latter arrangement is an approach I apply for runners training for shorter or longer races; since it is early in the season, **R** sessions are important and an occasional **T** session would be useful. For a runner who has fewer than 4 weeks of running in phase I, I would limit phase II to having only Q1 and Q2 **R**s and move Q2 to Thursday of that week.

1	2	3	4	5	6	7
L	Q1 E	(Q1) E OR Q1	Q2 (Q2) E OR Q1	E	E	Q3 (Q3) Race (Q)

Figure 6.3 Sample training week showing different approaches for including quality, **E**, and **L** days.

When you're not dealing with weekly races, I suggest Q1, Q2, and Q3 days on days 2, 4, and 7 of each week, or on days 3, 4, and 7 if you find the back-to-back training system works well. Of course, the Q3 session could also be a race, which is definitely a quality day of training.

Regardless of the phase of training, always make Q1 the most important workout of the week, focusing on the type of training being emphasized at that time of the season. I like to do this so that if poor weather or other undesirable circumstances interfere with a week of training, you do get in what is most important for that phase even if it means only one Q session that week.

An example of a week in phase III might be an **I** session for Q1, followed by **T** training (plus a few **R**s) for Q2, and either another **I** session or a race for Q3. In phase IV, for shorter-distance runners, Q1 and Q2 could both be **T** plus **R**, and Q3 could be a race or a solid **R** session. For longer-distance specialists, Q1 and Q2 are both **T** sessions and may be followed by a few short **R**s to finish off these sessions. If there is an important race on the coming weekend, I suggest that there be just a Q1 session (**T** plus a few **R**s) for all runners, best performed 4 days before the race, and the race is Q2 to finish that week.

SAMPLE SEASON PLAN

The following is a sample season plan for a runner training for fall cross country.

- Phase I : Sunday = **L** run; all other days of the week are **E** runs (+ strides on 3 days)
- Phase II: Sunday = **L** run; Q1 = session of **R** 200s; Q2 = combination of **R** 200s and **R** 400s; Q3 = session of **R** 400s; all other days are **E** run days
- Phase III: Sunday = **L** run; Q1 = **I** session of repeated 1,000-meter runs; Q2 = steady 20-minute run at **T** pace + 4 × **R** 200s; Q3 = race or session of **I** 1,200s
- Phase IV: Sunday = **L** run; Q1 = **T** plus some **R** 200s; Q2 = **T**; Q3 = race or combination of **T**, **I**, and **R**; if a race that week is important, then Q2 = the race and there is no Q3

Try to design each season's plan well ahead of the season start, and always feel free to make some adjustments over time based on race dates, weather changes, runner schedules, and possible setbacks. Training speeds may also be adjusted to meet each runner's current state of fitness. The overall plan is designed to introduce one new stress when moving from one phase of training to the next and new phases will also provide for maintenance of benefits earned in each previous phase.

An additional consideration when setting up a season of training is individual strengths and weaknesses, in keeping with the idea that we are not all the same. Some runners do better working more on speed, and others seem to benefit more from endurance work. I have developed what I call a speed versus endurance table, which is shown in table 6.1. This table has three columns of times for a few different distances. The left-hand column lists 400-meter times, the middle column has 800-meter times, and the right column lists both 1,500 and mile times. If you circle your best times in each of the three columns and then draw a line connecting the times you have circled, you will have a line that slopes down to the right, slopes up to the right, or goes straight across the page.

Table 6.1   Speed Versus Endurance Finder

400 m time	800 m time	1,500 m time/mile time
46.0	1:41.2	3:27.6/3:44.1
47.0	1:43.4	3:32.0/3:48.9
48.0	1:45.6	3:36.5/3:53.8
49.0	1:47.8	3:41.0/3:58.6
50.0	1:50.0	3:45.5/4:03.5
51.0	1:52.2	3:50.0/4:08.3
52.0	1:54.4	3:54.5/4:13.2
53.0	1:56.6	3:59.0/4:18.0
54.0	1:58.8	4:03.5/4:22.9
55.0	2:01.0	4:08.0/4:27.7
56.0	2:03.2	4:12.5/4:32.6
57.0	2:05.4	4:17.0/4:37.5
58.0	2:07.6	4:21.5/4:42.4
59.0	2:09.8	4:26.0/4:47.3
60.0	2:12.0	4:30.5/4:52.2
61.0	2:14.2	4:35.0/4:57.1
62.0	2:16.4	4:39.5/5:02.0
63.0	2:18.6	4:44.0/5:06.8
64.0	2:20.8	4:48.5/5:11.7
65.0	2:23.0	4:53.0/5:16.6
66.0	2:25.2	4:57.5/5:21.5
67.0	2:27.4	5:02.0/5:26.3

(continued)

Table 6.1   Speed Versus Endurance Finder   *(continued)*

400 m time	800 m time	1,500 m time/mile time
68.0	2:29.6	5:06.5/5:31.2
69.0	2:31.8	5:11.0/5:36.0
70.0	2:34.0	5:15.5/5:40.9
71.0	2:36.2	5:20.0/5:45.7
72.0	2:38.4	5:24.5/5:50.6
73.0	2:40.6	5:29.0/5:55.5
74.0	2:42.8	5:33.5/6:00.4
75.0	2:45.0	5:38.0/6:05.2
76.0	2:47.2	5:42.5/6:10.1
77.0	2:49.4	5:47.0/6:14.9
78.0	2:51.6	5:51.5/6:19.8
79.0	2:53.8	5:56.0/6:24.7
80.0	2:56.0	6:00.5/6:29.6
81.0	2:58.2	6:05.0/6:34.4
82.0	3:00.4	6:09.5/6:39.3
83.0	3:02.6	6:14.0/6:44.2
84.0	3:04.8	6:18.5/6:49.1
85.0	3:07.0	6:23.0/6:53.9
86.0	3:09.2	6:27.5/6:58.8
87.0	3:11.4	6:32.0/7:03.6
88.0	3:13.6	6:36.5/7:08.5
89.0	3:15.8	6:41.0/7:13.4
90.0	3:18.0	6:45.5/7:18.3
91.0	3:20.2	6:50.0/7:23.1
92.0	3:22.4	6:54.5/7:28.0
93.0	3:24.6	6:59.0/7:32.8
94.0	3:26.8	7:03.5/7:37.7
95.0	3:29.0	7:08.0/7:42.5
96.0	3:31.2	7:12.5/7:47.4
97.0	3:33.4	7:17.0/7:52.3
98.0	3:35.6	7:21.5/7:57.2
99.0	3:37.8	7:26.0/8:02.0
1:40	3:40.0	7:30.5/8:06.9
1:41	3:42.2	7:35.0/8:11.8

400 m time	800 m time	1,500 m time/mile time
1:42	3:44.4	7:39.5/8:16.6
1:43	3:46.6	7:44.0/8:21.5
1:44	3:48.8	7:48.5/8:26.4
1:45	3:51.0	7:53.0/8:31.3
1:46	3:53.2	7:57.5/8:36.1
1:47	3:55.4	8:02.0/8:41.0
1:48	3:57.6	8:06.5/8:45.9
1:49	3:59.8	8:11.0/8:50.8
1:50	4:02.0	8:15.5/8:55.7

If your line goes straight across, I would consider you equal in speed and endurance. If your line slopes down to the right, which is typical for most young runners, this suggests that your speed is better than your endurance. Of course, sloping up to the right indicates better endurance than speed. If your line goes down from the 400 to the 800 and back up to the 1,500, this means you have better speed and better endurance than your 800 suggests, and you should be able to race a better 800 than you have so far.

Other lines that go up and down, rather than straight in a linear fashion, usually mean an event that is lower than the others has not been raced as often or is of less interest; when one event is higher than the others, your body is better designed (possibly by muscle fiber type) for that distance than for the others, or this event has been raced most often or with greater enthusiasm.

Let's take an example of a runner with a best 400 time of 60 seconds, a best 800 of 2:20.8, and a best 1,500 of 5:06. This suggests that speed is better than endurance, and the logical approach to training may be to work more on endurance. After a season of endurance training, if the slope of your curve doesn't flatten out a little more, you may be the type of runner who will usually remain better at speed than endurance, and the next approach to training may be to work more on the speed factor.

Working on speed for a runner like this may improve both speed and endurance, seen if the slope of the line connecting best times remains at about the same angle of slope. So try working on the weakness first, but if that doesn't bring some positive results, concentrate on your strength, and that may well improve both strength and weakness. If nothing else, referring to this table at the end of each season will show how your speed and endurance are adjusting to the training you are carrying out.

7

Fitness Training

Running is something you can enjoy for your entire life.

I often refer to the great physical education program at my high school, and the most memorable part was the color system we followed, which assigned white, red, blue, purple, and gold gym shorts based on fitness levels achieved during tests administered in the fall and spring of each school year. I have followed a similar route by writing up four training plans distinguished by color for runners at different levels of training. These are a white plan for beginner runners and for those who ran years before but have not been running recently and want to give it another try; a red plan for runners who are involved in some running but to a rather limited degree; a blue plan for serious runners who want to increase their dedication to the sport; and a gold plan for very serious runners who want to be involved in a structured program and who have adequate time for serious participation.

Actually, the gold plan would be more than adequate for preparing for some serious racing, and, in fact, so would the blue plan. A runner who's spent some time on either the blue plan or gold plan could easily move to one of the more structured event training programs provided in the later chapters of this book.

Before initiating a running program, beginners should first get a physical exam to ensure their body's readiness to handle the stress of the activity. In that regard, please review the early chapters of this book where I explain how the body responds and adapts to new stressors. Also, new runners should consult qualified running coaches and knowledgeable, experienced runners before investing too much on shoes and other apparel.

The less fit a person is when starting a running program, the more he will benefit from a low-stress regimen. It is only after the runner attains a high fitness level that workouts will need to be very demanding for improvements to be made. So, especially at the start, you should stick to your training program and try not to overdo it. Following are a few more pieces of advice that pertain to all runners—beginners to the most highly fit and experienced:

- Rest—but not avoidance—is an essential part of your training.
- Consistency with regard to rest, nutrition, and training is the key to achieving maximum benefits from a program.
- Never train when injured or ill.

WHITE STARTING PLAN

As you read through the white plan, you will notice that I have not indicated you must run every day, but there is no problem with some running on a daily basis, and those who have adequate time may want to run more often. Again, people who are not in very good shape when starting out in a running program do not need to train very hard, or often, to gain considerable benefit.

If you have not been running at all, there is no doubt that getting in some running on 3 or 4 days of each week will produce positive results. I do suggest that when running only 3 days each week, it might be better to spread those 3 days over at least a 5-day period rather than doing 3 days of running in a row and then having 4 days in a row of no running. However, if your situation requires 3 consecutive days of running, followed by 4 days of no running, that approach is certainly better than not running at all. I have bolded the workouts in the workout tables that are recommended for minimum participation.

The 16-week white plan begins by asking for 30 minutes of your time each day of training and reaches a high of only 45 minutes in any of the training days. Basically, as time goes by, you'll spend more of the total time actually running and less time walking.

Later in the white plan, I have you add strides (light, quick runs of short duration, with full recovery between the individual strides) throughout some training sessions. These strides help improve running economy and prepare you for faster running as you progress in fitness. Sometimes mixing strides with some **E** running gives a nice break from just steady running, and it may also allow you to arrive at different locations during an **E** run where the footing is flat and soft, where strides become more comfortable.

Some people who decide to take up the white plan may think the training is not demanding enough, and for some who have been involved in other types of exercise, it may not be. If you are one of these people, try the phase

I training for a couple of weeks, and if it is really of minimal stress for you, jump ahead into one of the subsequent phases of the white plan. If phase IV of the white plan is still of minimal discomfort, maybe you are capable of handling the red plan, which gets into more advanced types of training.

Once you have completed the 16-week white plan, you may be completely satisfied with how you feel and with your current level of fitness, and if that is the case, I'd recommend just repeating the phase IV training plan and seeing how comfortably you can perform at that level. Or maybe you found one or two of the daily training sessions (in any of the phases of the white plan) to be of particular interest; if so, you can just repeat your favorite sessions whenever you go out for a run.

After completing the white plan you could probably participate in some low-key road races, but make your first road race not too long (hopefully no longer than about 40 minutes), and remember it is perfectly fine to walk a little during a road race if the stress of running gets a little harder than you were ready for. Make a point of starting any races a little slower than you think is the pace you can handle for the full distance; it's always better, after you finish a race, to believe you could have gone a little faster than to wish you had started out a little slower.

Table 7.1 details the white plan. In the table, **W** stands for walk and **E** stands for easy running. Strides (ST) are light, quick 20 sec runs (*not* sprinting); take 60 sec rest between strides.

Table 7.1   White Plan Phase I: Weeks 1-4

Day	Workout	Running min	Total min
1	**5 min W + 10 × 1 min E w/1 min W recoveries + 5 min W**	**10**	**30**
2	If you train today, repeat day 1 workout	10	30
3	**5 min W + 7 × 2 min E w/1 min W recoveries + 4 min W**	**14**	**30**
4	If you train today, repeat day 3 workout	14	30
5	**5 min W + 6 × 1 min E w/30 sec W + 8 × 30 sec E w/1 min W + 4 min W**	**10**	**30**
6	If you train today, repeat day 5 workout	10	30
7	If you train today, repeat day 1 workout	10	30

(continued)

Table 7.1   White Plan   *(continued)*

White Plan Phase II: Weeks 5-8

Day	Workout	Running min	Total min
1	**3 min E + 3 min W + 10 × 2 min E w/1 min W recoveries + 4 min W**	**23**	**40**
2	If you train today, repeat day 1 workout	23	40
3	**3 min E + 3 min W + 6×3 min E w/2 min W recoveries + 4 min W**	**21**	**40**
4	If you train today, repeat day 3 workout	23	40
5	**3 min E + 3 min W + 20 × 1 min E w/30 sec W recoveries + 4 min W**	**23**	**40**
6	If you train today, repeat day 5 workout	23	40
7	If you train today, repeat day 1 workout	23	40

White Plan Phase III: Weeks 9-12

Day	Workout	Running min	Total min
1	**10 min E + 3 min W + 10 min E + 3 min W + 10 min E + 4 min W**	**30**	**40**
2	If you train today, repeat day 1 workout	30	40
3	**2 min W + 4 × 8 min E w/1 min W recoveries + 2 min W**	**32**	**40**
4	If you train today, repeat day 3 workout	32	40
5	**5 min W + 20 min E + 5 min W + 10 min E + 5 min W**	**30**	**45**
6	Day 5 session can be done on either day 5, day 6, or both	0	0
7	If you train today, make it a 30 min W	0	30

White Plan Phase IV: Weeks 13-16

Day	Workout	Running min	Total min
1	**30 min E + 6 ST + 6 min E**	**36**	**44**
2	If you train today, repeat day 1 workout	36	44
3	**10 min E + 5 ST + 10 min E + 5 ST + 10 min E***	**30**	**43**
4	If you train today, repeat day 3 workout	30	43
5	**Repeat day 1 workout**	**36**	**44**
6	Day 5 session can be done on either day 5, day 6, or both	36	44
7	If you train today, make it a 30 min W	0	30

RED INTERMEDIATE PLAN

The red plan is designed for runners who have completed the four levels of the white plan, or for those who have been doing some running and believe they are able to handle a little more stress than what the white plan offers. This red plan should do a pretty good job of preparing a runner for some recreational track or road races, even if the distance to be covered in a race is an hour or a little longer.

If you decide to start out with the red plan without first spending time in the less demanding white plan, I suggest that you at least read through the white plan to get a feel for what has been recommended in the program. You might also want to look into the more demanding blue plan to see if you are up to that level of training, or at least to see what lies ahead for those who complete the red plan and want to be challenged a little more.

After completing this red plan, you will certainly be ready to handle some short races, but I would recommend a little more training before jumping into a marathon. I have dedicated an entire chapter to marathon training programs, and if that is your primary reason for getting started with some training, it would be a good idea to read through chapter 14.

This red plan is designed for a minimum of 4 days of training each week, and these 4 training days are bolded in table 7.2. If you decide to train more than the suggested 4 days, there are suggestions as to what to add on any additional days. Feel free to shuffle the training days around to take advantage of days when you have more time or to avoid having to train when weather conditions may be adverse.

When training just on 4 days each week, try to avoid training 3 days in a row when possible, and if training 5 days per week, generally try to separate the 2 nontraining days, but 2 days off in a row is not necessarily a bad approach.

Be familiar with how I describe the various workouts, which I do at the start of each of the four levels of the training plan. If you happen to participate in any races during your training, identify the VDOT values associated with race times, and use the associated training paces (found in the VDOT tables in chapter 5) in your training session of this red plan.

Once you complete the red plan, you should be very familiar with how you feel when running at **E**, **T**, and **I** paces and how you feel during an **L** run. You may want to try a more challenging program (blue and gold plans are next in order, if that is your desire), or you may want to try training for some specific distances as outlined in later chapters.

Also, you may decide to take a little break from structured training and just spend some time going out for **E** runs of different durations. You may even take a total break from running for a while. If you do decide to take some weeks off completely, it is best to start back again with a few weeks of just **E** running before adding any quality sessions to your training.

Table 7.2 provides a detailed structure of the red training plan. **E** represents easy running, and **L** represents a long run that is easy and steady. Strides (ST) are light, quick 20-second runs (not sprints) with 60 seconds of rest between each. Intervals (**I**) are hard runs that you could race at for 10 to 15 minutes. **T** represents threshold pace, which is comfortably hard, and jogs (jg) should be run at an easy pace. 1K means 1 kilometer.

Table 7.2   Red Plan Phase I: Weeks 1-4

Day	Workout	Running min	Total min
1	**30 min E + 6 ST**	**~32**	**~40**
2	If you run today, repeat day 1 workout	~32	~40
3	**10 min E + 3 × 1 mile T w/1 min rests between the T-pace miles + 10 min E**	**~40**	**~45**
4	If you run today, repeat day 1 workout	~32	~40
5	**10 min E + 6 × 1K T w/1 min rests between the T-pace Ks + 10 min E**	**~50**	**~55**
6	If you run today, repeat day 1 workout	~32	~40
7	**E run of the lesser of 40 min and 6 miles**	**~40**	**~40**

Red Plan Phase II: Weeks 5-8

Day	Workout	Running min	Total min
1	**30 min E + 6 ST**	**~32**	**~40**
2	If you run today, repeat day 1 workout	~32	~40
3	**10 min E + 2 mile T + 2 min rest + 1 mile T + 10 min E**	**~40**	**~42**
4	If you run today, repeat day 1 workout	~32	~40
5	**10 min E + 2 × 1 mile T w/1 min rests after each + 2 × 1K T w/1 min rest + 10 min E**	**~42**	**~45**
6	If you run today, repeat day 1 workout	~32	~40
7	**40-50 min L run at steady E pace**	**~40**	**~50**

Red Plan Phase III: Weeks 9-12

Day	Workout	Running min	Total min
1	**30 min E + 6 ST**	**~32**	**~40**
2	If you run today, repeat day 1 workout	~32	~40
3	**10 min E + 6 ST + 5 × 3 min hard w/2 min jg recoveries after each + 10 min E**	**~47**	**~50**
4	If you run today, repeat day 1 workout	~32	~40
5	**10 min E + the lesser of 3 miles and 20 min steady at T pace + 10 min E**	**40**	**40**
6	If you run today, repeat day 1 workout	~32	~40
7	**40-50 min L run at steady E pace**	**40-50**	**40-50**

Red Plan Phase IV: Weeks 13-16

Day	Workout	Running min	Total min
1	**30 min E + 8 ST**	**~32**	**~40**
2	If you run today, repeat day 1 workout	~32	~40
3	**10 min E + 4 ST + 2 × (5 min I + 4 min jg + 3 min I + 2 min jg) + 10 min E**	**~50**	**~53**
4	If you run today, repeat day 1 workout	~32	~40
5	**10 min E + 6 ST + 2 mile T + 2 min rest + 2 mile T + 10 min E**	**~50**	**~55**
6	If you run today, repeat day 1 workout	~32	~40
7	**40-50 min L run + 4 ST**	**40-50**	**40-50**

BLUE ADVANCED PLAN

The blue plan is for runners who have recently completed the red plan or who have considerable running experience, including some races now and then. Runners following this plan will be asked to train 5 to 7 days each week, with the possibility of running more than once on some days if it is necessary to accumulate desired weekly mileage goals. The recommended quality days of training are bolded so it is easy to see when you have something other than an easy or rest day in the schedule.

In this blue plan, weekly mileage ranges from about 40 to 52 miles per week (64 to 84 km, or 4.5 to more than 7 hours per week, depending on the speeds at which you are training). If you schedule any races while following the blue plan, rearrange the training schedule so you have at least 2 **E** days of training before any races. This may even mean deleting a day of training now and then. Remember, races are a very important part of training, and they play a significant role in improving your fitness.

If, while pursuing this blue plan, you believe the training is asking a little too much of you, consider going back to the red plan or even taking a break from running for a few weeks before getting back into a structured program. If you do choose to take a break for a while, read through chapter 15, which outlines how to transition back into training from a period of little or no activity.

After completing the blue plan, you will be familiar with different intensities of training and how you feel during and after the various types. Even though you will have considerable experience with a variety of training amounts and intensities, you may not yet be prepared to tackle a marathon. However, you certainly will be fit enough to consider a marathon, so if that is your goal, look into the marathon training programs presented later in this book. I have also outlined training programs for many distance events in the event you want to pursue training for a specific race distance.

For those who find the blue plan stimulates you to train even harder, look into the gold plan, which is next in this chapter. Many runners who feel qualified for the gold plan may also want to consider looking into a more specific program, designed for a particular race distance, and there are plenty of those available in chapters ahead.

Table 7.3 details the blue training program. **E** represents easy running, and **L** represents a long run that is easy and steady. Strides (ST) are light, quick 20-second runs (not sprints) with 60 seconds of rest between each. **R** represents repetition running at a pace that you could race at for 5 minutes. *Hard* runs are interval in nature and at a pace you could race at for 10-15 minutes. **T** represents threshold pace, which is comfortably hard, and jogs (jg) should be run at an easy pace. K refers to kilometer.

Table 7.3　Blue Plan Phase I: Weeks 1-4

Day	Workout	Running min	Total min
1	**60 min E (can be 1 or 2 runs to total 60 min)**	**60**	**60**
2	**10 min E + 8 × 400 R pace w/400 recovery jg + 10 min E**	**~50**	**~50**
3	If you run today, repeat day 1 workout	60	60
4	**30-45 min E + 8 ST**	**40**	**55**
5	**15 min E + 4 × 4 min hard w/3 min jg for recovery + 15 min E**	**~60**	**~60**
6	If you run today, repeat day 4 workout	40	55
7	**60-90 min L run**	**60**	**90**

Blue Plan Phase II: Weeks 5-8

Day	Workout	Running min	Total min
1	**60 min E run (can be 1 or 2 runs to total 60 min)**	**60**	**60**
2	**15 min E + 4 × (200 R + 200 jg + 200 R + 200 jg + 400 R + 400 jg) + 15 min E**	**~60**	**~60**
3	If you run today, repeat day 1 workout	60	60
4	**30-45 min E + 8 ST**	**30-45**	**50**
5	**15 min E + 20 min T + 4 ST + 15 min E**	**55**	**55**
6	If you run today, repeat day 4 workout	30-45	50
7	**60-90 min L run**	**60-90**	**60-90**

Blue Plan Phase III: Weeks 9-12

Day	Workout	Running min	Total min
1	**60 min E**	**60**	**60**
2	**15 min E + 6 ST + 6 × (400 R + 400 jg + 200 R + 200 jg) + 15 min E**	**~65**	**~65**
3	If you run today, run 30 min **E** + 6 ST	~35	~35
4	**30-45 min E + 8 ST**	**~40**	**55**
5	**15 min E + 4 × 4 min hard w/3 min jg for recovery + 15 min E**	**~60**	**~60**
6	If you run today, repeat day 4 workout	~40	55
7	**60-90 min L run**	**60-90**	**60-90**

Blue Plan Phase IV: Weeks 13-16

Day	Workout	Running min	Total min
1	**60 min E run**	**60**	**60**
2	**15 min E + 3 × 1K T w/1 min rests + 3 × 3 min hard w/2 min jg + 15 min E**	**~60**	**~ 65**
3	If you run today, run 30 min **E** + 4 ST	~32	~35
4	**30-45 min E + 6 ST**	**~35**	**50**
5	**20 min E + 2 × 200 R w/200 jg + 3 × 1K T w/1 min rest + 2 × 200 R w/200 jg + 5 min E**	**~50**	**~55**
6	If you run today, repeat day 4 workout	~35	50
7	**60-90 min L run**	**60-90**	**60-90**

GOLD ELITE PLAN

The gold plan is designed for runners who have completed level IV of the blue plan or who have considerable experience and time for training and want to feel prepared for races over a variety of distances. Runners who tackle this gold plan should be willing to accept 6 or 7 days of running each week and even some days when they may run twice in the same day. Weekly mileage will typically be more than 60 miles (97 km) per week, but this certainly can vary as weather and personal commitments dictate. Although you could use this gold plan to train for a marathon, I recommend looking into one of the specific marathon training programs provided in chapter 14.

In the gold plan, six workouts are scheduled for each week (bolded in the programs). Day 4 of each week is listed as an optional training day, but feel free to make any day of the week a day off if conditions or personal obligations so dictate. I also typically indicate Sunday as being day 1 of each week, but you can make day 1 whatever day best suits your schedule.

In addition to the time allocated for each training session, you should allow additional time for yourself for stretching, supplemental training, showering, changing clothes, traveling to a training site, and so on. I don't want to give the impression that the time indicated for the various training sessions is all you have to set aside for completing this program.

When following this program, give yourself 2 or 3 **E** days of training before any races and 1 **E** day after races for every 3,000 meters of race distance (e.g., 3 **E** days after a 10K race; 5 **E** days after a 15K race). I also recommend making your last quality training session before any races a **T** session that totals three 1-mile runs at **T** pace, with 2 minutes of rest between the **T**-pace runs.

The gold plan (as detailed in table 7.4) should prepare you for racing over almost any distance, but you still may want to look into more distance-specific training programs in the later chapters of this book when you are preparing for an important race.

Any runner who has completed the gold plan should be capable of handling any type of workout or training program. If this program proves too demanding, just move back to a less demanding plan, or select specific parts of any of the training plans I have presented and work on those as time permits. There are many ways to achieve your absolute ability, and what works best for one person may not be best for another. What I try to do is provide a variety of approaches and types of training sessions and hope each person finds what feels and works best.

Table 7.4 Gold Plan Phase I: Weeks 1-4

Day	Workout	Running min	Total min
1	**75 min E run (can be done in 1 or 2 runs)**	**75**	**75**
2	**20 min E + 10 × 400 R w/400 jg +10 min E**	**~60**	**~60**
3	**60 min E (can be 1 or 2 runs) + 6 ST**	**~62**	**~65**
4	If you run today, repeat day 3 workout	~62	~65
5	**20 min E + 6 ST + 20 min T + 6 ST + 10 min E**	**~65**	**~70**
6	**60 min E run**	**60**	**60**
7	**120 min L run**	**120**	**120**

Gold Plan Phase II: Weeks 5-8

Day	Workout	Running min	Total min
1	**75 min E run**	**75**	**75**
2	**20 min E + 5 × 3 min hard w/2 min recovery jg + 20 min E**	**65**	**65**
3	**1 or 2 E runs of 30-40 min each + 6 ST**	**30**	**80**
4	If you run today, repeat day 3 workout	30	80
5	**20 min E + 6 ST + 8 × 200 R w/200 jg + 5 min E + 8 × 200 R w/200 jg + 5 min E**	**~55**	**~55**
6	**60 min E run (to be done in 1 or 2 runs)**	**60**	**~60**
7	**120 min L run**	**120**	**120**

Gold Plan Phase III: Weeks 9-12

Day	Workout	Running min	Total min
1	**75 min E run (to be done in 1 or 2 runs)**	**75**	**75**
2	**20 min E + 6 ST + 5 × 4 min hard w/3 min jg + 20 min E**	**80**	**80**
3	**75 min E run (to be done in 1 or 2 runs)**	**75**	**75**
4	If you run today, repeat day 3 workout	75	75
5	**20 min E + 5 × 1 mile T w/1 min rests + 6 ST + 10 min E**	**~70**	**~75**
6	**60 min E run (to be done in 1 or 2 runs)**	**60**	**60**
7	**120 min L run**	**120**	**120**

(continued)

Table 7.4   Gold Plan   *(continued)*

Gold Plan Phase IV: Weeks 13-16

Day	Workout	Running min	Total min
1	**75 min E run (preferably the total of 2 runs)**	**75**	**75**
2	**20 min E + 3 × 3 min hard w/2 min jg + 8 × 200 R w/200 jg + 10 min E**	**~60**	**~60**
3	**75 min E run (could be total of 2 runs)**	**75**	**75**
4	If you run today, repeat day 3 workout	75	75
5	**20 min E + 6 × 1K T w/1 min rests + 6 ST + 20 min E**	**~70**	**~75**
6	**60 min E run (to be total of 1 or 2 runs)**	**60**	**60**
7	**120 min L run**	**120**	**120**

8

Altitude Training

Find ways to benefit from adversity and
from less-than-desirable race results.

In recent years the demand for better and better athletic performance has escalated to the point that existing competition between athletes is not good enough. Audiences demand and respond positively to unusual performances or to regular performances by unusual athletes. To meet the demand, no stone that might reveal a better or quicker way to achieve the level of performance that will attract attention, money, or fame is left unturned.

Unfortunately, the greater the payback for outstanding performance, the more outlandish become the methods of achieving notoriety. Sport at almost every level is experiencing a universal attempt to reach success through the use of performance-enhancing drugs, and the supporters of this movement have often done a good job of staying ahead of those who would find ways to keep sport clean and healthy.

Still, there are fair-minded people who would like to stick with the rules, and they try to achieve success through every possible legal approach. A good example is the attempt to improve performances in distance running (and other endurance sports) through altitude training. The idea is that hypoxia (a lower pressure of oxygen in the air being breathed), or something else associated with altitude, will bring about some physiological (or maybe even psychological) changes that allow an athlete to reach a higher level of fitness than could otherwise be achieved without altitude training.

However, even in this case, the scientist replaces the coach, and training becomes less and less personalized. I began coaching distance runners the same year I began conducting research related to human performance, which followed 11 years as a competitive athlete, and I was fortunate enough to win a couple modern pentathlon Olympic medals along the way. Of the five modern pentathlon events (horseback riding, epee fencing, pistol shooting, swimming, and running), running was clearly my weak event, so I dedicated myself to learning everything I could about how to train to perform at my best. There is no doubt in my mind that I rank my personal accomplishments below the benefits I gained by studying with P.O. Åstrand and Bruno Balke.

These two men knew human performance, and Balke was one of the leading experts in the world on altitude.

So, I am in favor of scientific research, as it can legally be applied to athletic performance, but I am also convinced that coaches with good interpersonal traits but lacking in scientific understanding can produce outstanding athletes. A combination of scientific knowledge and good interpersonal traits is certainly a desirable quality in someone preparing elite athletes.

What concerns me regarding altitude training is that we tend to defer decisions to the scientists, who, once having gained attention, become the coaches. The two must work together—coaches and scientists—in the best interest of the athletes. It is my attempt here to spend a little time in the shoes of a researcher, who deals in probability and group data, but I want to spend more time in the role of a coach, who is likely to deal in absolutes and individual efforts, because I am concerned more about people enjoying their athletic careers than just the few championships they may win.

From a scientific perspective we most often discuss the possible changes in blood chemistry, $\dot{V}O_2$max, and minute ventilation, and as a coach or athlete the issues are usually more related to speed of training, types of training, and discomfort while at altitude. I like to add, as a coach, or as a scientist, that environmental conditions are of considerable importance.

ALTITUDE: THE BEST TRAINING GROUND?

What do most runners want available to them at any training site? Usually the things of importance are weather, training facilities, housing, food, medical attention, and a friendly social atmosphere. If you have all these things and are at altitude, is that better than all of these things at sea level? Which would you rather have, all of these accommodations at sea level or few or none of them at altitude? Would altitude be worth it if it is not a desirable place to spend time training?

Altitude training has become a very popular topic of conversation among distance runners and coaches. I am saddened when I hear a coach or athlete say that if you can't include altitude training in your program as a distance runner, you may as well not even try being a great distance runner. I also think this is a poor message to send to our youth, primarily because I don't believe it is a true statement that can be backed by facts.

If it is altitude that is associated with the best distance runners in the world, then why aren't there more great distance runners in several South American countries, where altitude is part of daily life for many residents? Maybe we should be penalizing youngsters from the Rocky Mountains in the United States for not becoming better at running. After all, they grow up and train at altitude all of their early years. Maybe it is not altitude that makes some East African runners so great; maybe it is living close to the equator and not altitude at all. However, if that is the case then we have to

Some runners are attracted to altitude training because of a possible positive impact on sea-level performance.

go back to Ecuador and ask where are all the great distance runners who live in Quito, which is right on the equator.

Maybe we have to spend more time looking at the successful runners and trying to understand what all the great ones have in common. It might be a good idea to consider social aspects or genetic characteristics. Maybe we need to eliminate the idea that if we aren't from a special place on earth, we won't ever have a great chance of being the best.

THE EFFECTS OF ALTITUDE ON PERFORMANCE

When we attempt to analyze how any type of training affects performance in any sport, it is important to understand what demands running places on the human body. Is speed of greatest importance, or strength and power, or is it endurance that is primary in the sport in question? No doubt being at altitude affects the body in a few different ways, and the following points are worthy of consideration.

1. Performance in low-speed endurance events (e.g., running events that last more than about 2 minutes) is slower at altitude than at sea level. Relatively speaking, running over medium and long distances involves slow movement against air resistance, and the slight benefit a runner gains by moving through the less dense air at altitude does not make

up for the loss in aerobic power caused by lower amounts of oxygen being delivered by the blood to the exercising muscles.

2. Performance in high-speed events, as in the case of sprinters, whether of short duration or prolonged, benefits from the less dense air encountered at altitude. In other words, the reduced air resistance more than makes up for the reduced pressure of oxygen.

3. With acclimatization to altitude (2 or more weeks), performance at altitude will improve in endurance events. I have seen some runners, after 3 weeks of acclimatization, race a mile at altitude more than 10 seconds faster than they were able to perform upon initial altitude exposure. You must remember, however, that some improvement comes though just learning how to run a race under altitude conditions.

4. Regardless of the length of time available for altitude acclimatization, low-speed endurance performance will never reach that which can be achieved at sea level.

5. In addition, some researchers have reported that sea-level performance will (or may) improve as a result of altitude training. Consider the following situation, one that I and, I am sure, other researchers have encountered: A group of runners have just finished a spring semester in college, where they have been studying for final exams; the weather is 90 degrees and 80 percent humidity. We take them to altitude, where it is 80 degrees and 10 percent humidity, and they have nothing to do but eat, sleep, and train, and upon return to sea level they run a new personal best time in a 5K race. Man, that altitude sure is the answer, isn't it? Was it being at altitude or all the other things that changed during this time?

Relative to racing at altitude, there are two types of acclimatization that take place with training at altitude (as mentioned in point 3); one is a physiological acclimatization and one a competitive acclimatization. A big difference between these two types of acclimatization is that the physiological benefits, such as learning to ventilate larger amounts of air, are lost after some time back at sea level, and much of the competitive benefits are not lost, even after some weeks or months back at sea level.

In other words, once you have gone through the process of learning how to race at altitude, that will stay with you fairly permanently; you tend to remember how best to race in this environment. You could compare this to learning to race a new distance. A 5K race is a fair bit different for a miler, but after running a few 5K races, the runner will have adjusted to competing at this distance.

I should clarify that in this discussion about altitude training and racing, I am referring to moderate altitude, which is generally considered altitudes between 1,200 and 2,500 meters, which are in the range of about 4,000 to 8,000 feet above sea level. Most of my studies and training of athletes at altitude have been at elevations of about 2,130 to 2,255 meters (7,000 to 7,400 feet). There's no question that 7,000 feet imposes almost double the stress than does 5,000 feet because the real problems with altitude don't begin until about 3,000 feet above sea level, so going from 5,000 to 7,000 is about the same as going from sea level to 5,000.

Upon arrival at altitude, one's aerobic capacity ($\dot{V}O_2$max) is reduced by about 12 to 16 percent, but a runner's performance is affected by only about 6 to 8 percent. This happens because the "cost" (aerobic demand) of running is less at altitude compared to sea level, as a result of the less dense air against which you are running. So you lose some in aerobic power but gain some back in running economy.

COMPARISON OF SWIMMERS AND RUNNERS

Figure 8.1 shows sea-level and altitude economy curves, $\dot{V}O_2$max values, and $v\dot{V}O_2$max values for a typical distance runner. Figure 8.2 shows the same information for swimmers who go to altitude. Interestingly, because of a difference in the slope of economy curves for swimmers and runners (see figure 8.3), athletes in both of these sports lose about the same time at altitude (as reflected by $v\dot{V}O_2$max values) compared with sea-level times during events of the same duration. The swimmers do not gain in economy, since they are working against water and not air, but the steeper slope of the swimming economy curve allows them to stay closer to sea-level speed with an equal drop in $\dot{V}O_2$max. The result is that a 12 percent drop in $\dot{V}O_2$max is about a 6 percent drop in $v\dot{V}O_2$max for both the swimmers and runners.

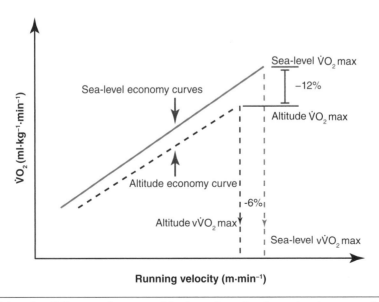

Figure 8.1   The differences between altitude and sea-level running in terms of $\dot{V}O_2$max, economy, and $v\dot{V}O_2$max.

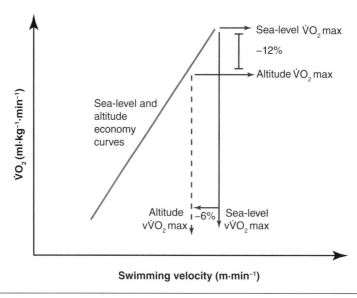

Figure 8.2   The differences between altitude and sea-level swimming in terms of $\dot{V}O_2$max, economy, and $v\dot{V}O_2$max.

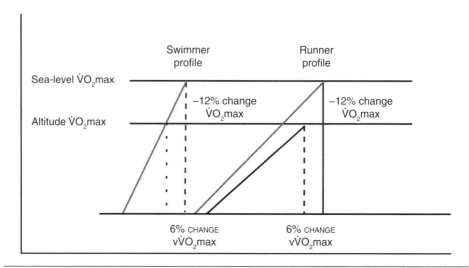

Figure 8.3   Comparison of running and swimming aerobic profiles at altitude and sea level.

The difference in economy-curve slopes between runners and swimmers helps explain why swimmers are able to perform closer to their maximum aerobic power than are runners. For example, most runners who can race 1 mile in 4 minutes are usually capable of running under 50 seconds for an all-out 400 meters, whereas many swimmers can swim a 400 in 4 minutes but may not go faster than low 50s for a 100.

Figures 8.1 and 8.2 illustrate this phenomenon by showing that a swimmer gains more energy than does a runner by slowing down just a little. The reverse of this comparison is that it requires a greater increase in energy for a swimmer to go a little faster than it does for a runner to increase speed by the same percentage. Cyclists and speedskaters sometimes can go faster at some altitudes, compared with sea level, because their speed of movement is so much faster than runners', and they benefit more from the reduced air resistance than they lose in aerobic power.

ALTITUDE TRAINING AND RACING CONSIDERATIONS

A usual question that athletes have when they decide to try some altitude training is how their training routines should be changed, if at all. I truly believe there is no need to change the amount of training that is typical at sea level. For example, a runner who is used to accumulating 80 miles (129 km) per week at sea level should be able to continue with that amount of running upon arrival at altitude. Further, the same amount of time spent on **T**, **I**, and **R** runs can also remain unchanged.

There is no need to reduce the time spent on any type of training because the speed of the various types of training will be a little slower—relative to a drop in aerobic power. With a reduction in aerobic power, all running speeds are now related to a different maximum power that is less than what was associated with sea-level running.

One type of training that should not have its speed adjusted when at altitude is running at **R** pace. For repetitions, sea-level speed can be matched when at altitude, but it may be necessary to increase the recovery time between **R** runs. This will not spoil the benefits of the workout because with repetitions the idea is to work on speed and economy, so adjust recovery to allow usual speed and economy to be practiced.

Incorporating Altitude Training

As someone who has competed, trained, performed research, and coached distance runners at altitude (and at sea level), here are some altitude training considerations I have learned:

1. I like training at altitude, with intermittent exposures to sea level for some days at a time, and even some exposure to higher altitudes now and then. The air is usually clean, dry, and cool, and in many cases, just going for an **E** run is more enjoyable than at sea level because of the very desirable weather conditions. It is not unlike having a refreshing cold front arrive in a typically warm and humid part of the country. It

is always a good idea to let your breathing pattern dictate how hard you are working when on an **E** run; are you breathing at a rate of perceived exertion that is no more stressful than is typical at sea level?

2. There is no need to reduce your training mileage upon initial exposure to altitude. However, don't immediately increase your mileage just because you have more available time. In other words, do normal amounts of training and increase mileage as you would when at sea level.

3. Run at normal sea-level speeds in **R** workouts, but maybe take a little longer time to recover between individual runs. With true **I** sessions, slow the speed of longer intervals by 3 or 4 seconds per 400 and take normal amounts of recovery. Also, slow **T** pace by about 12 to 16 seconds per mile (8 to 10 sec/km). During **E** and **L** runs, just go by feel and listen for a normal breathing pattern.

4. To race your best at altitude you need to get in some practice races so you become competitively acclimatized, even if this must be accomplished some months before the actual altitude competition.

5. Think of altitude training as one of a number of types of training stress to which you have access.

6. It is wise to allow for some adaptation to sea-level conditions after altitude training so that your body is adjusted to sea-level conditions.

7. Performance benefits that result from training at altitude should not be considered temporary in nature. Many athletes have raised their level of fitness a notch through altitude training and maintained that performance capability, even months after return to sea level. The key is to maintain what has been accomplished through new levels of stress in the overall training program. In other words, if your performances have improved as a result of altitude training, your body has made some improvements, and as long as your new level of fitness continues to be stressed—with increased speeds of training back at sea level—you will not lose that ability. It is no different from realizing an improvement as a result of increasing weekly mileage, but you have to continue stressing the body according to its fitness level, regardless of how improved fitness has been achieved.

8. Believe in altitude training if you decide to try it, but if it doesn't work, don't hesitate to make a change.

9. It is common for distance runners to fare better their first day at altitude than a few days after arrival. There is often a fair amount of dehydration during the first several days at altitude, and it is important to drink plenty of fluids, which helps maintain blood volume, and to get regular rest.

10. There appears to be a stress adaptation during continued exposure to altitude that is sped up by intermittent exposures to sea level. A study of adrenaline and noradrenaline values, measured through the collec-

tion of daily 24-hour urine samples, suggested that several days back at sea level reduced the daily stress levels upon return to altitude.

11. For lowlanders who are training at altitude for the purpose of preparing for a subsequent competition at altitude, it is beneficial to perform a time trial or race upon acute altitude exposure, which is in contrast to what is often recommended. The benefit of this trial effort is to face reality as soon as possible and therefore be more accepting of the changes that need to be made to race well at altitude. Further, a second test a couple of weeks later will invariably show an improvement in performance, and this is a real psychological boost—proof that progress is being made.

12. Training at altitude can be of normal amount and relative intensity without initially being more demanding than sea-level training. In an attempt to maintain normal speed during repetition workouts, remember that it is sometimes necessary to take longer periods of recovery after each faster run. If speed and economy of running are the purposes of a training session, then the runs being performed need to accomplish those purposes.

13. It is possible that endurance athletes training at altitude will not only adapt to altitude but also make a step up in fitness. If this is true, then it is not at all unusual to see sea-level as well as altitude performances improve.

Maintaining Speed at Altitude

Some will say you will lose speed when training at altitude, and this is troubling to me. Actually, I was part of a study that first suggested this may happen, but most people don't realize that the test group of runners spent 57 days at 13,000 feet (just under 4,000 meters) of altitude. First of all, some of the runners in that group were sick for a number of days at that altitude, and when they tried normal workouts they could not go anywhere near as fast as at sea level.

One person who often ran 16 400s in 64 seconds at sea level couldn't do more than 8 400s in 74 seconds. He tried to do them with normal amounts of sea-level rest between the faster runs, and it just didn't work. After 57 days of detraining his speed factor, it was decided that you lose speed by training at altitude. Now, as a coach I would have suggested that instead of running 16 400s in 64, why not run 32 200s in 32, and maybe with a little longer rest so you maintain the same speed as at sea level.

According to my math, 32×200 at 32 is the same as 16×400 at 64 (6,400 meters at the same speed), so there's no need to lose speed if you adjust training accordingly. In fact, it is well known that a person can run faster at altitude than at sea level because of the reduced air resistance, as mentioned earlier.

Remember, you must always be able to answer the question "What is the purpose of this workout?" No matter where you are, there are five intensities of training: **E** (easy) runs, **M** (marathon-pace runs, mostly for marathon specialists), **T** (threshold pace), **I** (interval pace), and **R** (repetition pace). Let's look at how altitude affects each of these types of training.

It is generally accepted that steady, prolonged runs at comfortable, even conversational, paces elicit tremendous benefits. Higher-intensity training is also employed for parts of a training season in order to stress various components of the overall physiological and biomechanical makeup of the athletes. Resistance training is often included, as are bounding drills and uphill runs, for the purpose of improving leg power. Faster runs of relatively short duration are included in the program to develop speed, power, and an economical running technique at faster racing speeds. **T**-pace runs and **I** runs are also included for the purpose of improving endurance and stressing the aerobic system to its limit.

The question is, during which type of training is the athlete being cheated in terms of leg power or speed? It certainly isn't that easy prolonged intensity of running that makes up about 85 percent of a week's total mileage. These **E** runs are performed at about 60 to 75 percent of $\dot{V}O_2$max, and if altitude makes you do a typical 60 percent effort at 68 percent of your reduced altitude max, then you are still moving along at the same pace. Further, I doubt that leg power or speed are associated very closely with running at 70 percent of max, so no difference relative to **E** runs.

Now consider the fast **R** training that is part of the program. It is well accepted that you can run faster at altitude than you can at sea level for short periods of time. The runs typically used in **R** sessions are about 30 seconds to 90 seconds, an amount of time that altitude doesn't negatively affect as long as you take adequate recovery time between runs; one of the purposes of repeating faster runs is to work on good mechanics and good speed, and to accomplish these goals you need to take adequate rest.

This brings us to longer **I** and **T** runs as the only types of training in which absolute speed is slower at altitude than at sea level. Keep in mind that even in a training phase when these types of training are being emphasized, it is unusual for an athlete to set aside more than about 10 percent of a week's training for these types of quality work. Also, remember that the primary purpose of **T** running is to teach the body how to better clear lactate from the system, and if that can be done at a little slower pace at altitude, the purpose of the workout is still being accomplished.

When it comes to the longer intervals that are a little slower at altitude, the purpose is to stress the aerobic system to its maximum, and certainly the central components (the lungs, heart, and blood vessels to deliver blood to the exercising muscles) of this system are working as hard at altitude as they do at sea level. Even though the cells do not receive as much oxygen for aerobic metabolism at altitude as they do at sea level, they are working as hard as they can with what they do have to work with.

Further, for anyone who is worried about losing speed or leg power because of a slower pace during $\dot{V}O_2$max **I** work, it would be fairly easy to find a slight downhill course for maintaining sea-level speed or to schedule this phase of training for a time when not at altitude. Personally, I think the learn-to-hurt aspect of intervals at altitude more than makes up for the slightly slower pace at which they are often performed.

An additional point about reduced intensity of training at altitude relates to overtraining and dealing with injury. I have seen several distance runners actually benefit from the reduced training intensity that altitude imposes during **T** runs and long **I** workouts. There are a couple of reasons for this:

- Many athletes train faster than is necessary to achieve a particular benefit, and at altitude they are reduced to a slower pace that is actually just right for them.
- Runners who are nursing minor injuries often find themselves injury free after a couple of weeks of training at altitude, where they must reduce the speed at which they are doing some of their runs.

What sometimes appears to have a negative impact on a person's training can become a positive one.

Racing at Altitude

When races are scheduled during a runner's time at altitude, there must be an adjustment in how the races are run. Most important is to avoid going out too fast at the beginning of a distance race, and by too fast, I mean don't try to match the speed you are used to going out for a sea-level race of the same distance.

Table 8.1 shows some approximate time adjustments for race durations at various altitudes. This will give you an idea of how much to adjust the pace of a race you are running at altitude for the first time. The times shown in table 8.1 are for runners who have spent some time at altitude, and if you are running an altitude race with no time for acclimatization, the pace will have to be a fair bit slower than what is shown in this table. The time to put a little more into an altitude race (if you think you are not working too hard) is after you are at least halfway into the race.

Sometimes runners will need to go all out at some altitude site. This doesn't happen often in championship races, but it is fairly common in races of moderate importance. The questions of considerable concern are as follows:

1. How much slower should times be at altitude?
2. What is the best approach to racing at altitude?

In answer to the first question, refer to table 8.1, which associates altitude and race duration with how much slower you might expect to run for different races.

Table 8.1   Time Adjustments for Races at Altitude

Altitude	1,000 m (3,281 ft)	1,500 m (4,921 ft)	2,000 m (6,562 ft)	2,250 m (7,382 ft)
Race duration (min)	*Added time (sec)*			
5	1.5	3.75	6.0	7.75
10	4.25	12.5	21.0	25.5
20	9.75	30.0	51.0	61.0
30	15.25	47.5	81.0	96.5

Table created by Jack Daniels' running calculator designed by the Run SMART Project.

In answer to the second question, the two most important factors are the duration of the altitude race and the best approach to attacking the race. It is pretty well known that short races are not affected by altitude, and by short I mean up to and including an 800-meter distance. It may hurt a little more than usual, but in a serious race you should perform the 800 at just about the same time you are used to running at sea level. In fact, in the 1968 Olympics in Mexico City, the winner (a sea-level native) of the 800 tied the Olympic record in the final of that race.

Obviously, tactics can play a major role in an altitude race, but aside from tactics, the best approach to a distance race at altitude is to be a little overly cautious during the early minutes of the race. Going out as fast as at sea level will definitely demand a fair greater amount of anaerobic energy, which will surely lead to a slower latter part of the race.

Alternating Between Altitude and Sea Level

Distance runners generally improve their altitude performances a considerable amount over a 2- or 3-week period of training at altitude. Greater improvement is realized when runners periodically train or race at sea level during a series of altitude stays. Getting back to sea level now and then helps athletes realize they have not lost their usual sea-level ability from being at altitude for prolonged periods.

For runners who have an opportunity to spend some time at altitude, it is beneficial to do some switching back and forth between altitude and sea level. Going up and down daily is not necessary, but a few weeks at altitude followed by a week or so at sea level and then back to altitude works well. A major benefit of this approach is that going down for a few days can give a psychological boost when you realize you haven't lost any fitness, as some of your altitude training sessions may be suggesting. In fact, during a few days at sea level you often can perform better than in previous sea-level outings.

I often refer to this advantage as having "learned to hurt" when at altitude, and that same level of hurt is now associated with a little faster time than previously run at sea level. In fact, I believe that one of the most significant benefits of spending some time training at altitude is that you do learn to hurt a little more.

Naturally, once the idea of going back to sea level for some extended training time is mentioned, then the topic of losing fitness upon return to sea level usually surfaces. You sometimes hear that you have only relatively few days back at sea level before losing what you may have gained while at altitude. I tend to think this is not the case at all.

Think of it this way—if while at altitude you increased your level of fitness, this simply means you are fitter than before, not that you are just temporarily fitter than before. I suppose you could compare it to increasing your mileage, and after some weeks of higher mileage you race better (some fitness factor has improved). As long as you continue to stress the necessary systems, there is no need to believe you will lose fitness because you back off a little in mileage.

The reason people say that after a few weeks back at sea level you will lose performance ability gained at altitude is that this is often the case; but why? Very often, runners go to altitude to prepare for a specific championship. They come down and compete, and then many of them are finished for the season; so have they lost fitness because they came back to sea level or because they quit training?

I have had athletes leave after a month at altitude, travel to race in Europe, and return to altitude where they raced faster (at altitude) than before they left for Europe. One runner spent 6 weeks at altitude and went home to set a personal best time in the 5K. He stayed at sea level for the next 10 months, during which time he ran many personal bests and was national champion and Pan American Games champion in his event, without ever returning to altitude. He didn't lose anything by not going back to altitude; but he did go faster with more time back at sea level.

For years I have argued that it is not unusual to see an endurance athlete leave the rigors of sea-level life (heat, humidity, possible study or job demands, and possible personal stresses), go to altitude for a period of training, and upon return to sea level, record some significant improvements in performance.

Racing at Sea Level After Training at Altitude

It usually takes a couple of weeks at altitude to see altitude performances improve. In terms of when is the best time to race upon return to sea level, there seems to be a fair bit of variation among athletes. One factor that affects how long back at sea level will produce the best sea-level performance is weather. Altitude weather is typically cool and dry, and if you return to sea level and have to race in warm, humid conditions, it may be best to give yourself a week or more to adjust to that type of environment. On the other hand, if a sea-level competition happens to be in cool, dry conditions, then you may be ready for a great race as soon as you come down from altitude.

How long you should be back at sea level before racing also varies with the event in question. In general, I believe that the longer the race, the longer you need to be down at sea-level conditions in order to perform your best.

One of my altitude subjects, an outstanding runner and close friend named Jim Ryun, ran a world-record mile (3:51.1 on June 23, 1967) on the evening of the day he returned to sea level after 3 weeks at altitude. A couple of weeks later, he set another world record in the 1,500 (3:33.1), a day after returning to sea level. Keep in mind these are fairly short races, and one thing that tends to happen upon return to sea level after some time at altitude is that you hyperventilate—breathe more than is necessary—because at altitude you definitely increase your breathing volume, and it takes some days back at sea level to realize you don't need to breathe quite so much. However, in a relatively short race, such as a 1,500 or mile, the race is pretty much over by the time you realize how hard you are breathing.

At the other end of the distance spectrum, the marathon, sea-level conditions can be very stressful compared with what you have been dealing with at altitude, especially in terms of heat and humidity. At altitude it is almost always dry and cooler than at sea level, and if you travel to a sea-level marathon and it is warm and humid, your body will not respond well to those conditions for 10 to 14 days. Also, over a number of days your breathing will settle down and things will feel much more comfortable.

For most other distances that are longer than the mile, a week or even more is probably better than just arriving at sea level in time for a race, especially when weather conditions differ from what was typical at altitude. Runners who have made several trips to sea level during a phase of training at altitude will generally have a better idea of how to prepare for a sea-level race than those who have spent considerable time at altitude with few or no intermittent trips to sea level.

I recommend making these sea-level trips for as much as a week at a time, both for the mental and physiological benefits that some time at sea level can provide. Table 8.2 shows some effects of various temperatures on two marathon race times.

Table 8.2 Effect of Different Air Temperatures on Marathon Times

Marathon time of 2:25

Temperature		Time added to total		Approximate fluid loss (ml)	
°F	°C	To total	Per 5K	Per min	Per 2:25
55	12.8	0:00	0 sec	13.0 ml	1,885 ml
60	15.6	1:07	8 sec	14.5 ml	2,105 ml
65	18.3	2:14	16 sec	15.7 ml	2,275 ml
70	21.1	3:21	24 sec	16.9 ml	2,450 ml
75	23.9	4:28	32 sec	18.1 ml	2,625 ml
80	26.7	5:35	40 sec	19.4 ml	2,815 ml
85	29.4	6:42	48 sec	20.7 ml	3,000 ml
90	32.2	7:49	56 sec	22.1 ml	3,200 ml

Marathon time of 2:07

Temperature		Time added to total		Approximate fluid loss (ml)	
°F	°C	To total	Per 5K	Per min	Per 2:25
55	12.8	0:00	0 sec	16.5 ml	2,145 ml
60	15.6	0:59	7 sec	18.1 ml	2,350 ml
65	18.3	1:58	14 sec	19.6 ml	2,550 ml
70	21.1	2:57	21 sec	21.2 ml	2,755 ml
75	23.9	3:56	28 sec	22.8 ml	2,965 ml
80	26.7	4:55	35 sec	24.4 ml	3,170 ml
85	29.4	5:54	42 sec	25.9 ml	3,370 ml
90	32.2	6:53	49 sec	27.5 ml	3,575 ml

Table created by Jack Daniels' running calculator designed by the Run SMART Project.

9

800-Meter Training

Good performances are the result of understanding
why you are doing what you are doing.

Often with the 800, and to a lesser extent in longer events, runners take either a speed or endurance approach to the race. In other words, some great 800 runners are almost primarily 400 specialists, and others rely more on endurance and less on all-out speed. That being said, the 800 is a very special track event, maybe one of the more difficult events to train for and certainly one of the most demanding. You might say that 800 runners are high-speed endurance athletes.

The 800 requires both great aerobic and anaerobic power, and it is not always easy to determine the better approach for each individual runner. I have been lucky enough to watch some great 800 runners over the years, including Peter Snell when he won at the Rome Olympics in 1960; Alberto Juantorena when he won the Montreal Olympics in 1976; and Joaquim Cruz leading all but about one lap of the 800s he ran in the Los Angeles Olympics in 1984. I also watched Jim Ryun break the 880-yard world record.

Snell and Ryun were more endurance oriented, Juantorena definitely a great 400 runner, and Cruz fairly well trained for both speed and endurance. I have designed some training programs that are flexible enough that parts of the training can be adjusted to cater to all 800 specialists, regardless of their preferred approach.

The better 800 runners include a fair amount of resistance training in their overall programs. Cruz was definitely involved in circuit training, and coach Bob Timmons had Ryun doing a good amount of weight training, even in his early training years.

In recent years it has become more popular to increase endurance training for 800 runners as it was shown that the aerobic contribution of an 800 race is greater than once thought. As with all of my training programs, I present a four-phase 24-week program, but the four phases may be cut down in order to fit into a shorter time frame.

Great 800-meter runners like Jim Ryun require ample aerobic and anaerobic power to be successful.

PHASE I

As explained in chapter 6, I prefer to break the season into four phases of training, and phase I is for the purpose of building a base and a resistance to injury. Resistance training, generally three times per week, should be included in phase I. Some coaches and runners prefer using free weights, while others like circuit training or body-resistance workouts (e.g., sit-ups, push-ups, bar dips, squat thrusts). The important thing about any resistance training is to learn technique first, with minimal resistance; heavier resistance should not be used until technique is of high quality.

The weeks available for phase I training may vary a great deal, with some high school runners having only a few weeks for this phase and other runners able to spend more than 2 months on phase I training. What's important is having an overall plan for the entire season and making sure that each new phase of training benefits from each previous phase.

PHASE II

Each week of phase II includes three Q (quality) sessions of training, although I do not specify which days of the week to set aside for each Q session. Generally, you may want to do Q1 and Q2 on Monday and Tuesday of each week and plan Q3 for Friday. Naturally if you are in a competitive season and have a race or two on most Fridays or Saturdays, you will not want to schedule a Q session for Friday; but remember that a race is a Q session, so eliminating a Friday Q session for a race is not minimizing the Q sessions you have in a week.

Some coaches and runners may prefer having Q sessions on Monday, Wednesday, and Friday or Saturday, or even Tuesday, Wednesday, and Saturday. It is worth trying different approaches for spreading out the Q sessions. I also like to add a fairly long run on weekends, whether after a meet on Saturday (as a prolonged cool-down after a race or two) or done separately on Sunday. The most important thing is to arrange the Q sessions so they fall when the runners are not feeling fatigued from a previous Q session or race. Remember, it is fine for a runner to skip a Q session now and then if not feeling up to a quality session—rest is part of training.

Phase II is not the most stressful part of a season, so always try to imagine you could do more in each workout than is actually scheduled for that session. It is much better to think you could have done more after each Q session than to wish it hadn't been so hard. Refer to chapter 4 for a review of the various types of training, and always try to have a reason for moving from one intensity of effort to a harder one (usually this is accomplished by racing faster than what earlier training was based on—see the VDOT tables in chapter 5).

PHASE III

Phase III introduces the hardest training. In this phase, I recommend a long run on each Saturday (if no race that day) or Sunday if there was a Saturday race the day before. As mentioned in my description of phase II, it is also possible to have a prolonged easy cool-down run after a Saturday track meet, and that can be used as your long run for the week.

For most runners, phase III comes during the middle of a competitive season, and with this being the time of hardest workouts, I recommend three Q sessions per week, with weekend **L** runs counting as Q sessions. With Saturday meets, the two mid-week Q sessions may be Monday and Wednesday or Tuesday and Wednesday, leaving Thursday and Friday as **E** days before the Saturday meet. With a Friday meet, consider Monday and Tuesday for the two mid-week Q sessions that week.

Use appropriate VDOT values to identify proper training paces for your workouts, but don't increase the speed of training any more often than every 3rd or 4th week, even if a race says it is time to go faster. Let your body have several weeks performing at one level of stress before going to the next level.

PHASE IV

Most weeks of this phase of training will have three Q sessions and often an additional Q day in weeks when you have a race. However, when a race in any week of phase IV is very important, such as a championship race or one that qualifies you for a championship, I suggest having just one mid-week Q session early in that week. This Q session should be of limited duration and not any faster than is usual for your recent training sessions.

All non-Q days are **E** days and on the **E** days you can run once, twice, or not at all, depending on desired weekly mileage. Learn to arrange your Q days and **E** days so you feel fresh for any important races.

Try to arrange **L** runs so they come right after any meets you race in, either immediately following a meet or early the next day. In race weeks, I like to schedule the final Q session 3 or even 4 days before the race, and that session should be **T**-pace effort with maybe some light repetitions of 200 meters each. During a season, it is always beneficial to try different approaches for the days leading up to races so you know what works best for you, and that may not be what works best for another runner on your team.

TRAINING SPEEDS

Since I strongly believe that 800 runners fall into one of two categories—400/800 types and 800/1,500 types—I present training speeds for each of the two different categories, and these are shown in table 9.1 (for 400/800 specialists) and table 9.2 (for those who fall more into the 800/1,500 classification).

The left-hand column of both tables lists current 800 racing ability, and as is the case with using the VDOT tables in chapter 5, the remainder of each table shows the recommended running speeds over various distances when doing workouts at **FR** (fast repetitions), **R**, **I**, and **T** intensities.

There is no difference between the two tables for **FR** and **R** training, but **I** and **T** paces are a little slower for the 400/800 specialists, who tend to be a little more anaerobically designed and usually have more trouble handling the **I** and **T** paces, which are a little more realistic for those who also are better at the 1,500. Sometimes 800/1,500 types have trouble with the **FR** paces and may need to do most of their training at **R** pace. As I have mentioned several times, when in doubt as to which of two training sessions to do, select the less stressful.

Table 9.1 Training Paces for 400/800 Specialists

Current 800 m time	FR (fast reps)				R (economy reps)					I (intervals)			T (threshold)		E (easy)
	200	300	400	600	200	300	400	600	800	400	1,000	1,600	1,000	1,600	Mile
1:42	25	38	51	1:16	29	44	59	1:27	1:56	69	2:53	4:36	3:18	5:16	6:06-6:36
1:44	26	39	52	1:18	30	45	60	1:30	2:00	70	2:55	4:40	3:20	5:20	6:10-6:40
1:46	26	39	53	1:19	30	45	61	1:31	2:02	71	2:58	4:44	3:23	5:24	6:14-6:44
1:48	27	40	54	1:21	31	46	62	1:33	2:04	72	3:00	4:48	3:25	5:28	6:18-6:48
1:50	27	41	55	1:22	31	47	63	1:34	2:06	73	3:03	4:52	3:27	5:32	6:22-6:52
1:52	28	42	56	1:24	32	48	64	1:36	2:08	74	3:05	4:56	3:30	5:36	6:26-6:56
1:54	28	42	57	1:25	32	48	65	1:37	2:10	75	3:08	5:00	3:33	5:40	6:30-7:00
1:56	29	43	58	1:27	33	49	66	1:39	2:12	76	3:10	—	3:35	5:44	6:34-7:04
1:58	29	44	59	1:28	33	50	67	1:40	2:14	77	3:13	—	3:38	5:48	6:38-7:08
2:00	30	45	60	1:30	34	51	68	1:42	2:16	78	3:15	—	3:40	5:52	6:42-7:12
2:02	30	45	61	1:31	34	51	69	1:43	2:18	79	3:18	—	3:43	5:56	6:46-7:16
2:04	31	46	62	1:33	35	52	70	1:45	2:20	80	3:20	—	3:45	6:00	6:50-7:20
2:06	31	47	63	1:34	35	53	71	1:46	2:22	81	3:23	—	3:48	6:04	6:54-7:24
2:08	32	48	64	1:36	36	54	72	1:48	2:24	82	3:25	—	3:50	6:08	6:58-7:28
2:10	32	48	65	1:37	36	54	73	1:49	2:26	83	3:28	—	3:52	6:12	7:02-7:32
2:12	33	49	66	1:39	37	55	74	1:51	2:28	84	3:30	—	3:55	6:16	7:06-7:36
2:14	33	50	67	1:40	37	56	75	1:52	2:30	85	3:33	—	3:58	6:20	7:10-7:40
2:16	34	51	68	1:42	38	57	76	1:54	2:32	86	3:35	—	4:00	6:24	7:14-7:44
2:18	34	51	69	1:43	38	57	77	1:55	2:34	87	3:38	—	4:03	6:28	7:18-7:48
2:20	35	52	70	1:45	39	58	78	1:57	2:36	88	3:40	—	4:05	6:32	7:22-7:52
2:22	35	53	71	1:46	39	59	79	1:58	2:38	89	3:43	—	4:08	6:36	7:26-7:56
2:24	36	54	72	1:48	40	60	80	2:00	2:40	90	3:45	—	4:10	6:40	7:30-8:00
2:26	36	55	73	1:50	40	61	81	2:02	2:42	91	3:48	—	4:13	6:44	7:34-8:04
2:28	37	56	74	1:52	41	62	82	2:04	2:44	92	3:50	—	4:15	6:48	7:38-8:08
2:30	37	56	75	1:53	41	62	83	2:05	2:46	93	3:53	—	4:18	6:52	7:42-8:12
2:32	38	57	76	1:54	42	63	84	2:06	2:48	94	3:55	—	4:20	6:56	7:46-8:16
2:34	38	58	77	1:56	42	63	85	2:07	2:50	95	3:58	—	4:23	7:00	7:50-8:20
2:36	39	59	78	1:58	43	64	86	2:09	2:52	96	4:00	—	4:25	7:04	7:54-8:24
2:38	39	59	79	1:59	43	65	87	2:10	2:54	97	4:03	—	4:28	7:08	7:58-8:28
2:40	40	60	80	2:00	44	66	88	2:12	2:56	98	4:05	—	4:30	7:12	8:02-8:32
2:42	40	61	81	2:02	44	67	89	2:14	2:58	99	4:08	—	4:33	7:16	8:06-8:36
2:44	41	62	82	2:04	45	68	90	2:16	3:00	1:40	4:10	—	4:35	7:20	8:10-8:40
2:46	41	62	83	2:05	45	68	91	2:17	3:02	1:41	4:13	—	4:38	7:24	8:14-8:44
2:48	42	63	84	2:06	46	69	92	2:18	3:04	1:42	4:15	—	4:40	7:28	8:18-8:48

(continued)

Table 9.1   Training Paces for 400/800 Specialists   *(continued)*

Current 800 m time	FR (fast reps)				R (economy reps)					I (intervals)			T (threshold)		E (easy)
	200	300	400	600	200	300	400	600	800	400	1,000	1,600	1,000	1,600	Mile
2:50	42	64	85	2:08	46	70	93	2:20	3:06	1:43	4:18	—	4:43	7:32	8:22-8:52
2:52	43	65	86	2:10	47	71	94	2:22	3:08	1:44	4:20	—	4:45	7:36	8:26-8:56
2:54	43	65	87	2:11	47	72	95	2:24	3:10	1:45	4:23	—	4:48	7:40	8:30-9:00
2:56	44	66	88	2:12	48	72	96	2:25	3:12	1:46	4:25	—	4:50	7:44	8:34-9:04
2:58	44	67	89	2:14	48	73	97	2:26	3:14	1:47	4:28	—	4:53	7:48	8:38-9:08
3:00	45	68	90	2:16	49	74	98	2:28	3:16	1:48	4:30	—	4:55	7:52	8:42-9:12
3:02	45	68	91	2:17	49	74	99	2:29	3:18	1:49	4:33	—	4:58	7:56	8:46-9:16
3:04	46	69	92	2:18	50	75	1:40	2:30	3:20	1:50	4:35	—	5:00	8:00	8:50-9:20
3:06	46	70	93	2:20	50	76	1:41	2:32	3:22	1:51	4:38	—	5:02	8:04	8:54-9:24
3:08	47	71	94	2:22	51	77	1:42	2:34	3:24	1:52	4:40	—	5:05	8:08	8:58-9:28
3:10	47	71	95	2:23	51	77	1:43	2:35	3:26	1:53	4:43	—	5:08	8:12	9:02-9:32

Table created by Jack Daniels' Running Calculator designed by the Run SMART Project.

Table 9.2   Training Paces for 800/1,500 Specialists

Current 800 m time	FR (fast reps)				R (economy reps)					I (intervals)			T (threshold)		E (easy)
	200	300	400	600	200	300	400	600	800	400	1,000	1,600	1,000	1,600	Mile
1:42	25	38	51	1:16	29	44	59	1:27	1:56	67	2:47	4:28	3:07	5:00	5:58-6:28
1:44	26	39	52	1:18	30	45	60	1:30	2:00	68	2:50	4:32	3:10	5:04	6:02-6:32
1:46	26	39	53	1:19	30	45	61	1:31	2:02	69	2:52	4:36	3:12	5:08	6:06-6:36
1:48	27	40	54	1:21	31	46	62	1:33	2:04	70	2:55	4:40	3:15	5:12	6:10-6:40
1:50	27	41	55	1:22	31	47	63	1:34	2:06	71	2:57	4:44	3:17	5:16	6:14-6:44
1:52	28	42	56	1:24	32	48	64	1:36	2:08	72	3:00	4:48	3:20	5:20	6:18-6:48
1:54	28	42	57	1:25	32	48	65	1:37	2:10	73	3:02	4:52	3:22	5:24	6:22-6:52
1:56	29	43	58	1:27	33	49	66	1:39	2:12	74	3:05	4:56	3:25	5:28	6:26-6:56
1:58	29	44	59	1:28	33	50	67	1:40	2:14	75	3:07	5:00	3:27	5:32	6:30-7:00
2:00	30	45	60	1:30	34	51	68	1:42	2:16	76	3:10	—	3:30	5:36	6:34-7:04
2:02	30	45	61	1:31	34	51	69	1:43	2:18	77	3:12	—	3:32	5:40	6:38-7:08
2:04	31	46	62	1:33	35	52	70	1:45	2:20	78	3:15	—	3:35	5:44	6:42-7:12
2:06	31	47	63	1:34	35	53	71	1:46	2:22	79	3:17	—	3:37	5:48	6:46-7:16
2:08	32	48	64	1:36	36	54	72	1:48	2:24	80	3:20	—	3:40	5:52	6:50-7:20

Current 800 m time	FR (fast reps)				R (economy reps)					I (intervals)			T (threshold)		E (easy)
	200	300	400	600	200	300	400	600	800	400	1,000	1,600	1,000	1,600	Mile
2:10	32	48	65	1:37	36	54	73	1:49	2:26	81	3:22	—	3:42	5:56	6:54-7:24
2:12	33	49	66	1:39	37	55	74	1:51	2:28	82	3:25	—	3:45	6:00	6:58-7:28
2:14	33	50	67	1:40	37	56	75	1:52	2:30	83	3:27	—	3:47	6:04	7:02-7:32
2:16	34	51	68	1:42	38	57	76	1:54	2:32	84	3:30	—	3:50	6:08	7:06-7:36
2:18	34	51	69	1:43	38	57	77	1:55	2:34	85	3:32	—	3:52	6:12	7:10-7:40
2:20	35	52	70	1:45	39	58	78	1:57	2:36	86	3:35	—	3:55	6:16	7:14-7:44
2:22	35	53	71	1:46	39	59	79	1:58	2:38	87	3:37	—	3:57	6:20	7:18-7:48
2:24	36	54	72	1:48	40	60	80	2:00	2:40	88	3:40	—	4:00	6:24	7:22-7:52
2:26	36	55	73	1:50	40	61	81	2:02	2:42	89	3:43	—	4:03	6:28	7:26-7:56
2:28	37	56	74	1:52	41	62	82	2:04	2:44	90	3:45	—	4:05	6:32	7:30-8:00
2:30	37	56	75	1:53	41	62	83	2:05	2:46	91	3:48	—	4:08	6:36	7:34-8:04
2:32	38	57	76	1:54	42	63	84	2:06	2:48	92	3:50	—	4:10	6:40	7:38-8:08
2:34	38	58	77	1:56	42	63	85	2:07	2:50	93	3:53	—	4:13	6:44	7:42-8:12
2:36	39	59	78	1:58	43	64	86	2:09	2:52	94	3:55	—	4:15	6:48	7:46-8:16
2:38	39	59	79	1:59	43	65	87	2:10	2:54	95	3:58	—	4:18	6:52	7:50-8:20
2:40	40	60	80	2:00	44	66	88	2:12	2:56	96	4:00	—	4:20	6:56	7:54-8:24
2:42	40	61	81	2:02	44	67	89	2:14	2:58	97	4:03	—	4:23	7:00	7:58-8:28
2:44	41	62	82	2:04	45	68	90	2:16	3:00	98	4:05	—	4:25	7:04	8:02-8:32
2:46	41	62	83	2:05	45	68	91	2:17	3:02	99	4:08	—	4:28	7:08	8:06-8:36
2:48	42	63	84	2:06	46	69	92	2:18	3:04	1:40	4:10	—	4:30	7:12	8:10-8:40
2:50	42	64	85	2:08	46	70	93	2:20	3:06	1:41	4:13	—	4:33	7:16	8:14-8:44
2:52	43	65	86	2:10	47	71	94	2:22	3:08	1:42	4:15	—	4:35	7:20	8:18-8:48
2:54	43	65	87	2:11	47	72	95	2:24	3:10	1:43	4:18	—	4:38	7:24	8:22-8:52
2:56	44	66	88	2:12	48	72	96	2:25	3:12	1:44	4:20	—	4:40	7:28	8:26-8:56
2:58	44	67	89	2:14	48	73	97	2:26	3:14	1:45	4:23	—	4:43	7:32	8:30-9:00
3:00	45	68	90	2:16	49	74	98	2:28	3:16	1:46	4:25	—	4:45	7:36	8:34-9:04
3:02	45	68	91	2:17	49	74	99	2:29	3:18	1:47	4:28	—	4:48	7:40	8:38-9:08
3:04	46	69	92	2:18	50	75	1:40	2:30	3:20	1:48	4:30	—	4:50	7:44	8:42-9:12
3:06	46	70	93	2:20	50	76	1:41	2:32	3:22	1:49	4:33	—	4:53	7:48	8:46-9:16
3:08	47	71	94	2:22	51	77	1:42	2:34	3:24	1:50	4:35	—	4:55	7:52	8:50-9:20
3:10	47	71	95	2:23	51	77	1:43	2:35	3:26	1:51	4:38	—	4:58	7:56	8:54-9:25

Table created by Jack Daniels' Running Calculator designed by the Run SMART Project.

TRAINING ON 20 TO 30 MILES (32 TO 48 KM) PER WEEK

Phase I.   Phase I involves three Q sessions per week, with **L** runs counting as a Q session. I do not specify which days to schedule the Q sessions because circumstances and weather may affect the days. Feel free to fit in the three Q sessions where appropriate for you.

All non-Q days are for **E** running, and an **E** day can be little or no running if a day off is desired now and then. Use the **E** days to accumulate desired weekly mileage totals. When there is a weekly race, have 2 **E** days before any races and 3 **E** days before championship or equally important races.

Use a recent race time to determine your current VDOT value for setting training paces (see chapter 5 for VDOT details). If no recent races are available, make a conservative estimate of current race time for 1 mile, and consider that to be your **R** pace. Make **I** pace 8 seconds per 400 slower than **R**, and make **T** pace 8 seconds per 400 slower than **I**.

Strides (ST) are light, quick 10- to 20-second runs (not sprints) with 40 to 50 seconds of recovery between. Feel free to perform strides on a gradual uphill course; be careful coming back down between uphill strides. **M** pace is about 20 to 30 seconds per mile faster than typical **E** (**L**) pace.

Phase II.   During phase II, make Q1 each week a 40- to 60-minute **L** run (not more than 30 percent of the week's total mileage) plus six ST, and add six to eight ST (which can be gradual uphill runs if desirable) to the middle or end of two of your weekly **E** runs.

Phase III.   During phase III, make **R** pace 1 second per 200 (2 seconds per 400 and 3 seconds per 600) faster than during the last 3 weeks of phase II training. Set **I** pace based on recent race and associated VDOT values, or make **I** pace 8 seconds per 400 slower than the new **R** pace. **FR** (fast repetitions) are to be 3 seconds per 200, 6 seconds per 400, and 12 seconds per 600 faster than current **R** pace. **T** pace is to be 16 seconds per 400 slower than the new **R** pace (8 seconds per 400 slower than **I** pace). Include eight ST (flat or uphill) during two of your weekly **E** runs. Hard (**H**) is **I**-pace effort.

In any weeks ending in races, eliminate Q3 of the training plan and consider races as replacing Q3 for that week. On low-stress race days (and with adequate time), consider adding 6 × 200 **R** w/200 jg after the final race of the day.

Phase IV.   During phase IV, make **R** pace 1 second per 200 (2 seconds per 400 and 3 seconds per 600) *faster* than during the last 3 weeks of phase III training. The information for phase III applies for phase IV as well.

Table 9.3 summarizes a 24-week training program for 800-meter runners whose weekly training totals 20 to 80 miles (32-48 km) per week.

Table 9.3 800-Meter Training Plan for 20 to 30 Miles (32 to 48 km) per Week

Phase I

Week	Q1	Q2	Q3
1	40-45 min **L** run	20 min **E** + 8 ST + 10 min **E**	20 min **E** + 8 ST + 10 min **E**
2	40-45 min **L**	30 min **E** + 8 ST + 10 min **E**	10 min **E** + 8 ST + 20 min **E**
3	45 min **L**	10 min **E** + 8 ST + 20 min **E**	30 min **E** + 8 ST + 10 min **E**
4	40 min **M** run	40 min **E** + 8 ST + 5 min **E**	10 min **E** + 10 ST + 20 min **E**
5	45 min **L** + 6 ST	20 min **E** + 20 min **M** + 6 ST	20 min **E** + 10 ST + 10 min **E**
6	40 min **M** + 6 ST	40 min **E** + 8 ST + 5 min **E**	10 min **E** + 10 ST + 20 min **E**

Phase II

Week	Q1	Q2	Q3
7	40-60 min **L** + 6 ST	20 min **E** + 6 × 200 **R** w/200 jg + 10 min **E**	10 min **E** + 8 × 200 **R** w/200 jg + 10 min **E**
8	40-60 min **L** + 6 ST	20 min **E** + 4 × 200 **R** w/200 jg + 2 × 400 **R** w/400 jg + 10 min **E**	20 min **E** + 8-10 × 200 **R** w/200 jg + 10 min **E**
9	40-60 min **L** + 6 ST	10 min **E** + 4 × 400 **R** w/400 jg + 10 min **E**	10 min **E** + 4-6 × 200 **R** w/200 jg + 10 min **E** + 4-6 × 200 **R** w/200 jg + 5 min **E**
10	40-60 min **L** + 6 ST	10 min **E** + 3 sets of (200 **R** + 200 jg + 200 **R** + 400 jg + 400 **R** + 200 jg) + 10 min **E**	10 min **E** + 4-6 × 400 **R** w/400 jg + 10 min **E**
11	40-60 min **L** + 6 ST	20 min **E** + 2 × 200 **R** w/200 jg + 2 × 600 **R** w/600 jg + 4 × 200 **R** w/200 jg + 10 min **E**	10 min **E** + 4 ST + 600 **R** + 600 jg + 2 × 400 **R** w/400 jg + 4 × 200 **R** w/200 jg + 10 min **E**
12	40-60 min **L** + 6 ST	10 min **E** + 4 × 200 **R** w/200 jg + 2 × 400 **R** w/400 jg + 1 × 600 **R** + 15 min **E**	10 min **E** + 6 × 200 **R** w/200 jg + 4 × 300 **R** w/300 jg + 20 min **E**

Phase III

Week	Q1	Q2	Q3
13	60 min **L** run + 6 ST	15 min **E** + 5 × 3 min **H** w/2 min jg + 4 × 200 FR w/200 jg + 15 min **E**	10 min **E** + 3 sets of (600 **R** + 30 sec rest + 200 FR + 7 min **E**) + 20 min **E**
14	20 min **E** + 3 × 1 **T** w/2 min rests + 20 min **E**	15 min **E** + 4 × 800 **I** w/3 min jg + 6 ST + 15 min **E**	10 min **E** + 600 **R** + 600 jg + 500 **R** + 500 jg + 400 FR + 400 jg + 2 × 300 FR w/300 jg + 10 min **E**
15	60 min **L** run + 6 ST	15 min **E** + 8 × 2 min **H** w/1 min jg + 1 **E** + 4 × 200 **R** w/200 jg + 15 min **E**	20 min **E** + 3 × 400 **R** w/400 jg + 4 × 300 FR w/300 jg + 10 min **E**
16	15 min **E** + steady 3 **T** + 4 × 200 **R** w/200 jg + 10 min **E**	15 min **E** + 4 × 1K **I** w/3 min jg + 6 ST + 20 min **E**	20 min **E** + 2 × 400 **R** w/400 jg + 2 × 600 **R** w/600 jg + 2 × 300 FR w/300 jg + 15 min **E**

(continued)

Phase III

Week	Q1	Q2	Q3
17	60 min **L** run + 8 ST	20 min **E** + 4 × 4 min **H** w/3 min jg + 10 min **E**	10 min **E** + 4 × 400 FR w/400 jg + 10 min **E** + 4 × 400 **R** w/400 jg + 10 min **E**
18	10 min **E** + 40 min **M** + 6 ST	15 min **E** + 4 × 1,200 **I** w/3 min jg + 6 ST + 10 min **E**	10 min **E** + 3 sets of (600 **R** + 30 sec rest + 200 FR + 7 min **E**) + 20 min **E**

Phase IV

Week	Q1	Q2	Q3
19	45-60 min **L** run + 8 ST	10 min **E** + 4 ST + steady 20 min **T** + 4 × 200 **R** w/200 jg + 10 min **E**	20 min **E** + 600 FR + 1K jg + 600 FR + 1K jg + 600 FR + 15 min **E**
20	50-60 min **L** run + 6 ST	10 min **E** + 4 × 200 **R** w/200 jg + 2 × 1 **T** w/2 min rest + 6 ST + 10 min **E**	20 min **E** + 600 FR + 1K jg + 2 × 400 FR w/400 jg + 4 × 200 **R** w/200 jg + 10 min **E**
21	20 min **E** + steady 3 **T** + 8 ST + 20 min **E**	20 min **E** + 3 × 1 **T** w/2 min rests + 6 × 200 **R** w/200 jg	20 min **E** + 600 FR + 600 jg + 2 × 300 FR w/500 jg + 3 × 200 **R** w/200 jg + 10 min **E**
22	60 min **L** run + 8 ST	20 min **E** + 5 × 1K **T** w/1 min rests + 6 × 200 **R** w/200 jg + 10 min **E**	20 min **E** + 8 × 200 FR w/200 jg + 20 min **E**
23	60 min **L** run + 6 ST	10 min **E** + 3 × 1 **T** w/2 min rests + 6 × 200 **R** w/200 jg + 20 min **E**	20 min **E** + 2 × 200 FR w/400 jg + 2 × 600 FR w/1K jg + 4 × 200 **R** w/200 jg + 10 min **E**
24	50 min **L** run + 6 ST	10 min **E** + 2 × 200 **R** w/200 jg + 2 × 1 **T** w/2 min rest + 2 × 200 **R** w/200 jg + 10 min **E**	20 min **E** + ST + important race day

Table created by Jack Daniels' Running Calculator designed by the Run SMART Project.

154

TRAINING ON 40 MILES (64 KM) PER WEEK

Phase I. Phase I involves three Q sessions per week, with **L** runs counting as a Q session. I do not specify which days to schedule the Q sessions because circumstances and weather may affect the days. Feel free to fit in the three Q sessions where appropriate for you.

All non-Q days are for **E** running, and an **E** day can be little or no running if a day off is desired now and then. Use the **E** days to accumulate desired weekly mileage totals. When there is a weekly race, have 2 **E** days before any races and 3 **E** days before championship or equally important races.

Use a recent race time to determine your current VDOT value for setting training paces (see chapter 5 for VDOT details). If no recent races are available, make a conservative estimate of current race time for 1 mile, and consider that to be your **R** pace. Make **I** pace 8 seconds per 400 slower than **R**, and make **T** pace 8 seconds per 400 slower than **I**.

Strides (ST) are light, quick 10- to 20-second runs (not sprints) with 40 to 50 seconds of recovery between. Feel free to perform strides on a gradual uphill course; be careful coming back down between uphill strides. **M** pace is about 20 to 30 seconds per mile faster than typical **E** (**L**) pace.

Phase II. During phase II, make Q1 each week a 60-minute **L** run (but not more than 25 percent of the week's total mileage) plus six ST, and add six to eight ST (which can be gradual uphill runs if desirable) to the middle or end of two of your weekly **E** runs.

Phase III. During phase III, make **R** pace 1 second per 200 (2 seconds per 400 and 3 seconds per 600) faster than during the last 3 weeks of phase II training. Set **I** pace based on recent race and associated VDOT values, or make **I** pace 8 seconds per 400 slower than the new **R** pace. **FR** (fast repetitions) are to be 3 seconds per 200, 6 seconds per 400, and 12 seconds per 600 faster than current **R** pace. **T** pace is to be 16 seconds per 400 slower than the new **R** pace (8 seconds per 400 slower than **I** pace).

Include eight ST (flat or uphill) during two of your weekly **E** runs. Hard (**H**) is **I**-pace effort. In any weeks ending in races, eliminate Q3 of the training plan, and consider races as replacing Q3 for that week. On low-stress race days (and with adequate time), consider adding 6 × 200 **R** w/200 jg after the race.

Phase IV. During phase IV, make **R** pace 1 second per 200 (2 seconds per 400 and 3 seconds per 600) faster than during the last 3 weeks of phase III training. The information for phase III applies for phase IV as well. Table 9.4 summarizes a 24-week training program for 800-meter runners whose weekly training totals about 40 miles (64 km) per week.

Table 9.4 800-Meter Training Plan for 40 Miles (64 km) per Week

Phase I

Week	Q1	Q2	Q3
1	60 min **L** run	30 min **E** + 8 ST + 20 min **E**	20 min **E** + 8 ST + 10 min **E**
2	60 min **L** run	40 min **E** + 8 ST + 10 min **E**	10 min **E** + 8 ST + 20 min **E**
3	60 min **L** run	30 min **E** + 8 ST + 20 min **E**	30 min **E** + 8 ST + 10 min **E**
4	50 min **M** run	40 min **E** + 8 ST + 10 min **E**	10 min **E** + 10 ST + 20 min **E**
5	70 min **L** + 6 ST	30 min **E** + 20 min **M** + 6 ST	20 min **E** + 10 ST + 10 min **E**
6	50 min **M** + 6 ST	40 min **E** + 8 ST + 5 min **E**	10 min **E** + 10 ST + 20 min **E**

Phase II

Week	Q1	Q2	Q3
7	60 min **L** + 6 ST	20 min **E** + 8 × 200 **R** w/200 jg + 20 min **E**	20 min **E** + 8 × 200 **R** w/200 jg + 10 min **E**
8	60 min **L** + 6 ST	20 min **E** +6 × 200 **R** w/200 jg + 4 × 400 **R** w/400 jg + 10 min **E**	20 min **E** + 10 × 200 **R** w/200 jg + 20 min **E**
9	60 min **L** + 6 ST	20 min **E** + 6 × 400 **R** w/400 jg + 20 min **E**	20 min **E** + 6 × 200 **R** w/200 jg + 10 min **E** + 6 × 200 **R** w/200 jg + 10 min **E**
10	60 min **L** + 6 ST	15 min **E** + 4 sets of (200 **R** + 200 jg + 200 **R** + 400 jg + 400 **R** + 200 jg) + 10 min **E**	15 min **E** + 6 × 400 **R** w/400 jg + 15 min **E**
11	60 min **L** + 6 ST	20 min **E** + 4 × 200 **R** w/200 jg + 2 × 600 **R** w/600 jg + 4 × 200 **R** w/200 jg + 10 min **E**	15 min **E** + 4 ST + 600 **R** + 600 jg + 3 × 400 **R** w/400 jg + 6 × 200 **R** w/200 jg + 10 min **E**
12	60 min **L** + 6 ST	15 min **E** + 4 × 200 **R** w/200 jg + 4 × 400 **R** w/400 jg + 1 × 600 **R** + 20 min **E**	15 min **E** + 6 × 200 **R** w/200 jg + 6 × 300 **R** w/300 jg + 20 min **E**

Phase III

Week	Q1	Q2	Q3
13	60 min **L** run + 8 ST	20 min **E** + 6 × 3 min **H** w/2 min jg + 6 × 200 FR w/200 jg + 15 min **E**	20 min **E** + 3 sets of (600 **R** + 30 sec rest + 200 FR + 7 min **E**) + 20 min **E**
14	15 min **E** + 4 × 1 **T** w/2 min rests + 15 min **E**	15 min **E** + 6 × 800 **I** w/3 min jg + 6 ST + 15 min **E**	15 min **E** + 600 **R** + 600 jg + 500 **R** + 500 jg + 400 FR + 400 jg + 3 × 300 FR w/300 jg + 10 min **E**

Phase III

Week	Q1	Q2	Q3
15	60 min **L** run + 6 ST	15 min **E** + 8 × 2 min **H** w/1 min jg + 1 mile **E** + 4 × 200 **R** w/200 jg + 2 × 200 FR w/200 jg + 15 min **E**	20 min **E** + 4 × 400 **R** w/400 jg + 4 × 300 FR w/300 jg + 10 min **E**
16	15 min **E** + steady 3 **T** + 6 × 200 **R** w/200 jg + 10 min **E**	15 min **E** + 5 × 1K **I** w/3 min jg + 6 ST + 20 min **E**	20 min **E** + 2 × 400 **R** w/400 jg + 3 × 600 **R** w/600 jg + 2 × 300 FR w/300 jg + 15 min **E**
17	60 min **L** run + 8 ST	20 min **E** + 4 × 4 min **H** w/3 min jg + 10 min **E**	20 min **E** + 4 × 400 FR w/400 jg + 10 min **E** + 4 × 400 **R** w/400 jg + 10 min **E**
18	10 min **E** + 40 min **M** + 6 ST	15 min **E** + 5 × 1,200 **I** w/3 min jg + 6 ST + 10 min **E**	10 min **E** + 3 sets of (600 **R** + 30 sec rest + 200 FR + 7 min **E**) + 20 min **E**

Phase IV

Week	Q1	Q2	Q3
19	60 min **L** run + 8 ST	15 min **E** + 4 ST + steady 20 min **T** + 6 × 200 **R** w/200 jg + 10 min **E**	20 min **E** + 600 FR + 1K jg + 600 FR + 1K jg + 600 FR + 20 min **E**
20	60 min **L** run + 6 ST	15 min **E** + 6 × 200 **R** w/200 jg + 2 × 1 **T** w/2 min rest + 6 ST + 10 min **E**	20 min **E** + 600 FR + 1K jg + 2 × 400 FR w/400 jg + 4 × 200 FR w/200 jg + 10 min **E**
21	20 min **E** + steady 3 **T** + 8 ST + 20 min **E**	20 min **E** + 4 × 1 **T** w/2 min rests + 6 × 200 **R** w/200 jg	20 min **E** + 600 FR + 600 jg + 3 × 300 FR w/500 jg + 3 × 200 **R** w/200 jg + 10 min **E**
22	60 min **L** run + 8 ST	20 min **E** + 4 × 1 **T** w/1 min rests + 8 × 200 **R** w/200 jg + 10 min **E**	20 min **E** + 8 × 200 FR w/200 jg + 20 min **E**
23	60 min **L** run + 6 ST	10 min **E** + 3 × 1 **T** w/2 min rests + 6 × 200 **R** w/200 jg + 20 min **E**	20 min **E** + 4 × 200 FR w/400 jg + 2 × 600 FR w/1K jg + 4 × 200 **R** w/200 jg + 10 min **E**
24	50 min **L** run + 6 ST	10 min **E** + 4 × 200 **R** w/200 jg + 2 × 1 **T** w/2 min rest + 2 × 200 **R** w/200 jg + 10 min **E**	20 min **E** + ST + important race day

Table created by Jack Daniels' Running Calculator designed by the Run SMART Project.

TRAINING ON 50 TO 60 MILES (80 TO 97 KM) PER WEEK

Phase I.   During phase I training, for those who are comfortable running around 50 or 60 miles (80 to 97 km) each week, running twice on several days of the week is recommended. This means you may have a second run on the same day as a Q session. When adding a morning run to your schedule, make it a minimum of 30 minutes of **E** running, plus 8 to 10 ST in the middle of, or after, the run.

During phase I, runners can determine whether afternoon runs feel better on the days with or without morning runs. If your daily study or work schedule is very demanding, try adding morning runs to the days when you have adequate rest or recovery time throughout the day. Experiment with which days work best for morning runs; it could be every other day or 2 consecutive days followed by 1, 2, or even 3 days in a row without any morning runs.

The key is to arrange a running schedule that suits you and to use morning runs (or second runs at any time of day aside from the Q sessions) to achieve the desired weekly mileage totals. Always feel free to reduce total weekly mileage in the case of a health problem or undue stress.

The phase I schedule is basically the same as was presented for those running about 40 miles per week, with the exception that distances rather than time durations are listed for the Q sessions. Remember, when no distance unit is listed, assume miles (e.g., 10 **L** = 10-mile **L** run).

Phase II.   During phase II, make Q1 each week the lesser of 10 miles (16 km) and 25 percent of the week's total mileage + 8 ST. Also, add six to eight ST (which can be gradual uphill runs if desirable) to the middle or end of two of your weekly **E** runs.

Phase III.   During phase III, make **R** pace 1 second per 200 (2 seconds per 400 and 3 seconds per 600) faster than during the last 3 weeks of phase II training. Set **I** pace based on recent race and associated VDOT values, or make **I** pace 8 seconds per 400 slower than the new **R** pace. **FR** (fast repetitions) are to be 3 seconds per 200, 6 seconds per 400, and 12 seconds per 600 faster than current **R** pace. **T** pace is to be 16 seconds per 400 slower than the new **R** pace (8 seconds per 400 slower than **I** pace).

Include eight ST (flat or uphill) during two of your weekly **E** runs. Hard (**H**) is **I**-pace effort. In any weeks ending in races, eliminate Q3 of the training plan, and consider races as replacing Q3 for that week. On low-stress race days (and with adequate time), consider adding 6 × 200 **R** w/200 jg after the race.

Phase IV.   During phase IV, make **R** pace 1 second per 200 (2 seconds per 400 and 3 seconds per 600) faster than during the last 3 weeks of phase III training. The information for phase III applies for phase IV as well. Table 9.5 summarizes a 24-week training program for 800-meter runners who are running 50 to 60 miles (80-97 km) per week.

Table 9.5 800-Meter Training Plan for 50 to 60 Miles (80 to 97 km) per Week

Phase I

Week	Q1	Q2	Q3
1	10 **L**	3 **E** + 8 ST + 2 **E**	3 **E** + 8 ST + 2 **E**
2	8 **L**	3 **E** + 8 ST + 3 **E**	2 **E** + 8 ST + 3 **E**
3	10 **L**	3 **E** + 8 ST + 2 **E**	3 **E** + 8 ST + 2 **E**
4	8 **M**	3 **E** + 8 ST + 3 **E**	2 **E** + 10 ST + 3 **E**
5	12 **L** + 6 ST	3 **E** + 3 **M** + 6 ST	3 **E** + 10 ST + 2 **E**
6	8 **M** + 6 ST	4 **E** + 8 ST + 1 **E**	2 **E** + 10 ST + 3 **E**

Phase II

Week	Q1	Q2	Q3
7	10 **L** + 6 ST	3 **E** + 10 × 200 **R** w/200 jg + 3 **E**	3 **E** + 12 × 200 **R** w/200 jg + 3 **E**
8	10 **L** + 6 ST	3 **E** + 8 × 200 **R** w/200 jg + 6 × 400 **R** w/400 jg + 2 **E**	3 **E** + 12 × 200 **R** w/200 jg + 2 **E**
9	10 **L** + 6 ST	3 **E** + 8 × 400 **R** w/400 jg + 3 **E**	3 **E** + 8 × 200 **R** w/200 jg + 1 **E** + 8 × 200 **R** w/200 jg + 2 **E**
10	10 **L** + 6 ST	2 **E** + 5 sets of (200 **R** + 200 jg + 200 **R** + 400 jg + 400 **R** + 200 jg) + 2 **E**	2 **E** + 8 × 400 **R** w/400 jg + 2 **E**
11	10 **L** + 6 ST	3 **E** + 4 × 200 **R** w/200 jg + 4 × 600 **R** w/600 jg + 4 × 200 **R** w/200 jg + 2 **E**	2 **E** + 4 ST + 2 × 600 **R** w/600 jg + 4 × 400 **R** w/400 jg + 6 × 200 **R** w/200 jg + 2 **E**
12	10 **L** + 6 ST	2 **E** + 6 × 200 **R** w/200 jg + 6 × 400 **R** w/400 jg + 2 × 600 **R** + 2 **E**	2 **E** + 6 × 200 **R** w/200 jg + 8 × 300 **R** w/300 jg + 2 **E**

Phase III

Week	Q1	Q2	Q3
13	10 **L** + 8 ST	3 **E** + 7 × 3 min **H** (or 6 × 1K **I**) w/2 min jg + 6 × 200 FR w/200 jg + 2 **E**	3 **E** + 4 sets of (600 **R** + 30 sec rest + 200 FR + 1 **E**) + 3 **E**
14	2 **E** + 5 × 1 **T** w/2 min rests + 2 **E**	2 **E** + 8 × 800 **I** w/2 min jg + 6 ST + 2 **E**	2 **E** + 600 **R** + 600 jg + 500 **R** + 500 jg + 400 FR + 400 jg + 3 × 300 FR w/300 jg + 2 **E**

(continued)

Table 9.5   800-Meter Training Plan for 50 to 60 Miles (80 to 97 km) per Week   *(continued)*

Phase III

Week	Q1	Q2	Q3
15	10 **L** + 8 ST	2 **E** + 10 × 2 min **H** w/1 min jg + 1 **E** + 4 × 200 **R** w/200 jg + 4 × 200 FR w/200 jg + 2 **E**	3 **E** + 6 × 400 **R** w/400 jg + 4 × 300 FR w/300 jg + 2 **E**
16	2 **E** + steady 3 **T** + 6 × 200 **R** w/200 jg + 2 **E**	2 **E** + 6 × 1K **I** w/3 min jg + 6 ST + 3 **E**	3 **E** + 2 × 400 **R** w/400 jg + 4 × 600 **R** w/600 jg + 2 × 300 FR w/300 jg + 2 **E**
17	10 **L** + 8 ST	3 **E** + 5 × 4 min **H** w/3 min jg + 2 **E**	3 **E** + 4 × 400 FR w/400 jg + 10 min **E** + 4 × 400 **R** w/400 jg + 2 **E**
18	2 **E** + 8 **M** + 6 ST	2 **E** + 6 × 1,200 **I** w/3 min jg + 6 ST + 2 **E**	2 **E** + 4 sets of (600 **R** + 30 sec rest + 200 FR + 1 **E**) + 3 **E**

Phase IV

Week	Q1	Q2	Q3
19	10 **L** + 8 ST	2 **E** + 4 ST + 3 **T** + 8 × 200 **R** w/200 jg + 2 **E**	3 **E** + 600 FR + 1K jg + 600 FR + 1K jg + 600 FR + 3 **E**
20	10 **L** + 6 ST	2 **E** + 8 × 200 **R** w/200 jg + 3 × 1 **T** w/2 min rests + 6 ST + 2 **E**	3 **E** + 600 FR + 1K jg + 2 × 400 FR w/400 jg + 6 × 200 FR w/200 jg + 2 **E**
21	3 **E** + 3 **T** + 8 ST + 3 **E**	3 **E** + 5 × 1 **T** w/2 min rests + 8 × 200 **R** w/200 jg + 2 **E**	3 **E** + 600 FR + 600 jg + 4 × 300 FR w/500 jg + 4 × 200 **R** w/200 jg + 2 **E**
22	10 **L** + 8 ST	3 **E** + 5 × 1 **T** w/1 min rests + 10 × 200 **R** w/200 jg + 2 **E**	3 **E** + 6 × 200 FR w/200 jg + 1 **E** + 4 × 200 FR w/200 jg + 3 **E**
23	10 **L** + 6 ST	2 **E** + 3 × 1 **T** w/2 min rests + 6 × 200 **R** w/200 jg + 3 **E**	3 **E** + 4 × 200 FR w/400 jg + 2 × 600 FR w/1K jg + 4 × 200 **R** w/200 jg + 2 **E**
24	8 **L** + 6 ST	2 **E** + 4 × 200 **R** w/200 jg + 2 × 1 **T** w/2 min rest + 2 × 200 **R** w/200 jg + 2 **E**	3 **E** + ST + important race day

Table created by Jack Daniels' Running Calculator designed by the Run SMART Project.

10

....

1,500 to 2-Mile Training

Never miss a chance to tell your teammates
how good they look running.

....

As is true for many 800 runners who also race seriously over the 1,500 meter and mile distances, so do many 1,500 and mile runners race seriously over the 3K and 2-mile distances, so I propose a four-phase training plan that covers races from 1,500 to 2 miles. Some 1,500 runners are equally dedicated to racing the 800 (and the 1,000-meter distance during indoor seasons), and the training I outline in this chapter will do a good job of preparing runners for a variety of middle-distance events.

The 1,500 is a demanding aerobic event that also relies a great deal on speed and anaerobic energy systems, and the intensity of a hard-raced 1,500 requires an effort that is about 10 to 12 percent higher than an athlete's $v\dot{V}O_2max$, which I explain in chapter 3. The 3,000 and 2-mile distances are run right at an athlete's $v\dot{V}O_2max$, about the speed used during demanding **I** training sessions.

In plotting out a season of training for these events, I start phase I training pretty much the same as I do for the 800, with a good amount of **E** running plus some strides (ST) or uphill runs several times a week.

In races that last about 4 to 12 minutes, runners tend to get going too fast, too soon, so I strongly encourage runners to almost overdo going out cautiously. One approach to racing the 1,500 or mile, when trying for a good time (and tactics and adverse weather conditions are not of major concern), is to run the first lap conservatively and to make the second lap about 2 seconds faster than the first. This works well because it is very common for younger runners to go out several seconds too fast, which results in the second lap being quite a bit slower than the first.

If you watch a lot of mile races, you may have noticed that the third lap is often very equal to what the second lap was, and so going out fast with a major slowdown on lap two usually leads to a slow lap three and a missed

Tony Marshall/Press Association Images

Elite 1,500-meter runners like Hicham El Guerrouj rely on both speed and anaerobic energy to excel in an event that requires an effort 10 to 12 percent higher than an athlete's v$\dot{V}O_2$max.

opportunity for a good time. However, a more cautious first lap and a focused effort for a faster second lap often leads to a good third lap, and then it is just a matter of hanging on for that final lap. As is true for racing over any distance, it is good to try a variety of approaches to see what is best for you.

I have known many 1,500 and mile runners over the years, and I have made a point of asking how many of them like racing over shorter distances and how many prefer racing over longer distances, compared with the distance of their best event. It turns out they like doing both shorter and longer races, with a little more dedication to racing shorter. Certainly racing the mile makes the pace of a 2-mile race seem relatively comfortable, and racing a 2 mile or 3K makes a 1,500 or mile seem like a fairly short event.

PHASE I

Phase I in any of the programs I recommend is the time to work on easy mileage, to add some strides (ST) to easy days of running, and to be involved in some supplemental training (e.g., some light resistance training or circuit training). Try to avoid running immediately after supplemental exercises; it is better to either run before this other work or several hours afterward.

Since phase I is primarily **E** runs and nontimed running, it is easy for just about everyone to do this phase of training on his own, when it best fits into the daily schedule. Obviously, in a school team situation, usually all runners will be training at the same time. In this case it is important to divide the team into groups of equal fitness and ability so the not-so-fit runners aren't trying to keep up with others who are in much better shape and set a pace that is too demanding.

PHASE II

I start injecting some Q (quality) sessions into the program in this phase of training, as is typical in all the training programs I put together. These Q sessions include a weekly **L** run and a couple **R** workouts each week. Occasionally, runners can start with phase II of training if they have just come off of a season and are in good aerobic shape. For example, for runners who have just completed a fall cross country season of training and racing, that season has eliminated the need for a phase I, and this is a good time to go back to concentrating on **R** workouts, as is normal for my phase II training programs. End-of-season cross country runners are in top aerobic shape, and some time spent working on speed and economy will set them up well for an indoor track season, which normally involves racing over shorter distances.

In addition, **R** training is usually less stressful on the body than **I** training. Middle- and long-distance runners often look forward to spending some time with repetition training, seeing it as a break from the demands of intervals and important races over distances of 5 to 12 kilometers.

PHASE III

I believe phase III is the most demanding phase of the entire season. Along with the more stressful **I** workouts, I like to schedule weekly **T** sessions, which are good at improving endurance. It could be said that this period of training will determine how much better any runner is going to get in the season.

Being willing and able to handle the **I** sessions without trying to overdo anything is the key to improvement during this tough phase of training. It's always good to remember that the goal of **I** workouts is to achieve the maximum benefit from the least amount of work, and this definitely means relying on the training speeds your recent races have provided through the VDOT tables.

PHASE IV

During a competitive track season, it is sometimes hard to not overdo the racing. For runners who are specialists over 1,500, mile, 3K, and 2-mile distances, the key is to vary the race distances and to be willing to adjust the training schedule during weeks when you have several races. Try to think of 400, 800, and 1,000-meter (and even 1,500 and mile) races as stressing your anaerobic and speed capabilities more than do 3K and 2-mile races. So, take advantage of racing a variety of distances, which is a definite opportunity during track season (unlike the cross country season, when every race is about the same in duration).

Always be willing to vary scheduled workouts, especially during outdoor seasons, when weather conditions can have a major effect on what training will work best, both mentally and physiologically. Also, be willing to eliminate a scheduled training session if having two Q days in the same week will bring you into an important Friday or Saturday race not adequately recovered. It might be worth considering one of the special high-stress workouts shown in appendix D, but don't add one of these in the days before an important race. These high-stress workouts should be experimented with during less important times in the season.

TRAINING ON 30 MILES (48 KM) PER WEEK

Phase I.   Even though each week includes three Q sessions in phase I, none of the Q sessions are at all demanding, and I list them as Q sessions only because there is more than just an **E** run involved in each. One Q session is a relatively long **M**-pace run, and the other two Q sessions include some strides (ST), which are 15- to 20-second light, quick runs that can be done on the flat or up a gradual hill if available, but they are not meant to be all-out sprints in nature. If doing strides on a hill, try to finish the final two on a flat area or track so you can feel good leg turnover and light, quick movement. Always take full recoveries between all strides, whether uphill or on the flat.

When asked to run at **M** pace, just make that about 20 to 30 seconds per mile faster than you typically go in **E** and **L** runs. On all non-Q days, just take an **E** run of at least 30 minutes. Use **E** days to accumulate your desired weekly mileage; an **E** day may be no running if you can get in your weekly mileage without having to run every day. If you have not been running for a period of weeks before starting phase I, select the minimum amount of running recommended in the schedule.

Phase II.   During phase II, each week should have an **L** run, usually on Sunday, but you could also add several miles to the end of a Saturday session if Saturday was not a stress day. For people running approximately 30 miles (48 km) per week, **L** runs should be 30 percent of weekly mileage; if the day after an **L** run is an **E** day of training, add six to eight ST to the end of that **E** day. Also, add six to eight ST to the end of two other **E** days of training each week. As usual, these strides can be on the flat or up a gradual hill, but be careful coming down from all uphill strides.

Try to have 2 **E** days between the mid-week 2 Q days scheduled each week. Every second or third week, if all is going well, it would be OK to add an additional Q session to the week; if you do this, I recommend repeating Q1 as the additional Q session. In any week that you do have three mid-week Q sessions, the best days might be Monday, Thursday, and Friday, which would leave Saturday or Sunday for the weekly **L** run. In weeks with just two mid-week Q sessions, either Monday and Thursday or Tuesday and Friday would be the best approach. Base **R** pace on a conservative estimate of what you think you could currently race for 1 mile.

Phase III.   In phase III, increase **R** pace by 1 second per 200, 2 seconds per 400, and 3 seconds per 600, compared with the speeds you were using in phase II. If that is going well, increase another 1 second per 200 after finishing the 3rd week of phase III. Either set **I** pace based on a recent race VDOT or as 6 seconds per 400 slower than the **R** pace you have been handling well.

It is common to start having some races (as additional Q sessions) during this phase of training. During any weeks ending with a race, have mid-week Q sessions on Monday and Wednesday when a race comes Saturday and on Monday and Tuesday for a Friday race. On relatively easy race days, consider following your final race of the day with 6 x 200 **R** w/200 jg to end that day's session.

Phase IV.   In phase IV, adjust training paces according to recent race-predicted VDOT values, or if there have been no races to judge by, increase all training paces by 1 second per 400 of distance run. It is usual to have a weekend race most weeks of this training phase, so in weeks 19, 20, and 22, schedule Q2 and Q3 on Monday and Wednesday for Saturday races and on Monday and Tuesday for Friday races. Going with back-to-back Q days is often better than having an **E** day between two Q days, so I definitely suggest trying some back-to-back Q days (even Tuesday and Wednesday before a Saturday race). Table 10.1 summarizes the 4 phases of a 24-week training program for 1,500-meter to 2-mile runners who total about 30 miles (48 km) per week.

Table 10.1   1,500-Meter to 2-Mile Training Plan for 30 miles (48 km) per Week

Phase I		
Week	**Q1**	**Q2**	**Q3**
1	40-60 min **L**	20 min **E** + 8 ST + 20 min **E**	20 min **E** + 8 ST + 10 min **E**
2	40-60 min **L**	30 min **E** + 8 ST + 10 min **E**	10-20 min **E** + 8 ST + 20 min **E**
3	45 min **L**	20 min **E** + 8 ST + 20 min **E**	20-30 min **E** + 8 ST + 10 min **E**
4	40 min **M**	30 min **E** + 8 ST + 10 min **E**	20 min **E** + 10 ST + 20 min **E**
5	40-60 min **L** + 6 ST	20 min **E** + 20 min **M** + 6 ST	20 min **E** + 10 ST + 10 min **E**
6	40 min **M** + 6 ST	30-40 min **E** + 8 ST + 10 min **E**	10-20 min **E** + 10 ST + 20 min **E**

Phase II		
Week	**Q1**	**Q2**	**Q3**
7	20 min **E** + 8 × 200 **R** w/200 jg + 10 min **E**	10 min **E** + 10 × 200 **R** w/200 jg + 20 min **E**	—
8	20 min **E** +2 × 200 **R** w/200 jg + 4 × 400 **R** w/400 jg + 10 min **E**	20 min **E** + 10 × 200 **R** w/200 jg + 10 min **E**	—

(continued)

Table 10.1   1,500-Meter to 2-Mile Training Plan for 30 miles (48 km) per Week   *(continued)*

Phase II

Week	Q1	Q2	Q3
9	10 min **E** + 2 × 200 **R** w/200 jg + 6 × 400 **R** w/400 jg + 10 min **E**	10 min **E** + 6 × 200 **R** w/200 jg + 10 min **E** + 4 × 200 **R** w/200 jg + 10 min **E**	—
10	20 min **E** + 3 sets of (200 **R** + 200 jg + 200 **R** + 400 jg + 400 **R** + 200 jg) + 10 min **E**	10 min **E** + 6 × 400 **R** w/400 jg + 2 × 200 **R** w/200 jg + 10 min **E**	—
11	20 min **E** + 4 × 200 **R** w/200 jg + 2 × 600 **R** w/600 jg + 4 × 200 **R** w/200 jg + 10 min **E**	10 min **E** + 4 ST + 600 **R** + 600 jg + 2 × 400 **R** w/400 jg + 4 × 200 **R** w/200 jg + 20 min **E**	—
12	10 min **E** + 2 × 200 **R** w/200 jg + 2 × 400 **R** w/400 jg + 2 × 600 **R** w/600 jg + 15 min **E**	10 min **E** + 6 × 200 **R** w/200 jg + 4 × 300 **R** w/300 jg + 20 min **E**	—

Phase III

Week	Q1	Q2	Q3
13	60-70 min **L** + 8 ST	10 min **E** + 16 × 200 **R** w/200 jg + 1 **E**	20 min **E** + 4 × 600 **R** w/600 jg + 4 × 200 **R** w/200 jg + 15 min **E**
14	10 min **E** + 8 × 400 **R** w/400 jg + 20 min **E**	15 min **E** + 4 × 800 **I** w/3 min jg + 6 ST + 15 min **E**	20 min **E** + 3 × 1 **T** w/2 min rests + 20 min **E**
15	60- 70 min **L** + 8 ST	20 min **E** + 4 × 600 **R** w/600 jg + 4 × 200 **R** w/200 jg + 10 min **E**	15 min **E** + 8 × 2 min **H** w/1 min jg + 1 mile **E** + 4 × 200 **R** w/200 jg + 15 min **E**
16	20 min **E** + 8 × 400 **R** w/400 jg + 15 min **E**	20 min **E** + 4 × 1K **I** w/3 min jg + 6 ST + 15 min **E**	15 min **E** + steady 3 **T** + 6 × 200 **R** w/200 jg + 10 min **E**
17	60-70 min **L** + 8 ST	20 min **E** + 4 × 600 **R** w/600 jg + 4 × 200 **R** w/200 jg + 10 min **E**	10 min **E** + 4 × 800 **I** w/400 jg + 4 × 200 **R** w/200 jg + 20 min **E**
18	20 min **E** + 2 × 600 **R** w/600 jg + 3 × 400 **R** w/400 jg + 4 × 200 **R** w/200 jg + 10 min **E**	15 min **E** + 4 × 1,200 **I** w/3 min jg + 6 ST + 10 min **E**	10 min **E** + 4 × 1 **T** w/1 min rests + 4 × 200 **R** w/200 jg + 10 min **E**

Phase IV

Week	Q1	Q2	Q3
19	60 min **L** + 8 ST	10 min **E** + 4 × 600 **R** w/600 jg + 15 min **E**	20 min **E** + 2 **T** + 4 × 200 **R** w/200 jg + 2 × 1 **T** w/1 min rests + 4 × 200 **R** w/200 jg + 10 min **E**
20	60 min **L** + 6 ST	10 min **E** + 2 × 600 **R** w/1K jg + 2 × 400 **R** w/400 jg + 4 × 200 **R** w/200 jg + 10 min **E**	20 min **E** + 4 × 200 **R** w/200 jg + 4 × 400 **R** w/400 jg + 6 ST + 10 min **E**

		Phase IV	
Week	**Q1**	**Q2**	**Q3**
21	20 min **E** + steady 3 **T** + 8 ST + 20 min **E**	20 min **E** + 600 **R** + 600 jg + 2 × 400 **R** w/400 jg + 4 × 200 **R** w/200 jg + 10 min **E**	20 min **E** + 3 × 1 **T** w/2 min rests + 6 × 200 **R** w/200 jg (skip this if weekend race coming)
22	60 min **L** + 8 ST	20 min **E** + 8 × 400 **R** w/400 jg + 10 min **E**	20 min **E** + 3 × 1 **T** w/1 min rests + 8 × 200 **R** w/200 jg + 10 min **E**
23	10 min **E** + 4 × 1 **T** w/1 min rests + 4 × 200 **R** w/200 jg + 10 min **E**	20 min **E** + 2 sets of (1 **T** + 400 jg + 4 × 200 **R** w/200 jg) + 1 **E**	10 min **E** + 2 × 1K **I** w/3 min jg + 4 × 400 **R** w/400 jg + 15 min **E** (skip this if big race coming)
24	50 min **L** + 6 ST	10 min **E** + 2 × 200 **R** w/200 jg + 2 × 1 **T** w/2 min rests + 2 × 200 **R** w/200 jg + 10 min **E**	20 min **E** + ST + important race day

Table created by Jack Daniels' Running Calculator designed by the Run SMART Project.

TRAINING ON 45 MILES (72 KM) PER WEEK

Phase I.   Even though each week includes three Q sessions in phase I, none of the Q sessions are at all demanding, and I list them as Q sessions only because there is more than just an **E** run involved in each. One Q session is a relatively long **M**-pace run, and some of the other two Q sessions include some repetitions or strides (ST). Strides are 15- to 20-second light, quick runs that can be done on the flat or up a gradual hill if available, but they are *not* meant to be all-out sprints in nature. If doing strides on a hill, try to finish the final two on a flat area or track so you can feel good leg turnover and light, quick movement. Always take full recoveries between all strides, whether uphill or on the flat.

When asked to run at **M** pace, just make that about 20 to 30 seconds per mile faster than you typically go in **E** and **L** runs. On all non-Q days, just take an **E** run of at least 30 minutes. Use **E** days to accumulate your desired weekly mileage; an **E** day may be no running if you can get in your weekly mileage without having to run every day. It is assumed that any runners following this schedule have been running regularly for some weeks, and so the distances suggested are not too demanding.

Phase II.   During phase II, each week should have an **L** run, usually on Sunday, but you could also add several miles to the end of a Saturday session if Saturday was not a stress day. For people running approximately 45 miles (72 km) per week, **L** runs should be 25 percent of weekly mileage; if the day after an **L** run is an **E** day of training, add six to eight ST to the end of that **E** day. Also, add six to eight ST to the end of two other **E** days of training each week. As usual, these strides can be on the flat or up a gradual hill, but be careful coming down from all uphill strides.

In addition to a Sunday **L** run (Q1), there are two other Q days listed for each week; try to have 2 **E** days between these 2 Q days. Every second or third week, if all is going well, it would be OK to add another Q session to the week; if you do this, I recommend repeating Q1 as an additional Q session. In any week that you do have another Q session, the best days might be Monday, Thursday, and Friday, which would leave Saturday or Sunday for the weekly **L** run. In weeks with two Q sessions following a long run, either Monday and Thursday or Tuesday and Friday would be best.

Phase III.   In phase III, increase **R** pace by 1 second per 200, 2 seconds per 400, and 3 seconds per 600, compared with the speeds you were using in phase II. If all is going well, increase another 1 second per 200 after finishing the 3rd week of phase III. Set **I** pace either based on a recent race VDOT or as 6 seconds per 400 slower than the **R** pace you are currently handling well.

It is common to start having some races during this phase of training. When there are races at the end of weeks 14, 16, or 18, eliminate Q1 and have only Q2 and Q3 for that week, placing them on Monday and Wednesday (when a race comes Saturday). Place Q2 and Q3 on Monday and Tuesday for a Friday race. On relatively easy race days, consider adding 6 × 200 **R** w/200 jg after your final race of the day.

Phase IV.   During phase IV, adjust training paces according to recent race-predicted VDOT values; if there have been no races to judge by, increase all training paces by 1 second per 400 of distance run. It is usual to have a weekend race most weeks of this training phase, so in weeks 19, 20, and 22, schedule Q2 and Q3 on Monday and Wednesday for Saturday races and on Monday and Tuesday for Friday races. Going with back-to-back Q days is often better than having an **E** day between two Q days, so I definitely suggest trying some back-to-back Q days (even Tuesday and Wednesday before a Saturday race). Table 10.2 provides a summary of suggested training types and days for a 24-week plan, which can be reduced by some weeks if a full 24 weeks are not available.

Table 10.2   1,500-Meter to 2-Mile Training Plan for 45 Miles (72 km) per Week

Phase I

Week	Q1	Q2	Q3
1	10 **L** + 6 ST	3 **E** + 4 **M** + 8 ST + 2 **E**	3 **E** + 8 ST + 2 **E**
2	10 **L** + 6 ST	4 **E** + 8 ST + 4 **E**	3 **E** + 8 ST + 3 **E**
3	8-10 **L** + 8 ST	3 **E** + 5 **M** + 8 ST + 2 **E**	4 **E** + 8 ST + 3 **E**
4	1 **E** + 8 **M** + 6 ST	2 **E** + 8 × 200 **R** w/200 jg + 3 **E**	3 **E** + 8 × 200 **R** w/200 jg + 2 **E**
5	10 **L** + 8 ST	2 **E** + 8 × 200 **R** w/200 jg + 3 **E**	3 **E** + 8 × 200 **R** w/200 jg + 2 **E**
6	1 **E** + 10 **M** + 8 ST	2 **E** + 8 × 200 **R** w/200 jg + 3 **E**	3 **E** + 8 × 200 **R** w/200 jg + 2 **E**

Phase II

Week	Q1	Q2	Q3
7	—	2 **E** + 12 × 200 **R** w/200 jg + 1 **E** + 2 × 400 **R** w/400 jg + 2 **E**	2 **E** + 6 × 400 **R** w/200 jg + 4 × 200 **R** w/200 jg + 2 **E**
8	—	2 **E** + 4 sets of (200 **R** + 200 jg + 200 **R** + 200 jg + 400 **R** + 400 jg + 2 **E**	2 **E** + 10 × 200 **R** w/200 jg + 1 **E** + 6 × 200 **R** w/200 jg + 2 **E**
9	—	2 **E** + 4 × 200 **R** w/200 jg + 6 × 400 **R** w/400 jg + 2 **E**	2 **E** + 4 × 200 **R** w/200 jg + 1 **E** + 4 × 600 **R** w/600 jg + 2 **E**
10	—	2 **E** + 5 sets of (200 **R** + 200 jg + 200 **R** + 400 jg + 400 **R** + 200 jg) + 2 **E**	2 **E** + 8 × 400 **R** w/400 jg + 2 × 200 **R** w/200 jg + 2 **E**
11	—	2 **E** + 4 × 200 **R** w/200 jg + 2 × 600 **R** w/600 jg + 4 × 200 **R** w/200 jg + 2 **E**	2 **E** + 4 ST + 2 × 600 **R** w/600 jg + 3 × 400 **R** w/400 jg + 4 × 200 **R** w/200 jg + 2 **E**
12	—	2 **E** + 6 × 200 **R** w/200 jg + 6 × 300 **R** w/300 jg + 2 **E**	2 **E** + 5 × 600 **R** w/600 jg + 2 **E**

Phase III

Week	Q1	Q2	Q3
13	5 **E** + 8 ST + 5 **E** + 6 ST	2 **E** + 6 × 800 **I** w/400 jg + 2 **E**	2 **E** + 8 × 400 **R** w/400 jg + 2 **E**
14	2 **E** + 5 × 600 **R** w/600 jg + 4 × 200 **R** w/200 jg + 2 **E**	2 **E** + 5 × 1K **I** w/3 min jg + 6 ST + 2 **E**	2 **E** + 4 × 1 **T** w/2 min rests + 2 **E**
15	10 **L** + 8 ST	2 **E** + 6 × 3 min **H** w/2 min jg + 1 **E** + 4 × 200 **R** w/200 jg + 2 **E**	2 **E** + 5 × 600 **R** w/600 jg + 4 × 200 **R** w/200 jg + 2 **E**
16	2 **E** + 8 × 400 **R** w/400 jg + 2 **E**	2 **E** + 4 × 1K **I** w/3 min jg + 6 ST + 2 **E**	2 **E** + steady 3 **T** + 6 × 200 **R** w/200 jg + 2 **E**

(continued)

Table 10.2   1,500-Meter to 2-Mile Training Plan for 45 Miles (72 km) per Week   *(continued)*

Phase III

Week	Q1	Q2	Q3
17	10 **L** + 8 ST	2 **E** + 6 × 800 **I** w/400 jg + 4 × 200 **R** w/200 jg + 2 **E**	2 **E** + 5 × 600 **R** w/600 jg + 4 × 200 **R** w/200 jg +2 **E**
18	2 **E** + 2 × 600 **R** w/600 jg + 3 × 400 **R** w/400 jg + 4 × 300 **R** w/300 jg + 2 **E**	2 **E** + 4 × 1,200 **I** w/3 min jg + 6 ST + 2 **E**	2 **E** + 4 × 1 **T** w/1 min rests + 4 × 200 **R** w/200 jg + 2 **E**

Phase IV

	Q1	Q2	Q3
19	10 **L** + 8 ST	2 **E** + 5 × 600 **R** w/600 jg + 2 **E**	2 **E** + 2 **T** + 4 × 200 **R** w/200 jg + 3 × 1 **T** w/1 min rests + 4 × 200 **R** w/200 jg + 2 **E**
20	10 **L** + 6 ST	2 **E** + 2 × 600 **R** w/1K jg + 2 × 400 **R** w/400 jg + 3 × 300 **R** w/300 jg + 2 **E**	2 **E** + 4 × 200 **R** w/200 jg + 4 × 400 **R** w/400 jg + 2 × 200 **R** w/200 jg + 2 **E**
21	2 **E** + 2 × 200 **R** w/200 jg + steady 3 **T** + 6 × 200 **R** w/200 jg + 2 **E**	2 **E** + 1,200 **I** + 800 jg + 600 **R** + 600 jg + 1 **T** + 400 jg + 2 × 200 **R** w/200 jg + 2 **E**	2 **E** + 4 × 1 **T** w/2 min rests + 6 × 200 **R** w/200 jg + 2 **E** (skip this if weekend race coming)
22	10 **L** + 8 ST	2 **E** + 4 sets of (200 **R** + 200 jg + 200 **R** + 400 jg + 400 **R** + 200 jg) + 2 **E**	2 **E** + 3 **T** + 1 **E** + 6 × 200 **R** w/200 jg + 2 **E**
23	2 **E** + 3 sets of (1 **T** + 400 jg + 2 × 200 **R** w/200 jg) + 2 **E**	2 **E** + 3 × 1 **T** w/1 min rests + 4 × 200 **R** w/200 jg + 2 **E**	2 **E** + 2 × 1K **I** w/3 min jg + 4 × 400 **R** w/400 jg + 2 **E** (skip this if weekend race coming)
24	8 **L** + 6 ST	2 **E** + 2 × 200 **R** w/200 jg + 3 × 1 **T** w/2 min rests + 2 × 200 **R** w/200 jg + 2 **E**	2 **E** + ST + important race day

Table created by Jack Daniels' Running Calculator designed by the Run SMART Project.

TRAINING ON 60 MILES (97 KM) PER WEEK

For runners who are running 60 miles (97 km) per week, it is normal to assume they will have done a fair amount of running before starting this suggested program. Maybe they have moved up from a lower weekly mileage program or maybe they have recently taken a break from running for a couple of weeks, but they are familiar with doing weekly mileage up around 60.

Phase I.   For those who have been running a fair amount before starting this four-phase program, phase I may not be necessary, and they can go directly to phase II. However, if you are comfortable with higher weekly mileage amounts but have not recently done many quality workouts, it is a good idea to spend some time in the phase I program. It may be only a matter of 2 or 3 weeks in phase I before phase II is more logical.

It is always important to look ahead and see what you will be facing before deciding how advanced you can afford to be in your training program. If you have the time and want to build up to faster running, then go through the phase I program before advancing.

Always consider doing strides (ST) on a gradual uphill path, but also make a point of running the last couple of strides of any set on the flat. Many runners who are running 60 miles per week or more will feel more rested if they run twice on many days of the week. This allows the body to rehydrate and recover between runs, and you are more likely to feel and perform better than if trying to get all your daily mileage into one session.

Phase II.   Phase II introduces a fair amount of **R** training, and usually **R** workouts in the afternoon will feel better if they come several hours after a morning **E** run. For this reason, I am assuming regular morning runs most days of each week, and each morning run should be about 30 minutes and should also include 8 to 10 ST in the middle or at the end. It is better to make these morning-run strides on the flat. Make Q1 of each week (usually on Sunday) a comfortable **L** run of about 10 to 12 miles (16 to 19 km) plus 6 to 8 ST.

Phase III.   In most of my training programs, I like to introduce a fair amount of **I**-intensity running in phase III. The **I** work may involve specific distances at **I** pace or hard (**H**) runs for specified durations of time, and the idea is always to be working at an intensity that is one you feel you could maintain in a race lasting about 10 to 12 minutes.

Phase IV.   During phase IV, adjust training paces according to recent race-predicted VDOT values; if there have been no races to judge by, increase all training paces by 1 second per 400 of distance run. It is usual to have a weekend race most weeks of this training phase, so in weeks 19, 20, and 22, schedule Q2 and Q3 on Monday and Wednesday for Saturday races and on Monday and Tuesday for Friday races. Going with back-to-back Q days is often better than having an **E** day between two Q days, so I definitely suggest trying some back-to-back Q days (even Tuesday and Wednesday before a Saturday race). Use non-Q days and morning miles to accumulate desired weekly mileage totals. Table 10.3 summarizes the recommended workouts associated with the 4 phases of training for 1,500-meter to 2-mile events for runners who total about 60 miles (97 km) per week. It is OK to reduce the plan by some weeks in each phase if 24 weeks are not available.

Table 10.3 1,500-Meter to 2-Mile Training Plan for 60 Miles (97 km) per Week

	Phase I		
Week	Q1	Q2	Q3
1	10-12 **L** + 6 ST	2 **E** + 4 **M** + 8 ST + 2 **E**	2 **E** + 8 ST + 8 **E**
2	1 **E** + 10 **M** + 6 ST	4 **E** + 8 ST + 4 **E**	6 **E** + 8 ST + 3 **E**
3	10-12 **L** + 8 ST	2 **E** + 5 **M** + 8 ST + 2 **E**	4 **E** + 8 ST + 4 **E**
4	1 **E** + 8 **M** + 6 ST	4 **E** + 8 × 200 **R** w/200 jg + 3 **E**	3 **E** + 8 × 200 **R** w/200 jg + 2 **E**
5	10 **L** + 8 ST	2 **E** + 8 × 200 **R** w/200 jg + 3 **E**	3 **E** + 8 × 200 **R** w/200 jg + 2 **E**
6	1 **E** + 10 **M** + 8 ST	4 **E** + 8 × 200 **R** w/200 jg + 3 **E**	3 **E** + 8 × 200 **R** w/200 jg + 2 **E**
	Phase II		
Week	Q1	Q2	Q3
7	—	2 **E** + 5 sets of (200 **R** + 200 jg + 200 **R** + 200 jg + 400 **R** + 400 jg) + 2 **E**	2 **E** + 5 × 1 **T** w/1 min rests + 6 × 200 **R** w/200 jg + 2 **E**
8	—	2 **E** + 6 × 200 **R** w/200 jg + 4 × 600 **R** w/600 jg + 4 × 200 **R** w/200 jg + 2 **E**	2 **E** + 6 × 400 **R** w/400 jg + 6 × 200 **R** w/200 jg + 2 **E**
9	—	2 **E** + 4 × 200 **R** w/200 jg + 2 × 800 **R** w/800 jg + 4 × 200 **R** w/200 jg + 2 **E**	2 **E** + 4 × 200 **R** w/200 jg + 4 × 1 **T** w/1 min rests + 4 × 200 **R** w/200 jg + 2 **E**
10	—	2 **E** + 5 sets of (200 **R** + 200 jg + 200 **R** + 200 jg + 400 **R** + 400 jg) + 2 **E**	2 **E** + 2 × 800 **R** w/800 jg + 2 × 600 **R** w/600 **R** + 2 × 400 **R** w/400 jg + 2 × 200 **R** w/200 jg + 2 **E**
11	—	2 **E** + 4 × 200 **R** w/200 jg + 3 × 600 **R** w/600 jg + 6 × 200 **R** w/200 jg + 2 **E**	2 **E** + 2 × 400 **R** w/400 jg + 2 × 600 **R** w/600 jg + 2 × 800 **R** w/800 jg + 2 × 200 **R** w/200 jg + 2 **E**
12	—	2 **E** + 4 × 200 **R** w/200 jg + 3 **T** + 800 **E** + 4 × 200 **R** w/200 jg + 2 **E**	2 **E** + 3 sets of (200 **R** + 200 jg + 200 **R** + 200 jg + 800 **R** + 400 jg) + 2 **E**

Phase III

Week	Q1	Q2	Q3
13	5 **E** + 8 ST + 5 **E** + 6 ST	2 **E** + 6 × 800 **I** w/400 jg + 2 **E**	2 **E** + 8 × 400 **R** w/400 jg + 2 **E**
14	2 **E** + 5 × 600 **R** w/600 jg + 4 × 200 **R** w/200 jg + 2 **E**	2 **E** + 5 × 1K **I** w/3 min jg + 6 ST + 2 **E**	2 **E** + 4 × 1 **T** w/2 min rests + 2 **E**
15	10 **L** + 8 ST	2 **E** + 6 × 3 min **H** w/2 min jg + 1 **E** + 4 × 200 **R** w/200 jg + 2 **E**	2 **E** + 5 × 600 **R** w/600 jg + 4 × 200 **R** w/200 jg + 2 **E**
16	2 **E** + 8 × 400 **R** w/400 jg + 2 **E**	2 **E** + 4 × 1K **I** w/3 min jg + 6 ST + 2 **E**	2 **E** + steady 3 **T** + 6 × 200 **R** w/200 jg + 2 **E**
17	10 **L** + 8 ST	2 **E** + 6 × 800 **I** w/400 jg + 4 × 200 **R** w/200 jg + 2 **E**	2 **E** + 5 × 600 **R** w/600 jg + 4 × 200 **R** w/200 jg +2 **E**
18	2 **E** + 2 × 600 **R** w/600 jg + 3 × 400 **R** w/400 jg + 4 × 300 **R** w/300 jg + 2 **E**	2 **E** + 4 × 1,200 **I** w/3 min jg + 6 ST + 2 **E**	2 **E** + 4 × 1 **T** w/1 min rests + 4 × 200 **R** w/200 jg + 2 **E**

Phase IV

Week	Q1	Q2	Q3
19	10 **L** + 8 ST	2 **E** + 4 × 800 **R** w/800 jg + 2 **E**	2 **E** + 3 **T** + 4 × 200 **R** w/200 jg + 2 **T** w/1 min rests + 4 × 200 **R** w/200 jg + 2 **E**
20	10 **L** + 8 ST	2 **E** + 2 × 600 **R** w/1K jg + 2 × 400 **R** w/400 jg + 2 × 600 **R** w/600 jg + 2 **E**	2 **E** + 4 × 400 **R** w/400 jg + 3 × 1 **T** w/1 min rests + 4 × 200 **R** w/200 jg + 2 **E**
21	2 **E** + 1,200 **I** + 800 jg + 600 **R** + 600 jg + 1 **T** + 400 jg + 2 × 200 **R** w/200 jg + 2 **E**	2 **E** + 2 × 200 **R** w/200 jg + steady 3 **T** + 6 × 200 **R** w/200 jg + 2 **E**	2 **E** + 4 × 1 **T** w/2 min rests + 6 × 200 **R** w/200 jg **+ 2 E** (skip this workout if weekend race coming)
22	10 **L** + 8 ST	2 **E** + 4 sets of (200 **R** + 200 jg + 200 **R** + 400 jg + 400 **R** + 200 jg) + 2 **E**	2 **E** + 3 **T** + 1 **E** + 8 × 200 **R** w/200 jg + 2 **E**
23	2 **E** + 4 sets of (1 **T** + 400 jg + 2 × 200 **R** w/200 jg) + 2 **E**	2 **E** + 3 × 1 **T** w/1 min rests + 4 × 200 **R** w/200 jg + 2 **E**	2 **E** + 2 × 1K **I** w/3 min jg + 4 × 400 **R** w/400 jg + 2 **E** (skip this workout if weekend race coming)
24	8 **L** + 6 ST	2 **E** + 2 × 200 **R** w/200 jg + 3 × 1 **T** w/2 min rests + 2 × 200 **R** w/200 jg + 2 **E** (3 days prerace)	2 **E** + ST + important race day

Table created by Jack Daniels' Running Calculator designed by the Run SMART Project.

11

5K to 10K Training

Imagine something good about every race you run,
and learn to be an optimist.

Racing a 5K is very different from racing a 10K, but training can be similar for both these events. In fact, racing some 5Ks will help performance in a 10K, and 10K races make a 5K seem short. As I tend to feel about all race distances, the race actually starts about two-thirds of the way through that particular event. So, in a 5K, you need to be ready to race after the first couple miles, and in a 10K the race really begins at about the 4-mile mark. Up to that two-thirds point, you need to see how relaxed you can be while still sticking with the pace (or competitors) that your plan calls for.

Both the 5K and 10K are primarily aerobic events, with most 5K races performed at about 95 to 98 percent of $\dot{V}O_2$max and 10Ks at about 90 to 94 percent of $\dot{V}O_2$max. To be sure, these are not fun intensities to hold for prolonged periods, and the mental aspect of these distances is certainly important.

In chapter 3 I discuss the physiological systems involved in running, including $\dot{V}O_2$max, running economy, lactate threshold, and heart rate. Both 5K and 10K runners need to make sure their training maximizes aerobic power, economy of movement, and lactate threshold, which requires a good mix of **R** running, **I** training, and **T** running. These types of training are all important, but some runners find more success by concentrating on one of these systems, while others may be better off emphasizing another approach. This means runners must spend a fair amount of time emphasizing each of these systems, with the idea of learning which brings the most return for the time spent doing it.

Figure 3.2 in chapter 3 shows the profiles of three female runners who all raced at about the same speed in a middle-distance event yet varied a great deal in $\dot{V}O_2$max and running economy. Sometimes the difference in physiological values between two runners is a function of inherent capabilities, and other times it is a result of the training that has been emphasized. In any case, each type of training must be included in the program to make sure nothing is being overlooked or underemphasized.

Eric Bretagnon/Flash Press/Icon SMI

Kenenisa Bekele, world and Olympic record holder in both the 5,000-meter and 10,000-meter events, utilizes training that maximizes aerobic power, economy of movement, and lactate threshold.

In the past, it was typical for runners training for a 5K or 10K race to have already spent a fair amount of time training for shorter distances before deciding to move up to a longer track event or road race. That has changed a fair bit in recent years. Many people taking up the sport today register for a 5K or 10K race, or even a marathon, as their first serious event. With this in mind, I present a couple of approaches to training for one of these longer track or popular road races.

When training for any running event, you should schedule some weeks of relatively easy running before taking on more specific workouts, and this initial period of training may have to involve a combination of walking and running. Chapter 14 outlines a conservative approach to training for a first-time marathon that also works well for a runner preparing for her first 5K or 10K event; therefore those who fit into this beginner category should consider the approach outlined in chapter 14. The programs presented in this chapter (chapter 11) apply to runners who have some running background and are interested in moving up to a slightly longer event.

PHASE I

If you plan to start training for a 5K or 10K event and have been recently training for other running events, you can usually consider this other training to be sufficient to allow you to move right on to phase II. If you have had a recent break in training, then I recommend spending 4 to 6 weeks following this phase I program.

As I point out in chapter 2, some basics will serve you well when getting into a season of training. If you are not in very good shape, you do not have to run very hard (or very much) to gain big benefits, so take it easy on yourself. Plan a particular amount of running you think is a reasonable weekly average, and stick with that number for about 3 or 4 weeks before increasing to more mileage.

My suggestion for increasing weekly mileage is to go up 1 mile every 3rd or 4th week for the number of times you run each week. So, if running 5 times each week, go up 5 miles (8 km) when you increase your weekly mileage. If running 2 times each day (14 times per week), then I suggest increasing weekly mileage by a maximum of 10 miles (16 km) after 3 or 4 weeks at your previous mileage.

Since this phase of training is for building up some resistance to injury, when you start increasing the stress of some of your workouts, make sure to be conservative in your approach. Daily runs should be easy, comfortable runs; consider 30 minutes to be a good amount to start with. It is also a good idea to take on some supplemental training, which can be in the form of light resistance work with some weights or light plyometrics. I have had good success with circuit programs, which I explain in chapter 15. When starting any resistance training program, make sure you work first on technique; do not increase the resistance until you are comfortable with relatively light loads.

Three types of run workouts you can do during phase I are **E** runs, light uphill runs, and strides (ST), all of which I have referred to earlier. Make sure any strides you do are not all-out sprints but are light, quick runs that last about 10 to 15 seconds each, with about 45 seconds' rest after each stride.

The same thing applies to any uphill runs you do—keep them comfortable rather than "blasting" up a hill. It is also possible to do some light bounding up a gradual hill, but in any uphill running you do, be careful going back down because it is easy to overdo it and bring on a minor impact injury.

After a couple weeks of **E** running, it is a good idea to include one longer run in each week's schedule. Make this **L** run no more than 30 percent of your total weekly mileage. These **L** runs should be at a comfortable, conversational pace and should be terminated any time you start struggling with mechanics.

Remember to be conscious of your stride rate (go for 180 steps per minute) and breathing mechanics (use a comfortable 2-2 rhythm). To summarize, in phase I of training, do all runs at an **E** pace, include one **L** run in each week, and add 8 to 10 ST to the middle or end of three or four of the **E** runs each week. Also, get going on some supplemental training, with the emphasis being on technique and light resistance.

PHASE II

I always recommend that some **R** training be the first true quality work in this phase of training. Your runs at **R** pace should not exceed 5 percent of your week's total running mileage. To set the speed at which you run your repetitions, make a conservative estimate of how fast you think you can currently race for 1 mile, and make that speed your **R** pace.

If you are going into this phase of training from having recently raced some other distances, use one of those current race performances to identify the associated VDOT value and the proper **R** pace associated with it. You can also use the tables in chapter 4 to determine some **R** sessions and how much to include in each session.

PHASE III

For runners getting serious about 5K and 10K races, this phase of training is very appropriate and can also be demanding. This is where intervals (run at **I** pace) become of primary importance, and intervals are not particularly easy to perform. In each **I**-pace session, the total amount of running you do at **I** pace should not exceed 8 percent of your weekly mileage and not more than 10K regardless of weekly mileage.

Also, two sessions of **I** training are enough for any single week. As far as the proper speed for **I** pace, use a recent race and associated VDOT value; if you have no races to go by, make **I** pace 6 to 8 seconds per 400 slower than the **R** pace you have recently been using.

PHASE IV

Phase IV is that phase of training that should set you up to perform well over 5K and 10K distances. This phase should not be quite as demanding as phase III, and there will not be as much **I** training. The main emphasis now will be on **T**-pace workouts, with some **R** and **I** work added now and then.

If you have the opportunity to race a couple of times during this phase of training, a 5K may be a good tune-up for a more important 5K or for a coming 10K event. If you do have a race or two along the way, make sure to take 2 or 3 **E** days leading up to these races, which will mean dropping at least one of your Q training sessions that week.

I also suggest taking one **E** day after races for each 3K of race distance. So, take 3 **E** days after a 10K and 2 **E** days after a 5K for recovery. More recovery days will be needed if you happen to run a race that is even longer (e.g., 5 **E** days for a 15K).

I am presenting here two 5K/10K training programs but will show only phases II, III and IV, with the understanding that you will have already performed a phase I or are not in need of phase I because you have just completed a period of training and racing for other events.

One program is for runners who will be accumulating about 40 to 50 miles (64 to 80 km) per week, and the other is for those totaling about 60 to 70 miles (97 to 112 km) per week. More or less can be done, but these two plans should provide adequate information for designing a program with higher or lower weekly mileage totals. Remember that **E** days are used to accumulate your weekly mileage goals and can be a day off if needed.

TRAINING ON 40 TO 50 MILES (64 TO 80 KM) PER WEEK

Phase II.   Phase II has a 3-week cycle. Weeks 1 and 4 have an **L** run and two sets of **R** work; weeks 2 and 5 each have an **L** run, an **R** session, and a session including some **T** and some **R** work; and weeks 3 and 6 have an **M**-pace run plus an **R** session and an **I** session. As usual I recommend an emphasis on **R** work but also introduce a little **T** work and occasionally **M**-pace and **I**- or **H**-pace running, the latter of which will get you prepared for phase III.

Phase III.   In phase III, with any coming Saturday race, either move Q2 and Q3 to Tuesday and Wednesday, or for a more important Saturday race, eliminate Q2 and make the Q3 session your Q2 that week (place it on Tuesday).

If you do have some races in this phase, feel free to adjust your training VDOT value as races predict, but don't increase your VDOT any more often than every 3rd week, even if a race result suggests you should. In this phase, I alternate weeks of **L** and **M** runs and place the other two Q sessions on back-to-back days, with an **I** day followed by a **T** or a **T** and **R** day.

Phase IV.   During phase IV, it is assumed there will be some weekend races. If there is a possible Saturday race, follow what is written in the schedule. If there is to be a coming Sunday race, move Q2 to the Wednesday before the race (and have **E** days on Thursday, Friday, and Saturday, leading up to the Sunday race). Include warm-up runs before any Q2 and Q3 sessions. Table 11.1 provides 3 phases of training for races of 5 km to 10 km in distance, and for runners who total 40-50 miles (64-80 km) per week. Although specific days are suggested for Q sessions, days chosen for Q sessions can be rearranged to suit weather or personal demands.

Table 11.1   5K to 10K Training Plan for 40 to 50 Miles (64 to 80 km) per Week

Phase II

Week 1	Q session	Workout
Sunday	Q1	**L** run of the lesser of 25% of week's mileage and 120 min, whichever comes first
Monday		**E** day + 10 ST
Tuesday	Q2	2 **E** + 2 sets of (8 × 200 **R** w/200 jg) w/800 jg between sets + 2 **E**
Wednesday		**E** day + 8 ST
Thursday		**E** day
Friday	Q3	2 **E** + 4 × 200 **R** w/200 jg + 2 × 1 **T** w/1 min rests + 4 × 200 **R** w/200 jg + 2 **E**
Saturday		**E** day + 8 ST
Week 2	**Q session**	**Workout**
Sunday	Q1	**L** run of the lesser of 25% of week's mileage and 120 min, whichever comes first
Monday		**E** day + 10 ST
Tuesday	Q2	2 **E** + 4 sets of (200 **R** + 200 jg + 200 **R** + 200 jg + 400 **R** + 400 jg) + 2 **E**
Wednesday		**E** day + 8 ST
Thursday		**E** day
Friday	Q3	2 **E** + 3 × 1 **T** w/1 min rests + 6 × 200 **R** w/200 jg + 2 **E**
Saturday		**E** day + 8 ST
Week 3	**Q session**	**Workout**
Sunday	Q1	1 **E** + 9 **M** + 6 ST
Monday		**E** day + 10 ST
Tuesday	Q2	2 **E** + 4 × 200 **R** w/200 jg + 4 × 400 **R** w/400 jg + 4 × 200 **R** w/200 jg + 2 **E**
Wednesday		**E** day + 8 ST
Thursday		**E** day
Friday	Q3	2 **E** + 7 × 2 min **H** w/1 min jg + 2 **E**
Saturday		**E** day + 8 ST
Week 4	**Q session**	**Workout**
Sunday	Q1	**L** run of the lesser of 25% of week's mileage and 120 min, whichever comes first
Monday		**E** day + 10 ST
Tuesday	Q2	2 **E** + 4 × 400 **R** w/400 jg + 1 **E** + 4 × 400 **R** w/400 jg + 2 **E**
Wednesday		**E** day + 8 ST
Thursday		**E** day
Friday	Q3	2 **E** + 4 × 200 **R** w/200 jg + steady 3 **T** + 4 × 200 **R** w/200 jg + 2 **E**
Saturday		**E** day + 8 ST

Phase II

Week 5	Q session	Workout
Sunday	Q1	**L** run of the lesser of 25% of week's mileage and 120 min, whichever comes first
Monday		**E** day + 10 ST
Tuesday	Q2	2 **E** + 5 sets of (200 **R** + 200 jg + 200 **R** + 400 jg + 400 **R** + 200 jg) + 2 **E**
Wednesday		**E** day + 8 ST
Thursday		**E** day
Friday	Q3	2 **E** + 4 × 1 **T** w/1 min rests + 4 × 200 **R** w/200 jg + 2 **E**
Saturday		**E** day + 8 ST

Week 6	Q session	Workout
Sunday	Q1	1 **E** + 9 **M** + 6 ST
Monday		**E** day + 10 ST
Tuesday	Q2	2 **E** + 10 × 400 **R** w/400 jg + 2 **E**
Wednesday		**E** day + 8 ST
Thursday		**E** day
Friday	Q3	2 **E** + 3 × 3 min **H** w/2 min jg + 4 × 2 min **H** w/2 min jg + 2 **E**
Saturday		**E** day + 8 ST

Phase III

Week 1	Q session	Workout
Sunday	Q1	**L** run of the lesser of 25% of week's mileage and 120 min, whichever comes first
Monday		**E** day + 10 ST
Tuesday		**E** day
Wednesday	Q2	2 **E** + 4 × 1,200 **I** w/3 min jg + 2 **E**
Thursday	Q3	2 **E** + 4 × 1 **T** w/1 min rests + 2 **E**
Friday		**E** day + 8 ST
Saturday		**E** day + 6 ST

Week 2	Q session	Workout
Sunday	Q1	1 **E** + 10 **M** + 4 ST
Monday		**E** day + 10 ST
Tuesday		**E** day + 8 ST
Wednesday	Q2	2 **E** + 5 × 1K **I** w/400 jg + 2 **E**
Thursday	Q3	2 **E** + 3 **T** + 4 × 200 **R** w/200 jg + 2 **E**
Friday		**E** day
Saturday		**E** day + 8 ST

(continued)

Table 11.1   5K to 10K Training Plan for 40 to 50 Miles (64 to 80 km) per Week   *(continued)*

Phase III

Week 3	Q session	Workout
Sunday	Q1	**L** run of the lesser of 25% of week's mileage and 120 min, whichever comes first
Monday		**E** day + 10 ST
Tuesday		**E** day + 8 ST
Wednesday	Q2	2 **E** + 6 × 800 **I** w/400 jg + 2 **E**
Thursday	Q3	2 **E** + 5 × 1 **T** w/1 min rests + 6 ST + 1 **E**
Friday		**E** day
Saturday		**E** day + 8 ST
Week 4	**Q session**	**Workout**
Sunday	Q1	1 **E** + 5 **M** + 1 **E** + 5 **M**
Monday		**E** day + 10 ST
Tuesday		**E** day + 8 ST
Wednesday	Q2	2 **E** + 4 × 1,200 **I** w/3 min jg + 2 **E**
Thursday	Q3	2 **E** + 1 **T** + 2 min rests + 2 **T** + 1 min rests + 1 **T** + 4 × 200 **R** w/200 jg + 1 **E**
Friday		**E** day
Saturday		**E** day + 8 ST
Week 5	**Q session**	**Workout**
Sunday	Q1	**L** run of the lesser of 25% of week's mileage and 120 min, whichever comes first
Monday		**E** day + 10 ST
Tuesday		**E** day + 8 ST
Wednesday	Q2	2 **E** + 5 × 1K **I** w/400 jg + 2 **E**
Thursday	Q3	2 **E** + steady 3 **T** + 4 × 200 **R** w/200 jg + 1 **E**
Friday		**E** day
Saturday		**E** day + 8 ST
Week 6	**Q session**	**Workout**
Sunday	Q1	1 **E** + 10 **M** + 6 ST
Monday		**E** day + 10 ST
Tuesday		**E** day + 8 ST
Wednesday	Q2	2 **E** + 6 × 3 min **H** w/2 min jg + 2 **E**
Thursday	Q3	2 **E** + 5 × 1 **T** w/1 min rests + 6 ST + 1 **E**
Friday		**E** day
Saturday		**E** day + 8 ST

Phase IV

Week 1	Q session	Workout
Sunday	Q1	**L** run of the lesser of 25% of week's mileage and 120 min, whichever comes first
Monday		**E** day + 6 ST
Tuesday	Q2	3 × 1 **T** w/2 min rests (if coming Sat race); 5 × 1 **T** w/1 min rests (if no race) + 2 **E**
Wednesday		**E** day
Thursday		**E** day
Friday		If no weekend race coming, do Q3 = 6 × 1K **I** w/400 jg + 1 **E**; if race coming, today is **E** day
Saturday		If race today, then Q3 is the race; if no race, today is **E** day
Week 2	**Q session**	**Workout**
Sunday	Q1	**L** run of the lesser of 25% of week's mileage and 120 min, whichever comes first
Monday		**E** day + 6 ST
Tuesday	Q2	3 × 1 **T** w/2 min rests (if coming Sat race); steady 3 **T** (if no race) + 2 **E**
Wednesday		**E** day
Thursday		**E** day
Friday		If no weekend race coming, do Q3 = 5 × 1,200 **I** w/3 min jg + 1 **E**; if race coming, today is **E** day
Saturday		If race today, then Q3 is the race; if no race, today is **E** day
Week 3	**Q session**	**Workout** **(In any of the next 4 weeks with an important race, cut L run to 90 minutes)**
Sunday	Q1	**L** run of the lesser of 25% of week's mileage and 120 min, whichever comes first
Monday		**E** day + 6 ST
Tuesday	Q2	3 × 1 **T** w/2 min rests (if coming Sat race); 5 × 1 **T** w/1 min rests (if no race) + 2 **E**
Wednesday		**E** day
Thursday		**E** day
Friday		If no weekend race coming, do Q3 = 6 × 1K **I** w/400 jg + 1 **E**; if race coming, today is **E** day
Saturday		If race today, then Q3 is the race; if no race, today is **E** day

(continued)

Phase IV

Week 4	Q session	Workout
Sunday	Q1	**L** run of the lesser of 25% of week's mileage and 120 min, whichever comes first
Monday		**E** day + 6 ST
Tuesday	Q2	3 × 1 **T** w/2 min rests (if coming Sat race); steady 3 **T** (if no race) + 1 **E**
Wednesday		**E** day
Thursday		**E** day
Friday		If no weekend race coming, do Q3 = 5 × 1,200 **I** w/3 min jg + 1 **E**; if race coming, today is **E** day
Saturday		If race today, then Q3 is the race; if no race, today is **E** day
Week 5	**Q session**	**Workout**
Sunday	Q1	**L** run of the lesser of 25% of week's mileage and 120 min, whichever comes first
Monday		**E** day + 6 ST
Tuesday	Q2	3 × 1 **T** w/2 min rests (if coming Sat race); 2 × 2 **T** w/2 min rests between (if no race) + 2 **E**
Wednesday		**E** day
Thursday		**E** day
Friday		If no weekend race coming, do Q3 = 6 × 1K **I** w/400 jg + 1 **E**; if race coming, today is **E** day
Saturday		If race today, then Q3 is the race; if no race, today is **E** day
Week 6	**Q session**	**Workout**
Sunday	Q1	**L** run of the lesser of 25% of week's mileage and 120 min, whichever comes first
Monday		**E** day + 6 ST
Tuesday	Q2	3 × 1 **T** w/2 min rests (if coming Sat race)
Wednesday		**E** day
Thursday		**E** day
Friday		If no weekend race coming, do Q3 = 6 × 1K **I** w/400 jg + 1 **E**; if race coming, today is **E** day
Saturday		If race today, then Q3 is the race; if no race, today is **E** day

Table created by Jack Daniels' Running Calculator designed by the Run SMART Project.

TRAINING ON 60 TO 70 MILES (97 TO 112 KM) PER WEEK

Phase II.   Phase II has a 3-week cycle. Weeks 1 and 4 have an **L** run, an **R** session, and an **R** plus **T** plus **R** session; weeks 2 and 5 each have an **L** run, an **R** session, and a session including some **T** work and some **R** work; and weeks 3 and 6 have an **M**-pace run plus an **R** session and an **I** session. As usual, I recommend an emphasis on **R** work but also introduce a little **T** work and occasionally **M**-pace and **I**- or **H**-pace running, the latter of which will get you prepared for phase III.

Phase III.   In phase III, with any coming Saturday race, either move Q2 and Q3 to Tuesday and Wednesday, or for a more important Saturday race, eliminate Q2 and make the Q3 session your Q2 that week (place it on Tuesday).

If you do have some races in this phase, feel free to adjust your training VDOT value as races predict, but don't increase your VDOT any more often than every 3rd week, even if a race result suggests you should. In this phase, I alternate weeks of **L** and **M** runs and place the other two Q sessions usually on back-to-back days, with an **I** day followed by a **T** or a **T** and **R** day.

Phase IV.   During phase IV, it is assumed there will be some weekend races. If there is a possible Saturday race, follow what is written in the schedule. If there is to be a coming Sunday race, move Q2 to the Wednesday before the race (and have **E** days on Thursday, Friday, and Saturday, leading up to the Sunday race). Include warm-up runs before any Q2 and Q3 sessions. Table 11.2 summarizes phases II, III, and IV for 5 km to 10 km runners who total 60-70 miles (97-112 km) per week. Specified days for Q sessions can be changed to deal with weather or personal demands.

Table 11.2 5K to 10K Training Plan for 60 to 70 Miles (97 to 112 km) per Week

Phase II

Week 1	Q session	Workout
Sunday	Q1	**L** run of the lesser of 25% of week's mileage and 120 min, whichever comes first
Monday		**E** day + 10 ST
Tuesday	Q2	2 **E** + 4 × 200 **R** w/200 jg + 6 × 400 **R** w/400 jg + 4 × 200 **R** w/200 jg + 3 **E**
Wednesday		**E** day + 8 ST
Thursday		**E** day
Friday	Q3	2 **E** + 4 × 200 **R** w/200 jg + 4 × 1 **T** w/ 1 min rests + 4 × 200 **R** w/200 jg + 2 **E**
Saturday		**E** day + 8 ST
Week 2	**Q session**	**Workout**
Sunday	Q1	**L** run of the lesser of 25% of week's mileage and 120 min, whichever comes first
Monday		**E** day + 10 ST
Tuesday	Q2	2 **E** + 6 sets of (200 **R** + 200 jg + 200 **R** + 200 jg + 400 **R** + 400 jg) + 2 **E**
Wednesday		**E** day + 8 ST
Thursday		**E** day
Friday	Q3	2 **E** + 5 × 1 **T** w/1 min rests + 6 × 200 **R** w/200 jg + 2 **E**
Saturday		**E** day + 8 ST
Week 3	**Q session**	**Workout**
Sunday	Q1	1 **E** + 10 **M** + 6 ST
Monday		**E** day + 10 ST
Tuesday	Q2	2 **E** + 4 × 200 **R** w/200 jg + 8 × 400 **R** w/400 jg + 4 × 200 **R** w/200 jg + 2 **E**
Wednesday		**E** day + 8 ST
Thursday		**E** day
Friday	Q3	2 **E** + 10 × 2 min **H** w/1 min jg + 3 **E**
Saturday		**E** day + 8 ST
Week 4	**Q session**	**Workout**
Sunday	Q1	**L** run of the lesser of 25% of week's mileage and 120 min, whichever comes first
Monday		**E** day + 10 ST
Tuesday	Q2	2 **E** + 2 × 200 **R** w/200 jg + 10 × 400 **R** w/400 jg + 1 **E** + 4 × 200 **R** w/400 jg + 2 **E**
Wednesday		**E** day + 8 ST
Thursday		**E** day
Friday	Q3	2 **E** + 4 × 200 **R** w/200 jg + 3 **T** + 3 min rests + 2 × 1 **T** w/1 min rests + 4 × 200 **R** w/200 jg + 2 **E**
Saturday		**E** day + 8 ST

Phase II

Week 5	Q session	Workout
Sunday	Q1	**L** run of the lesser of 25% of week's mileage and 120 min, whichever comes first
Monday		**E** day + 10 ST
Tuesday	Q2	2 **E** + 6 sets of (200 **R** + 200 jg + 200 **R** + 400 jg + 400 **R** + 200 jg) + 3 **E**
Wednesday		**E** day + 8 ST
Thursday		**E** day
Friday	Q3	2 **E** + 6 × 1 **T** w/1 min rests + 4 × 200 **R** w/200 jg + 2 **E**
Saturday		**E** day + 8 ST
Week 6	**Q session**	**Workout**
Sunday	Q1	1 **E** + 10 **M** + 6 ST
Monday		**E** day + 10 ST
Tuesday	Q2	2 **E** + 12 × 400 **R** w/400 jg + 2 **E**
Wednesday		**E** day + 8 ST
Thursday		**E** day
Friday	Q3	2 **E** + 2 × 4 min **H** w/3 min jg + 3 × 3 min **H** w/2 min jg + 2 × 2 min **H** w/1 min jg + 2 **E**
Saturday		**E** day + 8 ST

Phase III

Week 1	Q session	Workout
Sunday	Q1	**L** run of the lesser of 25% of week's mileage and 120 min, whichever comes first
Monday		**E** day + 10 ST
Tuesday		**E** day
Wednesday	Q2	2 **E** + 6 × 1,200 **I** w/3 min jg + 3 **E**
Thursday	Q3	2 **E** + 6 × 1 **T** w/1 min rests + 2 **E** (try today, but may move this workout to Fri or Sat if so desired)
Friday		**E** day + 8 ST
Saturday		**E** day + 6 ST
Week 2	**Q session**	**Workout**
Sunday	Q1	4 **E** + 10 **M** + 4 ST
Monday		**E** day + 10 ST
Tuesday		**E** day + 8 ST
Wednesday	Q2	2 **E** + 5-8 × 1K **I** (not to total more than 24 min at **I** pace) w/400 jg + 2 **E**
Thursday	Q3	2 **E** + 3 **T** + 4 × 200 **R** w/200 jg + 2 **T** + 2 **E**
Friday		**E** day
Saturday		**E** day + 8 ST

(continued)

Table 11.2   5K to 10K Training Plan for 60 to 70 Miles (97 to 112 km) per Week   *(continued)*

Phase III

Week 3	Q session	Workout
Sunday	Q1	**L** run of the lesser of 25% of week's mileage and 120 min, whichever comes first
Monday		**E** day + 10 ST
Tuesday		**E** day + 8 ST
Wednesday	Q2	2 **E** + 8 × 3 min **H** w/2 min jg + 3 **E**
Thursday	Q3	2 **E** + 6 × 1 **T** w/1 min rests + 4 × 200 **R** w/200 jg + 1 **E**
Friday		**E** day
Saturday		**E** day + 8 ST
Week 4	**Q session**	**Workout**
Sunday	Q1	1 **E** + 8 **M** + 1 **T** + 2 **M** (make this a nonstop workout, w/no rests between **M** & **T** & **M**)
Monday		**E** day + 10 ST
Tuesday		**E** day + 8 ST
Wednesday	Q2	2 **E** + 4-6 × 1,200 **I** (total not more than 24 min **H** running) w/3 min jg + 2 **E**
Thursday		**E** day + 8 ST
Friday		**E** day
Saturday	Q3	2 **E** + 3 × 2 **T** + 2 min rests + 4 × 200 **R** w/200 jg + 2 **E**
Week 5	**Q session**	**Workout**
Sunday	Q1	**L** run of the lesser of 25% of week's mileage and 120 min, whichever comes first
Monday		**E** day + 10 ST
Tuesday		**E** day + 8 ST
Wednesday	Q2	2 **E** + 7 × 3 min **H** w/4 min jg + 2 **E**
Thursday	Q3	2 **E** + steady 3 **T** + 4 × 200 **R** w/200 jg + 3 **T** + 2 **E**
Friday		**E** day
Saturday		**E** day + 8 ST
Week 6	**Q session**	**Workout**
Sunday	Q1	1 **E** + 10 **M** + 2 **E** + 6 ST
Monday		**E** day + 10 ST
Tuesday		**E** day + 8 ST
Wednesday	Q2	2 **E** + 2 × 4 min **H** w/3 min jg + 3 × 3 min **H** w/2 min jg + 4 × 2 min **H** w/1 min jg + 2 **E**
Thursday	Q3	2 **E** + 4 × 1 **T** w/1 min rests + 2 **T** + 6 ST + 1 **E**
Friday		**E** day
Saturday		**E** day + 8 ST

Phase IV

Week 1	Q session	Workout
Sunday	Q1	**L** run of the lesser of 25% of week's mileage and 120 min, whichever comes first
Monday		**E** day + 6 ST
Tuesday	Q2	3 × 1 **T** w/2 min rests (if coming Sat race); 3 × 2 **T** w/2 min rests (if no race) + 3 **E**
Wednesday		**E** day
Thursday		**E** day
Friday		If no weekend race coming, do Q3 = 6 × 4 min **H** w/3 min jg + 1 **E**; if race coming, today is **E** day
Saturday		If race today, then Q3 is the race; if no race, today is **E** day

Week 2	Q session	Workout
Sunday	Q1	**L** run of the lesser of 25% of week's mileage and 120 min, whichever comes first
Monday		**E** day + 6 ST
Tuesday	Q2	3 × 1 **T** w/2 min rests (if coming Sat race); (if no race, do steady 3 **T** + 2 **E** + 2 **T** + 2 **E**)
Wednesday		**E** day
Thursday		**E** day
Friday		If no weekend race coming, do Q3 = 6 × 4 min **H** w/3 min jg + 1 **E**; if race coming, today is **E** day
Saturday		If race today, then Q3 is the race; if no race, today is **E** day

Week 3	Q session	Workout (In any of next 4 weeks with an important race, cut L run to 90 minutes)
Sunday	Q1	**L** run of the lesser of 25% of week's mileage and 120 min, whichever comes first
Monday		**E** day + 6 ST
Tuesday	Q2	3 × 1 **T** w/2 min rests (if coming Sat race); 3 × 2 **T** w/2 min rests (if no race) + 2 **E**
Wednesday		**E** day
Thursday		**E** day
Friday		If no weekend race coming, do Q3 = 6 × 4 min **H** w/3 min jg + 1 **E**; if race coming, today is **E** day
Saturday		If race today, then Q3 is the race; if no race, today is **E** day

(continued)

Table 11.2   5K to 10K Training Plan for 60 to 70 Miles (97 to 112 km) per Week   *(continued)*

Phase IV

Week 4	Q session	Workout
Sunday	Q1	**L** run of the lesser of 25% of week's mileage and 120 min, whichever comes first
Monday		**E** day + 6 ST
Tuesday	Q2	3 × 1 **T** w/2 min rests (if coming Sat race); (if no race, do steady 3 **T** + 2 min rests + 2 **T** + 1 **E**)
Wednesday		**E** day
Thursday		**E** day
Friday		If no weekend race coming, do Q3 = 8 × 3 min **H** w/2 min jg + 2 **E**; if race coming, today is **E** day
Saturday		If race today, then Q3 is the race; if no race, today is **E** day

Week 5	Q session	Workout
Sunday	Q1	**L** run of the lesser of 25% of week's mileage and 120 min, whichever comes first
Monday		**E** day + 6 ST
Tuesday	Q2	3 × 1 **T** w/2 min rests (if coming Sat race); (if no race do 2 × 2 **T** w/2 min rests between + 2 **E**)
Wednesday		**E** day
Thursday		**E** day
Friday		If no weekend race coming, do Q3 = 10 × 2 min **H** w/1 min jg + 1 **E**; if race coming, today is **E** day
Saturday		If race today, then Q3 is the race; if no race, today is **E** day

Week 6	Q session	Workout
Sunday	Q1	**L** run of the lesser of 25% of week's mileage and 120 min, whichever comes first
Monday		**E** day + 6 ST
Tuesday	Q2	3 × 1 **T** w/2 min rests (if coming Sat race); (if no coming race, run 6 × 1 **T** w/1min rests + 2 **E**)
Wednesday		**E** day
Thursday		**E** day
Friday		If no weekend race coming, do Q3 = 10 × 2 min **H** w/1 min jg + 1 **E**; if race coming, today is **E** day
Saturday		If race today, then Q3 is the race; if no race, today is **E** day

Table created by Jack Daniels' Running Calculator designed by the Run SMART Project.

12

....

Cross Country Training

You don't have control over other runners, nor do they
have control over your running.

....

Several things make cross country a different type of race than is experienced on a track, or even what is experienced in some road races. Cross country races involve large fields of competitors and the footing is varied, from hard surfaces to grass or even mud. In addition, many cross country courses include running up and down hills of various grades. A tough stretch of terrain or a headwind will play a role in how the race is run.

Even though wind is a factor in track races, the wind varies from headwind to tailwind during each lap around the track. In a cross country race, you may have to run against a head wind for several minutes at a time, and how that affects race strategy can be a major factor. You are better off drafting off of others when going into a wind because the same running pace would cost more energy if you are by yourself or leading a group of runners.

In some not-so-well-designed courses, the trail over which you are running may become quite narrow, allowing no more than one or two runners to run abreast, which stretches out the field of runners considerably. Before a cross country race, you will need to consider all the factors you may face. It is important to have an opportunity to go over the course on the day of competition (so you know what situations you will face on that particular day and when you might face them).

When training for cross country, certainly some if not most of the training should be conducted over typical terrain. It is difficult to race over soft footing if all your training has been performed on a track or hard road surface. Try to plan cross country training on surfaces similar to those you will experience in the most important races of the season.

When it comes to **I** training, some runners will get more out of running for durations of time rather than distance, especially if the training route is over difficult or hilly terrain. Trying to hit specific times for designated distances can be rather disappointing if the footing is poor or hilly. In a way this makes **I** training for cross country not unlike **I** training at altitude—rather than being disappointed for not hitting desired speeds for your work bouts, you just know you are working hard for a set amount of time, and that is accomplishing the purpose of the workout.

If a major race is to be conducted over your home course, then make a plan on how best to take advantage of your course in areas that might be difficult for the competition. For example, knowing how you react to a particular hill and what follows that hill can make it easier for you to know when to relax and when to push it a little, without the effort hurting you as much as someone who has never raced that course before.

Setting a team strategy for a race can be a challenge. In some easy races, it can help new runners to try running along with several others—running in a pack, as it is often referred to. Pack running often works very well for the first third or so of a race, at which point the better runners can break away from slower teammates to see how well they can do in the latter stages of the race. Sometimes this approach works to the benefit of both the better runners and those who are less experienced, as it keeps the better runners from going out too fast and helps the slower runners improve in confidence and tactics.

USING A CONSERVATIVE-START APPROACH

A major way that most cross country races vary from track races is how fast the field goes out at the start. It is very common, especially in high school cross country races, that the fastest few runners all go out too fast. They often end up slowing down a fair amount because of their too-fast start, but they still win because everyone else also went out too fast to stay with the pack. So, the winner went out too fast but still wins and therefore decides that going out fast is the best way to win a race. When one of the runners who is pretty good goes out at a more reasonable pace, that runner will beat the better runners who go out too fast.

I have always encouraged a more moderate beginning pace, and I saw the benefits of this approach one year at our national championship meet. I measured off the first 400 meters of the course, and the last thing I asked my women's team to do in preparation for the race was to run a solid 800 meters, going through that first 400 in 85 seconds, which would be about a 17:42 5K if held the whole way. I encouraged them to not go any faster when the race began, which was to be about 8 to 10 minutes after completing that solid 800 warm-up run.

When the race started, my seven runners all went through that first 400 between 84 and 87 and were the last seven runners in the field of more than 180 runners. Some of the front runners went out in under 75, and all others were between 75 and 82 at that first 400 mark. At the first 1-mile mark, one of my runners was leading the entire pack, and she went on to win by more than 20 seconds (with a time of about 17:20). My next few runners placed 5th, 8th, 15th, and 26th, and winning the team title was a cinch.

Following are a few things to keep in mind when using this conservative-start approach:

• Often, especially in high school races, the course narrows very early in the race, and this can make it tough to move past the fast-start leaders. You get squeezed back and often lose confidence that you can still catch up. However, there is usually plenty of time to make a move during the middle mile of the race, even after getting boxed out early, and battling the field to get a front spot early can take a lot of reserve energy that could better serve you later on.

• It is common for relatively young runners who try the slow-start approach to become mentally discouraged when they see a mass of others out in front of them just a couple of minutes into the race. However, if the coach holds practice sessions that involve a conservative start to practice this tactic in some early-season races, these young runners will quickly realize the benefits of such an approach. The day they are more cautious but still confident they will catch up with many of the too-fast starters, there will be a lot of happy runners on the team.

• A tactic that works well is to pass as many runners as possible (even to the extent of counting each runner passed) during the middle mile of the race. I am not particularly impressed with runners who, in the middle of the pack, outkick two or three others in the final 100 meters of a race, because this often means they were not working very hard in the middle of the race. According to my math, passing 20 others during the middle of the race and getting outkicked by 3 runners in the final sprint means you helped your team score by 17 points, whereas not passing any in the middle mile and outkicking 3 at the end means you gained 3 points for your team. Which approach produces the better team score is not hard to realize.

Remember, if you are running with a good number of runners in the middle of a cross country race and you aren't feeling particularly strong, you must realize all those others near you are also feeling as bad as you are or they wouldn't be with you—they would be running on by and leaving you behind.

An additional comment relative to going out fast in cross country races relates to how the initial pace seems to keep getting faster and faster the more important the race is. In other words, a conference race may go out too fast, but a regional championship goes out even faster, and the state or national championship goes out faster again, even if the competition involves the same group of runners you just faced last week. To me this says that controlling your pace at the start becomes more and more important as you progress into the championship portion of the season.

Being surrounded by many other runners is a major part of cross country races.

PREPARING FOR THE RACE

Coaches should not assume all the runners on a team are equal and must all follow the same warm-up routine. It doesn't make a lot of sense for all team members to run together in their warm-up unless they all have equal race times, and even then some do better with more, or less, activity than others.

Does it sound like equal treatment and equal preparation for a 4:30 miler to be going through the same warm-up routine as a teammate whose best mile is 5:30? Ideally, coaches will design a warm-up especially for each member of the team. I sometimes chuckle to myself when I see entire teams, all dressed in their clean team warm-up suits, jogging together, staying within arm's length of each other, then stretching and striding together, all being treated as equal performers.

Each runner and every coach should experiment with a variety of warm-up routines to see which works best for which members of the team. Chances are the entire team doesn't finish each race within a few strides of each other, and they probably don't all respond similarly to the same warm-up approach. Some runners don't feel ready to go until they have run a few miles, while others start getting tired of warming up after a much shorter run.

A warm-up should prepare each participant, both physiologically and mentally, for the task ahead, which means some serious thought needs to be part of the process. For some runners this means being alone, and for others it means running with a group. In my years of coaching, I have experienced athletes who didn't even want to talk or make eye contact with me during the final hour or so leading up to a race, while others wanted my attention right up to the time the gun went off.

A mental approach that works well for some runners is to go over in their minds a race in which they had a particularly positive experience. They remember what made that race so pleasing, and they can rerun that good race in their minds in a matter of 10 or 15 seconds just before the start of any new race. In other words, focus on positive experiences. Sometimes you can even rerun a disappointing race, with changes in the approach that would result in a more positive effort.

What about the physiological warm-up for a race? First of all, weather plays a significant role in the process. Cold weather demands that you wear more clothing until you get the muscles heated up some, but going with minimal clothing is necessary on a hot day so you don't become overheated and dehydrated before the race begins.

Most runners can feel when their muscles are warmed up and when they need a little more time going easy or going hard. It typically takes about 10 minutes for the running muscles to start increasing their temperature. A couple of degrees will aid performance, but increasing muscle temperature more than a couple of degrees can lead to subpar performance. For a relatively long race, you certainly don't want to start the race with body temperature too high or you will quickly become overheated. Just as different runners lose fluids at different rates, so do some warm up more quickly than others, and each member of a team needs to experiment with different warm-up routines to see which works best under different environmental conditions.

Beyond the best warm-up approach is the approach in the race itself, and here it is particularly important to focus on the task at hand. In other words, it is better to think about what you are doing (breathing rhythm and stride rate are two good things to think about) than to be worrying about how much farther you have to go or how far you have gone so far. Don't worry about runners you have beaten in earlier races being in front of you because they may be pacing their races poorly and will pay for it later.

It is also always possible that someone you have beaten earlier is having a particularly great day. You can't judge your race by what others are doing; judge by what you are doing and what you are feeling. Some runners like to charge up hills; I prefer asking my runners to see how little effort they can put into staying with others on uphill runs and then to concentrate on a solid effort after reaching the top of the hill, when others are often backing off to recover. I have told my runners to concentrate on a solid pace while counting 50 foot falls after reaching the top of the hill. After the 50 foot falls, runners have often recovered well from the hill while moving ahead of others.

I often encourage runners to practice using a good 2-2 breathing rhythm for the first two-thirds of their early-season races so this becomes a normal approach during more important races. How you feel or how you perceive your effort in a race is very important, and learning to go by feel helps a great deal in cross country races, especially when faced with varying terrain and maybe wind and mud, which can slow the pace considerably. Again, focus on the task at hand, and don't worry about times you hear along the way; who knows, they may not even be accurate representatives of the distance run.

DEVELOPING A SEASON PLAN

In most school situations, there are only 10 or 12 weeks for an entire cross country season, which certainly doesn't allow for four 6-week phases of training during the season. As I mentioned in chapter 6 in regard to setting up a season, you have a couple of options for dealing with only 10 or 12 weeks for cross country. My preferred approach is to encourage the runners to get all of phase I and phase II completed during the summer, before the start of school in the fall. This makes it possible to go into the third phase of training when school begins.

For those who are new or who didn't get in much running in the summer, it is a must to spend some time in phase I training, with little or no phase II training once school begins. These runners will get in some base work before hitting the more demanding **I** work and early-season races. The training plan I outline in this chapter contains four 6-week phases, with the understanding that parts (or even all) of phase II will be eliminated and a couple weeks of phase I also cut.

It is a must to adjust how much of each type of quality running each runner on the team performs, based on each person's weekly mileage. For example, I limit how much training is done in an **I** session to the lesser of 8 percent of weekly mileage and 10K. A runner who is running 30 miles (48 km) a week is limited to 2.4 miles (8 percent of 30) at **I** pace during any single **I** session; another runner who is totaling 60 miles (97 km) per week can run as much as 4.8 miles (8 percent of 60) at **I** pace in a single **I** session.

I also use a 5 percent rule for **R** sessions and a 10 percent rule for **T** sessions. Keep in mind that these suggested limits are per session, not per week; so if you have two **R** sessions in a single week, each session could go up to the suggested maximum. Also, realize that these percent values are not required amounts but suggested maximums that should not be exceeded.

Phase I

Plan on an **L** run on Sunday of each week, but limit that run to be the lesser of 30 percent of weekly mileage and 60 minutes. For the remaining days of each week, get in a minimum of 30 minutes of **E** running, and make the most you run in any day not more than 25 percent of the week's total mileage.

Runners who haven't been doing much running lately, or who are relative beginners, might consider phase IV of the white plan outlined in chapter 7 as their phase I for cross country season. The following is better suited for runners who haven't had a long break in training and who are not beginners. If you haven't been running for more than 4 weeks, eliminate an **L** run and keep weekly mileage down to about 20 miles (32 km) for 3 weeks and then at about 25 to 30 miles (40 to 48 km) for the next 3 weeks. Table 12.1 lays out a simple phase I training plan; one that can be shortened if 6 weeks are not available, but for relative beginners should be used for at least 3 or 4 weeks.

Table 12.1 Phase I Training Plan for Cross Country

Weeks 1-3	
Day	**Workout**
Sunday	**L** run of the lesser of 60 min and 30% of week's total mileage
Monday, Tuesday, Thursday, and Friday	**E** days of about 30 min each day
Wednesday and Saturday	30-40 min **E** + 6 ST
Weeks 4-6	
Day	**Workout**
Sunday	**L** run of the lesser of 60 min and 30% of week's total mileage
Monday, Tuesday, and Friday	**E** days of about 30-40 min each day
Wednesday, Thursday, and Saturday	20 min **E** + 8 ST + 10 min **E**

Table created by Jack Daniels' Running Calculator designed by the Run SMART Project.

Phase II

All who are training in this phase should have had some consistent running during the past several weeks and should be ready for some light **R** training. Each runner's total weekly mileage for this phase should not be greater than 10 miles (16 km) more than was covered in the final 3 weeks of phase I training. In addition, each runner is to limit the amount of running at **R** pace (in any session of **R**-pace running) to no more than 5 percent of the week's total mileage, or not more than 5 miles (8 km) if doing more than 100 miles (160 km) per week.

Refer to table 4.4 in chapter 4 for choices of workouts based on the amount of weekly mileage accumulated. For example, runners who are getting in about 35 miles per week should select from the **R** sessions listed under category B, and runners getting in about 50 miles a week choose from category C or

D. Use **E** days to accumulate desired weekly total mileage, and if mileage is not very high, an **E** day may be a day off now and then.

R workouts can be performed either on flat terrain or as uphill runs. Consider that uphill running helps improve speed and economy, and if important races late in the season are to be held on hilly terrain, then it is particularly important to make some **R** sessions on a hill. Obviously the speed will be slower on uphill runs, but go by feel and don't worry about how far you run; use time as the measuring factor.

For example, maybe today's workout is an **R** session that involves eight 60-second uphill runs with full recovery during the return to the bottom. Make sure the route back down is not steep because downhill running puts a lot of stress on the legs. I also like to finish a hill **R** session with a few flat **R** runs so the runner gets the feeling of moving fast again after the relatively slower uphill runs. I like to avoid uphill training during the final couple of weeks before an important race, as this usually allows for a little better recovery from the stress of the uphill runs.

I provide three options (**R1**, **R2**, and **R3**) for scheduling Q (**R**) sessions during each week. Try to keep **L** runs down to the lesser of 25 percent of weekly total mileage, and cut any **L** run short if your mechanics are not feeling well.

During any week when there is a race scheduled on Tuesday, if following **R1** or **R3** schedules, switch to **R2** for that week, making Q1 the Tuesday race, and keep Q2 the day after the race and Q3 on Saturday. In any weeks with a Friday race, follow the **R3** schedule, but move Q2 from Wednesday to Tuesday, and the Friday Q3 is replaced by the race. For weeks with a Saturday race, follow the **R2** schedule as it is, with the Saturday race replacing Q3.

In terms of where to train, I strongly recommend doing all Q sessions on the type of terrain on which the more important races of the season will be held—usually grass or dirt. **E** runs and **L** runs can be on roads or smooth paths. If important races are to be run on hilly courses, consider doing one or two Q sessions over partly hilly terrain, but try to always run the final couple of **R**-pace runs on flat footing. Basically, try to have 2 **E** days before any race (consider **L** being **E**-pace running), and during this early part of the season, don't hesitate to do a desired Q session the day after a race. Table 12.2 summarizes the 3 approaches (R1, R2, R3) to training during phase II of the season.

Table 12.2   Phase II Training Plan for Cross Country

Day	R1	R2	R3
Sunday	**L** run	**L** run	**L** run
Monday	Q1	**E** day + 8 ST	Q1
Tuesday	**E** day + 8 ST	Q1	**E** day + 8 ST
Wednesday	**E** day + 8 ST	Q2	Q2
Thursday	Q2	**E** day + 8 ST	**E** day + 8 ST
Friday	Q3	**E** day + 8 ST	Q3
Saturday	**E** day + 8 ST	Q3	**E** day + 8 ST

Table created by Jack Daniels' Running Calculator designed by the Run SMART Project.

Phase III

As I have indicated earlier, phase III is the most stressful of the various training phases, and there are often races thrown into this phase, and races will always replace a Q session in the week of a race. Refer to table 4.3 in chapter 4, and base the amount of running performed in any **I** session on total weekly mileage (which is shown for each of the various **I** workouts listed).

Also, do not include distances of the **I**-pace runs that will make you go longer than 5 minutes per work bout. For example, if a runner has a VDOT that dictates a 6:00 mile pace for **I** runs, don't have that runner run **I** miles; 1,200s would be the longest, but you could go up to 5-minute **H** runs if running more for time than for distance.

Phase III is set aside for a weekly **I** session, so make that session the first Q session of the week, after the **L** run that was performed over the weekend. It is also normal to have a race most weeks during this phase of training, and races are similar in physiological benefit to what is accomplished with a solid **I** session, so I prefer making Q1 the **I** session and Q2 a **T** session that ends with some **R** 200s or strides.

For **T** running during a cross country season, which I like to include during both phase III and phase IV, even though you will be racing over varied terrain, I prefer doing **T** workouts on a flat surface so it is easier to control the pace at which the workout is being run. It is possible to run over undulating terrain and use a heart-rate monitor to keep track of effort, but

I prefer avoiding heart-rate monitors because they do not always reflect the speed desired for a particular workout.

If there is no race scheduled during a week of phase III, then it is OK to include a Q3 if you are feeling good, and the best thing would be either an **I** session based on time (e.g., 5 or 6 × 3 min **H** w/2 min jg) rather than distance (e.g., 5 × 1,000 **I** w/2 min jg), or a combination of **T**, **I**, and **R** (e.g., 2 **T** + 3 × 2 min **H** w/1 min jg + 4 × 200 **R** w/200 jg). My favored schedule during phase III is outlined in table 12.3.

Table 12.3   Phase III Training Plan for Cross Country

Day	Workout
Sunday	**L** run
Monday	**E** day + 8 ST
Tuesday	Q1: **I** session
Wednesday	Q2: **T** session + 4 × 200 **R**
Thursday	**E** day
Friday	**E** day
Saturday	Q3: **T-I-R** or race

Table created by Jack Daniels' Running Calculator designed by the Run SMART Project.

If there is a Tuesday race, that race replaces the scheduled Q1 session, and if there is a Saturday race, that race replaces the scheduled Q3 session. If there is a Friday race, drop Q2 on Tuesday, make Q2 the Friday race, and drop Q3 on Saturday.

Table 12.4 shows an example of how I would suggest plotting a 40-mile week (1) with no race that week, (2) with a Saturday race, and (3) with Tuesday and Saturday races.

Table 12.4   Options for Phase III 40-Mile (64 km) Weeks

Day	No race week	Saturday race week	Tuesday and Saturday race week
Sunday	10 mile **L** run + 6 ST	10 mile **L** run + 6 ST	50 min **L** run + 6 ST
Monday	**E** day + 8 ST	**E** day + 8 ST	**E** day
Tuesday	2 **E** + 5 × 1K **I** w/2 min jg + 2 **E**	2 **E** + 5 × 1K **I** w/2 min jg + 2 **E**	Race day
Wednesday	1 **E** + 4 × 1 **T** w/1 min rests + 2 **E**	2 **E** + 3 × 1 **T** w/2 min rests + 1 **E**	1 **E** + 4 × 1 **T** w/1 min rests + 2 **E**
Thursday	**E** day + 8 ST	**E** day + 8 ST	**E** day + 8 ST
Friday	**E** day	**E** day	**E** day
Saturday	2 **E** + 4 × 4 min **H** w/3 min jg + 2 **E**	Race day	Race day

Table created by Jack Daniels' Running Calculator designed by the Run SMART Project.

Phase IV

There are often weekly races during phase IV training, and these races are usually important, with the need to be relatively rested. In general, for a less important Saturday race, I suggest following the phase III schedule for a week with a Saturday race (table 12.4). For an important Saturday race, I recommend a moderately long Sunday **L** run and a **T**-type workout on Tuesday (table 12.5). All other days are **E** days, and I even tend to stop doing strides after late-week **E** runs. Table 12.5 summarizes the ways of dealing with phase IV training weeks that have no races or those with an important weekend race.

Table 12.5   Phase IV Training Plan for Cross Country

Day	No race week	Important Saturday race week
Sunday	10 mile **L** run + 6 ST	50-60 min **L** run + 6 ST
Monday	**E** day + 8 ST	**E** day + 8 ST
Tuesday	2 **E** + 4 × 1 **T** w/1 min rests + 2 **E**	2 **E** + 3 × 1 **T** w/2 min rests + 4 × 200 **R** w/200 jg + 1 **E**
Wednesday	**E** day + 8 ST	**E** day + 6 ST
Thursday	**E** day + 8 ST	**E** day
Friday	2 **E** + 4 × 1,200 **I** w/3 min jg + 2 **E**	**E** day
Saturday	**E** day	Race day

Table created by Jack Daniels' Running Calculator designed by the Run SMART Project.

In summary, when training for cross country races, keep the following things in mind.

1. Get in a weekly **L** run, preferably on Sunday of each week.
2. Do much of your Q training sessions on grass or dirt trails that are similar to race conditions.
3. Try to get in 2 **E** days of running before most midseason races entered.
4. Make your last Q session before a weekly race mostly of **T** intensity.
5. Remember that races provide similar benefits to **I** sessions.
6. Stop hill work for the last several weeks leading up to important races.
7. Runners should have a reasonable goal for each race entered.
8. Avoid trying to train harder during the final few weeks of the season.
9. Start races conservatively, and be willing to work harder as the race progresses.
10. Focus on the task at hand.

13

Half-Marathon Training

With good nutrition and rest habits, the body's energy stores
will get you through a half marathon.

There is no question that running in a 10K race or a marathon—or even
just following a training program for either of these races—will do a
great job of preparing a runner for a half marathon. However, I truly believe
that optimal half-marathon preparation involves a relative middle ground
between 10K and marathon training.

What I present in this chapter is a four-phase program for runners with
a specific interest in racing a half marathon. Compared with a 10K race, the
pace you will use for a half is a fair bit slower, more along the lines of a
solid **T** (threshold) effort. In fact, elite runners will run a half marathon just
about at their **T** pace, which is about 12 to 15 seconds per mile faster than
their full marathon pace.

A big advantage of a half marathon over a full marathon is that with a
consistent diet, the body will store enough muscle glycogen to provide all the
energy needed to complete the race. So, if you enter a half with good rest and
nutrition, you should be able to make the full 13-plus miles without needing
any additional energy along the way. Intake of fluids, on the other hand, may
be necessary during a half marathon, depending on the weather. It is usually
good to plan on some fluid and electrolyte intake a couple of times during a
half, but this is something you should have first practiced to determine your
rate of fluid loss associated with a variety of ambient temperatures.

PHASE I

As I emphasize in earlier chapters, phase I is for building a base and getting
the muscles, tendons, and cardiovascular system ready for some relatively
demanding workouts. For runners who have been running fairly regularly,
say 5 or more days per week, and accumulating 30 or more miles (48 km)
per week for at least 4 weeks, I recommend moving right into phase II of

Eritrean long-distance runner Zersenay Tadese, current half-marathon world record holder, excels at finding a relative middle ground between 10K and marathon training.

Adam Davy/Press Association Images

the half-marathon program. For those who have not been running that much, I suggest going through a full phase I program as outlined here.

Keep in mind that most of the running to be done in phase I is easy in intensity, which means you should be able to do all your running with a comfortable 2-2 breathing rhythm, and of course stride rate should be up around the desired 180 steps per minute. Phase I is a good time to concentrate on stride rate and breathing if you have not done so in previous training programs.

The only variation I add to **E** runs during phase I is some light strides, which are 10- to 15-second runs at about the pace you estimate to be current 1-mile race pace. There's no need to go out and race a mile to find this pace because the speed is not that important, and it is better to underestimate rather than overestimate your current mile racing fitness. Take about 45 seconds' recovery between strides so each one feels as comfortable as the previous one.

With the assumption that you have been doing some running at least 3 days each week, I recommend that starting with phase I you make an effort to run 5 days each week, 6 or 7 days if possible. Also, set 30 miles (48 km) per week as your initial weekly mileage goal. If you have been doing more than 30 per week, then stay with what you have been averaging, but consider the following—each week get in one **L** run, which I recommend to be the lesser of 25 percent of your weekly mileage and 150 minutes. Also, add 10 strides to the middle, or at the end, of 3 of your **E** days each week. In fact, one of your sets of strides can be during, or at the end of, your weekly **L** run, if that works well for you.

If you were doing 30 miles per week at the start of phase I, try moving up to 35 miles (56 km) after the first 4 weeks of phase I. If your initial weekly mileage in phase I is not more than 50 miles (80 km) per week, I suggest increasing weekly mileage about every 4th week throughout phases I and II. Try increasing weekly mileage by 1 mile (1.6 km) for every running session you do each week (1 run on 4 days each week and 2 runs on 3 days each week total 10 runs, meaning your weekly mileage can go up 10 miles [16 km]), but don't increase by more than 10 miles regardless of the number of sessions you are running per week. Also, there is no need to go over 80 miles (129 km) per week, unless you are already used to that and may be planning for a marathon in the not-too-distant future.

PHASE II

As with other programs in earlier chapters, phase II includes some serious **R**-pace runs (table 13.1). If you have run races in the past month or two and training has not been interrupted in that time, then use a recent race to identify the proper pace for your **R** workouts. If you don't have any recent races to go by, make a reasonable conservative estimate of current mile race pace, and use that pace for your **R** workouts.

How much you run at **R** pace is determined by how much total running you do each week. My recommendation is to set a maximum amount of running at **R** pace of no greater than 5 percent of your weekly mileage, with 5 miles (8 km) at **R** pace being the most you would do in any single **R** session, even if you run more than 100 miles (160 km) per week. So, if I indicate that an **R** session is to be made up of sets of 200, 200, 400, with equal recovery jogs, and you are totaling 60 miles per week (which means a max of 3 miles at **R** pace in a single **R** session), you would do no more than six sets of that indicated workout (since each set involves 800 meters at **R** pace).

Regarding cruise interval **T** workouts, try to total at least 4 miles (6.4 km) of running at **T** pace but not more than 10 percent of your weekly mileage, and take 1 minute of recovery time after each 5 to 6 minutes of running at **T** pace.

Since the pace of a half-marathon race is very similar to **T** pace, in addition to a weekly **R** session in phase II, I add some **T**-pace running along with repetitions once each week. All listed **E** days are used to accumulate your desired weekly mileage. Remember to get in a comfortable warm-up before and cool-down after every Q (quality) session. I have also added a couple of runs at **M** pace (estimated marathon pace; see the VDOT tables in chapter 5), and these runs are not to be longer than 20 percent of your weekly mileage or 18 miles (29 km), whichever is the lesser amount.

Table 13.1 summarizes a 6-week, phase II program. Depending on how many total weeks you have for race preparation, this phase II could be shortened or lengthened, but try to follow this program for at least 4 weeks prior to moving on to phase VI.

Table 13.1 Phase II Training Plan for a Half Marathon

Week 7	Q session	Workout
Sunday	Q	**L** run of the lesser of 120 min and 25% of weekly mileage
Monday		**E** day
Tuesday	Q	Sets of 200 **R** + 200 jg + 200 **R** + 400 jg + 400 **R** + 200 jg
Wednesday		**E** day
Thursday		**E** day
Friday	Q	1 mile runs at **T** pace w/1 min rests after each mile + 4 × 200 **R** w/200 jg
Saturday		**E** day + 6 ST
Week 8	**Q session**	**Workout**
Sunday	Q	**L** run of the lesser of 120 min and 25% of weekly mileage
Monday		**E** day
Tuesday	Q	200 **R** w/200 jg for recovery
Wednesday		**E** day
Thursday		**E** day
Friday	Q	Repeated 2 mile runs at **T** pace w/2 min recoveries + 4 × 200 **R** w/200 jg
Saturday		**E** day
Week 9	**Q session**	**Workout**
Sunday	Q	**M** run to total not more than 10% of weekly mileage, but at least 4 miles
Monday		**E** day
Tuesday		**E** day
Wednesday	Q	Sets of 200 **R** + 200 jg + 200 **R** + 400 jg + 400 **R** + 200 jg
Thursday		**E** day
Friday		**E** day
Saturday	Q	Steady 3-4 mile run at **T** pace + 4 × 200 **R** w/200 jg
Week 10	**Q session**	**Workout**
Sunday	Q	**L** run of the lesser of 90 min and 25% of weekly mileage
Monday		**E** day
Tuesday	Q	400 **R** w/400 recovery jg
Wednesday		**E** day
Thursday		**E** day
Friday	Q	4 × 200 **R** w/200 jg + mile repeats at **T** pace w/1 min rests + 4 × 200 **R** w/200 jg
Saturday		**E** day + 6 ST

Week 11	Q session	Workout
Sunday	Q	**L** run of the lesser of 120 min and 25% of weekly mileage
Monday		**E** day
Tuesday	Q	Sets of 200 **R** + 200 jg + 200 **R** + 400 jg + 400 **R** + 200 jg
Wednesday		**E** day
Thursday		**E** day
Friday	Q	Repeated 2 mile runs at **T** pace w/2 min recoveries + 4 × 200 **R** w/200 jg
Saturday		**E** day + 6 ST
Week 12	**Q session**	**Workout**
Sunday	Q	**M** run to total not more than 10% of weekly mileage, but at least 4 miles
Monday		**E** day
Tuesday	Q	200 **R** w/200 jg for recovery
Wednesday		**E** day
Thursday		**E** day
Friday	Q	1 mile runs at **T** pace w/1 min rests + 4 × 200 **R** w/200 recovery jg
Saturday		**E** day

Table created by Jack Daniels' Running Calculator designed by the Run SMART Project.

PHASE III

As is usual, my phase III training is the toughest phase of the program because it replaces the usual **R** training emphasized in phase II with **I** workouts, which are to be run at your current **I** pace (determined by using the VDOT tables in chapter 5) or at about 6 seconds per 400 slower than your previous phase II **R** pace (table 13.2).

I indicate either **H** (hard) pace of running or **I** pace for **I** workouts. Keep in mind that **H** should be equal to **I** pace, but it does not involve running specific distances for time; rather you just run at a pace you believe you could race at for about 10 to 12 minutes. Relative to amount of running at **I** pace for each session, do not run more distance at **I** pace than the lesser of 10,000 meters and 8 percent of weekly mileage.

Limit the amount of total time run at **H** pace in a single session to not more than the lesser of how long it would take you to race about 10K and how long it would take you to race for 8 percent of your current weekly mileage at about your current 5K race pace. For example, if your weekly total is 50 miles (8 percent of which is 4 miles) and your current 5K race pace is 18:45 (6:00 per mile pace), you could total 4 × 6:00 = 24 minutes of running at **I** pace, which might be 8 × 3 min **H** or 6 × 4 min **H**, and so on. Remember that when doing **H** runs, the recovery time is spent jogging and the duration of each recovery is about equal to, or a little shorter than, the time just run in the previous work bout.

If you have a race in any of the weeks in phase III, eliminate the midweek **I** session, and move the midweek **T** session to 3 or 4 days before the coming race for that week.

Table 13.2 summarizes a 6-week phase III program. Depending on total weeks available before the coming race, phase III can be shortened or lengthened, but try to get in at least 4 weeks of this training.

Table 13.2   Phase III Training Plan for a Half Marathon

Week 13	Q session	Workout
Sunday		**L** run of the lesser of 120 min and 25% of weekly mileage
Monday		**E** day + 6 ST
Tuesday		**E** day
Wednesday	Q	Repeated **H** runs lasting 3 min each w/2 min recovery jg
Thursday	Q	Repeated 1 mile runs at **T** pace w/1 min rests between
Friday		**E** day
Saturday		**E** day + 6 ST
Week 14	**Q session**	**Workout**
Sunday	Q	**M** run to total not more than 10% of weekly mileage, but at least 4 miles
Monday		**E** day + 6 ST

Week 14	Q session	Workout
Tuesday		**E** day
Wednesday	Q	Repeated 1,000 m runs at **I** pace w/3 min recovery jg
Thursday	Q	Steady 20 min run at **T** pace + 6 × 200 **R** w/200 recovery jg
Friday		**E** day
Saturday		**E** day + 6 ST
Week 15	**Q session**	**Workout**
Sunday	Q	**L** run of the lesser of 120 min and 25% of weekly mileage
Monday		**E** day + 6 ST
Tuesday		**E** day
Wednesday	Q	Repeated 4 min runs at **H** pace w/3 min recovery jg
Thursday	Q	Repeated 2 mile runs at **T** pace w/2 min rests between
Friday		**E** day + 6 ST
Saturday		**E** day
Week 16	**Q session**	**Workout**
Sunday	Q	**M** run to total not more than 10% of weekly mileage, but at least 4 miles
Monday		**E** day + 6 ST
Tuesday		**E** day
Wednesday	Q	Repeated 2 min **H** runs w/1 min recovery jg
Thursday	Q	Steady 20 min run at **T** pace + 6 × 200 **R** w/200 jg
Friday		**E** day
Saturday		**E** day + 6 ST
Week 17	**Q session**	**Workout**
Sunday	Q	**L** run of the lesser of 120 min and 25% of weekly mileage
Monday		**E** day + 6 ST
Tuesday		**E** day
Wednesday	Q	Repeated 1,000 m runs at **I** pace w/3 min recovery jg
Thursday	Q	1 mile runs at **T** pace w/1 min rests plus 4 × 200 **R** w/200 jg
Friday		**E** day
Saturday		**E** day + 6 ST
Week 18	**Q session**	**Workout**
Sunday	Q	**M** run to total not more than 10% of weekly mileage, but at least 4 miles
Monday		**E** day + 6 ST
Tuesday		**E** day
Wednesday	Q	Repeated 5 min runs at **H** effort with 4 min recovery jg
Thursday	Q	Steady 20 min run at **T** pace + 4 × 200 **R** w/200 jg
Friday		**E** day
Saturday		**E** day

Table created by Jack Daniels' Running Calculator designed by the Run SMART Project.

PHASE IV

As I normally recommend, phase IV will drop most of the **I** sessions, and training will emphasize **T** runs and some combinations of **T** + **I** + **R** running (table 13.3). When I suggest a combination of **T** and **I** or **T** and **R**, use half of your normal amount of each type of training for that session. If there is a combination of **T** + **I** + **R** training, total one-third of each of the types of training that you would normally do. In weeks that include a race on the weekend, eliminate both midweek **R** and **I** sessions leading up to the race, and have a midweek **T** session that is about half the number of 1-mile runs you would usually total in a **T** session but normally don't do more than 3 or 4 1-mile runs.

After any races, take 1 **E** day for each 3,000 meters of race distance. So if you ran a 15K race, give yourself 5 days of **E** running to recover from that race, which may mean eliminating a Q session during the week after the race. Depending on weather or other demanding conditions, always feel free to adjust the specific days for the Q sessions, but make sure you have 2 or 3 **E** days before any races.

Table 13.3 summarizes the final weeks of a half-marathon program. This phase IV could be shortened or lengthened some depending on total time used in the 4-phase program, but try to have at least 4 weeks in phase IV.

Table 13.3   Phase IV Training Plan for a Half Marathon

Week 19	Q session	Workout
Sunday	Q	10 min **E** + 30 min **M** + 5 min **T** + 30 min **M** (no rest between intensities)
Monday		**E** day + 8 ST
Tuesday		**E** day
Wednesday		**E** day
Thursday	Q	2 × 10 min **T** w/1 min rests + 60 min **E** + 2 × 10 min **T** w/1 min rests between
Friday		**E** day + 6 ST
Saturday		**E** day
Week 20	**Q session**	**Workout**
Sunday	Q	**L** run of the lesser of 120 min and 25% of weekly mileage
Monday		**E** day + 8 ST
Tuesday		**E** day
Wednesday		**E** day
Thursday	Q	60 min **E** + 20 min **T** + 5 min **E** + 10 min **T** + 5 min **E** + 5 min **T**
Friday		**E** day + 6 ST
Saturday		**E** day

Week 21	Q session	Workout
Sunday	Q	45 min **E** + 30 min **M** + 20 min **T** (a nonstop workout with no rests)
Monday		**E** day + 8 ST
Tuesday		**E** day
Wednesday		**E** day
Thursday	Q	3 × 5 min **T** w/1 min rests = 3 × 3 min **I** w/2 min jg + 3 × 400 **R** w/400 jg
Friday		**E** day
Saturday		**E** day
Week 22	**Q session**	**Workout**
Sunday	Q	**L** run of the lesser of 110 min and 20% of weekly mileage
Monday		**E** day (no more ST before the half-marathon race)
Tuesday		**E** day
Wednesday	Q	Repeated 5 min runs at **T** pace w/1 min rests between
Thursday		**E** day
Friday		**E** day
Saturday	Q	Steady 60 min run at **M** pace
Week 23	**Q session**	**Workout**
Sunday		**E** day
Monday		**E** day
Tuesday		**E** day
Wednesday	Q	2 × 10 min at **T** pace w/2 min rests between + 2 × 5 min **T** w/1 min rest
Thursday		**E** day
Friday		**E** day
Saturday		7-day prerace run (today or tomorrow) for 90 min at **E** pace
Week 24	**Q session**	**Workout**
Sunday		45-60 min **E** run
Monday		**E** day of 45 min total
Tuesday	Q	3 × 1 mile at **T** pace w/2 min rests between the **T**-pace runs
Wednesday		**E** day of 40-45 min total
Thursday		**E** day of 30 min total, or can even be a rest day
Friday		**E** day of about 30 min total
Saturday	Q	Half-marathon race (today or tomorrow)*

Table created by Jack Daniels' Running Calculator designed by the Run SMART Project.

*Take at least a week of **E** running after the half-marathon race.

HALF-MARATHON RACE TACTICS

As I mentioned in the early part of this chapter, elite runners race a half marathon just about at their current **T** pace. Even fairly middle-of-the-pack runners will average only about 8 to 10 seconds per mile slower than their current **T** pace, so pay particular attention to the **T**-pace runs that are part of your training program. It is common for runners who take on a half-marathon race to later make their next goal a full marathon, and so it is important to also be serious about the **M**-pace workouts that are part of the half-marathon program.

During the middle part of your training schedule, you might consider entering a full marathon race with the idea of going only halfway or even a little longer; this is a good opportunity to get in a fairly long training run at **M** pace. It will also give you an idea of how running seriously will feel for a prolonged period of time among a lot of other runners. You could even try picking up the pace to your true **T** pace for a mile or two before you pull out of the race; this will give you an idea of how things are going to feel in the latter portion of your upcoming half marathon.

Another idea to consider when training for a half marathon is to enter a few shorter-distance road races during your training program. Racing a 10K will certainly make your half-marathon pace feel much easier, and remember, racing events that take 10 to 15 minutes to complete provide some useful benefits for your aerobic system.

To determine the pace you should use in your half-marathon race, use the VDOT tables in chapter 5 to predict what half-marathon time you should be capable of, based on some other recent races you have run. You can also use recent training paces (particularly your manageable **T** pace) along with the VDOT tables to get a good idea of the pace you should be capable of in your coming half marathon.

Breaking the tape, as Mary Jepkosgei Keitany does here at the EDF Energy Birmingham Half Marathon, can be the ultimate joy of a long race.

Nick Potts/PA Archive/Press Association Images

14

Marathon Training

*Run with your head for the first two-thirds of every race
and with your heart for the last third.*

Probably the most important thing I have learned about marathon training (or training for almost any running event, for that matter) is that each runner needs to have an individualized program. Some handle higher amounts of mileage, and some can't handle a tough Q session as often as others can handle the same work schedule. Then there are the raw beginners, including people who have never run or even ever performed any type of physical activity before taking up a marathon program.

In this chapter on marathon training, I provide six different approaches to the event, and within each of these approaches, a few variations relative to the amount of weekly mileage (or time spent running) that any person might be able to, or have the time to, handle. These approaches, with their prominent features and tips for choosing the program best for you, are shown in table 14.1.

Remember, each of us may react a little differently to the same training program, and there probably is not a single training program that is best for everyone. Always eat well, stay hydrated, get adequate rest, and believe that the training you are doing is not only helping you run better but also improving your health. Just running for the fun of it can make the day enjoyable, and I certainly hope everyone who does spend some time running enjoys it as much as I enjoy helping others with their running.

Table 14.1   Six Approaches to Marathon Training

Program	Features	Reason for choosing the program
Novice	Training 3-5 days per week	• You are a beginner runner or have little previous running training to rely on.
2Q	Two Q sessions per week	• You have been running fairly regularly. • You are able to set aside 2 days each week for a more demanding Q session of training.
4-week cycles	Two Q sessions per week for 3 of 4 weeks, with a 4th week of only **E** running	• You like having 2 Q sessions each week. • You also like the idea of a high-mileage week with no Q sessions every 4th week of the program.
5-week cycles	Five weeks of training that can be repeated as often as time allows	• You are interested in regular **L** and **M**-pace runs while concentrating on **T** runs. • This plan also keeps some **R** and **I** work in your training plan. • This plan allows you to select specific workouts designed for runners logging a variety of distances. • This can be a demanding program, so it is recommended that for the final 3 weeks before a marathon, you follow what is provided for runners in your mileage category in table 14.3.
Final 18 weeks	Programs based on miles, kilometers, or time	• You like having the opportunity of scheduling your training based on miles, kilometers, or maybe on time, rather than distances being run. • These programs are typically for runners who are logging a lot of mileage and prefer not to have 2 Q sessions each week. • Q sessions are scheduled for every 4th or 5th day, so some weeks have only one and others have two Q sessions.
Final 12 weeks	Some fairly demanding final weeks prior to a marathon	• You have been training regularly and would prefer a program that provides training for the final 12 weeks before your chosen marathon.

NOVICE TRAINING

There are probably more people who fit into the novice category than any other. As a coach, I consider this group to include two basic types of people— true beginners, who have never had any running training, and those who have done a fair amount of running training in the past, but it was years ago and they want to get back into it again carefully. I like to call this second group "Re-runs."

It is most important that Re-runs don't try to duplicate what they used to be able to do, at least until they have built up a reasonable base from which to work. Injuries tend to plague Re-runs more than they bother new beginners, because the true beginners don't know what is possible, and every bit of improvement is better than they ever imagined.

Table 14.2 shows an 18-week plan for novice runners. Weeks 18 through 10 are designed for training 3, 4, or 5 days each week (4 or 5 is preferable). If training 3 days a week, do sessions A, C, and E, with at least one day between each session. If training 4 days a week, do sessions A, C, E, and either B or D. If training 5 days a week, do all sessions. Strides (ST) are runs that last 15 to 20 seconds each at a comfortably fast pace that you might be able to race at for 1 mile; take 1-minute rests between strides. **T**-pace running is comfortably hard running at a pace you could keep up for at least 30 minutes.

During week 10, try to complete a steady 10K run. If you run the 10K as a race, make sure to take it very easy. Coming into the final 9 weeks, try to bump up or keep training for 5 days a week. There should be two Q sessions for the first 4 weeks of this last period. Fit these Q sessions in on days with nice weather and when you have a lot of time. Separate the two Q days by at least 2 **E** days. The other 5 days of each week should be **E** days, including potential rest days or **E** running for at least 30 minutes.

Table 14.2   18-Week Marathon Training Plan for Novices

18-16 weeks until race

Session	Workout
A	15 1 min easy runs, w/1 min walks between runs (written 15 × 1:00 **E** w/1:00 W) Above workout is the first of the week, to be done either yesterday or today
B	If you run today, repeat the previous workout
C	9 × 1:00 **E** w/1:00 W + 3 × 2:00 **E** w/2:00 W
D	If you run today, repeat the previous workout
E	9 × 1:00 **E** w/1:00 W + 2 × 3:00 **E** w/3:00 W Above WO was to be last of the week and was to be either yesterday or today

15-14 weeks until race

Session	Workout
A	4 × 5:00 **E** w/ 5:00 W Above WO is the first of the week, to be done either yesterday or today
B	If you run today, repeat the previous workout
C	10 × 2:00 **E** w/2:00 W
D	If you run today, repeat the previous workout
E	(–15 weeks) 5 × 4:00 **E** w/4:00 W (–14 weeks) 3 × 4:00 **E** w/4:00 W + 15:00-20:00 **E** + 6:00 W Above WO was to be last of the week and was to be either yesterday or today

13-12 weeks until race

Session	Workout
A	5:00 **E** + 3:00 W + 5 × 3:00 **T** pace, w/2:00 W following each **T** run + 10 ST Above WO is the first of the week, to be done either yesterday or today
B	If you run today, do 3 × 10:00 **E** w/5:00 W (take less than 5:00 W if feeling good)
C	If you train today, repeat the A workout of this week
D	3 × 10:00 **E** w/5:00 W (may take less W if not that much recovery is needed)
E	(–13 weeks) 5:00 **E** + 5:00 W + 3 × 5:00 **T** w/2:00 W recoveries + 15:00 **E** + 4:00 W (–12 weeks) 5:00 **E** + 5:00 W + 2 × 5:00 **T** w/2:00 W recoveries + 25:00-30:00 **E** + 6:00 W Day 6 workout was to be last of the week and could be either yesterday or today

11-10 weeks until race

Session	Workout
A	10:00 **E** + 5:00 W + 5 ST + 5:00 W + 2 × 10:00 **E** w/5:00 W Above workout is the first of the week, to be done either yesterday or today
B	If you train today, repeat the A workout of this week

C	5:00 **E** + 5:00 W + 20:00 **E** + 5:00 W + 5:00 **T** + 5:00 W + 5:00 **E** + 5:00 W
D	If you run today do 3 × 10:00 **E** w/5:00 W (may do less than 5:00 recoveries if desired)
E	(−11weeks) 10:00 **E** + 5:00 W + 5 ST + 5:00 W + 20:00 **T** + 5:00 W + 10 **E** (−10 weeks) 10:00 **E** + 5:00 W + 5 ST + 5:00 W + 20:00 **T** + 5:00 W + 20 **E** Day 6 WO was to be last of the week and could be either yesterday or today

9-2 weeks until race

Week	First Q session	Second Q session
9	Steady 90 min **L** run	10:00 **E** + 15:00 **T** + 5:00 **E** + 2 × (10:00 **T** w/2:00 W recoveries) + 5:00 **T** + 10:00 **E**
8	10:00 **E** + 4 × (6:00 **T** w/2:00 W) + 1 hr **E** + 2 × (8:00 **T** w/2:00 W recoveries)	10:00 **E** + 4 × (6:00 **T** w/2:00 W) + 10:00 W + 3 × (6:00 **T** w/2:00 W)
7	1 hour 45 min at **M** (could be in a shorter race, but if in a race, just run **M**, not faster)	10:00 **E** + 3 × (10:00 **T** w/2:00 W) + 40:00 **E**
6	Steady 2 hr **L** run	10:00 **E** + 6 × (6:00 **T** w/1:00 W) + 10:00 **E**
5	10:00 **E** + 4 × (6:00 **T** w/1:00 W) + 60:00 **E** + 3 × (6:00 **T** w/1:00 W)	10:00 **E** + 4 × (10:00 **T** w/2:00 W) + 10:00 **E**
4	Steady 2 hr 30 min **L** run	10:00 **E** + 4 × (10:00 **T** w/2:00 W) + 10:00 **E**
3	Steady 2 hr 15 min at **M**	10:00 **E** + 3 × (12:00 **T** w/2:00 W) + 10:00 **E**
2	Steady 2 hr 15 min **L** run	10:00 **E** + 7 × (6:00 **T** w/1:00 W) + 10:00 **E**

1 week until race

Day	Workout
7	90 min **E**
6	60 min **E**
5	10:00 **E** + 4 × (5:00 **T** w/2:00 W) + 10:00 **E**
4	30:00-45:00 **E**
3	30:00 **E** Feel free to take any one of these final 3 days off; may be a travel day
2	30:00 **E**
1	30:00 **E** Marathon is tomorrow

2Q PROGRAM

Before starting any 2Q 18-week program, you should have at least 6 weeks of running under your belt. All 2Q plans include two Q training sessions each week. Try to do some running on at least 6 days each week. It is suggested that Q1 be on Sunday, or the same day of the week on which your coming marathon will be run. With Q1 on Sunday, then Q2 is best located on Wednesday or Thursday. Feel free to rearrange your Q1 and Q2 sessions to fall on whichever days best suit your personal schedule, but make an effort to always have 2 or 3 **E** days between Q days.

E days are to be used for recovery and easy running and to accumulate your weekly mileage goals. **E** days may involve one, two, or more **E** runs each day, as needed. If you must, or desire to, take a day off from training now and then, just use the remaining **E** days of that week to reach your weekly mileage goal. Make a habit of adding six to eight strides to the middle or end of at least 2 **E** days each week. Strides (ST) are meant to be light, quick 10- to 20-second runs, with about 1-minute recovery between each. Strides are fast, controlled runs but not sprints.

If you include any races during this marathon plan, schedule them in place of your Q1 session for that week, but perform the displaced Q1 session at midweek and drop that week's Q2 altogether. This means a Sunday race would start the week with the race, followed by that week's Q1 (a few days later), and the next week starts with its Q1, as normal. Try to rearrange training so you get 3 **E** days before any race, and take 1 **E** day for each 3,000 to 4,000 meters of race distance (e.g., 3 **E** days after a 10K).

I typically suggest that weekly mileage vary from about 80 to 100 percent of peak (P) mileage, with P being the most mileage you plan to run in any single week of this program. For example, if you pick 40 miles as your peak weekly mileage, then, when I suggest .8P for a week, this means you run 80 percent of 40 (32 miles) for the week. Each week's suggested fraction of P is listed in the second column of the program.

If you use VDOT values to determine training speeds for **M**, **T**, **I**, and **R** paces, try to be realistic, and use a VDOT that comes from a race distance of at least 10K. The longer and more recent the race, the better. If it has been a while since a race, make a conservative estimate of what you think you can race over a course of similar terrain to what you will face in training and in your marathon. For the first 6 weeks of this program, use the lesser of the VDOT values that is equal to a recent race and 2 VDOT units lower than your anticipated marathon VDOT. During the second 6 weeks of this program, increase the VDOT value by 1 unit, and for the final 6 weeks, increase another VDOT unit for determining training intensities.

If not using VDOT units, choose a realistic goal **M** pace. Then, final **T** pace will be 15 seconds per mile faster than goal **M** pace. Final **I** pace will be 6 seconds per 400 meters faster than **T** pace. Final **R** pace will be 3 seconds per 200 meters faster than **I** pace. An example of using this method follows: Assume estimated **M** race pace is 6:00 per mile (3:43/km), which means your final **T** pace is 5:45/mile (about 86 sec/400 and 3:35/km). This makes final **I** pace 80 sec/400 or 3:20/km, and final **R** pace is 74/400 and 37/200.

For the first 6 weeks, use training paces that are 10 seconds per mile (6 sec/km) slower than your goal and final paces, and for the middle 6 weeks, bring the paces to within 4 seconds per mile (2.5 sec/km) of your goal and final paces (which are then to be used during the final 6 weeks of the overall 18-week program).

Table 14.3 shows programs for runners who are running from up to 40 miles (64 km) per week to about 120 miles (194 km) per week. I have bolded some quality sessions, which means if you feel overly tired or overwhelmed, the bolded session may be eliminated and replaced by an **E** day of training. The number listed before the training intensity is the number of miles that should be completed at that intensity. For example, 3 **E** means 3 miles at easy pace, 4 **M** means 4 miles at marathon pace, and 1 **T** means 1 mile at threshold pace.

Table 14.3   Two Quality Sessions Marathon Training Plan for 40 to 120 Miles (64 to 194 km) per Week

Up to 40 miles (64 km) per week			
Weeks until race	Fraction of peak	Workout	Miles for Q sessions
18	.8	Q1 = 3 **E** + 4 **M** + 1 **T** + 1 **M** + 2 **E** (nonstop workout if no rest shown)	11
		Q2 = 5 **E** + 2 **T** + 2 min rest + 1 **E** + 2 × (1 **T** w/1 min rest between) + 2 **E**	12
17	.8	**Q1 = 2 E + 2 × (1 T w/1 min rests) + 30 min E + 2 × (1 T w/1 min rests) + 2 E**	12
		Q2 = 3 **E** + 6 × (2 min **I** w/2 min jg between) + 4 × (1 min **R** w/2 min jg) + 2 **E**	9
16	.9	Q1 = steady **E** run of 90-110 min	11
		Q2 = 5 **E** + 4 × (1 **T** w/1 min rests) + 2 **E**	11
15	.9	Q1 = 2 **E** + 5 **M** + 1 **T** + 1 **M** + 2 **E**	11
		Q2 = 40 min E + 4 × (1 T w/1 min rests) + 2 E	9

(continued)

Up to 40 miles (64 km) per week

Weeks until race	Fraction of peak	Workout	Miles for Q sessions
14	.9	Q1 = 2 **E** + 2 × (1 **T** w/1 min rests) + 30 min **E** + 2 × (1 **T** w/1 min rests) + 2 **E**	11
		Q2 = 40 min **E** + 5 × (3 min **I** w/2 min jg recoveries) + 2 **E**	9
13	.9	Q1= steady **E** run of 90-120 min	12
		Q2 = 40 min **E** + 2 × (2 **T** w/2 min rests) + 2 **E**	10
12	1.0	Q1 = 4 **E** + 6 **M** + 1 **T** + 1 **E**	12
		Q2 = 6 E + 3 T + 3 min E + 1 T + 2 E	12
11	.9	Q1 = 8 **E** + 4 × (1 **T** w/1 min rests) + 1 **E**	13
		Q2 = 6 **E** + 3 × (4 min **I** w/3 min jg) + 4 × (1 min **R** w/2 min jg) + 2 **E**	11
10	1.0	Q1 = steady **E** run of 120-130 min	14
		Q2 = 6 **E** + 6 **M** + 2 **E**	14
9	1.0	**Q1 = 4 E + 1 T + 8 M + 2 E**	15
		Q2 = 4 **E** + 2 **T** + 2 min **E** + 2 **T** + 2 min **E** + 1 **T** + 2 **E**	11
8	.9	Q1 = 5 **E** + 9 **M** + 2 **E**	16
		Q2 = 8 **E** + 5 × (3 min **I** w/2 min recovery jg) + 3 × (2 min **I** w/1 min jg) + 2 **E**	13
7	.9	Q1 = steady **E** run of 130-150 min	16
		Q2 = 2 E + 10 M + 1 T + 2 E	15
6	1.0	Q1 = 3 **E** + 12 **M** + 1 **E**	16
		Q2 = 45 min **E** + 2 × (2 **T** w/2 min rests) + 1 **T** + 1 **E**	11
5	1.0	**Q1 = 2 E + 2 T + 60 min E + 2 × (1 T w/1 min rest between) + 2 E**	15
		Q2 = 6 **E** + 5 × (3 min **I** w/2 min jg) + 4 × (1 min **R** w/2 min jg) + 2 **E**	12
4	.9	Q1 = steady **E** run of 150 min	17
		Q2 = 6 **E** + 5 × (3 min **I** w/3 min jg) + 1 **T** + 4 **E**	14
3	.9	Q1 = 1 **E** + 8 **M** + 1 **E** + 6 **M** + 1 **E**	17
		Q2 = 6 E + 4 × (1 T w/1 min rests) + 2 E	12
2	.9	Q1 = 1 **E** + 2 × (2 **T** w/2 min rests) + 60 min **E**	12
		Q2 = 4 **E** + 1 **T** + 2 **M** + 1 **E** + 1 **T** + 2 **M** + 1 **E**	12

Up to 40 miles (64 km) per week

Weeks until race	Fraction of peak	Workout	Miles for Q sessions
1	—	7 days: Q1 = 90 min **E**	10
		6 days: 60 min **E**	7
		5 days: Q2 = 2 **E** + 5 × (800 **T** w/2 min **E** recovery jg) + 1 **E**	6
		4 days: 50 min **E**	6
		3 days: 30-40 min **E**	4
		2 days: 0-20 min **E**	2
		1 day: 20-30 min **E** (tomorrow is the race)	3

41-55 miles (66-89 km) per week

Weeks until race	Fraction of peak	Workout	Miles for Q sessions
18	.8	Q1 = 4 **E** + 8 **M** + 1 **T** + 1 **E** (a nonstop workout)	14
		Q2 = 8 **E** + 2 × (2 **T** w/2 min rests) + 1 **T** + 2 **E**	15
17	.8	**Q1 = 2 E + 3 T + 40 min E + 2 T + 1 E**	13
		Q2 = 6 **E** + 5 × (3 min **I** w/2 min jg recoveries) + 6 × (1 min **R** w/2 min jg) + 2 **E**	13
16	.9	Q1 = steady **E** run of 90-120 min	15
		Q2 = 6 **E** + 2 **T** + 2 min **E** + 2 **T** + 2 min **E** + 1 **T** + 2 **E**	13
15	.9	Q1 = 2 **E** + 8 **M** + 1 **E** + 2 **M** + 2 **E**	15
		Q2 = 40 min E + 3 × (2 T w/2 min rests) + 2 E	13
14	.9	Q1 = 1 **E** + 2 × (2 **T** w/2 min rests) + 60 min **E** + 1 **T** + 1 **E**	15
		Q2 = 6 **E** + 5 × (4 min **I** w/3 min jg recoveries) + 2 **E**	13
13	.9	Q1= steady **E** run of 100-120 min	16
		Q2 = 40 min **E** + 3 × (2 **T** w/2 min rests) + 2 **E**	13
12	1.0	Q1 = 2 **E** + 6 **M** + 1 **E** + 6 **M** + 1 **E**	16
		Q2 = 6 E + 3 T + 3 min E + 2 T + 2 min E + 1 T + 2 E	14
11	.9	Q1 = 10 **E** + 2 × (2 **T** w/2 min rests) + 2 **E**	15
		Q2 = 8 **E** + 5 × (3 min **I** w/2 min jg) + 6 × (1 min **R** w/2 min jg) + 2 **E**	15
10	1.0	Q1 = steady **E** run of 120 min	16
		Q2 = 2 **E** + 12 **M** + 2 **E**	16
9	1.0	**Q1 = 2 E + 6 M + 1 E + 4 M + 1 T + 1 E**	15
		Q2 = 5 **E** + 3 × (2 **T** w/2 min rests) + 1 **T** + 2 **E**	14

(continued)

41-55 miles (66-89 km) per week

Weeks until race	Fraction of peak	Workout	Miles for Q sessions
8	.9	Q1 = 60 min **E** + 8 **M** + 1 **E**	17
		Q2 = 8 **E** + 4 × (4 min **I** w/3 min recovery jg) + 3 **E**	14
7	.9	Q1 = steady **E** run of 120-150 min	17
		Q2 = 2 E + 8 M + 3 × (1 T w/1 min recovery between) + 2 E	15
6	1.0	Q1 = 2 **E** + 14 **M** + 1 **E**	17
		Q2 = 60 min **E** + 3 × (2 **T** w/2 min rests) + 1 **T** + 1 **E**	15
5	1.0	**Q1 = 2 E + 3 T + 60 min E + 2 T + 2 E**	17
		Q2 = 8 **E** + 5 × (3 min **I** w/2 min **E**) + 4 × (1 min **R** w/2 min jg) + 3 **E**	15
4	.9	Q1 = steady **E** run of 150 min	17
		Q2 = 6 **E** + 5 × (3 min **I** w/2 min **E**) + 4 **E**	13
3	.9	Q1 = 1 **E** + 8 **M** + 1 **E** + 6 **M** + 1 **E**	17
		Q2 = 4 E + 2 × (2 T w/2 min rests) + 3 × (1 T w/1 min rests) + 2 E	13
2	.9	Q1 = 1 **E** + 3 × (2 **T** w/2 min rests) + 60 min **E**	15
		Q2 = 4 **E** + 1 **T** + 2 **M** + 1 **E** + 1 **T** + 2 **M** + 2 **E**	13
1	—	7 days: Q1 = 90 min **E**	10
		6 days: 60 min **E**	8
		5 days: Q2 = 2 **E** + 3 × (1 **T** w/2 min rests) + 2 **E**	7
		4 days: 50 min **E**	6
		3 days: 30-40 min **E**	5
		2 days: 0-20 min **E**	2
		1 day: 20-30 min **E** (tomorrow is the race)	3

56-70 miles (90-113 km) per week

Weeks until race	Fraction of peak	Workout	Miles for Q sessions
18	.8	Q1 = 1 **E** + 6 **M** + 1 **E** + 6 **M** + 2 **E** (a nonstop workout)	16
		Q2 = 8 **E** + 3 **T** + 3 min rest + 2 **T** + 2 **E**	15
17	.8	**Q1 = 2 E + 3 T + 60 min E + 1 T + 1 E**	15
		Q2 = 4 **E** + 5 × (1 km **I** w/3 min jg recoveries) + 4 × (400 **R** w/400 mjg) + 2 **E**	13
16	.9	Q1 = steady **E** run of the lesser of 16 miles (26 km) and 120 min	16
		Q2 = 6 **E** + 3 **T** + 3 min **E** + 2 **T** + 2 min **E** + 1 **T** + 2 **E**	14

Weeks until race	Fraction of peak	Workout	Miles for Q sessions
15	.9	Q1 = 2 **E** + 8 **M** + 1 **E** + 3 **M** + 2 **E**	16
		Q2 = 40 min E + 3 × (2 T w/2 min rests) + 2 × (1 T w/1 min rests) + 1 E	15
14	.9	Q1 = 1 **E** + 2 × (2 **T** w/2 min rests) + 60 min **E** + 2 **T** + 1 **E**	16
		Q2 = 8 **E** + 6 × (1 km **I** w/3 min jg recoveries) + 2 **E**	14
13	.8	Q1 = steady **E** run of the lesser of 17 miles (27 km) and 120 min	17
		Q2 = 40 min **E** + 3 **T** + 2 min rest + 2 × (2 **T** w/1 min rest between) + 2 **E**	15
12	1.0	Q1 = 1 **E** + 8 **M** + 1 **E** + 6 **M** + 1 **E**	17
		Q2 = 4 E + 3 T + 3 min E + 2 T + 2 min E + 2 T + 2 min E + 1 T + 2 E	14
11	.9	Q1 = 12 **E** + 3 **T** + 1 **E**	16
		Q2 = 8 **E** + 5 × (1 km **I** w/2 min jg) + 4 × (400 **R** w/400 jg) + 1 **E**	15
10	.9	Q1 = steady **E** run of the lesser of 18 miles (29 km) and 130 min	18
		Q2 = 2 **E** + 12 **M** + 2 **E**	16
9	1.0	**Q1 = 3 E + 6 M + 1 E + 4 M + 1 T + 1 E**	16
		Q2 = 5 **E** + 4 × (2 **T** w/2 min rests) + 2 **E**	15
8	1.0	Q1 = 2 **E** + 2 **T** + 60 min **E** + 2 **T** + 2 **E** *or* 60 min **E** + 8 **M** + 1 **E**	17
		Q2 = 8 **E** + 6 × (1 km **I** w/3 min jg) + 2 **E**	16
7	.9	Q1 = steady **E** run of the lesser of 20 miles (32 km) and 150 min	20
		Q2 = 2 E + 8 M + 2 × (2 T w/2 min recovery between) + 2 E	16
6	1.0	Q1 = 3 **E** + 12 **M** + 2 **E**	17
		Q2 = 40 min **E** + 4 × (2 **T** w/2 min rests) + 2 × (1 **T** w/1 min rests) + 1 **E**	17
5	.9	**Q1 = 6 E + 2 T + 6 E + 2 T + 1 E**	17
		Q2 = 8 **E** + 5 × (1 km **I** w/3 min jg) + 6 × (200 **R** w/200 jg) + 2 **E**	16
4	.9	Q1 = steady **E** run of the lesser of 20 miles (32 km) and 150 min	20
		Q2 = 6 **E** + 5 × (1 km **I** w/3 min **E**) + 4 **E**	15
3	.8	Q1 = 2 **E** + 6 **M** + 1 **E** + 6 **M** + 2 **E**	17
		Q2 = 2 E + 4 × (2 T w/2 min E) + 2 E	12
2	.8	Q1 = 2 **E** + 3 × (2 **T** w/2 min rests) + 7 **E**	15
		Q2 = 3 **E** + 1 **T** + 2 **M** + 1 **T** + 2 **M** + 2 **E**	11

(continued)

56-70 miles (90-113 km) per week

Weeks until race	Fraction of peak	Workout	Miles for Q sessions
1	—	7 days: Q1 = 90 min **E**	13
		6 days: 60 min **E**	8
		5 days: Q2 = 3 **E** + 3 × (1 **T** w/2 min rests) + 2 **E**	8
		4 days: 50 min **E**	7
		3 days: 30-40 min **E**	5
		2 days: 0-20 min **E**	3
		1 day: 20-30 min **E** (race is tomorrow)	

71 to 85 miles (114-137 km) per week

Weeks until race	Fraction of peak	Workout	Miles for Q sessions
18	.8	Q1 = 5 **E** + 6 **M** + 1 **T** + 5 **M** + 1 **E** (a nonstop workout)	18
		Q2 = 8 **E** + 4 **T** + 4 min rest + 4 **T** + 1 **E**	17
17	.8	**Q1 = 3 E + 3 T + 60 min E + 2 T + 2 E**	18
		Q2 = 6 **E** + 5 × (1 km **I** w/2 min jg) + 6 × (400 **R** w/400 m recovery jg) + 2 **E**	15
16	.9	Q1 = steady **E** run of 18 miles (29 km)	18
		Q2 = 5 **E** + 4 **T** + 4 min **E** + 3 **T** + 3 min **E** + 2 **T** + 2 min **E** + 1 **T** + 2 **E**	17
15	.9	Q1 = 2 **E** + 8 **M** + 1 **T** + 2 **M** + 1 **E** + 2 **M** + 2 **E**	18
		Q2 = 6 E + 4 × (2 T w/2 min rests) + 2 E	16
14	.9	Q1 = 2 **E** + 2 × (2 **T** w/2 min rests) + 60 min **E** + 2 **T** + 2 **E**	18
		Q2 = 8 **E** + 8 × (1 km **I** w/2 min jg) + 2 **E** *or* 8 **E** + 5 × (1 **I** w/4 min jg) + 2 **E**	17
13	.8	Q1= steady **E** run of 19 miles (31 km)	19
		Q2 = 7 **E** + 4 × (2 **T** w/2 min rests) + 2 **E**	17
12	1.0	Q1 = 4 **E** + 8 **M** + 1 **T** + 4 **M** + 2 **E**	19
		Q2 = 4 **E** + 3 **T** + 4 min **E** + 3 **T** + 3 min **E** + 2 **T** + 2 min **E** + 1 **T** + 2 **E**	15
11	.9	Q1 = 8 **E** + 3 **T** + 8 **E**	19
		Q2 = 8 **E** + 6 × (1 km **I** w/2 min jg) + 4 × (400 **R** w/400 jg) + 2 **E**	17
10	.8	Q1 = steady **E** run of 20 miles (32 km)	20
		Q2 = 2 **E** + 14 **M** + 2 **E**	18
9	1.0	**Q1 = 4 E + 6 M + 1 T + 5 M + 2 E**	18
		Q2 = 5 **E** + 2 × (3 **T** w/3 min rests) + 2 **T** + 3 **E**	16

71 to 85 miles (114-137 km) per week

Weeks until race	Fraction of peak	Workout	Miles for Q sessions
8	.9	Q1 = 1 **E** + 3 **T** + 10 **E** + 3 **T** + 1 **E** *or* 4 **E** + 13 **M** + 1 **E**	18
		Q2 = 8 **E** + 8 × (1 km **I** w/2 min jg) + 2 **E**	17
7	.9	Q1 = steady **E** run of 20 miles (32 km)	20
		Q2 = 2 E + 8 M + 3 T + 2 E	15
6	1.0	Q1 = 2 **E** + 8 **M** + 1 **T** + 4 **M** + 1 **T** + 1 **M** + 1 **E**	18
		Q2 = 4 **E** + 4 × (2 **T** w/2 min rests) + 2 **E**	14
5	.9	**Q1 = 2 E + 2 T + 8 miles E + 2 T + 2 E**	16
		Q2 = 6 **E** + 5 × (1 km **I** w/2 min jg) + 4 × (400 **R** w/400 jg) + 2 **E**	14
4	.8	Q1 = steady **E** run of 18 miles	18
		Q2 = 3 **E** + 3 × (1 **T** w/1 min jg) + 3 × (1 km **I** w/2 min jg) + 3 × (400 **R** w/400 jg) + 2 **E**	12
3	.8	Q1 = 3 **E** + 6 **M** + 1 **T** + 6 **M** + 2 **E**	18
		Q2 = 2 E + 4 × (2 T w/2 min E) + 2 E	12
2	.7	Q1 = 2 **E** + 3 × (2 **T** w/2 min **E** recoveries) + 8 **E**	16
		Q2 = 4 **E** + 1 **T** + 2 **M** + 1 **T** + 2 **M** + 2 **E**	12
1	—	7 days: Q1 = 90 min **E**	13
		6 days: 60 min **E**	8
		5 days: Q2 = 4 **E** + 3 × (1 **T** w/2 min rests) + 2 **E**	9
		4 days: 50 min **E**	7
		3 days: 30-40 min **E**	5
		2 days: 0-20 min **E**	3
		1 day: 20-30 min **E** (tomorrow is the race)	3

86-100 miles (138-161 km) per week

Weeks until race	Fraction of peak	Workout	Miles for Q sessions
18	.8	Q1 = 5 **E** + 6 **M** + 1 **T** + 5 **M** + 1 **T** + 1 **M** + 1 **E** (a nonstop workout)	20
		Q2 = 8 **E** + 4 **T** + 4 min rest + 4 **T** + 2 **E**	18
17	.8	**Q1 = 4 E + 3 T + 60 min E + 3 T + 2 E**	21
		Q2 = 8 **E** + 5 × (1 km **I** w/2 min recovery jg) + 6 × (400 **R** w/400 m jg) + 2 **E**	17
16	.9	Q1 = steady **E** run of 22 miles (35 km)	22
		Q2 = 5 **E** + 4 **T** + 4 min rest + 3 **T** + 3 min rest + 2 **T** + 2 min rest + 1 **T** + 2 **E**	17

(continued)

86-100 miles (138-161 km) per week

Weeks until race	Fraction of peak	Workout	Miles for Q sessions
15	.9	Q1 = 2 **E** + 8 **M** + 1 **T** + 4 **M** + 1 **T** + 2 **M** + 2 **E**	20
		Q2 = 6 E + 4 × (2 T w/2 min rests) + 2 E	16
14	.8	Q1 = 2 **E** + 2 × (2 **T** w/2 min rests) + 60 min **E** + 3 **T** + 2 **E**	20
		Q2 = 8 **E** + 8 × (1 km **I** w/2 min jg) + 2 **E** or 8 **E** + 5 × (1 **I** w/4 min jg) + 2 **E**	17
13	.9	Q1 = steady **E** run of 21 miles (34 km)	21
		Q2 = 40 min **E** + 5 × (2 **T** w/2 min rests) + 2 **E**	18
12	1.0	Q1 = 4 **E** + 8 **M** + 1 **T** + 6 **M** + 1 **T** + 1 **E**	21
		Q2 = 6 E + 4 T + 4 min E + 3 T + 3 min E + 2 T + 2 min E + 1 T + 2 E	18
11	1.0	Q1 = 8 **E** + 4 **T** + 10 **E**	22
		Q2 = 8 **E** + 6 × (1 km **I** w/2 min jg) + 4 × (400 **R** w/400 jg) + 2 **E**	17
10	.8	Q1 = steady **E** run of 21 miles (34 km)	21
		Q2 = 2 **E** + 15 **M** + 2 **E**	19
9	1.0	**Q1 = 4 E + 6 M + 1 T + 6 M + 1 E**	18
		Q2 = 3 **E** + 4 **T** + 4 min rest + 3 **T** + 3 min rest + 3 **T** + 2 **E**	15
8	1.0	Q1 = 2 **E** + 4 **T** + 10 **E** + 4 **T** + 1 **E** *or* 5 **E** + 14 **M** + 2 **E**	21
		Q2 = 8 **E** + 3 × (1 **I** w/4 min jg) + 3 × (1 km **I** w/2 min jg) + 2 **E**	16
7	.9	Q1 = steady **E** run of 22 miles (35 km)	22
		Q2 = 2 E + 8 M + 4 T + 2 E	16
6	1.0	Q1 = 3 **E** + 8 **M** + 1 **T** + 4 **M** + 1 **T** + 1 **M** + 1 **E**	19
		Q2 = 3 **E** + 4 **T** + 4 min **E** + 3 × (2 **T** w/2 min rests) + 2 **E**	15
5	.8	**Q1 = 2 E + 3 T + 8 miles (13 km) E + 3 T + 2 E**	18
		Q2 = 6 **E** + 6 × (1 km **I** w/2 min jg) + 4 × (400 **R** w/400 jg) + 2 **E**	15
4	.9	Q1 = steady **E** run of 20 miles (32 km)	20
		Q2 = 6 **E** + 3 × (1 **T** w/1 min rests) + 3 × (1 km **I** w/2 min jg) + 3 × (400 **R** w/400 jg) + 2 **E**	15
3	.8	Q1 = 4 **E** + 6 **M** + 1 **T** + 6 **M** + 2 **E**	19
		Q2 = 2 E + 4 × (2 T w/2 min rests) + 2 E	12
2	.7	Q1 = 2 **E** + 3 × (2 **T** w/2 min rests) + 8 **E**	16
		Q2 = 4 **E** + 1 **T** + 2 **M** + 1 **T** + 2 **M** + 2 **E**	12

86-100 miles (138-161 km) per week

Weeks until race	Fraction of peak	Workout	Miles for Q sessions
1	—	7 days: Q1 = 90 min **E**	14
		6 days: 60 min **E**	9
		5 days: Q2 = 4 **E** + 3 × (1 **T** w/2 min rests) + 2 **E**	9
		4 days: 50 min **E**	7
		3 days: 30-40 min **E**	6
		2 days: 0-20 min **E**	3
		1 day: 20-30 min **E** (tomorrow is the race)	4

101-120 miles (163-194 km) per week

Weeks until race	Fraction of peak	Workout	Miles for Q sessions
18	.8	Q1 = 5 **E** + 6 **M** + 1 **T** + 5 **M** + 1 **T** + 1 **M** + 2 **E** (a nonstop workout)	21
		Q2 = 10 **E** + 4 **T** + 4 min rest + 4 **T** + 2 **E**	20
17	.8	**Q1 = 4 E + 3 T + 60 min E + 3 T + 2 E**	21
		Q2 = 8 **E** + 5 × (1 km **I** or 3 min **H** w/ 2 min jg) + 6 × (400 **R** w/ 400 m jg) + 2 **E**	17
16	.9	Q1 = steady **E** run of 23 miles (37 km)	23
		Q2 = 5 **E** + 4 **T** + 4 min **E** + 3 **T** + 3 min **E** + 2 **T** + 2 min **E** + 1 **T** + 2 **E**	18
15	.9	Q1 = 2 **E** + 8 **M** + 1 **T** + 4 **M** + 1 **T** + 3 **M** + 2 **E**	21
		Q2 = 8 E + 4 × (2 T w/2 min rests) + 2 E	18
14	.8	Q1 = 2 **E** + 2 × (2 **T** w/2 min rests) + 60 min **E** + 3 **T** + 2 **E**	20
		Q2 = 8 **E** + 8 × (1 km **I** w/2 min jg) + 3 **E** *or* 8 **E** + 5 × (1 **I** w/ 4 min jg) + 3 **E**	18
13	1.0	Q1 = steady **E** run of 20 miles (32 km)	20
		Q2 = 8 **E** + 5 × (2 **T** w/2 min rests) + 2 **E**	20
12	1.0	Q1 = 4 **E** + 8 **M** + 1 **T** + 6 **M** + 1 **T** + 2 **E**	22
		Q2 = 6 **E** + 4 **T** + 4 min rest + 3 **T** + 3 min rest + 2 **T** + 2 min rest + 1 **T** + 2 **E**	18
11	.9	Q1 = 10 **E** + 4 **T** + 8 **E**	22
		Q2 = 8 **E** + 6 × (1 km **I** w/2 min jg) + 4 × (400 **R** w/400 jg) + 2 **E**	17
10	.8	Q1 = steady **E** run of 21 miles (34 km)	21
		Q2 = 2 **E** + 16 **M** + 2 **E**	20

(continued)

101-120 miles (163-194 km) per week

Weeks until race	Fraction of peak	Workout	Miles for Q sessions
9	1.0	**Q1 = 4 E + 6 M + 1 T + 6 M + 2 E**	19
		Q2 = 3 E + 4 T + 4 min E + 4 T + 4 min E + 2 T + 2 E	16
8	.9	Q1 = 6 E + 13 M + 2 E	21
		Q2 = 8 E + 3 × (1,200 I w/3 min jg) + 3 × (1 km I w/3 min jg) + 2 E	17
7	1.0	Q1 = steady E run of 22 miles (35 km)	22
		Q2 = 3 E + 8 M + 4 T + 2 E	17
6	1.0	Q1 = 4 E + 8 M + 1 T + 4 M + 1 T + 1 M + 1 E	20
		Q2 = 3 E + 4 T + 4 min rest + 2 × (3 T w/3 min jg between) + 2 E	15
5	.8	**Q1 = 2 E + 4 T + 8 miles (13 km) E + 4 T + 2 E**	20
		Q2 = 6 E + 6 × (1 km I w/2 min jg) + 4 × (400 R w/400 jg) + 2 E	15
4	.9	Q1 = steady E run of 21 miles (34 km)	21
		Q2 = 5 E+ 3 × (1 T w/1 min jg) + 3 × (1 km I w/2 min jg) + 3 × (400 R w/400 jg) + 2 E	14
3	.8	Q1 = 4 E + 6 M + 1 T + 6 M + 1 T + 2 E	20
		Q2 = 4 E + 4 × (2 T w/2 min E) + 2 E	14
2	.7	Q1 = 2 E + 3 × (2 T w/2 min rests) + 8 E	16
		Q2 = 4 E + 1 T + 2 M + 1 T + 2 M + 2 E	12
1	—	7 days: Q1 = 90 min E	14
		6 days: 60 min E	9
		5 days: Q2 = 4 E + 3 × (1 T w/2 min rests) + 2 E	9
		4 days: 50 min E	7
		3 days: 30-40 min E	5
		2 days: 0-20 min E	3
		1 day: 20-30 min E (tomorrow is the race)	3

More than 120 miles (194 km) per week

Weeks until race	Fraction of peak	Workout	Miles for Q sessions
18	.8	Q1 = 5 E + 6 M + 1 T + 5 M + 1 T + 1 M + 2 E (a nonstop workout)	21
		Q2 = 10 E + 4 T + 1 E + 4 T + 2 E	21
17	.8	Q1 = 4 E + 3 T + 60 min E + 3 T + 2 E	21
		Q2 = 8 E + 6 × (1 km I w/2 min jg) + 6 × (400 R w/400 m jg) + 2 E	17

Weeks until race	Fraction of peak	Workout	Miles for Q sessions
16	.9	Q1 = steady **E** run of 23 miles (37 km)	23
		Q2 = 5 **E** + 4 **T** + 4 min **E** + 3 **T** + 3 min **E** + 2 **T** + 2 min **E** + 1 **T** + 2 **E**	18
15	.9	Q1 = 2 **E** + 8 **M** + 1 **T** + 4 **M** + 1 **T** + 3 **M** + 2 **E**	21
		Q2 = 8 E + 4 × (2 T w/2 min rests) + 2 E	18
14	.8	Q1 = 2 **E** + 2 × (2 **T** w/2 min rests) + 60 min **E** + 3 **T** + 2 **E**	20
		Q2 = 8 **E** + 8 × (1 km **I** w/2 min jg) + 3 **E** or 8 **E** + 5 × (1 **I** w/4 min jg) + 3 **E**	17
13	1.0	Q1 = steady **E** run of 20 miles (32 km)	20
		Q2 = 8 **E** + 5 × (2 **T** w/2 min rests) + 2 **E**	20
12	1.0	Q1 = 4 **E** + 8 **M** + 1 **T** + 6 **M** + 1 **T** + 2 **E**	22
		Q2 = 6 E + 4 min E + 3 T + 3 min E + 2 T + 2 min E + 1 T + 2 E	19
11	.9	Q1 = 10 **E** + 4 **T** + 8 **E**	22
		Q2 = 8 **E** + 8 × (1 km **I** w/2 min jg) + 4 × (400 **R** w/400 jg) + 2 **E**	18
10	.8	Q1 = steady **E** run of 21 miles (34 km)	21
		Q2 = 2 **E** + 16 **M** + 2 **E**	20
9	1.0	**Q1 = 4 E + 6 M + 1 T + 6 M + 2 E**	19
		Q2 = 3 **E** + 4 **T** + 4 min **E** + 4 **T** + 4 min **E** + 2 **T** + 2 **E**	16
8	1.0	Q1 = 6 **E** + 13 **M** + 3 **E**	22
		Q2 = 8 **E** + 3 × (1 **I** w/4 min jg) + 3 × (1 km **I** w/2 min jg) + 2 **E**	17
7	.9	Q1 = steady **E** run of 22 miles (35 km)	22
		Q2 = 4 E + 8 M + 4 T + 2 E	18
6	1.0	Q1 = 4 **E** + 8 **M** + 1 **T** + 4 **M** + 1 **T** + 1 **M** + 2 **E**	21
		Q2 = 3 **E** + 4 **T** + 4 min **E** + 2 × (3 **T** w/3 min rests) + 2 **E**	15
5	.8	**Q1 = 2 E + 4 T + 8 mile (13 km) E + 4 T + 2 E**	20
		Q2 = 6 **E** + 6 × (1 km **I** w/2 min jg) + 4 × (400 **R** w/400 jg) + 2 **E**	15
4	.9	Q1 = steady **E** run of 21 miles (34 km)	21
		Q2 = 5 **E** + 3 × (1 **T** w/1 min jg) + 3 × (1 km **I** w/2 min jg) + 3 × (400 **R** w/400 jg) + 2 **E**	15
3	.7	Q1 = 4 **E** + 6 **M** + 1 **T** + 6 **M** + 1 **T** + 2 **E**	20
		Q2 = 2 **E** + 4 × (2 **T** w/2 min jg) + 2 **E**	12

(continued)

Table 14.3   Two Quality Sessions Marathon Training Plan for 40 to 120 Miles (64 to 194 km) per Week   *(continued)*

		More than 120 miles (194 km) per week		
Weeks until race	**Fraction of peak**	**Workout**		**Miles for Q sessions**
2	.7	Q1 = 2 **E** + 3 × (2 **T** w/2 min rests) + 8 **E**		16
		Q2 = 4 **E** + 1 **T** + 2 **M** + 1 **T** + 2 **M** + 2 **E**		12
1	—	7 days: Q1 = 90 min **E**		14
		6 days: 60 min **E**		9
		5 days: Q2 = 4 **E** + 3 × (1 **T** w/2 min rests) + 2 **E**		9
		4 days: 50 min **E**		7
		3 days: 30-40 min **E**		6
		2 days: 30-40 min **E**		5
		1 day: 20-30 min **E** (tomorrow is the race)		3

Table created by Jack Daniels' Running Calculator designed by the Run SMART Project.

4-WEEK CYCLE

The following training programs provide 26 weeks of training and assume any runners who follow them have been running regularly before starting out. If you have sufficient training, it is certainly possible to jump in less than 26 weeks before the marathon for which you are preparing. I encourage you to look through the full program you believe best meets your needs in order to decide when to enter, and if you think you need a few weeks of base running before getting started, then do so.

All 4-week cycles are 2Q plans, designed to include two Q training sessions each week, for 3 consecutive weeks, followed by a 4th week of no Q sessions. The non-Q week contains just **E** running and also maximum (peak) weekly mileage.

It is suggested that Q1 be on Sunday, or the same day of the week on which your coming marathon will be run. With Q1 on Sunday, then Q2 is best located on Wednesday or Thursday. Feel free to rearrange your Q1 and Q2 sessions to fall on whichever days best suit your personal schedule, but make an effort to always have 2 or 3 **E** days between Q days.

E days are to be used for recovery and easy (non-Q) runs used to accumulate your weekly mileage goals. **E** days may involve one, two, or more **E** runs for each day, as needed. If you must, or desire to, take a day off from training now and then, just use the remaining **E** days of that week to reach your weekly mileage goal. Make a habit of adding six to eight strides to the middle or end of at least 2 **E** days every week. Strides (ST) are meant to be light, quick 10- to 20-second runs, with about 1-minute recovery between each. Strides are fast, controlled runs but not sprints. If you have a moderate hill available, feel free to run strides up the hill, but be careful jogging back down because downhill running can sometimes be a little stressful.

If you include any races during this marathon plan, schedule them in place of your Q1 session for that week, but perform the displaced Q1 session at midweek and drop that week's Q2 altogether. This means a Sunday race would start the week with the race, followed by that week's Q1 (a few days later), and the next week starts with its Q1, as normal. Try to rearrange training so you get 3 **E** days before any race, and take 1 **E** day for each 3,000 to 4,000 meters of race distance (e.g., 3 **E** days after a 10K).

I typically suggest that weekly mileage vary from 80 to 100 percent of peak (P) mileage, with P being the most mileage you plan to run in any single week, and most often every 4th week, as indicated in this program. For example, if you pick 60 miles as your peak weekly mileage, and I suggest .8P for a week, this means you run 80 percent of 60 (48 miles) for that week. Each week's suggested fraction of P is listed in the second column of the program.

If you use VDOT values to determine training speeds for **M**, **T**, **I**, and **R** paces, try to be realistic, and use a VDOT that comes from a race distance of at least 10K. The longer and more recent the race, the better. If it has been a while since a race, make a conservative estimate of what you think you can race over a course of similar terrain to what you will face in training and in your marathon. For the first 8 weeks of this program, use the lesser of the VDOT values that is equal to a recent race and 3 VDOT units lower than your anticipated marathon VDOT. During each additional 8 weeks of this program, increase the VDOT value by 1 unit. If you run a race or two that suggest your VDOT is greater than what you would get by adding 1 to the previous value, feel free to use the race VDOT, particularly if you believe the course was legitimate.

If not using VDOT units, choose a realistic goal **M** pace. Then, final **T** pace will be 15 seconds per mile faster than goal **M** pace. Final **I** pace will be 6 seconds per 400 meters faster than **T** pace. Final **R** pace will be 3 seconds per 200 meters faster than **I** pace. An example of using this method follows: Assume estimated **M** race pace is 6:00 per mile (3:43/km), which means your final **T** pace is 5:45/mile (about 86 sec/400 and 3:35/km). This makes final **I** pace 80 sec/400 or 3:20/km, and final **R** pace is 74/400 and 37/200.

For the first 8 weeks, use training paces that are 10 seconds per mile slower than your goal and final paces, and for the middle 8 weeks, bring the paces to within 4 seconds per mile of your goal and final paces (which are then to be used during the final 10 weeks of the overall 26-week program).

Table 14.4 provides 4-week cycles for runners running from up to 40 miles (64 km) per week to about 120 miles (194 km) per week. Remember, if no units of distance are indicated, the distance is miles. For example, 8 **M** means to run 8 miles at **M** pace and 3 × 1 **T** means to run three 1-mile runs at **T** pace.

Table 14.4 4-Week-Cycle Marathon Training Plan for 40 to 120 Miles (64 to 194 km) per Week

		Up to 40 miles (64 km) per week	
Weeks until race	**Fraction of peak**	**First Q session**	**Second Q session**
26	.9	No Q sessions this week; **E** runs all week + add 6-8 ST on 2 days	
25	.9	**L** = lesser of 12 miles (19 km) & 90 min	2 **E** + 2 × 1 **T** w/1 min rests + 3 × 3 min **H** (**I** pace) w/2 min jg + 4 × 200 **R** w/200 jg + 1 **E**
24	.8	30 min **E** + 6 **M**	1 **E** + 3 **M** + 1 **E** + 3 **M** + 1 **E**
23	.9	2 **E** + 4 × 1 **T** w/1 min rests + 2 **E**	2 **E** + 3 × 1 **T** w/1 min rests + 8 × 200 **R** w/200 jg + 1 **E**
22	1.0	No Q sessions this week; **E** runs all week + add 6-8 ST on 2 days	
21	.8	**L** = lesser of 13 miles (21 km) & 90 min	2 **E** + 2 × 1 **T** w/2 min rests + 3 × 1 km **I** w/3 min jg + 6 × 200 **R** w/200 jg + 1 **E**
20	1.0	30 min **E** + 8 **M**	1 **E** + 5 **M** + 1 **E** + 4 **M** + 1 **E**
19	.9	2 **E** + 4 × 1 **T** w/1 min rests + 2 **E**	2 **E** + 3 × 1 **T** w/1 min rests + 8 × 200 **R** w/200 jg + 2 **E**
18	1.0	No Q sessions this week; **E** runs all week + add 6-8 ST on 2 days	
17	.8	**L** = lesser of 14 miles (23 km) & 2 hr	2 **E** + 2 **T** + 2 min rest + 3 × 3 min **H** w/3 min jg + 8 × 200 **R** w/200 jg + 1 **E**
16	.9	3 **E** + 10 **M**	2 **E** + 6 **M** + 1 **E** + 4 **M** + 1 **E**
15	.8	2 **E** + 2 × 1 **T** w/1 min rests	2 **E** + 4 × 1 **T** w/1 min rests + 8 × 200 **R** w/200 jg + 2 **E** + 2 **T** + 2 min rest + 1 **T** + 1 **E**
14	1.0	No Q sessions this week; **E** runs all week + add 6-8 ST on 2 days	
13	.9	**L** = lesser of 15 miles (24 km) & 2 hr	2 **E** + 2 **T** + 2 min rest + 3 × 3 min **H** w/2 min jg + 8 × 200 **R** w/200 jg + 1 **E**
12	.8	20 min **E** + 12 **M**	2 **E** + 6 **M** + 1 **E** + 5 **M** + 1 **E**
11	.7	2 **E** + 2 × 1 **T** w/1 min rests + 2 **T**	2 **E** + 4 × 1 **T** w/1 min rests + 8 × 200 **R** w/200 jg + 2 **E** + 2 min rest + 1 **T** + 1 **E**
10	1.0	No Q sessions this week; **E** runs all week + add 6-8 ST on 2 days	
9	.9	**L** = lesser of 15 miles (24 km) & 130 min	2 **E** + 2 **T** + 2 min rest + 2 **T** + 2 min rest + 3 × 3 min **H** w/2 min jg + 6 × 200 **R** w/200 jg + 1 **E**
8	1.0	30 min **E** + 12 **M**	3 **E** + 6 **M** + 1 **E** + 4 **M** + 1 **E**
7	.8	30 min **E** + 3 × 2 **T** w/2 min rests + 2 **E**	2 **E** + 4 × 1 **T** w/1 min rests + 8 × 200 **R** w/20 jg + 2 **E**

Up to 40 miles (64 km) per week

Weeks until race	Fraction of peak	First Q session	Second Q session
6	1.0	No Q sessions this week; **E** runs all week + add 6-8 ST on 2 days	
5	.9	**L** = lesser of 15 miles (24 km) & 130 min	2 **E** + 2 × 1 **T** w/1 min rests + 3 × 3 min **H** w/2 min jg + 8 × 200 **R** w/200 jg + 1 **E**
4	.9	20 min **E** + 12 **M**	3 **E** + 5 **M** + 1 **E** + 5 **M** + 1 **E**
3	.8	60 min **E** + 3 **T** + 2 min rest + 2 **T** + 2 **E**	2 **E** + 4 × 1 **T** w/1 min rests + 8 × 200 **R** w/200 jg + 2 **E**
2	.7	No Q sessions this week; **E** runs all week + add 6-8 ST on 2 days	
1	—	• 7 days: 90 min **E** • 6 days: 60 min **E** • 5 days: 3 × 1 **T** w/2 min rests • 4 days: 60 min **E** • 2 days: 30 min **E** • 1 day: 30 min **E** (tomorrow is the marathon race)	

41-55 miles (66-89 km) per week

Weeks until race	Fraction of peak	First Q session	Second Q session
26	.8	No Q sessions this week; **E** runs all week + add 6-8 ST on 2 days	
25	.9	**L** = lesser of 13 miles (21 km) & 90 min	2 **E** + 3 × 1 **T** w/1 min rests + 3 × 3 min **H** (**I** pace) w/2 min recovery jg + 4 × 200 **R** w/200 jg + 1 **E**
24	.8	30 min **E** + 7 **M**	1 **E** + 5 **M** + 1 **E** + 2 **M** + 1 **E**
23	.9	2 **E** + 5 × 1 **T** w/1 min rests + 2 **E**	2 **E** + 4 × 1 **T** w/1 min rests + 4 × 400 **R** w/400 jg + 1 **E**
22	1.0	No Q sessions this week; **E** runs all week + add 6-8 ST on 2 days	
21	.8	**L** = lesser of 14 miles (23 km) & 90 min	2 **E** + 3 × 1 **T** w/2 min rests + 3 × 3 min **H** w/2 min jg + 4 × 200 **R** w/200 jg + 1 **E**
20	1.0	30 min **E** + 9 **M**	2 **E** + 5 **M** + 1 **E** + 4 **M** + 2 **E**
19	.9	2 **E** + 5 × 1 **T** w/1 min rests + 2 **E**	2 **E** + 4 × 1 **T** w/1 min rests + 4 × 400 **R** w/400 jg + 1 **E**
18	1.0	No Q sessions this week; **E** runs all week + add 6-8 ST on 2 days	
17	.8	**L** = lesser of 15 miles (24 km) & 100 min	2 **E** + 3 × 1 **T** + 3 min rest + 3 × 3 min **H** w/2 min jg + 8 × 200 **R** w/200 jg + 1 **E**

(continued)

41-55 miles (66-89 km) per week

Weeks until race	Fraction of peak	First Q session	Second Q session
16	.9	3 **E** + 10 **M**	2 **E** + 6 **M** + 1 **E** + 5 **M** + 1 **E**
15	.8	2 **E** + 2 × 2 **T** w/2 min rests + 2 **E**	2 **E** + 3 **T** + 3 min rest + 2 **T** + 2 min rest + 8 × 200 **R** w/200 jg + 2 × 1 **T** w/1 min rests + 1 **E** + 2 **E**
14	1.0	No Q sessions this week; **E** runs all week + add 6-8 ST on 2 days	
13	.9	**L** = lesser of 16 miles (26 km) & 2 hr	2 **E** + 3 × 1 **T** w/1 min rests + 3 min rest + 3 × 1 km **I** w/3 min jg + 4 × 400 **R** w/400 jg + 1 **E**
12	.8	3 **E** + 13 **M**	1 **E** + 6 **M** + 1 **E** + 5 **M** + 1 **E** + 2 **M** + 1 **E**
11	.7	2 **E** + 2 × 2 **T** w/2 min rests	2 **E** + 3 **T** + 3 min rest + 2 **T** + 2 min rest + 2 × 400 **R** w/400 jg + 2 × 1 **T** w/1 min rest + 1 **E** + 4 × 200 **R** w/200 jg + 1 **E**
10	1.0	No Q sessions this week; **E** runs all week + add 6-8 ST on 2 days	
9	.9	**L** = lesser of 16 miles (26 km) & 140 min	2 **E** + 3 × 1 **T** w/1 min rests + 4 × 3 min **H** w/2 min jg + 6 × 200 **R** w/200 jg + 1 **E**
8	1.0	20 min **E** + 14 **M**	1 **E** + 6 **M** + 1 **E** + 7 **M** + 1 **E**
7	.8	4 **E** + 3 × 2 **T** w/2 min rests + 1 **T** + 1 **E**	2 **E** + 2 × 2 **T** w/2 min rests + 8 × 200 **R** w/20 jg + 4 × 1 **T** w/1 min rests + 2 **E**
6	1.0	No Q sessions this week; **E** runs all week + add 6-8 ST on 2 days	
5	.9	**L** = lesser of 16 miles (26 km) & 140 min	2 **E** + 2 × 3 **T** w/3 min rests + 2 **T** + 3 min rest + 4 × 3 min **H** w/2 min jg + 8 × 200 **R** w/200 jg + 1 **E**
4	.9	10 min **E** + 14 **M**	1 **E** + 8 **M** + 1 **E** + 5 **M** + 1 **E**
3	.8	60 min **E** + 3 × 2 **T** w/2 min rests + 1 **T**	2 **E** + 2 × 2 **T** w/2 min rests + 2 × 1 **T** w/1 min rests + 2 **E** 8 × 200 **R** w/ 200 jg + 2 **E**
2	.7	No Q sessions this week; **E** runs all week + add 6-8 ST on 2 days	
1	—	• 7 days: 90 min **E** • 6 days: 60 min **E** • 5 days: 3 × 1 mile **T** w/2 min rests • 4 days: 60 min **E** • 3 days: 45 min **E** • 2 days: 30 min **E** • 1 day: 30 min **E** (tomorrow is the marathon race)	

56-70 miles (90-113 km) per week

Weeks until race	Fraction of peak	First Q session	Second Q session
26	.8	No Q sessions this week; **E** runs all week + add 6-8 ST on 2 days	
25	.9	**L** = lesser of 14 miles (23 km) & 100 min	2 **E** + 3 × 1 **T** w/1 min rests + 4 × 3 min **H** (**I** pace) w/2 min recovery jg + 6 × 200 **R** w/200 jg + 1 **E**
24	.8	30 min **E** + 8 **M**	1 **E** + 5 **M** + 1 **E** + 3 **M** + 1 **E**
23	.9	2 **E** + 6 × 1 **T** w/1 min rests + 2 **E**	2 **E** + 5 × 1 **T** w/1 min rests + 8 × 200 **R** w/200 jg + 1 **E**
22	1.0	No Q sessions this week; **E** runs all week + add 6-8 ST on 2 days	
21	.8	**L** = lesser of 15 miles (24 km) & 105 min	2 **E** + 3 × 1 **T** w/2 min rests + 5 × 3 min **H** w/2 min jg + 8 × 200 **R** w/200 jg + 1 **E**
20	1.0	30 min **E** + 10 **M**	2 **E** + 6 **M** + 1 **E** + 4 **M** + 2 **E**
19	.9	2 **E** + 3 × 1 **T** w/1 min rests + 2 **T**	2 **E** + 6 × 1 **T** w/1 min rests + 8 × 200 **R** w/200 jg + 1 **E** + 2 × 1 **T** w/1 min rest + 1 **E**
18	1.0	No Q sessions this week; **E** runs all week + add 6-8 ST on 2 days	
17	.8	**L** = lesser of 16 miles (26 km) & 2 hr	2 **E** + 3 × 1 **T** + 3 min rest + 5 × 3 min **H** w/2 min jg + 8 × 200 **R** w/200 jg + 1 **E**
16	.9	4 **E** + 12 **M**	2 **E** + 6 **M** + 1 **E** + 6 **M** + 1 **E**
15	.8	2 **E** + 3 × 2 **T** w/2 min rests	2 **E** + 6 × 1 **T** w/1 min rests + 4 × 200 **R** w/200 jg + 2 × 1 **T** w/1 min rests + 1 **E** + 4 × 400 **R** w/400 jg + 2 **E**
14	1.0	No Q sessions this week; **E** runs all week + add 6-8 ST on 2 days	
13	.9	**L** = lesser of 17 miles (27 km) & 130 min	2 **E** + 2 × 2 **T** w/2 min rests + 5 × 3 min **H** w/2 min jg + 4 × 400 **R** w/400 jg + 1 **E**
12	.8	**M** = 3 **E** + 14 **M**	1 **E** + 8 **M** + 1 **E** + 6 **M** + 1 **E**
11	.7	**T** = 4 **E** + 4 × 2 **T** w/2 min rests + 2 **E**	2 **E** + 6 × 1 **T** w/1 min rests + 4 × 200 **R** w/200 jg + 4 × 400 **R** w/400 jg + 1 **E**
10	1.0	No Q sessions this week; **E** runs all week + add 6-8 ST on 2 days	
9	.9	**L** = lesser of 18 miles (29 km) & 140 min	2 **E** + 3 **T** + 3 min rest + 2 **T** + 2 min rest + 5 × 3 min **H** w/2 min jg + 6 × 200 **R** w/200 jg + 1 **E**
8	1.0	30 min **E** + 15 **M**	2 **E** + 8 **M** + 1 **E** + 6 **M** + 2 **E**
7	.8	4 **E** + 4 × 2 **T** w/2 min rests + 1 **T** + 1 **E**	2 **E** + 3 × 2 **T** w/2 min rests + 8 × 200 **R** w/200 jg + 2 **T** + 2 **E**

(continued)

56-70 miles (90-113 km) per week

Weeks until race	Fraction of peak	First Q session	Second Q session
6	1.0	No Q sessions this week; **E** runs all week + add 6-8 ST on 2 days	
5	.9	**L** = lesser of 18 miles (29 km) & 140 min	2 **E** + 3 **T** + 3 min rest + 2 **T** + 3 min rest + 5 × 3 min **H** w/2 min jg + 8 × 200 **R** w/200 jg + 1 **E**
4	.9	50 min **E** + 16 **M**	4 **E** + 10 **M** + 1 **E** + 6 **M** + 2 **E**
3	.8	60 min **E** + 4 × 3 **T** w/3 min rests + 1 **E**	2 **E** + 2 × 3 **T** w/3 min rests + 8 × 200 **R** w/ 200 jg + 2 **E**
2	.7	No Q sessions this week; **E** runs all week + add 6-8 ST on 2 days	
1	—	• 7 days: 90 min **E** • 6 days: 60 min **E** • 5 days: 3 × 1 mile **T** w/2 min rests • 4 days: 60 min **E** • 3 days: 45 min **E** • 2 days: 30 min **E** • 1 day: 30 min **E** (tomorrow is the marathon race)	

71-85 miles (114-137 km) per week

Weeks until race	Fraction of peak	First Q session	Second Q session
26	.9	No Q sessions this week; **E** runs all week + add 6-8 ST on 2 days	
25	.9	**L** = lesser of 15 miles (24 km) & 100 min	2 **E** + 4 × 1 **T** w/1 min rests + 4 × 3 min **H** (**I** pace) w/2 min recovery jg + 8 × 200 **R** w/200 jg + 2 **E**
24	.8	40 min **E** + 8 **M**	3 **E** + 5 **M** + 1 **E** + 3 **M** + 3 **E**
23	.9	2 **E** + 3 × 1 **T** w/1 min rests + 2 **T** + 2 min rest + 2 × 1 **T** w/1 min rests	2 **E** + 6 × 1 **T** w/1 min rests + 8 × 200 **R** w/200 jg + 2 **E**
22	1.0	No Q sessions this week; **E** runs all week + add 6-8 ST on 2 days	
21	.8	**L** = lesser of 17 miles (27 km) & 2 hr	2 **E** + 3 × 1 **T** w/2 min rests + 5 × 3 min **H** w/2 min jg + 8 × 200 **R** w/200 jg + 2 **E**
20	1.0	30 min **E** + 10 **M**	2 **E** + 6 **M** + 1 **E** + 4 **M** + 2 **E**
19	.9	2 **E** + 3 × 1 **T** w/1 min rests + 2 **T** + 2 × 1 **T** w/1 min rest + 1 **E**	2 **E** + 6 × 1 **T** w/1 min rests + 8 × 200 **R** w/200 jg + 1 **E**
18	1.	No Q sessions this week; **E** runs all week + add 6-8 ST on 2 days	
17	.8	**L** = lesser of 18 miles (29 km) & 130 min	2 **E** + 4 × 1 **T** w/1 min rests + 5 × 3 min **H** w/2 min jg + 6 × 200 **R** w/200 jg + 2 **E**

71-85 miles (114-137 km) per week

Weeks until race	Fraction of peak	First Q session	Second Q session
16	.9	40 min **E** + 12 **M**	**4 E** + **6 M** + **1 E** + **6 M** + **1 E**
15	.8	2 **E** + 4 × 2 **T** w/2 min rests + 2 **T** + 2	2 **E** + 3 × 2 **T** w/2 min rests + 8 × 200 **R** w/200 jg 1 **T** + 2 **E**
14	1.0	No Q sessions this week; **E** runs all week + add 6-8 ST on 2 days	
13	.9	**L** = lesser of 19 miles (31 km) & 2.5 hr	2 **E** + 5 × 1 **T** w/1 min rests + 6 × 3 min **H** w/2 min jg + 4 × 400 **R** w/400 jg + 2 **E**
12	.8	4 **E** + 14 **M**	2 **E** + 8 **M** + 1 **E** + 6 **M** + 1 **E**
11	.7	4 **E** + 5 × 2 **T** w/2 min rests + 1 **E**	2 **E** + 3 × 2 **T** w/1 min rests + 8 × 200 **R** w/200 jg + 2 **T** + 2 **E**
10	1.0	No Q sessions this week; **E** runs all week + add 6-8 ST on 2 days	
9	.9	**L** = lesser of 20 miles (32 km) & 2.5 hr	2 **E** + 3 × 2 **T** w/3 min rests + 2 **T** + 2 min rest + 6 × 3 min **H** w/2 min jg + 8 × 200 **R** w/200 jg + 1 **E**
8	1.0	30 min **E** + 16 **M**	2 **E** + 8 **M** + 1 **E** + 8 **M** + 1 **E**
7	.8	4 **E** + 3 × 3 **T** w/3 min rests + 2 **T** + 1 **E**	2 **E** + 4 × 2 **T** w/2 min rests + 8 × 200 **R** w/200 jg + 1 **T** + 2 **E**
6	1.0	No Q sessions this week; **E** runs all week + add 6-8 ST on 2 days	
5	.9	**L** = lesser of 20 miles (32 km) & 2.5 hr	2 **E** + 3 × 2 **T** w/2 min rests + 6 × 3 min **H** w/2 min jg + 8 × 200 **R** w/200 jg + 2 **E**
4	.9	30 min **E** + 16 **M**	4 **E** + 8 **M** + 1 **E** + 6 **M** + 1 **E**
3	.8	60 min **E** + 3 × 3 **T** w/3 min rests + 2 **T** + 1 **E**	2 **E** + 4 × 2 **T** w/2 min rests + 8 × 200 **R** w/ 200 jg + 1 **T** + 2 **E**
2	.7	No Q sessions this week; **E** runs all week + add 6-8 ST on 2 days	
1	—	• 7 days: 90 min **E** • 6 days: 60 min **E** • 5 days: 3 × 1 **T** w/2 min rests • 4 days: 60 min **E** • 3 days: 45 min **E** • 2 days: 30 min **E** • 1 day: 30 min **E** (tomorrow is the marathon race)	

86-100 miles (138-161 km) per week

Weeks until race	Fraction of peak	First Q session	Second Q session
26	.8	No Q sessions this week; **E** runs all week + add 6-8 ST on 2 days	

(continued)

86-100 miles (138-161 km) per week

Weeks until race	Fraction of peak	First Q session	Second Q session
25	.9	**L** = lesser of 16 miles (26 km) & 2 hr	2 **E** + 2 × 2 **T** w/2 min rests + 5 × 3 min **H** (**I** pace) w/2 min recovery jg + 8 × 200 **R** w/200 jg + 2 **E**
24	.8	40 min **E** + 9 **M**	3 **E** + 5 **M** + 1 **E** + 3 **M** + 3 **E**
23	.9	2 **E** + 2 × 1 **T** w/1 min rests + 2 × 2 **T** w/2 min rest + 2 × 1 **T** w/1 min rest + 2 **E**	2 **E** + 6 × 1 **T** w/1 min rests + 8 × 200 **R** w/200 **E** + 2 × 2 **T** w/2 min jg + 2 **E**
22	1.0	No Q sessions this week; **E** runs all week + add 6-8 ST on 2 days	
21	.8	**L** = lesser of 18 miles (29 km) & 130 min	2 **E** + 3 × 1 **T** w/2 min rests + 5 × 3 min **H** w/2 min jg + 8 × 200 **R** w/200 jg + 1 **E**
20	1.0	50 min **E** + 11 **M**	2 **E** + 6 **M** + 1 **E** + 4 **M** + 2 **E**
19	.9	2 **E** + 3 × 1 **T** w/1 min rests + 2 × 2 **T** w/2 min rest + 2 × 1 **T** w/1 min rest + 2 **E**	2 **E** + 6 × 1 **T** w/1 min rests + 8 × 200 **R** w/200 jg + 2 **E**
18	1.0	No Q sessions this week; **E** runs all week + add 6-8 ST on 2 days	
17	.8	**L** = lesser of 19 miles (31 km) & 2.5 hr	2 **E** + 4 × 1 **T** w/1 min rests + 5 × 3 min **H** w/2 min jg + 6 × 200 **R** w/200 jg + 2 **E**
16	.9	40 min **E** + 13 **M**	4 **E** + 6 **M** + 1 **E** + 6 **M** + 1 **E**
15	.8	2 **E** + 4 × 2 **T** w/2 min rests + 2 × 1 **T** w/1 min rests + 2 **E**	2 **E** + 3 × 2 **T** w/2 min rests + 8 × 200 **R** w/200 jg + 2 **T** + 2 **E**
14	1.0	No Q sessions this week; **E** runs all week + add 6-8 ST on 2 days	
13	.9	**L** = lesser of 20 miles (32 km) & 2.5 hr	2 **E** + 5 × 1 **T** w/1 min rests + 6 × 3 min **H** w/2 min jg + 4 × 400 **R** w/400 jg + 1 **E**
12	.8	30 min **E** + 15 **M**	2 **E** + 8 **M** + 1 **E** + 6 **M** + 1 **E**
11	.7	4 **E** + 4 × 2 **T** w/2 min rests + 3 × 1 **T** w/1 min rests + 1 **E**	2 **E** + 3 × 2 **T** w/1 min rests + 8 × 200 **R** w/200 jg + 2 **T** + 2 **E**
10	1.0	No Q sessions this week; **E** runs all week + add 6-8 ST on 2 days	
9	.9	**L** = lesser of 22 miles (35 km) & 2.5 hr	2 **E** + 3 × 2 **T** w/2 min rests + 2 **T** + 2 min rest + 6 × 3 min **H** w/2 min jg + 4 × 400 **R** w/400 jg + 1 **E**
8	1.0	40 min **E** + 16 **M**	4 **E** + 8 **M** + 1 **E** + 8 **M** + 1 **E**
7	.8	4 **E** + 6 × 2 **T** w/2 min rests + 1 **E**	2 **E** + 2 × 3 **T** w/3 min rests + 8 × 200 **R** w/20 jg + 4 × 1 **T** w/ 1 min rests + 2 **E**

86-100 miles (138-161 km) per week

Weeks until race	Fraction of peak	First Q session	Second Q session
6	1.0	No Q sessions this week; **E** runs all week + add 6-8 ST on 2 days	
5	.9	**L** = lesser of 22 miles (35 km) & 2.5 hr	2 **E** + 3 × 2 **T** w/2 min rests + 6 × 3 min **H** w/2 min jg + 4 × 400 **R** w/400 jg + 1 **E**
4	.9	**M** = 40 min **E** + 16 **M**	4 **E** + 8 **M** + 1 **E** + 8 **M** + 1 **E**
3	.8	60 min **E** + 6 × 2 **T** w/2 min rests	2 **E** + 3 × 2 **T** w/2 min rests + 8 × 200 **R** w/ 200 jg + 3 × 1 **T** w/1 min rests + 2 **E**
2	.7	No Q sessions this week; **E** runs all week + add 6-8 ST on 2 days	
1	—	• 7 days: 90 min **E** • 6 days: 60 min **E** • 5 days: 3 × 1 **T** w/2 min rests • 4 days: 60 min **E** • 3 days: 45 min **E** • 2 days: 30 min **E** • 1 day: 30 min **E** (tomorrow is the marathon race)	

101-120 miles (163-194 km) per week

Weeks until race	Fraction of peak	First Q session	Second Q session
26	.8	No Q sessions this week; **E** runs all week + add 6-8 ST on 2 days	
25	.9	**L** = lesser of 17 miles & 2 hr	2 **E** + 2 × 2 **T** w/2 min rests + 1 **T** + 3 min rest + 5 × 3 min **H** w/2 min jg + 6 × 200 **R** w/200 jg + 2 **E**
24	.8	50 min **E** + 10 **M**	3 **E** + 6 **M** + 1 **E** + 4 **M** + 3 **E**
23	.9	3 **E** + 3 **T** + 3 min rest + 3 × 2 **T** w/2 min rests + 2 **E**	2 **E** + 3 **T** + 3 min rest + 2 **T** + 2 min rest + 1 **T** + 2 min rest + 8 × 200 **R** w/200 jg + 1 **T** + 2 **E**
22	1.0	No Q sessions this week; **E** runs all week + add 6-8 ST on 2 days	
21	.8	**L** = lesser of 18 miles (29 km) & 130 min	2 **E** + 5 × 1 **T** w/1 min rests + 6 × 3 min **H** w/2 min jg + 6 × 200 **R** w/200 jg + 3 **E**
20	1.0	50 min **E** + 12 **M**	3 **E** + 6 **M** + 1 **E** + 6 **M** + 3 **E**
19	.9	3 **E** + 5 × 2 **T** w/2 min rests + 2 **E**	2 **E** + 3 × 2 **T** w/2 min rests + 8 × 200 **R** w/200 jg + 2 **T** + 1 **E**
18	.9	No Q sessions this week; **E** runs all week + add 6-8 ST on 2 days	
17	.8	**L** = lesser of 20 miles (32 km) & 2.5 hr	2 **E** + 3 × 2 **T** w/2 min rests + 6 × 3 min **H** w/2 min jg + 6 × 200 **R** w/200 jg + 2 **E**

(continued)

101-120 miles (163-194 km) per week

Weeks until race	Fraction of peak	First Q session	Second Q session
16	.9	40 min **E** + 14 **M**	4 **E** + 8 **M** + 1 **E** + 6 **M** + 1 **E**
15	.8	3 **E** + 2 × 3 **T** w/3 min rests + 2 × 2 **T** w/2 min rests + 1 **T** + 2 **E**	3 **E** + 4 × 2 **T** w/2 min rests + 8 × 200 **R** w/200 jg + 2 **T** + 2 **E**
14	1.0	No Q sessions this week; **E** runs all week + add 6-8 ST on 2 days	
13	.9	**L** = lesser of 21 miles (34 km) & 2.5 hr	2 **E** + 3 × 2 **T** w/2 min rests + 6 × 3 min **H** w/2 min jg + 4 × 400 **R** w/400 jg + 2 **E**
12	.8	40 min **E** + 15 **M**	4 **E** + 8 **M** + 1 **E** + 7 **M** + 1 **E**
11	.7	4 **E** + 4 × 3 **T** w/3 min rests + 2 **E**	2 **E** + 4 × 2 **T** w/1 min rests + 8 × 200 **R** w/200 jg + 2 **T** + 2 **E**
10	.6	No Q sessions this week; **E** runs all week + add 6-8 ST on 2 days	
9	.9	**L** = lesser of 23 miles (37 km) & 2.5 hr	2 **E** + 4 × 2 **T** w/2 min rests + 6 × 3 min **H** w/2 min jg + 8 × 200 **R** w/200 jg + 3 **E**
8	1.0	40 min **E** + 16 **M**	4 **E** + 10 **M** + 1 **E** + 6 **M** + 2 **E**
7	.8	4 **E** + 3 × 3 **T** w/3 min rests + 2 × 2 **T** w/2 min rests + 1 **E**	2 **E** + 2 × 3 **T** w/3 min rests + 8 × 200 **R** w/200 jg + 4 × 1 **T** w/ 1 min rests + 2 **E**
6	.9	No Q sessions this week; **E** runs all week + add 6-8 ST on 2 days	
5	.9	**L** = lesser of 23 miles (37 km) & 2.5 hr	2 **E** + 2 × 3 **T** w/3 min rests + 2 **T** + 3 min rest + 6 × 3 min **H** w/2 min jg + 8 × 200 **R** w/200 jg + 1 **E**
4	.9	40 min **E** + 16 **M**	4 **E** + 8 **M** + 1 **E** + 8 **M** + 2 **E**
3	.8	60 min **E** + 3 × 3 **T** w/3 min rests	2 **E** + 2 × 3 **T** w/3 min rests + 8 × 200 **R** w/ 200 jg + 3 × 1 **T** w/2 min rests + 2 **E**
2	.7	No Q sessions this week; **E** runs all week + add 6-8 ST on 2 days	
1	—	• 7 days: 90 min **E** • 6 days: 60 min **E** • 5 days: 3 × 1 **T** w/2 min rests • 4 days: 60 min **E** • 3 days: 45 min **E** • 2 days: 30 min **E** • 1 day: 30 min **E** (tomorrow is the marathon race)	

More than 120 miles (194 km) per week

Weeks until race	Fraction of peak	First Q session	Second Q session
26	.8	No Q sessions this week; **E** runs all week + add 6-8 ST on 2 days	
25	.9	**L** = lesser of 18 miles (29 km) & 2 hr	2 **E** + 3 **T** + 3 min rest + 2 **T** + 2 min rest + 1 **T** + 1 min rest + 5 × 3 min **H** w/2 min jg + 8 × 200 **R** w/200 jg + 2 **E**
24	.8	60 min **E** + 10 **M**	4 **E** + 6 **M** + 1 **E** + 4 **M** + 3 **E**
23	.9	3 **E** + 5 × 2 **T** w/2 min rests + 3 **E**	3 **E** + 3 **T** + 3 min rest + 2 **T** + 2 min rest + 1 **T** + 2 min rest + 8 × 200 **R** w/200 jg + 2 **T** + 2 **E**
22	1.0	No Q sessions this week; **E** runs all week + add 6-8 ST on 2 days	
21	.8	**L** = lesser of 19 miles (31 km) & 135 min	3 **E** + 6 × 1 **T** w/1 min rests + 6 × 3 min **H** w/2 min jg + 8 × 200 **R** w/200 jg + 2 **E**
20	1.0	50 min **E** + 12 **M**	4 **E** + 6 **M** + 1 **E** + 6 **M** + 3 **E**
19	.9	3 **E** + 3 × 3 **T** w/3 min rests + 2 **T** + 2 **E**	3 **E** + 4 × 2 **T** w/2 min rests + 8 × 200 **R** w/200 jg + 1 **T** + 2 **E**
18	.9	No Q sessions this week; **E** runs all week + add 6-8 ST on 2 days	
17	.8	**L** = lesser of 21 miles (34 m) & 2.5 hr	3 **E** + 3 × 2 **T** w/2 min rests + 6 × 3 min **H** w/2 min jg + 4 × 400 **R** w/400 jg + 2 **E**
16	.9	50 min **E** + 14 **M**	**4 E + 8 M + 1 E + 6 M + 2 E**
15	.8	3 **E** + 6 × 2 **T** w/2 min rests + 2 **E**	2 **E** + 4 × 2 **T** w/2 min rests + 8 × 200 **R** w/200 jg + 2 **T** + 2 **E**
14	1.0	No Q sessions this week; **E** runs all week + add 6-8 ST on 2 days	
13	.9	**L** = lesser of 22 miles (35 km) & 2.5 hr	3 **E** + 3 **T** + 3 min rest + 2 × 2 **T** w/2 min rests + 6 × 3 min **H** w/2 min jg + 8 × 200 **R** w/200 jg + 1 **E**
12	.8	50 min **E** + 15 **M**	4 **E** + 8 **M** + 1 **E** + 7 **M** + 2 **E**
11	.7	4 **E** + 3 **T** + 3 min rest + 5 × 2 **T** w/2 min rests + 2 **E**	3 **E** + 2 × 3 **T** w/3 min rests + 8 × 200 **R** w/200 jg + 2 × 2 **T** w/2 min rests + 2 **E**
10	.6	No Q sessions this week; **E** runs all week + add 6-8 ST on 2 days	
9	.9	**L** = lesser of 23 miles (37 km) & 2.5 hr	2 **E** + 2 × 3 **T** w/3 min rests + 2 **T** + 2 min rest + 6 × 3 min **H** w/2 min jg + 8 × 200 **R** w/200 jg + 1 **E**

(continued)

More than 120 miles (194 km) per week

Weeks until race	Fraction of peak	First Q session	Second Q session
8	1.0	40 min **E** + 16 **M**	4 **E** + 10 **M** + 1 **E** + 6 **M** + 2 **E**
7	.8	4 **E** + 3 × 3 **T** w/3 min rests + 2 × 2 **T** w/2 min rests + 1 **E**	3 **E** + 2 × 3 **T** w/3 min rests + 8 × 200 **R** w/200 jg + 4 × 1 **T** w/ 1 min rests + 2 **E**
6	.9	No Q sessions this week; **E** runs all week + add 6-8 ST on 2 days	
5	.9	**L** = lesser of 23 miles (37 km) & 2.5 hr	2 **E** + 2 × 3 **T** w/3 min rests + 2 **T** + 3 min rest + 6 × 3 min **H** w/2 min jg + 8 × 200 **R** w/200 jg + 2 **E**
4	.9	40 min **E** + 16 **M**	4 **E** + 10 **M** + 1 **E** + 6 **M** + 2 **E**
3	.8	60 min **E** + 3 × 3 **T** w/3 min rests	2 **E** + 2 × 3 **T** w/3 min rests + 8 × 200 **R** w/200 jg + 3 × 1 **T** w/2 min rests + 2 **E**
2	.7	No Q sessions this week; **E** runs all week + add 6-8 ST on 2 days	
1	—	• 7 days: 90 min **E** • 6 days: 60 min **E** • 5 days: 3 × 1 **T** w/2 min rests • 4 days: 60 min **E** • 3 days: 45 min **E** • 2 days: 30 min **E** • 1 day: 30 min **E** (tomorrow is the marathon race)	

Table created by Jack Daniels' Running Calculator designed by the Run SMART Project.

5-WEEK CYCLE

Five-week cycles are repeated as many times as necessary to build up to an important race. How much of each type of training is performed is a function of current fitness and weekly mileage.

R sessions should total no more than the lesser of 5 percent of weekly mileage and 5 miles (8 km) at **R** pace. Recovery time between fast **R** running bouts should be two to three times as long as is the **R**-pace run time. **I** sessions can total no more than the lesser of 8 percent of weekly mileage and 10,000 meters at **I** pace. Recovery time between **I**-pace work bouts should be equal to, or a little less than, time spent at **I** pace. In combined **I/R** sessions, limit time at **R** and **I** paces to half that set aside for individual **R** and **I** sessions.

T sessions should total no more than the lesser of 10 percent of weekly mileage and 15 miles (24 km) at **T** pace, but consider 3 miles (4.8 km) at **T** pace to be the minimum for any **T** session. Recovery between bouts of **T**-pace running should be 1 minute for each 5 to 6 minutes of running time.

Limit total duration of **M**-pace running, in a single session, to not more than the lesser of 18 miles (29 km) and 20 percent of weekly mileage if doing more than 40 miles (64 km) per week, and not more than 30 percent of weekly mileage if less than 40. See chapter 4 for **R**, **I**, **T**, and **M** sessions to choose from.

With a weekend race, replace the back-to-back midweek sessions with one relatively comfortable **T** session 4 days before the race. After races, plan on 1 day of easy recovery running for each 3,000 meters of race distance. For example, take 3 **E** days after a 10K, 5 **E** days after a 15K, 7 **E** days after a half marathon, and 14 **E** days after a full marathon.

E is easy, conversational-pace running, and **E** pace is used in most **L** runs and during warm-up, cool-down, and recovery runs between faster work bouts. **L** runs are to be 30 percent of weekly mileage if running 40 miles (64 km) or less per week and 25 percent of weekly mileage if totaling more than 40 miles per week. Make **L** runs the lesser of 150 minutes and the amount determined by the 25 percent and 30 percent rules.

T is threshold-pace running, which is comfortably hard. You can estimate **T** pace from the VDOT tables in chapter 5. Cruise intervals are repeated runs at **T** pace, with short periods of rest between the **T**-pace runs. **I**, or interval pace, is subjectively hard—a pace you could race at for 10 to 12 minutes. Get **I** pace from the VDOT tables.

R is repetition-pace running and is at current mile or 1,500 race pace. **M** is marathon-pace running, determined by anticipated **M** race pace or VDOT tables.

In general, **I** pace is about 6 to 8 seconds per 400 slower than **R** pace, and **T** pace is 6 to 8 seconds per 400 slower than **I** pace. **M** pace is 12 seconds per mile slower than **T** for faster runners and 15 to 20 seconds per mile slower than **T** for slower runners.

Strides (ST) are 10- to 20-second light, quick (or uphill) runs with 30 to 60 seconds of rest between them.

Table 14.5 provides an overall description of how to follow the training program. In the last three weeks before the race, eliminate weekly strides and run mostly on flat terrain to get the feeling of floating over the ground. In the final two weeks before the race, eliminate any hill training and follow the first week of the training program, making the final week's **L** run a 90-minute effort. Instead of completing the **R** sessions, just focus on the **L** and **T** sessions, completing the **T** session four or five days prior to the race.

Table 14.5   5-Week Cycle Marathon Training Plan

Week	Day	Workout
1	Sunday	**L** run
	Monday	**E** + 8 ST
	Tuesday	E
	Wednesday	**T** session
	Thursday	**R** session
	Friday	E
	Saturday	**E** + 6 ST
2	Sunday	**M** run
	Monday	**E** + 6 ST
	Tuesday	E
	Wednesday	**T** session
	Thursday	**R** session
	Friday	E
	Saturday	**E** + 8 ST
3	Sunday	**L** run
	Monday	**E** + 8 ST
	Tuesday	E
	Wednesday	**T** session
	Thursday	**I** session
	Friday	E
	Saturday	**E** + 6 ST

Week	Day	Workout
4	Sunday	**M** run
	Monday	**E** + 6 ST
	Tuesday	E
	Wednesday	**T** session
	Thursday	**R** session
	Friday	E
	Saturday	**E** + 8 ST
5	Sunday	**L** run
	Monday	**E** + 8 ST
	Tuesday	E
	Wednesday	**T** session
	Thursday	**I** & **R** session
	Friday	E
	Saturday	**E** + 8 ST

Table created by Jack Daniels' Running Calculator designed by the Run SMART Project.

FINAL 18-WEEK PROGRAMS

There isn't always a specific amount of time available for training that prepares a runner for a marathon, and certainly some people have, and may also need, more time than others. Current state of fitness, weather, and the date of the marathon will all affect how much time may be necessary or available. I tend to write 18-week programs, but some runners like more time than that, especially if they want to run some special shorter races along the way. Some runners who are in great shape may want to race a marathon that's only a couple of months away, and in such a case, they could jump into the middle of a longer training schedule or even pick out weeks within a longer schedule that look desirable to them.

Some runners preparing for a marathon are logging high mileage and prefer not to try getting in two or three Q sessions in one week. Additionally, some runners want the distances in their training program to be written in miles, while others prefer dealing with distances written in kilometers. A third approach is to follow a program that is written in time spent performing different workouts.

With all this in mind, I present three different 18-week programs, all of which follow a similar approach to how the Q sessions are presented, but the first program is written so all the training distances are done in miles; the second program has all the training written in kilometers; and the third program has all the training expressed in amounts of time rather than distances of various intensities of training. It is possible to change training between a distance-based program and a time-based program just to see which might impose the least stress on a runner.

18-Week Program in Miles

This program is designed for the final 18 weeks leading up to a marathon. It assumes you are putting in a fair amount of time running and feel better *not* scheduling 2 Q runs each week; rather, a Q session is scheduled about every 4th or 5th day. The program assumes you are capable of handling a single steady run of at least 2 hours and a week that totals 100 or more miles. First, pick what you think is a reasonable maximum (peak, or P) weekly mileage. Each week I suggest a fraction of your chosen P mileage to achieve for that week (e.g., if you are doing 100 miles as a peak amount of weekly mileage, .8P = 80 miles). An E day means 1 or 2 E runs or no run if a rest day is needed (use E days to allow you to reach your weekly distance goals). I pace is the speed you could race for about 2.5 to 3 miles, or it is taken from the VDOT tables. On 2 E days each week, run six to eight 20-second ST (about mile [R] race pace, not sprints). R pace is current mile race pace.

On the E days, just do as much running as necessary to allow you to achieve your weekly distance goal. If sometimes you need a rest day, then use one of the E days for rest and just get the week's total distance in the other 6 days. If you have time for the longer training sessions only on weekends, then move the days around a little, but try to get in all the workouts that are written in detail.

Table 14.6 details an 18-week marathon training program in miles. The schedule is flexible, so the workouts can be arranged to best fit any schedule. The most important thing is to keep the quality training sessions in the order listed, even if they are not completed on the specific day in the table.

Table 14.6   18-Week Marathon Training Plan in Miles

Week	Workout
1	**16-18 mile (not more than 2.5 hr) long run (referred to as L) at easy (E) pace**
	E day (total .8P of running this week)
	E day
	E day
	10 min E + 10-12 miles at current estimated marathon (M) pace
	E day
	E day
2	E day (total .9P this week)
	E day
	10 min E + 2 × 3 miles T w/3 min rest between (T pace is 12-16 sec/mile faster than M, or can be selected from VDOT tables) + 60 min E
	E day
	E day
	E day
	E day
3	**10 min E + 4 × 2 mile T w/2 min rests + 30 min E**
	E day (total .8P this week)
	E day
	E day
	17-20 mile (not more than 2.5 hr) L run
	E day
	E day
4	**30 min E + 5 × 1 km I w/3 min jg + 4 × 400 R w/400 jg + 30 min E**
	E day (total .9P this week)
	E day
	E day
	E day
	10 min E + 4 × (2 mile at T w/2 min rests) + 40 min E
	E day

(continued)

Table 14.6   18-Week Marathon Training Plan in Miles   *(continued)*

Week	Workout
5	**E** day (total 1.0P this week)
	E day
	18-20 mile L run (not more than 2.5 hr)
	E day
	E day
	E day
	10 min **E** + 10-12 miles **M** + 30 min **E**
6	**E** day (total .8P this week)
	E day
	E day
	E day
	20 min E + 4 × (2 mile at T w/2 min rests) + 60 min E
	E day
	E day
7	**E** day (total 1.0P this week)
	E day
	30 min E + 12 miles M + 30 min E
	E day
	E day
	E day
	E day
8	**60 min E + 6 × 1 km I w/400 jg recovery + 2 miles T + 10 min E**
	E day (total .9P this week)
	E day
	E day
	E day
	20-23 mile L run (not more than 2.5 hr)
	E day

Week	Workout
9	**E** day (total .9P this week)
	E day
	E day
	30 min E + 14 miles M + 20 min E
	E day
	E day
	E day
10	**30 min E + 2 × (3 mile T w/3 min rests) + 2 × (2 mile T w/2 min rests) + 20 min E**
	E day (total .8P this week)
	E day
	E day
	E day
	30 min E + 6 × 1,200 I w/3 min jg + 2 mile T + 30 min E
	E day
11	**E** day (total .9P this week)
	E day
	E day
	20-23 mile L run (not more than 2.5 hr)
	E day
	E day
	E day
12	**10 min E + 80-90 min M (total .8P this week)**
	E day
	E day
	E day
	E day
	10 min E + 5 × (1 mile T w/1 min rests) + 60 min E
	E day

(continued)

Table 14.6   18-Week Marathon Training Plan in Miles   *(continued)*

Week	Workout
13	**E** day (total 1.0P this week)
	E day
	E day
	10 min E + 3 mile T + 4 × 1 km I w/400 jg + 2 mile T + 10 min E
	E day
	E day
	E day
14	**20-23 mile L run (not more than 2.5 hr) (total .9P this week)**
	E day
	E day
	E day
	E day
	20 min E + 6 miles M + 10 min E + 3 mile T + 10 min E
	E day
15	**E** day (total .8P this week)
	E day
	E day
	10 min E + 6 mile M + 1 mile T + 6 mile M + 2 mile T + 10 min E
	E day
	E day
	E day
16	**10 min E + 12-14 miles M + 50 min E (total .7P this week)**
	E day
	E day
	E day
	E day
	10 min E + 5 × (1 mile T w/1 min rests) + 60 min E
	E day

Week	Workout
17	**E** day (total .6P-.7P this week)
	E day
	E day
	30 min E + 3 × (2 mile T w/2 min rests) + 20 min E
	E day
	E day
	E day
18	90 min L
	60 min **E**
	20 min E + 3-4 × (1 mile T w/2 min rests) + 10 min E
	50 min **E**
	30 min **E**
	30 min **E** or rest day (especially if a travel day)
	30 min **E** (marathon race tomorrow)

Table created by Jack Daniels' Running Calculator designed by the Run SMART Project.

18-Week Program in Kilometers

This program is designed for the final 18 weeks leading up to a marathon. It assumes you have been running fairly seriously for some time before starting the following specific workouts and that you are capable of handling a single steady run of at least 2 hours and a week that totals at least 125 kilometers. Use VDOT tables to determine proper **M** and **T** training paces. Each **E** day is one or two **E** runs, or a day off if needed. Use **E** days to achieve weekly distance goals.

This program demands a Q day of running every 4th or 5th day. If you have time for the longer training sessions only on weekends, then move the days around a little, but try to get in all the workouts that are written in detail.

Pick what you think is a reasonable peak (P) weekly mileage for this 18-week program, and for each week I suggest totaling a fraction of that P. For example, if you think 120 km is a good peak amount for you and I suggest .8P for a week, that means you should strive to total 96 km (.8 × 120) that week.

Table 14.7 details an 18-week marathon training program in kilometers. The schedule is flexible, so the workouts can be arranged to best fit any schedule. The most important thing is to keep the quality training sessions in the order listed, even if they are not completed on the specific day in the table.

Table 14.7   18-Week Marathon Training Plan in Kilometers

Week	Workout
1	**25-30K (not more than 2.5 hr) long run (referred to as L) at easy (E) pace**
	E day (total .8P of running this week)
	E day
	E day
	10 min E + 15-18K at projected marathon (M) pace
	E day
	E day
2	**E** day (total .9P this week)
	E day
	10 min E + 2 × 5K T w/3 min rest between (T pace is 8-10 sec/km faster than M) + 60 min E
	E day
	E day
	E day

Week	Workout
3	**Possible road race today, or 10 min E + 4 × 3K T w/2 min rests + 30 min E**
	E day (total .8P this week)
	E day
	E day
	25-30K L run (not more than 2.5 hr)
	E day
	E day
4	**E** day (total .9P this week)
	30 min E + 5 sets of (1 km T + 400 jg) + 30 min E
	E day
	E day
	E day
	10 min E + 4 × (3K at T w/2 min rests) + 40 min E
	E day
5	**E** day (total 1.0P this week)
	E day
	30K L run (not more than 2.5 hr)
	E day
	E day
	E day
	10 min **E** + 15K **M** + 30 min **E**
6	**E** day (total .8P this week)
	E day
	E day
	E day
	20 min E + 4 × (3K at T w/2 min rests) + 60 min E
	E day
	E day

(continued)

Table 14.7   18-Week Marathon Training Plan in Kilometers   *(continued)*

Week	Workout
7	**E** day (total 1.0P this week)
	E day
	30 min E + 18K M + 30 min E
	E day
	E day
	E day
	E day
8	**60 min E + 4K T + 30 min E + 3K T + 10 min E**
	E day (total .9P this week)
	E day
	E day
	E day
	30-35K L run (not more than 2.5 hr)
	E day
9	**E** day (total .9P this week)
	E day
	E day
	30 min E + 20K M + 20 min E
	E day
	E day
	E day
10	**30 min E + 4 × (3K T w/2 min rests) + 30 min E**
	E day (total .8P this week)
	E day
	E day
	E day
	10 min E + 4K T + 10 min E + 4k T + 40 min E
	E day

Week	Workout
11	**E** day (total .9P this week)
	E day
	E day
	30-35K L (not more than 2.5 hr)
	E day
	E day
	E day
12	**10 min E + 20K M (total .8P this week)**
	E day
	E day
	E day
	E day
	10 min E + 5 × (2K T w/2 min rests) + 60 min E
	E day
13	**E** day (total 1.0P this week)
	E day
	E day
	10 min E + 4 × (3K T w/2 min rests) + 10 min E
	E day
	E day
	E day
14	**30-35K L (total .9P this week)**
	E day
	E day
	E day
	E day
	20 min E + 10K M + 10 min E + 4K T + 10 min E
	E day

(continued)

Table 14.7   18-Week Marathon Training Plan in Kilometers   *(continued)*

Week	Workout
15	**E** day (total .8P this week)
	E day
	E day
	10 min E + 5K T + 10 min E + 4k T + 10 min E + 3K T
	E day
	E day
	E day
16	**10 min E + 20K M + 50 min E (total .7P this week)**
	E day
	E day
	E day
	E day
	10 min **E** + 4 × (2K **T** w/2 min rests) + 60 min **E**
	E day
17	**E** day (total .6-.7P this week)
	E day
	E day
	30 min E + 3 × (3K T w/2 min rests) + 20 min E
	E day
	E day
	E day
18	90 min **L**
	60 min **E**
	20 min E + 3 × (2K T w/2 min rests) + 10 min E
	400 min **E**
	30 min **E**
	30 min **E** or rest day (especially if a travel day)
	30 min **E** (marathon race tomorrow)

Table created by Jack Daniels' Running Calculator designed by the Run SMART Project.

18-Week Program in Time

Whether it is an advantage or a disadvantage for any particular runner, running workouts in which all the training is expressed in time rather than distance encourages the runner to learn to run by feel rather than always knowing exactly how fast every mile or kilometer is being covered. No doubt being able to feel how hard or how easy you are stressing yourself can be a big advantage in a race, especially if the terrain is undulating or it is a windy day; in these cases, it may be difficult to rely on timed distances to determine how hard you are stressing yourself. I encourage runners to try different workouts based on time, even in good conditions, so they become knowledgeable about relating how they feel with how hard they are working.

For this 18-week program by time, the total minutes are shown for each type of run. **L** is a long **E** run. In most **T** cases, break the total into repeated runs. For example, **T** 40 means 40 minutes at **T** pace, which can be 8 × 5 min, 5 × 8 min, 4 × 10 min, and so on (with 1 or 2 min rests). **TL** 40-70 means 40 total minutes at **T** pace (maybe 4 × 10 min w/2 min rests) plus a 70-minute **L** (**E**) run.

TIR 15-10-5 means a total of 15 minutes (e.g., 3 × 5 min) at **T** pace (w/1 min rests) plus a total of 10 minutes at **I** pace (maybe 5 × 2 min **hard** w/ equal-time recovery jg) plus a total of 5 minutes at **R** pace (e.g., 5 × 1 min **R** pace—maybe 4-5 × 400 or 8-10 × 200 w/double-time rests).

M is projected marathon pace, so **MT** 80-20 would be a steady 80-minute run at **M** plus 20 total minutes at **T** (maybe 4 × 5 min w/1 min rests or 2 × 10 min w/2 min rests). **ME** 80-60 would be an 80-minute run at **M** followed immediately by a 60-minute **E** run. T_{race} up to 25K means try to find a race of medium distance (15 to 25K), and switch days around if none is available that particular weekend. If there are no races near this time, then pick a favorite workout to do.

No warm-up is needed for **E**, **L**, or **M** sessions, but do a warm-up for workouts that start with **T**. All days of the week not specified are **E** days, so run however much is needed to achieve desired weekly mileage goals (you may not need to run on all days). Do six to eight strides (ST) on 2 of each week's untimed days. **T** pace is 15 to 20 seconds per mile faster than **M** pace, **I** pace is 6 seconds per 400 faster than **T** pace, and **R** pace is 6 seconds per 400 faster than **I** pace. Numbers refer to minutes of time running.

Table 14.8 details an 18-week marathon training program in minutes. The schedule is flexible, so the workouts can be arranged to best fit any schedule. The most important thing is to keep the quality training sessions in the order listed.

Table 14.8   18-Week Marathon Training Program in Time

Week	Workout and time
1	**L** 120-150 min
	TIR 15-10-5 min
2	**EM** 60-40 min
	TL 40-60 min
3	**TIR** 20-15-6 min
4	**MT** 60-15 min
	L 120-150 min
5	**TIR** 20-10-10 min
6	**TL** 40-70 min
	T$_{race}$ up to 25K
7	**MT** 80-15 min
8	**TIR** 20-10-8 min
	T 20-20-10-10 min
9	**T** 40 min
10	**TIR** 20-15-10 min
	L 150 min
11	**MT** 80-20 min
12	**TIR** 20-10-10 min
	L 150 min
13	**TIR** 20-15-10 min
14	Big **T** 20-20-15-12-6 min
15	**L** 150 min
	I$_{race}$ 5-10K
16	**ME** 80-60 min
17	**TL** 40-80 min
	T 40 min

Week	Workout and time
18	**L** 1.5 hr **E**
	1 hr
	T 20 min
	1 hr **E**
	40 min **E**
	30 min or rest day **E**
	30 min **E**
	Marathon race day

Table created by Jack Daniels' Running Calculator designed by the Run SMART Project.

FINAL 12-WEEK PROGRAM

This plan allows for two **Q** days each week (whichever days best fit your schedule). All other days call for **E** running to allow you to accumulate your desired weekly mileage goal. The numbers followed by *P* (e.g., 1.0P, .9P, .8P) indicate what fraction of your peak weekly miles to run that week.

For example, if you have decided that 110 is a great enough weekly mileage, then .8P means 88 miles that week. So set a peak weekly mileage that you think is reasonable for you for this season. The following training is for sea level; at an altitude of 7,000 feet (2,130 m), keep the **R** pace the same as at sea level, but **M**, **T**, and **I** paces will all be 4 seconds per 400 (10 sec/km, 16 sec/mile) slower than at sea level. Adjust training speeds to meet conditions, such as adverse weather like wind, heat, or poor footing.

If no distance units are shown, assume miles (8 **M** = 8 miles at **M** pace). If you are not using VDOT units, choose a realistic goal **M** pace. Then, final **T** pace will be 15 seconds per mile faster than goal **M** pace. Final **I** pace will be 6 seconds per 400 meters faster than **T** pace. Final **R** pace will be 3 seconds per 200 meters faster than **I** pace.

Table 14.9 details a demanding final 12-week marathon training plan with 2 Q sessions per week. These Q sessions can be planned anywhere in the week depending on schedule and weather constraints, but try to have at least 2 **E** days between the Q sessions.

Table 14.9 Final 12-Week Marathon Training Plan

Week	Fraction of peak	Workout	Total miles	Type
12	.8-1.0	Q1 = 4 **E** + 8 **M** + 1 **T** + 6 **M** + 1 **T** + 2 **E**	22	**MT**
		Q2 = 2 **E** + 4 **T** + 4 min **E** + 3 **T** + 3 min **E** + 2 **T** + 2 min **E** + 1 **T** + 2 **E**	15	**T**
11	.9	Q1 = 2 **E** + 4 **T** + 10 miles **E** + 2 × 2 **T** w/2 min rests + 2 **E**	22	**TLT**
		Q2 = 2 **E** + 6 × 1 km **I** or 4 × 1 **I** w/2 or 4 min **E** + 4 × 400 **R** w/3 min **E** + 2 **E**	13	**IR**
10	.8	Q1 = steady **E** run of 20 miles	20	**L**
		Q2 = 12 mile accelerating steadily to **T** pace for the final 3 miles + 2 **E**	14	**T**
9	1.	Q1 = 6 **E** + 6 **M** + 1 **T** + 6 **M** + 1 **T** + 2 **E**	22	**MT**
		Q2 = 2 **E** + 5 **T** + 5 min **E** + 4 **T** + 4 min **E** + 3 **T** + 3 min **E** + 1 **T** + 2 **E**	23	Big **T**
8	.9	Q1 = 2 **E** + 4 **T** + 10 **E** + 4 **T** + 2 **E**	22	**TLT**
		Q2 = 2 **E** + 3 × 1 mile **I** w/4 min **E** + 3 × 1,000 **I** w/2 min **E** + 2 **E**	10	**I**
7	.7	Q1 = steady **E** run of 22 mile	22	**L**
		Q2 = 8 **E** + 8 **M** + 1 **T** + 4 **M** + 1 **T** + 1 **M**	23	**MT**
6	1.0	Q1 = 10 mile accelerating to **T** pace the final 4 miles + 2 **E**	12	**T**
		Q2 = 2 **E** + 5**T** + 5 min **E** + 4**T** + 4 min **E** + 3**T** + 3 min **E** + 2 **T** + 2 min **E** + 1 **T** + 2 **E**	21	Big **T**
5	.8	Q1 = 2 **E** + 4 **T** + 10 miles **E** + 2 × 2**T** w/2 min rest between + 2 **E**	22	**TLT**
		Q2 = 2 **E** + 6 × 1 km **I** w/2 min **E** + 4 × 400 **R** w/400 jg + 3 min **E**	11	**IR**
4	.7	Q1 = steady **E** run of 22 miles	22	**L**
		Q2 = 2 **E** + 3 × 1 **T** w/1 min **E** + 3 × 1 km **I** w/2 min **E** + 3 × 400 **R** w/400 jog + 2 **E**	11	**TIR**
3	.7	Q1 = 6 **E** + 6 **M** + 1 **T** + 6 **M** + 1 **T** + 2 **E**	22	**MT**
		Q2 = 2 **E** + 4 × 2 **T** w/2 min **E** + 2 **E**	12	**T**

Week	Fraction of peak	Workout	Total miles	Type
2		Q1 = 2 **E** + 3 × 2 **T** (or 2 × 3 **T**) w/2 min **E** recoveries + 10 miles **E**	18	**TL**
		Q2 = 2 **E** + 3 × 2 **T** w/2 min **E** + 2 **E**	10	**T**
1		7 days: Q1 = 90 min **E**	13	**E**
		6 days: 1 hr **E**	9	**E**
		5 days: Q2 = 2 **E** + 4 × 1,200 **T** w/2 min **E** + 2 **E**	7	**T**
		4 days: 50 min **E**	7	**E**
		3 days: 30-40 min **E**	6	**E**
		2 days: 0-20 min **E**	3	**E**
		1 day: 20-30 min **E** (tomorrow is the marathon race)	3	**E**

Table created by Jack Daniels' Running Calculator designed by the Run SMART Project.

15

Training Breaks
and Supplemental Training

It's not winning that is most important; it's getting to participate
that counts the most.

I have made a point of emphasizing that rest can be considered part of
training, rather than an avoidance of training, and I want to also say there
may be times when a full break from training can be beneficial. By a full
break I mean ceasing running completely for an extended period (from several days to weeks or even a month or two).

Some breaks from training may be considerably longer than others. For
example, a major injury that requires surgery can easily mean being away
from running for an extended time, and becoming frustrated with how training is going can also lead to a relatively long break from running.

In a sense, there are two categories of breaks from training—planned
breaks and unplanned breaks. The main difference between these two types
of breaks is that during some of the unplanned ones, you may not be able to
do any running or even alternate exercises because of a particular injury or
illness. In planned breaks, running is always still a possibility, as are other
types of training.

Regardless of the reason for a break from regular training, it is not advisable to jump right back into the volume of training you were doing before
the time off started. Training will have to be adjusted because there has
been some loss of fitness, and always remember that when your fitness is
down a little, training doesn't have to be as hard as it was before the break
to still gain benefits. In other words, don't try to work extra hard to make
up for lost time.

TAKING BREAKS

I don't believe I have ever met a runner who hasn't taken a break from training at some time in his career. You can even think of a day or two of rest from a hard training session as a break in training. Or what about tapering for an event, during which training is substantially reduced; is that a break in training?

The greatest example of taking breaks when needed was a good friend of mine who was an NCAA national champion, a Pan American Games champion, and an Olympian. He also, by the way, broke 30 minutes in a 10K the year he turned 40. What is so interesting about this runner is that I tested him at age 24, and his $\dot{V}O_2$max was a high 78.6. I also tested him 25 years later, the year he turned 50, and his $\dot{V}O_2$max at that age was 76.0. I have never heard of someone that age with such outstanding aerobic power.

When I asked him how many days he thought he had taken off from training during those 25 years between tests, he said he had kept track of every day he took off, and they totaled more than 1,200 days. He basically took a few days off every time he had a little injury or illness, and it clearly didn't hurt him any to take that many breaks in training over the years.

In addition, this great runner hardly ran during the winter months; instead he did a lot of cross-country skiing, proving that supplemental training did a great job of helping him maintain fitness for running (skiing days were not considered days off from training, even though he was not running during those days).

This documented case is a great example of what the human body can maintain even with many little breaks. It certainly tells me that you are better off taking a few rest days in order to heal an injury than to try to work through that injury and just prolong the healing process (the same with minor illnesses, which can cause a major setback if you try to train through them).

Regardless of the reason for a break in training, it is always advisable to consider what is happening to the body when it is away from daily activity. Fitness will drop off, but usually not as much or as fast as expected, because many of the physiological benefits that have been earned during regular training are rather slow to go away.

For example, when the heart muscle, or running muscles for that matter, have increased in strength over weeks of training, the loss in muscle is slow to take place. Little changes in the muscle fibers and in the blood vessels feeding those fibers are retained for a while as well.

Figure 15.1 shows a simplified example of how training benefits occur over time and how those benefits are lost over time. In other words, when just starting a program, relatively little training produces sizable benefits that taper off over time; with a stop in training, the benefits are lost slowly at first, so a few days off now and then won't have much of a negative effect, if any at all. After all, it is common to taper (back off, with more rest) for an important race, with the idea that it will produce a better-than-usual performance.

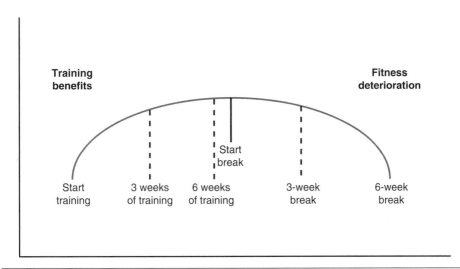

Figure 15.1 Reactions to training and taking a break from training.

A major consideration during breaks, especially for those who have been accumulating a high number of weekly miles, is that runners are used to consuming a certain amount of calories per day and maintaining a desired body weight. It is rather common to keep caloric intake the same during a break, which can easily lead to putting on weight. For some, this may be good, but at some point during a prolonged break there must be a change in eating habits so that the body doesn't gain excess fat tissue. Staying healthy is rule number 1 when you are not exercising as much as you normally do.

Nonplanned Breaks

A few things must be considered when faced with a nonplanned break in training. Most important is to accept the fact that a break is necessary and to do whatever needs to be done to fix the problem. Also, if returning to serious training is important, supplemental training may minimize loss of fitness during the break from running.

In fact, some types of cross-training will actually build up resistance to further problems once back to regular running, with the result that running will be better than before. For example, resistance training may improve body balance and lead to a more economical running technique. Some research has shown that performing half-squats with relatively light weights can improve running performance. In a sense, an unplanned break may end up being a blessing in disguise, especially if it leads to finding some new modes of exercise that result in overall improvement in running performance.

When an injury is the culprit leading to a break, there are usually two types—those that prevent continued use of the legs and those that allow aerobic involvement of some of the running muscles in the legs. For example,

An elliptical trainer is one option you can use to supplement your training if you aren't able to withstand the high impact of running for a period of time.

a broken leg will definitely prevent any activity involving impact on that leg, and the only type of aerobic training that may be possible will involve using the arms—swimming, for example. An ankle or foot injury may prevent running but may allow deep-water running, which allows the hip and many leg muscles to be trained fairly seriously.

Elliptical trainers and cycles may be an approach to exercise that doesn't involve impact, and even uphill walking on a tread-mill may work for some runners when they are not able to actu-ally run. The important thing when performing cross-training is to make sure that what you are doing is not aggravating the problem further, thus prolong-ing the time off from true run training. With any injury that lasts more than just a couple of days, it is a good idea to consult with a physical therapist, ath-letic trainer, or medical doctor. Something that seems very minor to you could be a major problem down the road, and sometimes what seems major is a simple issue to deal with, with proper advice.

Planned Breaks

Most runners will plan a year of training so that they get some time off, and this is a good idea. First of all, I like to think of time off from training as part of the training process. Just as the body reacts positively to easy days of training between quality sessions, so can a bit of time away from training allow the body, and mind, to reach a new level of performance once back to a regular training schedule.

It is best to base your training break on what races you anticipate run-ning in coming months. In other words, have a long-range training plan that includes desired breaks, fully understanding that an unplanned break may alter that plan.

The length of a planned break depends on how stressful training has been in the preceding weeks and months. If you have taken a few minor injury or illness breaks throughout the year, then a planned break may not even be needed, but don't be pessimistic and assume there will be injury or illness breaks in the months ahead, so there is no need to plan a break.

I tend to favor 2 weeks as the minimum time for a planned break, with about 6 weeks being the maximum, provided you plan to continue with serious running. Obviously, an unplanned break may be even longer.

Table 15.1 is a guide for adjusting training intensity based on time away from running training. This table allows adjustments in training speeds as determined by VDOT values. Current VDOT dictates training speeds, and as you race better, your training VDOT increases. On the other hand, as you spend time away from training, current VDOT will also deteriorate to some degree.

Table 15.1 shows how to adjust your VDOT value as dictated by time away from training and whether or not you have engaged in some leg-associated aerobic training. If you haven't been doing any leg-associated aerobic training, you should use the values under the heading of FVDOT-1, but if your time off has included this type of exercise, then use column FVDOT-2.

Table 15.1   VDOT Adjustments for Training Breaks

Training break	FVDOT-1	FVDOT-2
Up to 5 days	1.000	1.000
6 days	.997	.998
7 days	.994	.997
10 days	.985	.992
14 days	.973	.986
21 days	.952	.976
28 days	.931	.965
35 days	.910	.955
42 days	.889	.944
49 days	.868	.934
56 days	.847	.923
63 days	.826	.913
70 days	.805	.902
72 days or more	.800	.900

If you go down to the values associated with 6 weeks (42 days) off from running, you see that, if not doing some leg training, your VDOT has dropped by about 11 percent (.889 fraction of the starting value when in good shape). With some good cross-training, FVDOT-2 suggests that the loss in VDOT is just about half of that 11 percent drop associated with not doing anything during the time off (.944 fraction of the VDOT value when in good shape).

As shown in table 15.1, there is no loss with only 5 days without any training. After about 10 weeks off from running, you probably have lost about as much as you are going to lose, about 20 percent. However, to say that 20 percent is about all you can lose is misleading because if you gain a fair amount of unnecessary weight, then the VDOT value can be negatively affected further until you are back to ideal running weight. To calculate how much change can be expected in your returning VDOT value, complete the steps in figure 15.2.

FIGURE 15.2
Estimating Return VDOT Value

Enter presetback weight in kilograms in *A*
(pounds × .454 = kg).   **(A)** _____

Enter presetback VDOT in *B* (from recent race time).   **(B)** _____

Multiply *A* × *B* to get C.   **(C)** _____

Divide *C* by current weight in kilograms to get **D**.   **(D)** _____

D is your weight-adjusted VDOT. Apply the appropriate FVDOT value from table 15.1 to your D value from the above calculation to determine the VDOT value on which you should base your comeback training. Of course, once you start racing you can determine the most accurate VDOT to use for continued training. An example of VDOT adjustment associated with a change in weight follows:

If presetback weight was 132.2 pounds, then *A* = 60 kg (132.2 × .454).

If presetback VDOT was 50, then *B* = 50, and A × B (50 × 60) = *C* = 3,000.

If current weight is 139 pounds (139 × .454 = 63.1 kg), then *D* = 3,000/63.1 = 47.5 (adjusted VDOT).

From J. Daniels, 2014, *Daniels' running formula*, 3rd ed. (Champaign, IL: Human Kinetics).

ADJUSTING MILEAGE OR DURATION OF TRAINING

Table 15.2 provides a guide, and some examples, for adjusting the amount of training you should schedule after a prolonged break, planned or not. I have indicated four categories of adjustments, and these are based on time

Table 15.2   Adjustments to Training Loads After a Break

Category	Time off	Adjustment to work load	% of prebreak VDOT
1	Up to 5 days	5 days **E** @ no more than 100% load	100%
2	6-28 days	1st half **E** @ 50% load	93.1-99.7% or 96.5-99.8% (see table 15.1)
		2nd half **E** @ 75% load	93.1-99.7% or 96.5-99.8% (see table 15.1)
	6 days	3 days **E** @ 50% load + 3 days **E** @ 75%	99.7-99.8%
	28 days	14 days **E** @ load 50% + 14 days **E** @ 75% load	93.1-96.5%
3	4-8 weeks	1st 3rd **E** @ 33% load	84.7-93.1% or 92.3-96.5% (see table 15.1)
		2nd 3rd **E** @ 50% load	84.7-93.1% or 92.3-96.5% (see table 15.1)
		Final 3rd **E** @ 75% load	84.7-93.1% or 92.3-96.5% (see table 15.1)
	29 days	9 days @ 33% load + 10 days @ 50% load + 10 days @ 75% load + some strides (ST)	93.0-96.4%
	8 weeks	18 days **E** @ 33% load + 19 days **E** @ 50% +19 days **E** @ 75% load + some ST	84.7-92.3%
4	8 weeks or more	3 weeks **E** @ 33% load, but not more than 30 miles/wk	80.0-84.7% or 90.0-92.3% (see table 15.1)
		3 weeks **E** @ 50% load, but not more than 40 miles/wk	80.0-84.7% or 90.0-92.3% (see table 15.1)
		3 weeks **E** @ 70% load + ST, but not more than 60 miles/wk	80.0-84.7% or 90.0-92.3% (see table 15.1)
		3 weeks **E** @ 85% load + ST & **R**, but not more than 75 miles/wk	80.0-84.7% or 90.0-92.3% (see table 15.1)
		3 weeks **E** at 100% load w/ST & **T** & **R**, but not more than 90 miles/wk	80.0-84.7% or 90.0-92.3% (see table 15.1)

missed from running: 5 days or fewer (category I); up to 4 weeks (category II); between 4 and 8 weeks (category III); and more than 8 weeks (category IV).

For runners who fit into category II, for the first half of their return-to-training time, they should not run a total weekly mileage that is more than 50 percent of what they were doing before missing training, and the second half of their return time can total 75 percent of prebreak mileage. If these runners did not engage in any cross-training during time off, then the return VDOT value would be 93.1 percent of prebreak VDOT, from column FVDOT-1 in table 15.1.

Runners who missed 6 weeks of run training but who diligently performed cross-training involving some aerobic leg exercises would be placed in category III. Their cross-training drops their VDOT to 94.4 percent of the presetback value (from table 15.1), and from table 15.2, the first third of their return mileage should not be more than 33 percent of presetback mileage. If they were previously totaling 60 miles per week, these first 2 weeks would total not more than 20 miles each. Then the next 2 weeks could total 30 miles per week, and the final 2 weeks of return mileage could be 45 per week. In addition, these runners could include some regular strides during or after some of their **E** runs.

After adjusting training loads and intensities for a return to training following a setback, it should be OK to engage in whatever normal amount of training was typical before the setback. Do make any adjustments to return VDOT that may be a result of weight gain, as outlined earlier in this chapter.

ADDING SUPPLEMENTAL TRAINING

When people decide to take up running, the first thing they usually consider is how much time they can commit to running, both in terms of time per day and days per week or per month. Certainly it is important to schedule time for running, but often little or no time is set aside for other activities that may also lead to better running. These nonrunning activities include such things as stretching, resistance training, massage, ice baths, and yoga. Unfortunately, some of these things take time and some even cost money, but if you do have the time and finances, they may be beneficial.

One type of supplemental training that has been shown to result in better running performance is resistance training, and I encourage all runners to include some resistance training in their weekly program.

If you have access to a gym with weight machines, a few exercises that can help your running include hamstring curls, knee extensions, hip abduction and adduction exercises, and abdominal and back exercises. If you have the time and inclination, some arm exercises often make you feel better in general, although they are usually of no real benefit in terms of helping you run. If you decide to do resistance training with free weights, concentrate first on proper technique, and add resistance gradually over time.

Possibly the greatest benefit of leg strengthening is to build a resistance to common running injuries. In other words, resistance training may not improve your running as much as it builds resistance to injury, which allows you to run more or faster without getting hurt. Then the harder running training makes you a better runner. Running is probably associated with more minor injuries than most other sports, and in fact, a research study conducted in the 1990s found that the sport associated with the most injuries among high school students is girls' cross country.

In addition to helping ward off injuries, some resistance work can actually improve running economy (lessen the energy demand of running). The reasons are not clear, but it is assumed that being a little stronger gives you a more solid base, more controlled stride, and less unnecessary movement in running technique. Hill running, both uphill and downhill, can also be useful in building strength and running economy.

A warning about downhill running is appropriate at this point because running on too steep of a downhill course or on hard road surfaces can increase your chance of hurting some areas in your hips, knees, and feet. The key to downhill running is to use a gradual hill, one of only 2 or 3 percent of slope (for comparison, the steepest hill allowed on interstate highways is 6 percent, so make it a fair bit less than those steeper highway hills). When running downhill, it is important to avoid overstriding; instead, concentrate on a light, fast leg turnover. Make downhill running feel as if you are "rolling" down the hill rather than bounding down, and it may help to land rear-footed, rather than up on the balls of your feet.

On the other hand, uphill running can be on just about any steepness of slope because you are not really pounding into the ground as hard as on a flat surface, so you get the benefit of strengthening the pushing-off muscles and the hip flexors, while reducing the landing shock associated with flat or downhill running. If you do uphill running on a hill outside, take it very easy running back down to the bottom. This brings up a great advantage of doing uphill runs on a treadmill; you can run up for any period of time, and when you need a break, you just hop off the treadmill and don't have to run down to start the next uphill run.

Some people refer to supplemental training as cross-training. The term used doesn't really matter; the point is to stress some areas of your body that may take a beating while running, especially high-mileage running. If you take on runs that are longer than you have built up to at a gradual pace, your good running mechanics may deteriorate, and nothing leads to running injury more quickly than poor running mechanics. In fact, any time you feel you are getting "sloppy" with your running technique, it is time to terminate that run. Spend a little more time in the weight room or doing some circuit training or some other activity, and you will see your running become more enjoyable and you will feel yourself getting stronger during your regular workout sessions.

Just as you need to carefully increase the amount and speed of your running workouts, so do you need to carefully increase the stress of any supplemental training you include in your overall program. My general rule is that you give your body a good 4 weeks at one level of training stress before increasing that stress—it's better to undertrain than to overtrain. For example, when considering run mileage, you are better to stay at a set amount of weekly mileage for a good 4 weeks before increasing that amount, but when you do increase, the increase can be a little more than just adding 2 or 3 miles to your weekly total. Take the same approach to resistance training: Stay at one level of stress for about four weeks before moving to a greater stress.

In summary, consider adding some supplemental training to your overall program, even if it is just some exercises you can do in your house or backyard. Getting stronger will increase your confidence, will improve your running economy, and will help ward off those little injuries that often plague runners at all levels of proficiency.

I have included a relatively simple circuit routine that does not require any equipment, so all the resistance is body weight. You will notice that stations 1 and 4 involve performing half of a 1-minute maximum. For example, station 1, a push-up station, asks for you to perform half of your 1-minute maximum, which means, before getting involved in the circuit, you first need to establish how many push-ups you can do in 1 minute so you know how many to do each time you arrive at station 1.

Push-Ups

The circuit starts with half of your 1-minute maximum of push-ups. Support the body on hands and toes in a plank position. The arms should extend straight down to the floor from the shoulder. Lower the body until the chest nearly touches the floor. Using the arms, push the body back up to the starting position.

Side Leg Lifts

At station 2, do 10 side leg lifts with each leg. Lie on one side with legs straight. Support the body with one arm bent at the elbow with weight resting on the forearm. Raise the top leg so that the foot is above shoulder height. Return to the starting position.

High Knees

For station 3, do 30 high knee lifts with each leg while running in place(figure 15.3). Start in a standing position and quickly bring one knee up. Alternate right and left knees to maintain a continuous motion.

Figure 15.3 High knee.

Crunches

For station 4 do half of your 1-minute maximum of crunches. Lie on the back with knees bent and feet on the floor. Place hands behind the head (without holding the head), behind the ears, or across the chest. Steadily raise the head and shoulders off of the floor to an upright position and return to the starting position.

Recovery Run and Stretch

Station 5 is a one-minute run or a 400 m run. At station 6 do 2 minutes of stretching of any kind.

Squat Thrusts

At station 7, do 10 squat thrusts (burpees). Start from a standing position and drop into a squat with both hands touching the ground outside the feet (figure 15.4*a*). Jump the legs back so that the body is in a push up position (figure 15.4*b*), and then jump back into the squatting position. Jump back to a standing position to complete one repetition (figure 15.4*c*).

Figure 15.4 Squat thrust.

Leg Lifts

For station 8, complete 10 leg lifts with each leg, first resting on forearms and facing upward with the hips off the ground. Bend one leg for balance and lift the other leg to at least the height of the bent leg. Then, turn over and rest on the forearms while facing downward. Keeping one leg straight, raise the other leg up off of the ground as far as is comfortable. Complete 10 leg lifts with each leg.

Arm and Leg Flapping

At station 9, lie on the stomach with arms over the head and legs straight out. Alternately flap the arms and legs up and down until both arms and legs have been raised and lowered 20 times.

Recovery Run

For station 10, run for 2 minutes or for 800 m.

I recommend that people following this routine go through the entire circuit three times, preferably two or three times each week. Stations 5 and 10 are runs of 1 minute and 2 minutes. These are recovery stations, so the runs are not to be particularly fast. The goal is to allow you to recover from some resistance work before going to the next resistance station.

For those who use this circuit routine, it is a good idea to time yourself every few weeks for the full three times through. You will be surprised how much faster you will learn to get through the entire 10 stations three times.

Aerobic Profile Test Protocol

Submaximal Test

The following procedure is for running on a treadmill.

1. Perform a typical warm-up, including at least 10 minutes of **E** running and any other usual stretching, striding, and so on. It is best to do this on the treadmill to familiarize yourself with running on that surface.

2. Get fitted with any equipment to be used during the test—headgear, mouthpiece, nose clip, heart-rate monitor.

3. Determine the fastest test speed to be used: Determine current 10K race pace from the chart. The corresponding velocity in meters per minute (or slightly faster—to fit one of the standard test speeds) will be the fastest submax test speed.

Test Speeds to Be Used in Submax Running Tests

m/min	170	190	210	230	250	270	290	310	330	350	370
10K time	58:50	52:38	47:37	43:29	40:00	37:02	34:29	32:15	30:18	28:34	27:02
MPH	6.4	7.1	7.8	8.6	9.3	10.1	10.8	11.6	12.3	13.0	13.8

4. Once the fastest test speed is determined, then count back four test speeds to determine the starting test speed (slowest). For example, a 28:30 10K runner will select 13 mph as fastest and 10.1 mph as slowest (initial) test speed.

5. The treadmill speed must be accurately timed by measuring the running belt length to the nearest millimeter and timing 10 revolutions of the belt (while the runner is running on the belt). Timing 10 revolutions must be done with every runner at every speed to record the actual speed being run in each case. The belt length won't vary, but the accuracy of the speedometer will, so you can't just go by the mph reading (mph is just to put you in the ballpark).

6. Run the first submax test at the slowest test speed, as determined in step 4. Each submax run should last 5 minutes, with the 5th-minute $\dot{V}O_2$ and heart rate used to represent that particular running velocity.

7. If blood lactate data is being collected, a finger-stick blood sample is taken immediately upon completion of each submax run and analyzed for blood lactate, to represent that speed of submax running.

8. Take a 2- to 3-minute rest between submax runs (during which time the blood lactate can be evaluated and $\dot{V}O_2$ determined if not using an online system).

9. Perform all submax speeds, in ascending order, and repeat the procedure.

10. The final submax test is to be the one earlier determined as the fastest test speed, or that speed at which a blood lactate of 4.0 mmol/liter or higher is recorded (if this occurs before the earlier indicated fastest test speed). In the example shown above, for a 28:30 10k runner, the submax speeds to be used would be 270, 290, 310, and 330 (and 350, if 4.0 mmol lactate had not yet been reached).

11. If blood lactates are not being monitored, then the fastest submax run could be determined based on the subject's perceived exertion (15 or greater on Borg's 6 to 20 scale).

12. A 5- to 10-minute break is given between any submax and max test.

On a track, have the runner run four or five 5-minute runs at specific steady submaximal speeds, and collect expired air samples during the 5th minute of each run to determine the $\dot{V}O_2$ associated with that specific speed. Allow 3 minutes' rest and go to the next speed. Try to get four different speeds.

$\dot{V}O_2$max Test

The following procedure is for running on a treadmill.

1. If the max test follows a submax test or a series of submax tests, then the submax tests serve as a warm-up for the max test. If not after submax testing, then the subject should first perform a thorough warm-up, followed by fitting of all the necessary test equipment.

2. The running speed to be used for the max test is that speed determined to be the fastest speed used for a submax test (see submax treadmill testing protocol), but not faster than 350 meters per minute, which is getting pretty fast for max testing on a treadmill (additional grade will provide the necessary stress).

3. The max test begins on 0 percent grade and either at the fastest submax speed or a slightly slower speed (the latter sometimes allows a more gradual adjustment for the test). If the fastest submax speed is the ini-

tial max-test speed, then stay 2 minutes at 0 percent grade; if a slightly slower speed is used, then stay at 0 percent at that speed for 1 minute and 0 percent at the fastest submax speed for 1 minute.

4. At the end of minute 2 of the test, the treadmill grade is increased to 1 percent for the 3rd minute (speed is not changed after the 2nd minute).

5. During the final 10 seconds of the 3rd minute (and any subsequent minutes that the test lasts), ask the subject if at least 1 more minute is possible. With a positive response—thumbs up by the subject—treadmill grade is increased by 1 percent. After a negative response—horizontal waving of a hand—ask the subject if half a minute more is possible. If so, the final half minute is run at the same grade; if not, the test is terminated. (The max test, following this protocol, will typically last 5 to 8 minutes in total.)

6. If using an online system, $\dot{V}O_2$ is monitored throughout the entire max test. If collecting expired air samples for later evaluation, start collecting after the completion of 3 minutes of the test (usually 45- or 30-second samples are best when using the bag-collection technique).

7. Determine $\dot{V}O_2$max as the greatest 1-minute value reached during the test (which may be the average of two consecutive 30-second collections, or if monitoring online every 20 seconds, use the three consecutive 20-second readings that produce the highest mean $\dot{V}O_2$).

8. Max heart rate is the highest value reached throughout the test.

9. Take the final finger stick 2 minutes after the termination of the max test, and use this to indicate blood lactate associated with $\dot{V}O_2$max (not necessarily max blood lactate, because this is an aerobic test).

10. When presenting data for R and V_E, take care to indicate if the values being presented are max R and max V_E or if these are the R and V_E values associated with v$\dot{V}O_2$max (higher R and V_E may come after peaking for $\dot{V}O_2$max).

On a track, have the runner run five laps: The first lap is comfortable, followed by three laps at 5K race pace and a final fifth lap all out. Collect 30- to 45-second expired air samples during the fourth and fifth laps to determine a $\dot{V}O_2$max value.

Times for Varying Distances at the Same Pace

400	1 km	Mile	3 km	5 km	10 km	15 km	10 mile	20 km	Half marathon	Marathon
50	2:05	3:21	6:15	10:25	20:50	31:15	33:31	41:40	43:57	1:27:54
51	2:07	3:25	6:22	10:37	21:15	31:52	34:12	42:30	44:50	1:29:40
52	2:10	3:29	6:30	10:50	21:40	32:30	34:52	43:20	45:42	1:31:25
53	2:12	3:33	6:37	11:02	22:05	33:07	35:32	44:10	46:35	1:33:10
54	2:15	3:37	6:45	11:15	22:30	33:45	36:12	45:00	47:28	1:34:56
55	2:17	3:41	6:52	11:27	22:55	34:22	36:53	45:50	48:21	1:36:41
56	2:20	3:45	7:00	11:40	23:20	35:00	37:33	46:40	49:13	1:38:27
57	2:22	3:49	7:07	11:52	23:45	35:37	38:13	47:30	50:06	1:40:12
58	2:25	3:53	7:15	12:05	24:10	36:15	38:53	48:20	50:59	1:41:58
59	2:27	3:57	7:22	12:17	24:35	36:52	39:33	49:10	51:52	1:43:43
60	2:30	4:01	7:30	12:30	25:00	37:30	40:14	50:00	52:44	1:45:29
61	2:32	4:05	7:37	12:42	25:25	38:07	40:54	50:50	53:37	1:47:14
62	2:35	4:09	7:45	12:55	25:50	38:45	41:34	51:40	54:30	1:49:00
63	2:37	4:13	7:52	13:07	26:15	39:22	42:14	52:30	55:23	1:50:45
64	2:40	4:17	8:00	13:20	26:40	40:00	42:55	53:20	56:15	1:52:31
65	2:42	4:21	8:07	13:32	27:05	40:37	43:35	54:10	57:08	1:54:16
66	2:45	4:25	8:15	13:45	27:30	41:15	44:15	55:00	58:01	1:56:02
67	2:47	4:29	8:22	13:57	27:55	41:52	44:55	55:50	58:54	1:57:47
68	2:50	4:33	8:30	14:10	28:20	42:30	45:36	56:40	59:46	1:59:33
69	2:52	4:37	8:37	14:22	28:45	43:07	46:16	57:30	1:00:39	2:01:18
70	2:55	4:41	8:45	14:35	29:10	43:45	46:56	58:20	1:01:32	2:03:04
71	2:57	4:45	8:52	14:47	29:35	44:22	47:36	59:10	1:02:24	2:04:49
72	3:00	4:49	9:00	15:00	30:00	45:00	48:16	1:00:00	1:03:17	2:06:35
73	3:02	4:53	9:07	15:12	30:25	45:37	48:57	1:00:50	1:04:10	2:08:20

(continued)

400	1 km	Mile	3 km	5 km	10 km	15 km	10 mile	20 km	Half marathon	Marathon
74	3:05	4:57	9:15	15:25	30:50	46:15	49:37	1:01:40	1:05:03	2:10:06
75	3:07	5:01	9:22	15:37	31:15	46:52	50:17	1:02:30	1:05:55	2:11:51
76	3:10	5:05	9:30	15:50	31:40	47:30	50:57	1:03:20	1:06:48	2:13:37
77	3:12	5:10	9:37	16:02	32:05	48:07	51:38	1:04:10	1:07:41	2:15:22
78	3:15	5:14	9:45	16:15	32:30	48:45	52:18	1:05:00	1:08:34	2:17:08
79	3:17	5:18	9:52	16:27	32:55	49:22	52:58	1:05:50	1:09:26	2:18:53
80	3:20	5:22	10:00	16:40	33:20	50:00	53:38	1:06:40	1:10:19	2:20:39
81	3:22	5:26	10:07	16:52	33:45	50:37	54:19	1:07:30	1:11:12	2:22:24
82	3:25	5:30	10:15	17:05	34:10	51:15	54:59	1:08:20	1:12:05	2:24:10
83	3:27	5:34	10:22	17:17	34:35	51:52	55:39	1:09:10	1:12:57	2:25:55
84	3:30	5:38	10:30	17:30	35:00	52:30	56:19	1:10:00	1:13:50	2:27:41
85	3:32	5:42	10:37	17:42	35:25	53:07	57:00	1:10:50	1:14:43	2:29:26
86	3:35	5:46	10:45	17:55	35:50	53:45	57:40	1:11:40	1:15:36	2:31:12
87	3:37	5:50	10:52	18:07	36:15	54:22	58:20	1:12:30	1:16:28	2:32:57
88	3:40	5:54	11:00	18:20	36:40	55:00	59:00	1:13:20	1:17:21	2:34:43
89	3:42	5:58	11:07	18:32	37:05	55:37	59:40	1:14:10	1:18:14	2:36:28
90	3:45	6:02	11:15	18:45	37:30	56:15	1:00:21	1:15:00	1:19:07	2:38:14
91	3:47	6:06	11:22	18:57	37:55	56:52	1:01:01	1:15:50	1:19:59	2:39:59
92	3:50	6:10	11:30	19:10	38:20	57:30	1:01:41	1:16:40	1:20:52	2:41:45
93	3:52	6:14	11:37	19:22	38:45	58:07	1:02:21	1:17:30	1:21:45	2:43:30
94	3:55	6:18	11:45	19:35	39:10	58:45	1:03:02	1:18:20	1:22:38	2:45:16
95	3:57	6:22	11:52	19:47	39:35	59:22	1:03:42	1:19:10	1:23:30	2:47:01
96	4:00	6:26	12:00	20:00	40:00	1:00:00	1:04:22	1:20:00	1:24:23	2:48:47
97	4:02	6:30	12:07	20:12	40:25	1:00:37	1:05:02	1:20:50	1:25:16	2:50:32
98	4:05	6:34	12:15	20:25	40:50	1:01:15	1:15:43	1:21:40	1:26:09	2:52:18
99	4:07	6:38	12:22	20:37	41:15	1:01:52	1:16:23	1:22:30	1:27:01	2:54:03
1:40	4:10	6:42	12:30	20:50	41:40	1:02:30	1:07:03	1:23:20	1:27:54	2:55:48
1:41	4:12	6:46	12:37	21:02	42:05	1:03:07	1:07:43	1:24:10	1:28:47	2:57:34
1:42	4:15	6:50	12:45	21:15	42:30	1:03:45	1:08:23	1:25:00	1:29:40	2:59:20
1:43	4:17	6:54	12:52	21:27	42:55	1:04:22	1:09:04	1:25:50	1:30:32	3:01:05
1:44	4:20	6:58	13:00	21:40	43:20	1:05:00	1:09:44	1:26:40	1:31:25	3:02:50
1:45	4:22	7:02	13:07	21:52	43:45	1:05:37	1:10:24	1:27:30	1:32:18	3:04:36
1:46	4:25	7:06	13:15	22:05	44:10	1:06:15	1:11:04	1:28:20	1:33:11	3:06:22
1:47	4:27	7:10	13:22	22:17	44:35	1:06:52	1:11:45	1:29:10	1:34:03	3:08:07

400	1 km	Mile	3 km	5 km	10 km	15 km	10 mile	20 km	Half marathon	Marathon
1:48	4:30	7:14	13:30	22:30	45:00	1:07:30	1:12:25	1:30:00	1:34:56	3:09:52
1:49	4:32	7:18	13:37	22:42	45:25	1:08:07	1:13:05	1:30:50	1:35:49	3:11:38
1:50	4:35	7:22	13:45	22:55	45:50	1:08:45	1:13:45	1:31:40	1:36:42	3:13:24
1:51	4:37	7:26	13:52	23:07	46:15	1:09:22	1:14:26	1:32:30	1:37:34	3:15:09
1:52	4:40	7:30	14:00	23:20	46:40	1:10:00	1:15:06	1:33:20	1:38:27	3:16:54
1:53	4:42	7:34	14:07	23:32	47:05	1:10:37	1:15:46	1:34:10	1:39:20	3:18:40
1:54	4:45	7:38	14:15	23:45	47:30	1:11:15	1:16:26	1:35:00	1:40:12	3:20:25
1:55	4:47	7:42	14:22	23:57	47:55	1:11:52	1:17:07	1:35:50	1:41:05	3:22:11
1:56	4:50	7:46	14:30	24:10	48:20	1:12:30	1:17:47	1:36:40	1:41:58	3:23:56
1:57	4:52	7:50	14:37	24:22	48:45	1:13:07	1:18:27	1:37:30	1:42:51	3:25:42
1:58	4:55	7:54	14:45	24:35	49:10	1:13:45	1:19:07	1:38:20	1:43:43	3:27:27
1:59	4:57	7:58	15:52	24:47	49:35	1:14:22	1:19:48	1:39:10	1:44:36	3:29:13
2:00	5:00	8:02	15:00	25:00	50:00	1:15:00	1:20:28	1:40:00	1:45:29	3:30:58
2:01	5:02	8:06	15:07	25:12	50:25	1:15:37	1:21:08	1:40:50	1:46:22	3:32:44
2:02	5:05	8:10	15:15	25:25	50:50	1:16:15	1:21:48	1:41:40	1:47:14	3:34:29
2:03	5:07	8:14	15:22	25:37	51:15	1:16:52	1:22:28	1:42:30	1:48:07	3:36:15
2:04	5:10	8:19	15:30	25:50	51:40	1:17:30	1:23:09	1:43:20	1:49:00	3:38:00
2:05	5:12	8:23	15:37	26:02	52:05	1:18:07	1:23:49	1:44:10	1:49:53	3:39:46
2:06	5:15	8:27	15:45	26:15	52:30	1:18:45	1:24:29	1:45:00	1:50:45	3:41:31
2:07	5:17	8:31	15:52	26:27	52:55	1:19:22	1:25:09	1:45:50	1:51:38	3:43:17
2:08	5:20	8:35	16:00	26:40	53:20	1:20:00	1:25:50	1:46:40	1:52:31	3:45:02
2:09	5:22	8:39	16:07	26:52	53:45	1:20:37	1:26:30	1:47:30	1:53:24	3:46:48
2:10	5:25	8:43	16:15	27:05	54:10	1:21:15	1:27:10	1:48:20	1:54:16	3:48:33
2:11	5:27	8:47	16:22	27:17	54:35	1:21:52	1:27:50	1:49:10	1:55:09	3:50:19
2:12	5:30	8:51	16:30	27:30	55:00	1:22:30	1:28:31	1:50:00	1:56:02	3:52:04
2:13	5:32	8:55	16:37	27:42	55:25	1:23:07	1:29:11	1:50:50	1:56:55	3:53:50
2:14	5:35	8:59	16:45	27:55	55:50	1:23:45	1:29:51	1:51:40	1:57:47	3:55:35
2:15	5:37	9:03	16:52	28:07	56:15	1:24:22	1:30:31	1:52:30	1:58:40	3:57:20
2:16	5:40	9:07	17:00	28:20	56:40	1:25:00	1:31:11	1:53:20	1:59:33	3:59:06
2:17	5:42	9:11	17:07	28:32	57:05	1:25:37	1:31:52	1:54:10	2:00:26	4:00:52
2:18	5:45	9:15	17:15	28:45	57:30	1:26:15	1:32:32	1:55:00	2:01:18	4:02:37
2:19	5:47	9:19	17:22	28:57	57:55	1:26:52	1:33:12	1:55:50	2:02:11	4:04:22
2:20	5:50	9:23	17:30	29:10	58:20	1:27:30	1:33:52	1:56:40	2:03:04	4:06:08
2:21	5:52	9:27	17:37	29:22	58:45	1:28:07	1:34:33	1:57:30	2:03:57	4:07:54

(continued)

400	1 km	Mile	3 km	5 km	10 km	15 km	10 mile	20 km	Half marathon	Marathon
2:22	5:55	9:31	17:45	29:35	59:10	1:28:45	1:35:13	1:58:20	2:04:49	4:09:39
2:23	5:57	9:35	17:52	29:47	59:35	1:29:22	1:35:53	1:59:10	2:05:42	4:11:24
2:24	6:00	9:39	18:00	30:00	1:00:00	1:30:00	1:36:33	2:00:00	2:06:35	4:13:10
2:25	6:02	9:43	18:07	30:12	1:00:25	1:30:37	1:37:14	2:00:50	2:07:27	4:14:55
2:26	6:05	9:47	18:15	30:25	1:00:50	1:31:15	1:37:54	2:01:40	2:08:20	4:16:41
2:27	6:07	9:51	18:22	30:37	1:01:15	1:31:52	1:38:34	2:02:30	2:09:13	4:18:26
2:28	6:10	9:55	18:30	30:50	1:01:40	1:32:30	1:39:14	2:03:20	2:10:06	4:20:12
2:29	6:12	9:59	18:37	31:02	1:02:05	1:33:07	1:39:55	2:04:10	2:10:58	4:21:57
2:30	6:15	10:03	18:45	31:15	1:02:30	1:13:45	1:40:35	2:05:00	2:11:51	4:23:43

C

Time and Pace Conversions

Table A Time Conversions

min:sec/400 m	sec/400 m	m/sec	m/min	sec/100 m	min:sec/1,000 m
7:00	420	.95	57	105.0	17:30
6:45	405	.99	59	101.3	16:52
6:30	390	1.03	62	97.5	16:15
6:15	375	1.07	64	93.8	15:37
6:00	360	1.11	67	90.0	15:00
5:50	350	1.14	69	87.5	14:35
5:40	340	1.18	71	85.0	14:10
5:30	330	1.21	73	82.5	13:45
5:20	320	1.25	75	80.0	13:20
5:10	310	1.29	77	77.5	12:55
5:00	300	1.33	80	75.0	12:30
4:50	290	1.38	82	72.5	12:05
4:40	280	1.43	85	70.0	11:40
4:30	270	1.48	88	67.5	11:15
4:20	260	1.54	92	65.0	10:50
4:10	250	1.60	96	62.5	10:25
4:00	240	1.67	100	60.0	10:00
3:50	230	1.74	104	57.5	9:35
3:40	220	1.82	109	55.0	9:10
3:30	210	1.90	114	52.5	8:45
3:20	200	2.00	120	50.0	8:20
3:10	190	2.11	126	47.5	7:55
3:00	180	2.22	133	45.0	7:30
2:50	170	2.35	141	42.5	7:05
2:40	160	2.50	151	40.0	6:40
2:30	150	2.67	160	37.5	6:15

(continued)

min:sec/400 m	sec/400 m	m/sec	m/min	sec/100 m	min:sec/1,000 m
2:20	140	2.86	171	35.0	5:50
2:10	130	3.08	185	32.5	5:25
2:00	120	3.33	200	30.0	5:00
1:50	110	3.64	218	27.5	4:35
1:45	105	3.81	229	26.3	4:22
1:40	100	4.00	240	25.0	4:10
1:35	95	4.21	253	23.8	3:57
1:30	90	4.44	267	22.5	3:45
1:25	85	4.71	282	21.3	3:32
1:20	80	5.00	300	20.0	3:20
1:15	75	5.33	320	18.8	3:07
1:10	70	5.71	342	17.5	2:55
1:05	65	6.15	369	16.3	2:42
1:00	60	6.67	400	15.0	2:30
0:58	58	6.90	414	14.5	2:25
0:56	56	7.14	429	14.0	2:20
0:54	54	7.41	444	13.5	2:15
0:53	53	7.55	453	13.2	2:12
0:52	52	7.69	462	13.0	2:10
0:51	51	7.84	471	12.8	2:07
0:50	50	8.00	480	12.5	2:05
0:49	49	8.16	490	12.2	2:02
0:48	48	8.33	500	12.0	2.00
0:47	47	8.51	511	11.7	1:57

Table B   Pace Conversions

mph	kph	min:sec/1,000 m	min:sec/mile	sec/400 m
1.0	1.61	37:17	60:00	895
2.0	3.22	18:38	30:00	447
3.0	4.83	12:26	20:00	298
4.0	6.44	9:19	15:00	224
5.0	8:05	7:27	12:00	179
6.0	9.66	6:13	10:00	149
7.0	11.27	5:20	8:34	128
8.0	12.87	4:40	7:30	112
9.0	14.48	4:09	6:40	99
10.0	16.09	3:44	6:00	89
11.0	17.70	3:23	5:27	81
12.0	19.31	3:06	5:00	75
13.0	20.92	2:52	4:37	69
14.0	22.53	2:41	4:17	64
15.0	24.14	2:29	4:00	59.6
16.0	25.75	2:20	3:45	55.9
17.0	27.36	2:12	3:32	52.6
18.0	28.97	2:04	3:20	49.7
19.0	30.58	1:58	3:09	47.1
20.0	32.19	1:52	3:00	44.7
21.0	33.80	1:47	2:51	42.6
22.0	35.41	1:42	2:44	40.7
23.0	37.01	1:37	2:37	38.9
24.0	38.62	1:33	2:30	37.3
25.0	40.23	1:29	2:24	35.8
26.0	41.85	1:26	2:18	34.4
27.0	43.45	1:23	2:13	33.1
28.0	45.06	1:20	2:09	32.0
29.0	46.67	1:17	2:04	30.9
30.0	48.28	1:15	2:00	29.8
31.0	49.89	1:12	1:56	28.9
32.0	51.50	1:10	1:52	28.0
33.0	53.11	1:08	1:49	27.1
34.0	54.72	1:06	1:46	26.3

(continued)

mph	kph	min:sec/1,000 m	min:sec/mile	sec/400 m
35.0	56.33	1:04	1:43	25.6
36.0	57.94	1:02	1:40	24.9
37.0	59.55	1:00	1:37	24.2
38.0	61.16	0:59	1:35	23.6
39.0	62.76	0:57	1:32	22.9
40.0	64.37	0:56	1:30	22.4
41.0	65.98	0:55	1:28	21.8
42.0	67.59	0:53	1:26	21.3
43.0	69.20	0:52	1:24	20.8
44.0	70.81	0:51	1:22	20.3
45.0	72.42	0:50	1:20	19.9
46.0	74.03	0:49	1:18	19.5
47.0	75.64	0:48	1:17	19.0
48.0	77.25	0:47	1:15	18.6
49.0	78.86	0:46	1:13	18.3
50.0	80.47	0:45	1:12	17.9

High-Stress Workouts

High-Stress Workout 1

Warm up and then perform the following:

1. 1,600 4 sec/200 slower than current mile race pace; 5 min recovery (keep moving—walk or jog—during recovery bouts)
2. 1,000 2 sec/200 slower than current mile race pace, or 2 sec/200 faster than in the 1,600 above; 4 min recovery
3. 800 at current mile race pace; 3-min recovery
4. 600 1 sec/200 faster than for the 800 above; 2.5 min recovery
5. 400 1 sec/200 faster than for the 600 above; 2 min recovery
6. 300 1 sec/200 faster than for the 400 above; 1.5 min recovery
7. 200 1 sec/200 faster than for the 300 above

Cool down and go home. This workout is about a 31-minute session (excluding warm-up and cool-down).

High-Stress Workout 2

Warm up and then perform the following:

1. 800 at current mile race pace; 3 min recovery
2. 600 at 2 sec/200 faster than in the 800 above; 2 min recovery
3. 400 at 1 sec/200 faster than in the 600 above; 1.5 min recovery
4. 300 at 1 sec/200 faster than in the 400 above; 1 min recovery
5. 200 at 1 sec/200 faster than in the 300 above

Cool down. This is about a 15-minute session (excluding warm-up and cool-down)

High-Stress Workout 3

The total time for each of the five 800s listed here is to be at a pace that is 6 seconds per 800 slower than current 1,500 or mile race ability. For example, if current mile race ability is 4:40, this is a 2:20 per 800 pace, so for the following workout, each 800 is to total 2:26. The pace of each 800 is changed so each 800 starts a little slower and finishes a little faster. The following uses a 4:40 mile as an example.

Warm up and then perform the following:

1. 36.5 + 36.5 + 36.5 + 36.5 = 2:26 *or* 73 + 73 = 2:26
   Recovery = 200jg + 200 at 36.5 + 200 jg
2. 37 + 37 + 36 + 36 = 2:26 *or* 74 + 72 = 2:26
   Recovery = 200 jg + 200 at 36.5 + 200 jg
3. 38 + 37 + 36 + 35 = 2:26 *or* 75 + 71 = 2:26
   Recovery = 200 jg + 200 at 36.5 + 200 jg
4. 38 + 38 + 35 + 35 = 2:26 *or* 76 + 70 = 2:26
   Recovery = 200 jg + 200 at 36.5 + 200 jg
5. 39 + 38 + 35 + 34 = 2:26 *or* 77 + 69 = 2:26

Cool down. This is about a 25-minute session (excluding warm-up and cool-down)

High-Stress Workout 4

This is an 800-600-400-200 at 3-2.5-1.5 sec/200 faster speeds.

Warm up and then perform the following:

1. 800 at current **T** pace, followed by a 200 jg
2. 600 at 3 sec/200 faster than the pace of the 800 above, followed by a 200 jg
3. 400 at 2.5 sec/400 faster than the pace of the 600 above, followed by a 200 jg
4. 200 at 1.5 sec faster than the pace of the 400 above

If up to it, take a 10-minute recovery period and run the same session in the reverse order, starting with the 200, and do each run at the same speed you did them on the way down in distance.

Cool down. This is about a 9-minute session, but about a 28-minute session if the reverse order follows the initial 4 increasing-speed runs and the 10-minute recovery run.

High-Stress Workout 5

Warm up and then perform the following:

1. 2 × 600 at 1 sec/200 slower than current mile race pace, with 600 jg after each
2. 3 × 400 at current mile race pace, with 400 jg after each

3. 4 × 300 at 1 sec/200 faster than current mile race pace, with 300 jg after each

4. 6 × 200 at current 800 race pace, with 200 jg after each

Cool down. This is about a 35-minute session (excluding warm-up and cool-down)

High-Stress Test Session

- If current 1,600 race time is 4:40 or faster (VDOT greater than 63.8), do 10 × 400 with as fast an average time as possible, with 1-minute rests. The pace you can average should be attainable for a 1,600 or 1,500-meter race.

- If current 1,600 race time is 4:41 to 5:20 (VDOT between 54.8 and 63.7), do 9 × 400 with as fast an average pace as possible, with 1-minute rests. This should provide you with the pace you can race at for 1,600 or 1,500 meters.

- If current 1,600 race time is 5:21 to 6:12 (VDOT between 46.3 and 54.7), do 8 × 400 with as fast an average pace as possible, with 1-minute rests. This should provide you with the pace you can race at for 1,600 or 1,500 meters.

- If current 1,600 race time is slower than 6:12 (VDOT less than 46.3), do 7 × 400 with as fast an average pace as possible, with 1-minute rests. This should provide you with the pace you can race for 1,600 or 1,500 meters.

Index

Note: The italicized *f* and *t* following page numbers refer to figures and tables, respectively.

About the Author

Jack Daniels has been called the world's best coach by *Runner's World* magazine. He has more than 50 years of experience coaching and mentoring some of world's top distance runners at both the collegiate and postcollegiate levels, including Jim Ryun, Penny Werthner, Ken Martin, Jerry Lawson, Alicia Shay, Peter Gilmore, Lisa Martin, Magdalena Lewy Boulet, and Janet Cherobon-Bawcom. He also won two Olympic medals and one world championship medal in the men's modern pentathlon.

Daniels has decades of experience as a track and cross country coach at institutions such as Oklahoma City University, the University of Texas, Brevard College, and the State University of New York at Cortland. Under his guidance, Cortland runners won 8 NCAA Division III national championships, 30 individual national titles, and more than 130 All-America awards. He was named Women's Cross Country Coach of the 20th Century by the NCAA Division III.

Since 1997 Daniels has been the national running coach advisor for the Leukemia/Lymphoma Society's Team in Training program, which involves coaching thousands of marathon runners each year. He has also enjoyed coaching members of the Nike Farm Team and the Chasquis, a group of Peruvian marathoners. Jack also coaches numerous runners online at runsmartproject.com

Daniels has logged years of graduate study and research on distance running in both the United States and Sweden. He holds a doctoral degree in exercise physiology from the University of Wisconsin at Madison. He also studied exercise science at the Royal Gymnastics Central Institute in Stockholm under renowned sport scientist Per-Olaf Åstrand.

In recent years, Daniels has been an associate professor in the human movement program at A.T. Still University in Mesa, Arizona, in addition to coaching Olympic runners.

Of all his accomplishments, Daniels is most proud of his two daughters and being married to his wife, Nancy.